Dialogues and Games of Logic

Volume 3

Logic of Knowledge

Theory and Applications

Volume 1
How to Play Dialogues: An Introduction to Dialogical Logic
Juan Redmond and Matthieu Fontaine

Volume 2
Dialogues as a Dynamic Framework for Logic
Helge Rückert

Volume 3
Logic of Knowledge. Theory and Applictions
Cristina Barés Gómez, Sébastien Magnier, and Francisco J. Salguero, eds.

Dialogues and Games of Logic Series Editors
Shahid Rahman   shahid.rahman@univ-lille3.fr
Nicolas Clerbout
Matthieu Fontaine

Logic of Knowledge

Theory and Applications

Cristina Barés Gómez,
Sébastien Magnier,
and
Francisco J. Salguero

editors

ISBN 978-1-84890-074-5

College Publications
Scientific Director: Dov Gabbay
Managing Director: Jane Spurr
Department of Informatics
King's College London, Strand, London WC2R 2LS, UK

www.collegepublications.co.uk

Original cover design by Laraine Welch
Printed by Lightning Source, Milton Keynes, UK

DIALOGUES AND THE GAMES OF LOGIC: A PHILOSOPHICAL PERSPECTIVE

http://www.collegepublications.co.uk/dialogues/

Series edited by:
Shahid Rahman (Univ. Lille 3, UMR 8163 STL)
Nicolas Clerbout (Univ. Lille 3, UMR 8163 STL)
Matthieu Fontaine (Univ. Lille 3, UMR 8163 STL)

For more than two decades now the scientific community has seen a growing number of important results in the emerging field centered on the interactions between game theory and logic. We feel that it is time for the philosopher to assess in which ways those results bear on the fundamental questions of the philosophy of logic. In particular, what insight have we gained on such central notions such as meaning, truth, validity, proof, proposition, form and formality, logicality. We would thus like to open a series of books that we conceive as a gathering place where philosophical ideas concerning those topics can be expressed, scrutinized and confronted. We therefore invite submissions related to all aspects of the philosophical consequences of the interactions between games and logic. More specific topics include (but are not limited to): game-theoretical and game semantics, dialogical logic, ludics, Ehrenfeucht-Fraïssé games, game-theoretical notions of logical form, game-theoretical notion of proposition, logical games between semantics and proof theory, games and modal logic.

Submission Details. Authors are strongly encouraged to use LATEX, using the usual 'article' document class. Acceptable formats are (in order of preference): LATEX(.tex), gereral text formats (.rtf and .txt), OpenOffice (.odt), Word (.doc). For proposals contact Shahid Rahman with the subject matter "GDL-proposal".

Other Volumes in the Series

Volume 1, 2011. Redmond, J. and Fontaine, M. *How to Play Dialogues. An Introduction to Dialogical Logic.*

Volume 2, 2011. Rückert, H. *Dialogues as a Dynamic Framework for Logic.*

FOREWORD

This volume includes revised versions of presentations at the *International Symposium - Argumentation in Intensional contexts: Knowledge, Belief, Dialogue* organised by the UMR 8163 "Savoirs, Textes, Langage", Université Lille 3, France; and the "Grupo de Lógica, Lenguaje e Información" (HUM-609), Universidad de Sevilla, Spain. We are grateful to these two institutions for their supports. The congress was held in Sevilla, Facultad de Filosofía, May 20th-21th 2010.

Through this foreword, we thank all of the authors included here for taking part in the Workshop, for getting their papers in on time, and for revising them according to referees' recommendations. We owe a large debt of gratitude to all blind reviewers who collaborated to improve the papers. We are particularly grateful for their helpful comments and various suggestions on previous version of each paper. Without those silent contributions such a publication would not be possible. We also address our thanks to Nicolas Clerbout for his hard-work in the final edition of the book.

This book would not have been possible without the constant support and encouragement of the heads of both research groups: Pr. Dr. Shahid Rahman and Pr. Dr. Ángel Nepomuceno. Thanks for all.

The Editors.

Table of Contents

Preface

Shahid RAHMAN*

Since the times of the ancient Greece, where the agora emerged as the
first public space for discussion and decision-making on diverse and
serious matters, and after the crucial influence of the Sophists, of Plato
and of Aristotle argumentation won a place in our understanding of
science and constitution of a society which it ever lost any more. More
generally and beyond the western tradition arguments played and still
play an important role in the processes of acquisition of knowledge
and decision making not only in science but also in our every day
life, when acting and interacting as members of a society. In other
words, argumentation seems to be closely related to our very concept
of reasoning and rational acting in both a cognitive and epistemological
sense. Moreover, one could see the development of different sciences
as involving the development of different and interweaving reasoning
skills in our pursuit of knowledge. The study of these argumentation
skills is thus, according to one of our main conceptual views, pluralistic
and interdisciplinary by its very nature: different argumentation forms
for different contexts.

The link between logic and argumentation is that argumentation provides to logic the dynamics required to model agent-based knowledge
constituted by inferential interaction. However, after Aristotle, logic
and argumentation theory followed different paths and with it the dynamic aspects of logic were lost. Furthermore, during the years that
followed immediately after the failure of the logical positivism project
the links between science as a body of knowledge and science as process by which knowledge is achieved were cut off. Indeed, it looks as
a ban on the logical analysis of science as a dynamic process, which in
traditional philosophy was overtaken by 'gnoseology', produced a gap
between sciences and logic (including philosophy of science). In gnoseology the main notion was the one of judgement rather than that of
proposition. Judgement delivered the epistemic aspect of logic, namely

*Université de Lille, UMR 8163: STL

the relation between an (epistemic) agent and a proposition.[1] This represented the basis of the Kantian approach to logic, which seemed to be in conflict with the post-Fregean approach where only relations between propositions are at stake and where the epistemic aspect is seen as outside logic.[2]

As it happens quite often in philosophy, the echoes of the old traditions come back and point to the mistakes of the younger iconoclast movements. This is indeed the case in the relation between logic and knowledge where the inclusion or exclusion of the epistemic moment as linked with the concept of proposition provoked a heated debate since the 1960s. In 1955 Paul Lorenzen proposed an *operative* approach that delved into the conceptual and technical links between *procedure* and knowledge.[3] The insights of Lorenzen's *Operative Logik* had lasting consequences in the literature on proof-theory and still deserve attention nowadays. Indeed, the notion of *harmony* formulated by the logicians that favoured the epistemic approaches and particularly by Dag Prawitz[4] has been influenced by Lorenzen's notions of *admissibility*; *eliminability* and *inversion*.[5] The epistemic approaches, which started to call themselves, following Michael Dummett, 'antirealism', found their formal argument in the mathematics of Brouwer and intuitionistic logic while the others persisted with the formal background of the Frege-Tarski tradition, where Cantorian set theory is linked via model theory to classical logic. This picture is, however, incomplete:

> On one hand, already in the 1960s appeared *Dialogical logic* developed by Paul Lorenzen and Kuno Lorenz, as a solution to some of the problems that arouse in Lorenzen's *Operative*

---

[1]Cf. Sundholm, B.G.: "Inference versus Consequence". *The Logica Yearbook*, 1998, pp. 26-36. Also in http://www.springerlink.com/content/q34027wh7w816r3r/fulltext.pdf. Sundholm, B.G. "A Century of Judgment and Inference: 1837-1936". In: Haaparanta, L. (Ed.), *The Development of Modern Logic*, pp. 263-317. Oxford: Oxford University Press, 1999.

[2]Cf. S. Rahman/G. Primiero/M. Marion: *The Realism, Antirealism Debate in the Age of Alternative Logics*, Dordrecht : Springer, 2012, pp. vii-ix.

[3]P. Lorenzen: *Einführung in die operative Logik und Mathematik*. Berlin, Göttingen, Heidelberg: Springer, 1955.

[4]D. Prawitz, D: "Proofs and the meaning and completeness of the logical constants". In J. Hintikka, I. Niiniluoto/E. Saarinen (editors): *Essays on Mathematical and Philosophical Logic*, Dordrecht: Reidel, 1979, pp. 25–40.

[5]Cf. P. Schröder-Heister,: "P. Lorenzen's operative justification of intuitionistic logic". In M. van Atten/P. Boldini/M. Bourdeau/G. Heinzmann (eds.), *One Hundred Years of Intuitionism* (1907-2007), Basel: Birkhäuser 2008.

Logik (1955). Herewith, the epistemic turn initiated by the proof theoretic was tackled with the notion of games. Inspired by Wittgenstein's *meaning as use* the basic idea of the dialogical approach to logic is that the meaning of the logical constants is given by the norms or rules for their use; and it provides an alternative to both model theoretic and proof-theoretic semantics. The dialogical approach to logic is not a specific logical system but rather a rule-based semantic framework in which different logics can be developed, combined and compared. The point is that those rules that fix meaning may be of more than one type, and that they determine the kind of reconstruction of an argumentative and/or linguistic practice that a certain kind of language games called dialogues provide. This feature of its underlying semantics quite often motivated the dialogical approach to be understood as a *pragmatist* semantics. More precisely, in a dialogue two parties argue about a thesis respecting certain fixed rules. The player that states the thesis is called Proponent (**P**), his rival, who puts into question the thesis is called Opponent (**O**). In its original form, dialogues were designed in such a way that each of the plays end after a finite number of moves with one player winning, while the other loses. Actions or moves in a dialogue are often understood as *utterances* or as speech-acts. The point is that the rules of the dialogue do not operate on expressions or sentences isolated from the act of uttering them. The rules are divided into particle rules or rules for logical constants (*Partikelregeln*) and structural rules (*Rahmenregeln*). The structural rules determine the general course of a dialogue game, whereas the particle rules regulate those moves (or utterances) that are requests (to the moves of a rival) and those moves that are answers (to the requests).[6]

---

[6]The main original papers are collected in P. Lorenzen/K. Lorenz: *Dialogische Logik*, Darmstadt: WBG, 1978. A detailed account of recent developments can be found in S. Rahman, S./L. Keiff: "On how to be a dialogicians". In D. Vanderveken (ed.), *Logic, Thought and Action*, Dordrecht: Kluwer, 2004, pp. 359-408; L. Keiff: "Dialogical Logic". Stanford Encyclopaedia of Philosophy, 2009, http://plato.stanford.edu/entries/logic-dialogical/; For a textbook presentation J. Redmond/M. Fontaine 2011: *How to Play Dialogues. An Introduction to Dialogical Logic*. London: College Publications, London

Crucial for the dialogical approach are the following points:[7]

1. The distinction between *local* (rules for logical constants) and *global* meaning (included in the structural rules that determine how to play).

2. The player independence of local meaning.

3. The distinction between the play level (local winning or winning a play) and the strategic level (existence of a winning strategy).

4. A notion of validity that amounts to winning strategy *independently of any model* instead of winning strategy for *every* model.

5. The notion of winning in a *formal play* instead of winning strategy in a model.

On the other hand, Jaakko Hintikka combined the model-theoretical and the epistemic and the game-based traditions by means of the development what is now known as 'explicit epistemic logic', where the epistemic content is introduced into the object language as an operator which yield propositions from propositions rather than as metalogical constraint on the notion of inference. These kind of operators were rapidly generalized covering several propositional attitudes including notably knowledge and belief. Furthermore, Hintikka developed *game theoretical semantic* that is an approach to formal semantics that, like in the dialogical framework, grounds the concepts of truth or validity on game-theoretic concepts, such as the existence of a winning strategy for a player, though differently to the dialogical framework it is build up on the notion of model.[8] The simplest application

and H. Rückert: *Dialogues as Dynamic Framework for Logic*. London: Collegue Publications, 2011.

[7]Cf. S. Rahman: "Negation in the Logic of First-Degree-Entailment and Tonk. A Dialogical Study". In S. Rahman/G. Primiero/M. Marion: *The Realism, Antirealism Debate in the Age of Alternative Logics*, Dordrecht : Springer, 2012, pp. 213-250.

[8]J. Hintikka: *Knowledge and Belief: An Introduction to the Logic of the Two Notions*. Cornell: Cornell University Press; J. Hintikka, Logic, *Language-Games and Information: Kantian Themes in the Philosophy of Logic*, Oxford: Clarendon Press, 1973; J. Hintikka, *The Principles of Mathematics Revisited*, N. York: Cambridge University Press, 1996; J. Hintikka / Gabriel Sandu, "Game-theoretical semantics", in *Handbook of Logic and*

of game semantics is to propositional logic. Each formula of
this language is interpreted as a game between two players,
known as the "Verifier" and the "Falsifier". In the case of
a disjunction, the Verifier has the choice of the subformula
to be played, and the Falsifier is likewise given the choice
in the case of a conjunction. Each move of the game consists of allowing the player who has the choice in relation
to the dominant connective to pick one of its branches; the
play will then continue in that subformula, with whichever
player controls its dominant connective making the next
move. Play ends when a primitive proposition has been
so chosen by the two players; at this point the Verifier is
deemed the winner if the resulting proposition is true in the
model, and the Falsifier is deemed the winner if it is false
in the *model*. The original formula will be considered true
precisely when the Verifier has a winning strategy, while it
will be false whenever the Falsifier has the winning strategy. Negation induces a switch of players. More generally,
game semantics may be applied to predicate logic; the new
rules allow a dominant quantifier to be removed by the one
has the choice (the Verifier for existential quantifiers and
the Falsifier for universal quantifiers) and its bound variable replaced at all occurrences by an object drawn from
the quantification domain by the player who has the choice.
Thus, one could say in some sense that GTS is the result of
applying agent interaction to a model.[9]

Games, as stressed by Johan van Benthem, involve a tight interplay
of what agents know and how they act, and the rise of this paradigm
inside logic is unmistakeable. But note again that this development
also involves a major extension of a classical viewpoint. Games are
typically an interactive process involving several agents, and indeed,
many issues in logic today are no longer about zero-agent notions like
truth, or single-agent notions like proof, but rather about processes
of verification, argumentation, communication, or general *interaction*.

Language, ed. Johan van Benthem and Alice ter Meulen, Elsevier, Amsterdam ,1997,
pp. 361-410.
   [9]S. Rahman/T. Tulenheimo: "From Games to Dialogues and Back: Towards a General
Frame for Validity". In O. Majer, A-V. Pietarinen and T. Tulenheimo (editors), *Games:
Unifying Logic, Language and Philosophy*, Part III, Dordrecht, Springer, 2009.

Actually, this new impulse where epistemic operators are combined with a game-theoretical approach experienced a parallel renewal in the fields of theoretical computer science, computational linguistics, artificial intelligence and the formal semantics of programming languages triggered by the work of Johan van Benthem[10] and collaborators in Amsterdam who not only looked thoroughly at the interface between logic and games but also provided new and powerful tools to tackle the issue of the *expressivity* of a language – in particular the capability of propositional modal logic to express some undecidable fragments of first-order logic.[11] New results in linear logic by J-Y. Girard in the interfaces between mathematical game theory and proof theory on one hand and argumentation theory and logic on the other hand resulted in the work of many others, including S. Abramsky, J. van Benthem, A. Blass, H. van Ditmarsch, D. Gabbay, M. Hyland, W. Hodges, R. Jagadessan, G. Japaridze, E. Krabbe, L. Ong, H. Prakken, G. Sandu, D. Walton, and J. Woods who placed game semantics in the center of new concept of logic in which logic is understood as a dynamic instrument of inference.[12]

The papers that constitute the present volume are a result of the movements mentioned above where flow of information, agentivity, and the dialogical approach interweave in new and exciting ways in the context of what van Benthem calls the dynamic turn. Moreover one can read the present volume as providing different complementary variations and perspectives that should motivate and render future new cross-fertilizing dialogues between explicit epistemic and dialogical approaches. Indeed, according to this reading we could distinguish the following pairs of interlocutors:

> While the papers of F. Soler-Toscano & F. R. Velázquez-Quesada and Laura Leónides explore the dynamics induced

---

[10]J. van Benthem: *Exploring Logical Dynamics*. Amsterdam: ILLC, 1996; J. van Benthem: *Logic in Games*. Amsterdam: ILLC, 2009; J. van Benthem: *Logical Dynamics of Information and Interaction*. Cambridge: CUP, 2010. H. van Ditmarsch/W. van der Hoek/B. Kooi: *Dynamic-Epistemic Logic*. Berlin: Synthese Library 337, 2007.

[11]J. van Benthem: "Correspondence Theory". In D. Gabbay/F. Guenthner, eds.: *Handbook of Philosophical Logic*, Vol. II., Reidel, Dordrecht, 167–247. (Reprint with addenda in D. Gabbay, ed., 2001, *Handbook of Philosophical Logic*, vol. III., Kluwer, Dordrecht, 325–408.)

[12]See among others, A. Blass A: "A Game Semantics for Linear Logic", *Annals of Pure and Applied Logic* 56, pp. 183–220, 1992; S. Abramsky/P.-A. Melliès, "Concurrent Games and Full Completeness". *14th Annual Symposium on Logic in Computer Science*, Trento, Italy, IEEE Computer Society Press, 1999, pp. 431–442, J.-Y. Girard: "From foundations to ludics". *Bulletin of Symbolic Logic* 9, 2003, pp. 131-168.

by the arrival of new information in scientific processes such as abduction by means of non-monotonic approaches to reasoning and knowledge, V. Fiutek studies the other side of the coin of non-monotonic reasoning, namely belief revision, in a dialogical setting.

While the paper of P. Seban and H. van Ditmarsch develop a model theoretic semantics for a generalization of Public Announcement Logic (PAL) in order to formalize the concept of 'having the permission to say something to somebody'. S. Magnier provides the semantic basis for the dialogical perspective on a multi-agent public announcement logic with common knowledge.

While the paper of T. Tulenheimo explores the expressivity of interval-based temporal logic, N. Clerbout studies the expressivity of the dialogical approach in relation to a modal logic with actuality operator. Another study of the expressivity power of dialogical logic is the contribution of Fontaine and Redmond who show how the inferential properties of the standard free logics can be expressed in the dialogical framework by delving in the local meaning of the quantifiers.

The papers of C. Barés Gómez and of A. Popek present a new feature of the dynamic turn, namely its sensitivity and ability to deal with historic studies such as the study of conditionals in Ugaritic language and the reconstruction of the medioeval theory of Obligationes.

It is not easy to say what philosophy is, and any statement about it might be contentious. However, philosophy seems to be closely related to the possibility to constitute knowledge and rationality in the interaction with the others in such a way that, on one hand, it is the perspective of the others that constitutes my own, and on the other hand my perspective constitutes their own. It is this what I think the contributions of this volume are about.

PART I

INTENSIONAL CONTEXTS: INTERACTION AND MODELS

A Logical Framework for Individual Permissions on Public Announcements

Hans Van DITMARSCH* & Pablo SEBAN†

ABSTRACT. We propose a formalization of the concept of 'having the permission to say something to somebody'. For it, we introduce a notion of private announcement and define a permission operator with agency. We prove that this can be seen as a generalisation of the notion of permitted *public* announcement Balbiani and Seban (2011). We also add a notion of obligation with a new intuition. We illustrate the logic with an example of communication in the french medical system. We axiomatize the logic and give some of its properties.

Introduction

A medical laboratory (L) gets the results of the blood analysis of a patient called Michel (M). This confirms that Michel does not have AIDS (A). But of course, the results could have been different. To prevent that patients commit suicide when they learn that they are ill, French laboratories are not allowed to inform a patient directly of the results of a blood analysis (by email, by post, or whatever inconvenient form of impersonal or unprofessional communication). They have to inform a doctor (D), who will receive the patient in his office, and then inform the patient. This protocol has to be followed when the patient has AIDS , but also when he does not have AIDS, otherwise having an appointment with the doctor could already be interpreted as confirmation of the disease, and we still get the terrible situation of lonely people in distress, that are a suicide risk.

Our aim is to be able to formalize this kind of situation in which agents can communicate with each other, and where there are restrictions, that can be deontic, moral or hierarchical.

*Universidad de Sevilla, Spain.
†IRIT, Université de Toulouse, France.

The logic of public announcements (*PAL*) proposed by Plaza in Plaza (1989) is an extension of epistemic logic. It permits to express how agents update their knowledge after public announcements of true propositions. We can write in this language $\langle\psi\rangle\varphi$ which means that after the truthful public announcement of ψ, φ is true. This logic has been largely studied and extended van Ditmarsch et al. (2007). One of these extensions (Baltag and Moss (2004)) allows us to consider other kind of informative events than public announcements, as private ones (announcement that give information to a subgroup of the entire group of agents, with partial information given publicly).

To formalize the concept of 'having the permission to say something to somebody' we extend a variant of Plaza's public announcement logic, which we could call 'private announcement logic', with a modal operator P_i^G for permission, where $P_i^G\varphi$ expresses that agent i is allowed to say φ to the agents of the group G. This can be seen as an adaption of the dynamic logic of permission proposed by van der Meyden in van der Meyden (1996), and later elaborated by Pucella and Weissman (2004). In van der Meyden's work, $\Diamond(\alpha, \varphi)$ means *"there is a way to execute α which is permitted and after which φ is true"*. We treat the particular case where actions are truthful announcements. Thus, for α in van der Meyden's $\Diamond(\alpha, \varphi)$ we take an announcement $\psi!$ such that $\Diamond(\psi!, \varphi)$ now means "it is permitted to announce ψ, after which φ is true". This suggests an equivalence with $P_i^{AG}\psi \wedge \langle\psi!\rangle\varphi$, but our operator behaves slightly differently, because we assume that if you have the permission to say something, you also have the permission to say something weaker, *i.e.* a something that gives less information. We also introduce an obligation operator $O_i^G\psi$, meaning that the agent is obliged to say ψ to the group G.

Our work relates to the extension of public announcement logic with protocols by van Benthem et al. (2009). In their approach, one cannot just announce anything that is true, but one can only announce a true formula that is part of the *protocol*, i.e., that is the first formula in a sequence of formulas (standing for a sequence of successive announcements) that is a member of a set of such sequences called the protocol. In other words, one can only announce *permitted* formulas. We don't have this limitation in our framework: as in their one, we consider only truthful announcement, but we can distinguish an announcement that cannot be done (because its content is false) from an announcement that is feasible but forbidden.

The permissions we model here are permissions for individual agents modelled in a multi-agent system. For example, if we have three agents a, b, c, we want to formalize that a has permission to say p to b, but not to c. We chose to model permission for agents using the standard method that agents only announce what they know: so, saying p, agent a says $K_a p$. This leaves open what c learns from this interaction, and we could imagine many possibilities Baltag et al. (1998). The solution we chose is similar to the semi-public announcements where agents not involved in the communicative interaction at least are aware of the topic of conversation and of the agents involved in it: if a actually announces p to b, c considers it possible that a announces $K_a p$ to b, or that he announces $\neg K_a p$ to the same b. These notions are presented in details in Section 1.2. We also model such permissions and obligations of individual agents towards other agents in the system, or to groups of other agents.

1 Logic of permitted and obligatory private announcements

1.1 Starting from public announcements

The work that we present here is based on a previous work Balbiani and Seban (2011), where we considered exclusively public announcements. Let us present it briefly. The logic *POPAL* of permitted and obligatory public announcement was an extension of public announcement logic, with two new binary operators P and O. More precisely, the language $\mathcal{L}_{popal}$ over a countable set of agents AG and a countable set of propositions Θ is defined inductively as follow:

$$\varphi ::= \bot \mid p \mid \neg\varphi \mid \psi \vee \varphi \mid K_i\varphi \mid [\psi]\varphi \mid P(\psi, \varphi) \mid O(\psi, \varphi)$$

where $i \in AG$ and $p \in \Theta$. We interpret these new operators as "after the (public) announcement of ψ, it is permitted (resp. obligatory) to announce χ". We add the usual boolean abbreviations (in particular $\top := \neg\bot$) and the following ones: $\hat{K}_i\varphi := \neg K_i\neg\varphi$, $\langle\psi\rangle\varphi := \neg[\psi]\neg\varphi$.

The models of this logic (permission Kripke models) are tuples of the form $\mathcal{M} = (S, \mathcal{R}, V, \mathcal{P})$ where $(S, \mathcal{R}, V)$ is a classical Kripke model and $\mathcal{P}$ is a subset of $\mathcal{T} = \{(s, S', S'') \in S \times 2^S \times 2^S \mid s \in S'' \subseteq S'\}$. The semantics of knowledge and announcement are the classical ones Plaza (1989), the new operators having the following semantics:

$\mathcal{M}, s \models P(\psi, \chi)$ iff for some $(s, \llbracket\psi\rrbracket_{\mathcal{M}}, S'') \in \mathcal{P}$, $S'' \subseteq \llbracket\langle\psi\rangle\chi\rrbracket_{\mathcal{M}}$

$\mathcal{M}, s \models O(\psi, \chi)$ iff for all $(s, \llbracket\psi\rrbracket_{\mathcal{M}}, S'') \in \mathcal{P}$, $S'' \subseteq \llbracket\langle\psi\rangle\chi\rrbracket_{\mathcal{M}}$.

For all formula $\chi \in \mathcal{L}_{popal}$, we note $P\chi := P(\top, \chi)$ and $O\chi := O(\top, \chi)$. The following proposition allows us to consider the simpler equivalent language restricted to these 'unary' operators (for which we explain the intuition):

Proposition 1.1. *The language $\mathcal{L}_{popal}$ is expressively equivalent to the language with unary operators $P\varphi$ and $O\varphi$.*

Proof. Clearly, $\mathcal{L}_{popal}$ is at least as expressive as this language. To prove the equivalence, it is sufficient to prove that for all $\psi, \varphi \in \mathcal{L}_{popal}$, $\models P(\psi, \varphi) \leftrightarrow \langle \psi \rangle P\varphi$ and $\models O(\psi, \varphi) \leftrightarrow \langle \psi \rangle O\varphi$. We know already that $\models [\psi]P(\top, \varphi) \leftrightarrow P(\psi, \varphi)$ and $\models [\psi]O(\top, \varphi) \leftrightarrow O(\psi, \varphi)$ (see Balbiani and Seban (2011) for details). It remains to prove that $\models P(\psi, \varphi) \rightarrow \psi$ (and analogously for O). But by definition of $\mathcal{T}$, if $(s, [\![\psi]\!]_{\mathcal{M}}, S'') \in \mathcal{P}$ then $s \in [\![\psi]\!]_{\mathcal{M}}$, then we have the wanted result. ∎

We then have:

$$\mathcal{M}, s \models P\chi \text{ iff for some } (s, S, S'') \in \mathcal{P}, S'' \subseteq [\![\chi]\!]_{\mathcal{M}}$$

$$\mathcal{M}, s \models O\chi \text{ iff for all } (s, S, S'') \in \mathcal{P}, S'' \subseteq [\![\chi]\!]_{\mathcal{M}}.$$

How to read this intuition of permission? They say that it is permitted to announce χ if there is a restriction (S'') "in $\mathcal{P}$" that is more restrictive than the announcement of χ. The obligation says that all the restrictions that are in $\mathcal{P}$ are more restrictive than the announcement of χ. In other words, it is permitted to say χ if *something* can be said (following $\mathcal{P}$) that gives more information than χ, and it is obligatory if *all* that can be said says more than χ.

As we will see in Proposition 1.2, the notion of permission of our new logic with private announcements can be seen as an extension of this one, if the group that 'receives' the announcement is always the whole group of agents AG. It is not true for obligation, given that we have a different intuition of obligation in this paper.

1.2 Introducing agency and individual permission

Private Announcements

We want to consider private announcements, *i.e.* informative events in which an agent gives an information that she has to another agent (or to a group of agents). Some choices have to be made. First, we consider that the content of an announcement is true, second we consider that the agent who is speaking can speak only about her own knowledge (it is the only thing she can actually know to be true), third we consider that the agents who hear the announcement believe that it was true before it was announced (and update their knowledge in consequence). This third point implies, in our understanding, that if the receiver of the announcement is a group then the information will be common to all its agents: anyone of them knows that any other one modified her knowledge. These points, except maybe the second, are classical in the field of dynamic epistemic logic (van Ditmarsch et al. (2007)). But one characteristic of 'private announcement' still has to be fixed: what do the other agents learn. Indeed, the announcement can be hidden (and the others may believe that nothing is happening), or it may be the case that the other agents see who is communicating with who, without knowing anything about the content of the message. They may also know both the agents involved and the topic of the announcement, without knowing its truth value.

In Baltag and Moss (2004) and Baltag et al. (1998) the authors propose a general framework to express these different kinds of announcements. The main idea is that an announcement is represented by a graph: its states are deterministic events (and are labelled by formulas of the language that express the piece of information contained in the message, that we call *precondition*); a relation between two states, labeled by an agent i, is like in Kripke models an uncertainty for this agent about which of the two messages is given. With this formalism the previous examples of announcement can be represented as follow (in these examples i gives the information φ to j, the actual event being double-surrounded):

Public announcement:

Hidden private announcement :

Visible private announcement: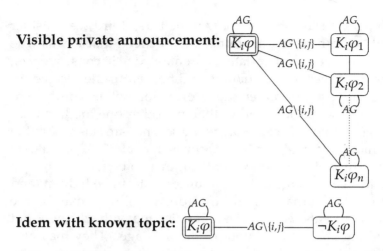

Idem with known topic: $\boxed{\boxed{K_i\varphi}}$ ———$AG\backslash\{i,j\}$——— $\boxed{\neg K_i\varphi}$

For both technical and practical reasons we restrict our formalism to the last kind of announcements, in which both the agents involved and the topic of the message are publicly known. In this context, we consider announcements of the type $!_i^G\varphi$ with $\varphi \in \mathcal{L}_{el}$, $i \in AF$ and $G \subseteq AG$. This formula represents the semi-private announcement by i to the group G of what she knows about φ. That can be "I know that φ is true", "I don't know if φ is true" (analogously to the treatment of questions in work by Groenendijk Groenendijk and Stokhof (1997)). Our formalism does not use event models, announcements are simply modelled as models restrictions, but the result of such an announcement is bisimilar to the result of the action of the corresponding event model as described previously:

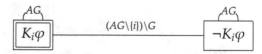

You can read it in the following way: The actual action is that i says "I know that φ" and the agents in the group G know it, but every other agent that is not in G cannot distinguish this action from i saying "I don't know that φ".

It is worth noting that every state of every model satisfies only one of the two previous preconditions: in every state, either i knows φ, or she does not know φ. This implies that the action of $!_i^G\varphi$ on an epistemic model is only a copy of it with less epistemic arrows (if j learns that i knows φ, she does not consider anymore the states in which $\neg K_i\varphi$ was true). Note that $!_i^G\varphi$ is identical to $!_i^G K_i\varphi$ and that $!_i^G\neg K_i\varphi$ is the same action model but pointed in the other state.

Such semi-public announcements can be modelled as restrictions on accessibility relations, while keeping the entire domain intact.

In the following subsection, instead of working with a permission relation that is the same for all agents, we define individual permission relations, one for each agent, and based on these structures we propose operators (let us take the one argument version) $P_i^G \psi$ and $O_i^G \psi$ for "agent i is permitted to announce if she knows ψ to group G", and "agent i is obliged to announce if she knows ψ to group G". The more general form of obligation is $O_i^{\vec{G}} \vec{\psi}$, where i has obligations $(\vec{\psi} =) \psi_1, ..., \psi_n$ to groups of agents $(\vec{G} =) G_1, ..., G_n$.

Let us see it in details.

Syntax and Semantics

We first define the following partial language $\mathcal{L}_{pral}$:

Definition 1.1. The language of private announcement logic $\mathcal{L}_{pral}$ over a countable set of propositional atoms Θ and a countable set of agents AG is defined inductively as follows:

$$\psi ::= p \,|\, \bot \,|\, \neg\psi \,|\, \psi \vee \psi \,|\, K_i\psi \,|\, [!_i^G \psi]\psi$$

where $i \in AG$, $G \subseteq AG$, and $p \in \Theta$.

We are now able to introduce properly the syntax of our language:

Definition 1.2. The language of permitted and obligatory private announcements logic $\mathcal{L}_{popral}$ is defined inductively as follows:

$$\varphi ::= p \,|\, \bot \,|\, \neg\varphi \,|\, \varphi \vee \varphi \,|\, K_i\varphi \,|\, [!_i^G \psi]\varphi \,|\, P_i^G \psi \,|\, O_i^{\vec{G}} \vec{\psi}$$

where $i \in AG$, $G \subseteq AG$, $p \in \Theta$, $\psi \in \mathcal{L}_{pral}$, $\vec{\psi} = (\psi_1, \ldots, \psi_n)$ is a tuple of $\mathcal{L}_{pral}$-formulas and $\vec{G} = (G_1, \ldots, G_n)$ a tuple of subsets of AG. We call $\mathcal{L}_{ppral}$ the fragment of the language without obligation operators (and $\mathcal{L}_{pral}$ is the fragment of the language without permission and obligation operators).

The boolean operators have the classical reading, and $K_i\varphi$ is read "agent i knows that φ". We read $[!_i^G \psi]\varphi$ as "after the announcement by agent i to the group G that (she knows) ψ, where the agents not in G also consider possible that i announces that she does not know ψ, φ becomes true", $P_i^G \psi$ by "i is allowed to say ψ to the group G" and $O_i^{\vec{G}} \vec{\psi}$ by "i is obliged to say ψ_1 to G_1 or ... or ψ_n to G_n". The obligation is thus presented as a list of allowed announcements, and the agent satisfies her obligation by announcing one of them. This construction may seam complicated, and looks like a disjunction: isn't it possible to reduce $O_i^{\vec{G}}\vec{\psi}$ to some kind of $\bigvee_i O_i^{G_i}\psi_i$? The answer is no: the following example shows that you can have the obligation to announce one thing or one other without having the obligation to announce any of the two.

Example 1.1. In the Cluedo game,[1] a murder has been committed and every player has some information about the weapon that has been used, the murderer or the room where the murder took place. A player (A) makes a proposal: "I suggest it was Professor Plum (PP), in the library (L), with the candlestick (C)." If another player (B) knows that this proposal is not correct, she has to show to A one card that invalidate it (for example showing the card that says that Professor Plum is innocent). B is thus obliged to give an information to A, but she has no obligation to give one particular information. Suppose that B knows that the three propositions PP, L and C are false. Therefore we have (considering $\vec{A} = (A, A, A)$) :

$$O_B^{\vec{A}}(\neg PP, \neg L, \neg C) \wedge \neg(O_B^A(\neg PP) \vee O_B^A(\neg L) \vee O_B^A(\neg C)).$$

The following technical notation will allow us to define the notion of *strong* obligation: Let $k, n \in \mathbb{N}$, let $\begin{cases} \vec{\psi} := (\psi_1, \ldots, \psi_n) \\ \vec{G} := (G_1, \ldots, G_n) \end{cases}$ and

let $\begin{cases} \vec{\psi}' := (\psi'_1, \ldots, \psi'_k) \\ \vec{G}' := (G'_1, \ldots, G'_k) \end{cases}$. We note $(\vec{\psi}', \vec{G}') < (\vec{\psi}, \vec{G})$ if $(\vec{\psi}', \vec{G}') \neq (\vec{\psi}, \vec{G})$ and there exist $j_1, \ldots, j_k \in \mathbb{N}$ such that $1 \leqslant j_i < \cdots < j_k \leqslant n$ and for all $l \in \{1, \ldots, k\}$, $\begin{cases} \psi_{j_l} = \psi'_l \\ G_{j_l} := G'_l \end{cases}$. This notation can be understood as the fact that the announcements (formula and group) of the first couple are announcements of the second. In particular, $k < n$.

We can now introduce the following useful abbreviations:

- $\langle !_i^G \psi \rangle \varphi := \neg [!_i^G \psi] \neg \varphi$.

- $[!_i^G \psi^\sim] \varphi := [!_i^G \psi] \varphi \wedge [!_i^G \neg K_i \psi] \varphi$: whatever i announces to G about her knowledge on ψ, φ becomes true after the announcement.

---

[1]For a complete explanation of the rules of this game: www.cluedofan.com/origrule.htm

- *Strong* obligation: $O_i^{\vec{G}}\vec{\psi} := O_i^{\vec{G}}\vec{\psi} \wedge \bigwedge_{(\vec{\psi'},\vec{G'})<(\vec{\psi},\vec{G})} \neg O_i^{\vec{G'}}(\vec{\psi'})$.

- (Finite) sequence of announcements: an announcement $!_i^G\psi$ is a sequence of announcements, and if σ_1, σ_2 are sequences of announcements, then $\sigma_1; \sigma_2$ is a sequence of announcements.

- For all sequences of announcements σ_1, σ_2, we define $[\sigma_1; \sigma_2]\varphi := [\sigma_1][\sigma_2]\varphi$ and $[(\sigma_1; \sigma_2)^\sim]\varphi := [\sigma_1^\sim][\sigma_2^\sim]\varphi$.

- If the tuple of groups (and announcements) are made of a unique element, we abbreviate in the following way: $O_i^G\varphi := O_i^{(G)}(\varphi)$.

The first operator is the dual of $[!_i^G\psi]$. As we will see, it is equivalent to $[!_i^G\psi]\varphi$ with the supplementary condition that i can announce ψ. The second construction, $[!_i^G\psi^\sim]\varphi$, means that whatever i knows about ψ, if she says it to G then φ becomes true. The third one defines a stronger (and in our opinion more realistic) notion of obligation: not only a list of announcements one of which you have to ensure, but the smallest such list. This strong obligation will guarantee us to avoid Ross' paradox, indeed with this interpretation if you are (strongly) obliged to make an announcement you are not (strongly) obliged to make this announcement or another one. The forth definition allows us to consider every sequence of announcements σ. The fifth abbreviates the notation in the case where the considered tuples are 1-uples.

Finally let us consider the following operations on tuples:

- if $\vec{G} = (G_1, \ldots, G_n)$ is a tuple and G an element,

  then we define $G \circ \vec{G} := (G, G_1, \ldots, G_n)$

- if $\vec{\varphi} = (\varphi_1, \ldots, \varphi_n)$ is a tuple and η a permutation on $\{1, \ldots, n\}$ (*i.e.* a bijection on $\{1, \ldots, n\}$),

  then we define $\eta(\vec{\varphi}) := (\varphi_{\eta(1)}, \ldots, \varphi_{\eta(n)})$.

Semantics The models of our logic are epistemic models with an additional relation $\mathcal{P}$ between states and sets of relations, that represents, for each state, the announcements that are explicitly permitted to be done in this state. To define it properly, we need some notion of inclusion between binary relations.

Definition 1.3 (Inclusion between relations). Let $\mathcal{R} = \{R_i\}_{i \in AG}$ and $\mathcal{R}' = \{R_i'\}_{i \in AG}$ be two sets of equivalence relations on a domain S. We note:

- $\mathcal{R}' \subseteq \mathcal{R}$ if for all $i \in AG$, $R'_i \subseteq R_i$.

- for all $i \in AG$, $\mathcal{R}' \subseteq_i \mathcal{R}$ if $R'_i = R_i$ and for all $j \in AG \setminus \{i\}$, $R'_j \subseteq R_j$.

Remark 1.1. For all $i, G \in AG \times 2^{AG}$, we have that $\mathcal{R}' \subseteq_i \mathcal{R}$ only if $\mathcal{R}' \subseteq \mathcal{R}$. Note also that $\subseteq$ and $\subseteq_i$ are partial orders on the class of equivalence relations on S, in particular, they are transitive.

We can now define the *models* of our logic, that are epistemic models *augmented* in the following way.

Definition 1.4. A model is a structure $\mathcal{M} = (S, \mathcal{R} = \{R_i\}_{i \in AG}, V, \mathcal{P} = \{\mathcal{P}_i\}_{i \in AG})$ with S being a non-empty set of states, R_i being an equivalence relation between states of S, V mapping propositional atoms to subsets of S. Furthermore, $\mathcal{P} = \{\mathcal{P}_i\}_{i \in AG}$ is such that for all $i \in AG$, $\mathcal{P}_i \subseteq \mathcal{T}_i$ with $\mathcal{T}_i = \{(s, \mathcal{R}', \mathcal{R}'') : s \in S, \mathcal{R}'' \subseteq_i \mathcal{R}' \subseteq \mathcal{R}\}$.

The membership of $(s, \mathcal{R}', \mathcal{R}'')$ in $\mathcal{P}_i$ can be interpreted as follows: in state s, after every announcement that restricts the set of transitions to $\mathcal{R}'$, every i's announcement that restricts the set of transitions to $\mathcal{R}''$ is 'permitted'.

We can now define the update of a model $\mathcal{M}$ after the announcement $!^G_i \psi$ as the restriction $\mathcal{M}_{!^G_i \psi}$, and the interpretation of our logical language employing that model restriction. Remark that such a restriction is still a model (see Baltag et al. (1998) for details).

Definition 1.5 (satisfiability relation and restricted model). Let $\mathcal{M}$ be a model and s be a state of S. The satisfiability relation $\mathcal{M}, s \models \varphi$ is defined inductively on the structure of φ:

- $\mathcal{M}, s \models p$ iff $s \in V(p)$

- $\mathcal{M}, s \not\models \bot$

- $\mathcal{M}, s \models \neg\psi$ iff $\mathcal{M}, s \not\models \psi$

- $\mathcal{M}, s \models \psi_1 \vee \psi_2$ iff $(\mathcal{M}, s \models \psi_1$ or $\mathcal{M}, s \models \psi_2)$

- $\mathcal{M}, s \models K_i\psi$ iff for all $t \sim_i s$, $\mathcal{M}, t \models \psi$

- $\mathcal{M}, s \models [!^G_i \psi]\chi$ iff $\mathcal{M}, s \models K_i\psi$ implies $\mathcal{M}_{!^G_i \psi}, s \models \chi$

- $\mathcal{M}, s \models P^G_i \chi$ iff (there exists $\psi \in \mathcal{L}_{pral}$ s.t. $s \in [\![K_i\psi]\!]_{\mathcal{M}} \subseteq [\![K_i\chi]\!]_{\mathcal{M}}$ and $(s, \mathcal{R}, \mathcal{R}_{!^G_i \psi}) \in \mathcal{P}_i)$

- $\mathcal{M}, s \models O_i^{\vec{G}} \vec{\varphi}$ iff

    - for all k, $\mathcal{M}, s \models K_i \varphi_k$ and $(s, \mathcal{R}, \mathcal{R}_{!_i^{G_k} \varphi_k}) \in \mathcal{P}_i$, and

    - for all $(s, \mathcal{R}, \mathcal{R}_{!_i^G \chi}) \in \mathcal{P}_i$ there exists a k such that $\mathcal{R}_{!_i^G \chi} = \mathcal{R}_{!_i^{G_k} \chi}$ and $[\![K_i \chi]\!]_{\mathcal{M}} \subseteq [\![K_i \varphi_k]\!]_{\mathcal{M}}$

with for every model $\mathcal{M}$, $i \in AG$, $G \subseteq AG$ and $\psi \in \mathcal{L}_{pel}$, the *restriction* $\mathcal{M}_{!_i^G \psi} = (S', \mathcal{R}_{!_i^G \psi} = \{R'_j\}_{j \in AG}, V', \mathcal{P}')$ is:

- $S' = S$

- $V' = V$

- $R'_i = R_i$

- for all $j \notin G$, $R'_j = R_j$

- for all $j \in G$, $R'_j = \{(s,t) \in R_j \text{ s.t. } s \in [\![K_i \psi]\!]_{\mathcal{M}} \text{ iff } t \in [\![K_i \psi]\!]_{\mathcal{M}}\}$

- for all $j \in AG$, $\mathcal{P}'_j = \{(s, \mathcal{R}^1, \mathcal{R}^2) \in \mathcal{P}_j \text{ s.t. } \mathcal{R}^1 \subseteq \mathcal{R}_{!_i^G \psi}\}$

The semantics of the permission operator are thus the following: we say that i is allowed to say (that she knows) χ to G if there is something (ψ) that she knows, which announcement is more informative than the announcement of χ and gives a restriction that is in $\mathcal{P}_i$. The intuition hard encoded in the semantics for obligation is that given two different things that you are permitted to say, you should only have the obligation to announce the weaker of both. This explains the part "for all $(s, \mathcal{R}, \mathcal{R}_{!_i^G \chi}) \in \mathcal{P}_i$ there exists a k such that $\mathcal{R}_{!_i^G \chi} = \mathcal{R}_{!_i^{G_k} \chi}$ and $[\![K_i \chi]\!]_{\mathcal{M}} \subseteq [\![K_i \varphi_k]\!]_{\mathcal{M}}$" of the definition. This also intuitively entails that if you are obliged to do something then it should at least be permitted, and that intuition is indeed valid for the given semantics of obligation: for all $\varphi \in \mathcal{L}_{pral}$: $\models O_i^G \varphi \rightarrow P_i^G \varphi$.

But this notion of obligation still does not say what you are actually forced to say: indeed, adding formulas to the tuple $\vec{\varphi}$ would maintain this obligation. This pushed us to define the notion of 'strong obligation' as the smallest such $\vec{\varphi}$ satisfying the definiendum: $\mathcal{M}, s \models \mathbf{O}_i^{\vec{G}} \vec{\varphi}$ iff $\mathcal{M}, s \models O_i^{\vec{G}} \vec{\varphi}$ and for all $\vec{\varphi'} < \vec{\varphi}$, $\mathcal{M}, s \not\models O_i^{\vec{G'}}(\vec{\varphi'})$.

We define also $\mathcal{M}_{(!_i^G \psi; !_j^H \chi)} := (\mathcal{M}_{!_i^G \psi})_{!_j^H \chi}$, and we obtain inductively $\mathcal{M}_\sigma$ for every finite sequence of announcements σ. What is precisely the epistemic effect of the restriction $!_i^G \psi$? For every agent $j \in G$ after the announcement of $!_i^G \psi$ it becomes valid that j is able to distinguish the states where i knew ψ from the states where she did not know ψ.

1.3   Comparison with the *non-agent* version

As we announced in section 1.1, except for the notion of obligation that differs in the semantics, we can see this work as an extension of the previous work on permitted *public* announcement logic. More precisely, in the case where the group that receives the announcement is the entire group of agents AG, an announcement $!_i^{AG} \varphi$ has the same meaning as the public announcement of $K_i \varphi$. Even more precisely:

Proposition 1.2. *For every model* $\mathcal{M}$, *every state* $s \in S$, *every agent* $i \in AG$ *and every formula* $\varphi \in \mathcal{L}_{el}$, *if* $\mathcal{M}, s \models K_i \varphi$ *then* $\mathcal{M}_{!_i^{AG}\varphi}, s$ *is bisimilar to* $\mathcal{M}|K_i\varphi, s$.

Proof. The main idea is that in both models, the restriction to the states that are accessible from s is identical. Indeed, on one hand $\mathcal{M}|K_i\varphi$ is the restriction of $\mathcal{M}$ to the states that satisfy $K_i\varphi$ without modifying the relation between these states, on the other hand $\mathcal{M}_{!_i^{AG}\varphi}$ contains all the states of $\mathcal{M}$, but the $K_i\varphi$ -states are disconnected from the $\neg K_i\varphi$-ones, without modifying any relation inside these two sets of states.   ∎

To define the $\mathcal{P}_i$ sets of the public case from the private one, we can follow the following principle: we translate every triplet $(s, \mathcal{R}, \mathcal{R}_{!_i^{AG}\varphi})$ belonging to $\mathcal{P}_i$ into $(s, S, [\![K_i\varphi]\!])$ if $\mathcal{M}, s \models K_i\varphi$ and into $(s, S, [\![\neg K_i\varphi]\!])$ if $\mathcal{M}, s \models \neg K_i\varphi$. We can verify easily now that $\mathcal{M}, s \models P_i^{AG}\varphi$ only if $\mathcal{M}, s \models P(K_i\varphi)$.

We also have a different intuition than in Balbiani and Seban (2011) of what 'strong obligation' means. The obligation is here seen as a disjunction – the obligation to make *one of* the announcements of $\vec{\psi}$ – but as the minimal one, in the sense that every agent i has a *unique* obligation. Indeed, if i has two different obligations, then they are equivalent in a strong way: $\mathcal{M}, s \models O_i^{\vec{G}}(\vec{\varphi}) \wedge O_i^{\vec{H}}(\vec{\psi})$ implies there is a permutation η such that $\vec{\varphi} = \eta(\vec{\psi})$ and $\vec{G} = \eta(\vec{H})$.

1.4   Properties

Let us see some properties of our logic, and in particular a reduced language that is expressively equivalent.

Proposition 1.3. *For all* $p \in \Theta$, *all* $i \in AG$, *all* $G \subseteq AG$, *all* $\psi \in \mathcal{L}_{pral}$, *and all* $\varphi, \varphi_1, \varphi_2 \in \mathcal{L}_{popral}$

1. $\models [!_i^G \psi]p \leftrightarrow (K_i\psi \rightarrow p)$

2. $\models [!_i^G \psi]\bot \leftrightarrow \neg K_i\psi$

3. $\models [!_i^G \psi]\neg\varphi \leftrightarrow (K_i\psi \rightarrow \neg[!_i\psi^G]\varphi)$

4. $\models [!_i^G \psi](\varphi_1 \vee \varphi_2) \leftrightarrow ([!_i^G \psi]\varphi_1 \vee [!_i^G \psi]\varphi_2)$

5. *for all* $j \in G$, $\models [!_i^G \psi]K_j\varphi \leftrightarrow (K_i\psi \rightarrow K_j[!_i^G \psi]\varphi)$

6. *for all* $k \notin G$, $\models [!_i^G \psi]K_k\varphi \leftrightarrow (K_i\psi \rightarrow K_k([!_i^G \psi^\sim]\varphi))$

These equivalences need some explanation, let us see the first one. It says that p is true after every possible announcement by i of ψ iff if i knows ψ (and then he *can* announce it) thus p is true. This only says that an announcement cannot change the valuation.

Proof. This proof is very similar to the proof of reduction of *PAL* (see Plaza (1989) for details). Let us see the proof of the last two ones, with $\mathcal{R}' := \mathcal{R}_{!_i^G \psi}$.

5. ($\Rightarrow$) let $j \in G$, $s \in [\![K_i\psi]\!]_{\mathcal{M}}$ and t a state such that $(s,t) \in R'_j$ (which implies that $(s,t) \in R_j$ and $\mathcal{M}, t \models K_i\psi$ by definition of $\mathcal{R}'$) and $\mathcal{M}_{!_i^G \psi}, t \models \varphi$. Thus $\mathcal{M}, t \models [!_i^G \psi]\varphi$. As t is arbitrary, $\mathcal{M}, s \models K_j[!_i^G \psi]\varphi$.

   ($\Leftarrow$) let $j \in G$, $s \in [\![K_i\psi]\!]_{\mathcal{M}}$ and t a state such that $(s,t) \in R_k$ and $\mathcal{M}, t \models [!_i^G \psi]\varphi$. By definition of $\mathcal{R}'$, either $\mathcal{M}, t \models \neg K_i\psi$ and thus the implication is correct, or $(s,t) \in R'_j$ and thus $\mathcal{M}_{!_i^G \psi}, t \models K_j\varphi$.

6. ($\Rightarrow$) let $k \notin G$, $s \in [\![K_i\psi]\!]_{\mathcal{M}}$ and t a state such that $(s,t) \in R'_k$ (which implies that $(s,t) \in R_k$) and $\mathcal{M}_{!_i^G \psi}, t \models \varphi$. Now, either $\mathcal{M}, t \models K_i\psi$ and then $\mathcal{M}, t \models [!_i^G \psi]\varphi$ or $\mathcal{M}, t \models \neg K_i\psi$ and then $\mathcal{M}, t \models [!_i^G \neg K_i\psi]\varphi$. Thus $\mathcal{M}, t \models K_k([!_i^G \psi]\varphi \wedge [!_i^G \neg K_i\psi]\varphi)$, i.e. $\mathcal{M}, t \models K_k[!_i^G \psi^\sim]\varphi$.

   ($\Leftarrow$) let $k \notin G$, $s \in [\![K_i\psi]\!]_{\mathcal{M}}$ and t a state such that $(s,t) \in R_j$ and $\mathcal{M}, t \models [!_i^G \psi]\varphi \wedge [!_i^G \neg K_i\psi]\varphi$. Now, $(s,t) \in R'_j$ and in all cases, $\mathcal{M}_{!_i^G \psi}, t \models \varphi$, therefore, as it is true for every state t, $\mathcal{M}, s \models [!_i^G \psi]K_k\varphi$. ∎

Definition 1.6. We call $\mathcal{L}_{elPO}$ the following language:

$$\varphi ::= p\,|\,\bot\,|\,\neg\varphi\,|\,\varphi \vee \varphi\,|\,K_i\varphi\,|\,\langle\sigma\rangle P_i^G \psi\,|\,\langle\sigma\rangle \neg P_i^G \psi\,|\,\langle\sigma\rangle O_i^G \vec{\psi}\,|\,\langle\sigma\rangle \neg O_i^G \vec{\psi}$$

where $\psi \in \mathcal{L}_{el}$, $i \in AG$, $G \subseteq AG$, σ is a sequence of announcements and for all ψ_j, G_j in the tuples $\vec{\psi}, \vec{G}$, we have $\psi_j \in \mathcal{L}_{el}$ and $G_j \subseteq AG$. It is the restriction of $\mathcal{L}_{popral}$ to the fragment without announcements except a sequence before permission and obligation operators. We call $\mathcal{L}_{elP}$ the restriction of $\mathcal{L}_{elPO}$ to the fragment without obligation operators.

Corollary 1.1 (of Proposition 1.3). $\mathcal{L}_{elPO}$ *is expressively equivalent to* $\mathcal{L}_{popral}$. $\mathcal{L}_{elP}$ *is expressively equivalent to* $\mathcal{L}_{ppral}$. $\mathcal{L}_{el}$ *is expressively equivalent to* $\mathcal{L}_{pral}$.

This last language, $\mathcal{L}_{elP}$, will be used in Section 1.5 to prove the completeness of the given axiomatization.

Proof. We prove the first property, we can prove the other two properties in the same way). Clearly $\mathcal{L}_{popral}$ is at least as expressive as $\mathcal{L}_{elPO}$ (because the second is included in the first). To prove the other inclusion, let us define inductively the following translation *tr*:

- $tr(\bot) = \bot$ and for all atom $p \in \Theta$, $tr(p) = p$

- $tr(\neg\varphi) = \neg tr(\varphi)$; $tr(\varphi \vee \psi) = tr(\varphi) \vee tr(\psi)$; $tr(K_i\varphi) = K_i tr(\varphi)$

- $tr([!_i^G\psi]p) = K_i tr(\psi) \rightarrow p$; $tr([!_i^G\psi]\bot) = \neg K_i tr(\psi)$

- $tr([!_i^G\psi]\neg\varphi) = K_i tr(\psi) \rightarrow \neg tr([!_i^G\psi]\varphi)$

- $tr([!_i^G\psi](\varphi_1 \vee \varphi_2)) = tr([!_i^G\psi]\varphi_1) \vee tr([!_i^G\psi]\varphi_2)$

- for all $j \in G$, $tr([!_i^G\psi]K_j\varphi) = K_i tr(\psi) \rightarrow K_j tr([!_i^G\psi]\varphi)$

- for all $k \notin G$, $tr([!_i^G\psi]K_k\varphi) = K_i tr(\psi) \rightarrow K_k tr([!_i^G\psi^\sim]\varphi)$

- $tr(P_i^G\psi) = P_i^G tr(\psi)$; $tr(O_i^{\vec{G}}\vec{\psi}) = O_i^{\vec{G}}(tr(\psi_1), \ldots, tr(\psi_n))$.

We obtain the wanted result by Proposition 1.3.   ∎

Another interesting property of our semantics is that, without any additive assumption, the following proposition is true:

Proposition 1.4. *For all models* $\mathcal{M}$ *and all formulas* $\psi_1, \psi_2 \in \mathcal{L}_{pral}$ *all* $i, j \in AG$, *we have that if* $\mathcal{M} \models K_i\psi_1 \rightarrow K_i\psi_2$ *then* $\mathcal{M} \models P_i^G\psi_1 \rightarrow P_i^G\psi_2$.

Note that it translates our intuition that: if an agent is allowed to give some information to some group of agents, then she is also allowed to give less information to the same group.

Corollary 1.2. *If we have* $\mathcal{M} \models K_i(\psi_1 \rightarrow \psi_2)$ *then* $\mathcal{M} \models P_i^G \psi_1 \rightarrow P_i^G \psi_2$.

This corollary comes directly from axiom K.

Proof.[of Proposition 1.4] By definition of the semantics of P and by transitivity of the implication. More precisely: let $s \in S$, suppose that $\mathcal{M}, s \models P_i^G \psi_1$, we want to show that $\mathcal{M}, s \models P_i^G \psi_2$. Then let $\psi_0 \in \mathcal{L}_{pral}$ be such that $\mathcal{M}, s \models K_i \psi_0$, $\mathcal{M} \models K_i \psi_0 \rightarrow K_i \psi_1$ and $(s, \mathcal{R}, \mathcal{R}_{!G\psi_0}^i) \in \mathcal{P}_i$, the three conditions of the semantics. Then we can keep the first and the third one, and replace the second, by transitivity of the implication, by $\mathcal{M} \models K_i \psi_0 \rightarrow K_i \psi_2$. We then obtain $\mathcal{M}, s \models P_i^G \psi_2$. ∎

Let us see now what are the consequences of the composition of different obligations or permissions:

Proposition 1.5. *For all* $\psi \in \mathcal{L}_{popral}$, *all agent i and all group G, all n-uples* $\vec{\psi}$ *and* $\vec{G}$ *of* $\mathcal{L}_{popral}$-*formulas and groups,*

1. $\models P_i^G(\psi) \rightarrow K_i \psi$

2. $\models O_i^{\vec{G}} \vec{\psi} \longrightarrow \bigwedge_k P_i^{G_k} \psi_k$

3. $\models \mathcal{O}_i^{\vec{G}} \vec{\psi} \rightarrow O_i^{\vec{G}} \vec{\psi}$

4. *for all permutation* η, $\models (O_i^{\eta(\vec{G})} \eta(\vec{\psi}) \leftrightarrow O_i^{\vec{G}} \vec{\psi}) \wedge (O_i^{\eta(\vec{G})} \eta(\vec{\psi}) \leftrightarrow O_i^{\vec{G}} \vec{\psi})$

5. $\models P_i^{G_1} \psi \wedge O_i^{G_1 \circ \vec{G}}(\varphi_1 \circ \vec{\varphi}) \rightarrow P_i^{G_1}(\psi \wedge \varphi_1)$

Proof. The first proposition comes directly from $s \in [\![K_i \psi]\!]_\mathcal{M}$ in the semantics of $\mathcal{P}$, the second one from $(s, \mathcal{R}, \mathcal{R}_{!G_k \varphi_k}^i) \in \mathcal{P}_i$ in the semantics of O, the third and the fourth one are inducted by the semantics of $\mathcal{O}$ and O. For the fifth one, note that $[\![K_i \psi]\!] \cap [\![K_i \varphi_1]\!] = [\![K_i(\psi \wedge \varphi_1)]\!]$. ∎

Proposition 1.6. *For all models* $\mathcal{M}$ *and all formulas* $\psi \in \mathcal{L}_{pral}$ *all* $i, j \in AG$, *for all* $G \subseteq AG$, *we have that if* $\mathcal{M} \models K_i \psi \rightarrow K_j K_i \psi$ *then* $\mathcal{M} \models P_i^G \psi \leftrightarrow P_i^{G \cup \{j\}} \psi$.

Proof. It is easy to see that in both cases it is enough to show that for all model $\mathcal{M}$ such that $\mathcal{M} \models K_i \psi \rightarrow K_j K_i \psi$ we have $\mathcal{R}_{!G\psi}^i = \mathcal{R}_{!G \cup \{j\} \psi}^i$. Therefore let $\mathcal{M}$ be such a model. Note that if $j \in G$ the result is empty, let us then suppose $j \notin G$. Now,

- for all $k \notin G$ with $k \neq j$, $(\mathcal{R}_{!_i^G \psi})_k = \mathcal{R}_k = (\mathcal{R}_{!_i^{G \cup \{j\}} \psi})_k$

- for all $k \in G$, $(\mathcal{R}_{!_i^G \psi})_k = (\mathcal{R}_{!_i^{\{k\}} \psi})_k = (\mathcal{R}_{!_i^{G \cup \{j\}} \psi})_k$

- let us show now that $(\mathcal{R}_{!_i^{G \cup \{j\}} \psi})_j = (\mathcal{R}_{!_i^G \psi})_j$ showing that $(\mathcal{R}_{!_i^{G \cup \{j\}} \psi})_j = \mathcal{R}_j$. The direct inclusion is trivial, let then $(s, t) \in \mathcal{R}_j$, let us see that $s \in [\![K_i \psi]\!]_{\mathcal{M}}$ iff $t \in [\![K_i \psi]\!]_{\mathcal{M}}$. But $s \in [\![K_i \psi]\!]_{\mathcal{M}}$ implies $\mathcal{M}, s \models K_j K_i \psi$ that implies $\mathcal{M}, t \models K_i \psi$. And reciprocally.

∎

This proposition says that if is true everywhere in the model that some agent (j) would not learn anything if i announces ψ, then i is allowed to announce it to him, in addition with every group of agent for which this announcement was permitted.

Finally, here is a characterization of the link between a model and its reduction after an announcement:

Proposition 1.7. *For all formula φ, all model $\mathcal{M}$, all state s of the model and all sequence of announcements σ we have:* $\mathcal{M}_\sigma, s \models \varphi \iff \mathcal{M}, s \models [\sigma^\sim]\varphi$.

Proof. Let us first prove it for a single announcement $!_i^G \psi$:

$$\mathcal{M}_{!_i^G \psi}, s \models \varphi$$

iff $\begin{cases} \mathcal{M}, s \models K_i \psi \text{ implies } \mathcal{M}, s \models \langle !_i^G \psi \rangle \varphi \\ \mathcal{M}, s \models \neg K_i \psi \text{ implies } \mathcal{M}, s \models \langle !_i^G \neg K_i \psi \rangle \varphi \end{cases}$

iff $\mathcal{M}, s \models (K_i \psi \to \langle !_i^G \psi \rangle \varphi) \wedge (\neg K_i \psi \to \langle !_i^G \neg K_i \psi \rangle \varphi)$

iff $\mathcal{M}, s \models [!_i^G \psi] \varphi \wedge [!_i^G \neg K_i \psi] \varphi$ (because $\models \neg K_i \psi \leftrightarrow K_i \neg K_i \psi$)

iff $\mathcal{M}, s \models [!_i^G \psi^\sim] \varphi$.

By definition of $[.^\sim]$ the result extends to every sequence of announcements. ∎

1.5 Soundness and Completeness

In this section, we give a sound and complete axiomatization of our logic. For technical reasons, we restrict this proposal to the language without obligation operators $\mathcal{L}_{ppral}$. We conjecture that a complete axiomatisation for the whole logic exists, and plan to prove it in a further work.

Let *PPrAL* be the smallest logic in our language that contains all the tautologies of propositional logic, the schemata presented in table 1.1 and that is closed under modus ponens, under necessitation for every K_i

Table 1.1: The axiomatisation *PPrAL*

$K_i\varphi \to \varphi$	truth
$K_i\varphi \to K_iK_i\varphi$	positive introspection
$\neg K_i\varphi \to K_i\neg K_i\varphi$	negative introspection
$[!_i^G\psi]p \leftrightarrow (K_i\psi \to p)$	atomic permanence
$[!_i^G\psi]\bot \leftrightarrow \neg K_i\psi$	ann. and false
$[!_i^G\psi]\neg\varphi \leftrightarrow (K_i\psi \to \neg[!_i^G\psi]\varphi)$	ann. and negation
$[!_i^G\psi](\varphi_1 \vee \varphi_2) \leftrightarrow ([!_i^G\psi]\varphi_1 \vee [!_i^G\psi]\varphi_2)$	ann. and disjunction
if $j \in G \cup \{i\}$, $[!_i^G\psi]K_j\varphi \leftrightarrow (K_i\psi \to K_j[!_i^G\psi]\varphi)$	ann. and knowledge (1)
if $k \notin G \cup \{i\}$, $[!_i^G\psi]K_k\varphi \leftrightarrow (K_i\psi \to K_k[!_i^G\psi^{\sim}]\varphi)$	ann. and knowledge (2)
$\langle\sigma\rangle P_i^G\varphi \to \langle\sigma\rangle K_i\varphi$	rationality of permission

and every $[!_i^G\psi]$ where $!_i^G\psi$ is an announcement, and under the following inference rule:

$$\text{From } [\sigma^{\sim}](K_i\varphi \to K_i\varphi') \text{ infer } [\sigma^{\sim}](P_i^G\varphi \to P_i^G\varphi') \tag{R}$$

Proposition 1.8. *PPrAL is sound in all the models.*

Proof. The soundness of the tautologies of propositional logic, of modus ponens, of the first three axioms of table 1.1, and of the necesitation rule for every K_i comes from the fact that for every model $\mathcal{M} = (S, V, \mathcal{R}, \mathcal{P})$, $(S, V, \mathcal{R})$ is a Kripke model where every $R_i \in \mathcal{R}$ is an equivalence relation (see Fagin et al. (1995) for details). From the fourth to the ninth axiom, the soundness is proven by Propositions 1.3. For the tenth axiom we use propositions 1.5, and 1.7. Finally for the inference rule R we use propositions 1.4 and 1.7. ∎

Remark 1.2. Note that we have in particular that for all $\varphi \in \mathcal{L}_{ppral}$, $\vdash_{PPrAL} \varphi \leftrightarrow tr(\varphi)$. We use often this property in the following proofs, in particular to use φ instead of $tr(\varphi)$, for the sake of simplicity, when we need a $\mathcal{L}_{elP}$-formula.

To prove the completeness result, we define the canonical model for *PPrAL*:

Definition 1.7 (Canonical Model). The canonical model $\mathcal{M}^c = (S^c, \mathcal{R}_i^c, V^c, \mathcal{P}^c)$ is defined as follows:

- S^c is the set of all $\vdash_{PPrAL}$-maximal consistent sets

H. van Ditmarsch & P. Seban

- for every $p \in \Theta$, $V^c(p) = \{x \in S^c \mid p \in x\}$

- for every $i \in AG$, $x\mathcal{R}^c_i y$ iff $K_i x = K_i y$, where $K_i x = \{\varphi | K_i \varphi \in x\}$

- $\mathcal{T}^c_i = \{(x, \mathcal{R}^c_\sigma, \mathcal{R}^c_{\sigma!^G_i \chi}) : \chi \in \mathcal{L}_{pral}, \sigma$ a sequence of announcements, $G \subseteq AG\}$, and $\mathcal{P}^c_i = \mathcal{T}^c_i \setminus \{(x, \mathcal{R}^c_\sigma, \mathcal{R}^c_{\sigma!^G_i \chi}) :$ for some $\psi \in \mathcal{L}_{pral}, \vdash [\sigma^\sim](K_i\chi \rightarrow K_i\psi)$ and $\langle\sigma\rangle\neg P^G_i \psi \in x\}$

Remark 1.3. Note that to define $\mathcal{P}^c_i$ in the canonical model we need to define $\mathcal{R}_\sigma$ and $\mathcal{R}_{\sigma!^G_i \chi}$ which suppose that we are able to define properly what $\mathcal{M}^c, x \models \langle\sigma\rangle\top$ and $\mathcal{M}^c, x \models \langle\sigma\rangle K_i \chi$ mean . It would be a contradiction because we are defining the model $\mathcal{M}^c$. But as $\langle\sigma\rangle\top$ and $\langle\sigma\rangle K_i \chi$ are $\mathcal{L}_{pral}$-formulas and thus equivalent to $\mathcal{L}_{el}$-formulas (see Remark 1.2), $\mathcal{R}^c_\sigma$ and $\mathcal{R}_{\sigma!^G_i \chi}$ can be properly defined using exclusively the epistemic model $(S^c, V^c, \mathcal{R}^c)$. Thus $\mathcal{M}^c$ is properly defined.

Proposition 1.9. *The canonical model is a model.*

Proof. Indeed, S^c is a set, V^c, $\mathcal{P}^c_i$ and $\mathcal{R}^c_i$ for all i have the desired form. The only property we have to show is that if $(x, \mathcal{R}_1, \mathcal{R}_2) \in \mathcal{P}^c_i$ then $\mathcal{R}_2 \subseteq_i \mathcal{R}_1$. Thus, let us suppose that $(x, \mathcal{R}_1, \mathcal{R}_2) \in \mathcal{P}^c_i$, we have σ, χ, G such that $\mathcal{R}_1 = \mathcal{R}^c_\sigma$ and $\mathcal{R}_2 = \mathcal{R}^c_{\sigma|!^G_i \chi}$. By definition of $\subseteq_i$ we obtain the wanted result. ∎

In the canonical model, a state is thus a set of formulas. The link between the fact that a formula φ is in a set x and the fact that $\mathcal{M}^c, x \models \varphi$ is given by the following proposition:

Proposition 1.10 (Truth Lemma for $\mathcal{L}_{elP}$). *For all $\varphi \in \mathcal{L}_{elP}$ we have:*

$$\Pi(\varphi) : \textit{for all } x \in S^c, \mathcal{M}^c, x \models \varphi \textit{ iff } \varphi \in x$$

Proof. Let us prove it by induction on the number of occurrences of a P operator.

base case : If φ is a formula without permission, $\Pi(\varphi)$ is a known result, the canonical model considered here being an extension of the canonical model for $S5$ (see Blackburn et al. (2001) or Fagin et al. (1995) for details).

Let us then suppose that it is true for every formula with at most n occurrences of a permission operator. Note that by Remarks

1.1 and 1.2 we can suppose the result for every formula of $\mathcal{L}_{ppral}$ containing at most n occurrences of a permission operator.

Let us now prove the wanted result for every formula with at most $n + 1$ occurrences of a permission operator by induction on the structure of the formula φ:

- $\varphi = \neg\psi$: $\mathcal{M}_c, x \models \neg\psi$ iff $\mathcal{M}_c, x \not\models \psi$ iff $\psi \notin x$ (by IH) iff $\neg\psi \in x$ (by maximality of x).

- $\varphi = \varphi_1 \vee \varphi_2$: $\mathcal{M}_c, x \models \varphi_1 \vee \varphi_2$ iff $\mathcal{M}_c, x \models \varphi_1$ or $\mathcal{M}_c, x \models \varphi_2$ iff $\varphi_1 \in x$ or $\varphi_2 \in x$ (by IH) iff $\varphi_1 \vee \varphi_2 \in x$.

- $\varphi = K_i\psi$: Let us first suppose that $K_i\psi \in x$ and let y be such that $x\mathcal{R}_i^c y$, we want to show that $\mathcal{M}_c, y \models \psi$. Indeed we have $K_i\psi \in y$ and then $\psi \in y$, which implies (by IH) that $\mathcal{M}_c, y \models \psi$.

  Reciprocally, let us suppose that $\mathcal{M}_c, x \models K_i\psi$ and that $K_i\psi \notin x$. Then $K_i x \cup \{\neg\psi\}$ is consistent which means that there exists a y such that $x\mathcal{R}_i y$ and $\neg\psi \in y$. By IH we obtain $\mathcal{M}^c, y \not\models \psi$ and thus $\mathcal{M}^c, x \not\models K_i\psi$ which is a contradiction. Thus the hypothesis $K_i\psi \notin x$ was wrong and $K_i\psi \in x$.

- $\varphi = \langle\sigma\rangle P_i^G\chi$:

  ($\Rightarrow$) By the first IH, we have that for every $\mathcal{L}_{pral}$-formula $\theta, \langle\sigma\rangle\theta \in x$ iff $\mathcal{M}^c, x \models \langle\sigma\rangle\theta$ (∗). Let us suppose that $\langle\sigma\rangle P_i^G\chi \notin x$, i.e. $\neg\langle\sigma\rangle P_i^G\chi \in x$ by maximality, we want to show that $\mathcal{M}^c, x \not\models \langle\sigma\rangle P_i^G\chi$. Now, either $\langle\sigma\rangle\top \notin x$ and thus $\mathcal{M}^c, x \not\models \langle\sigma\rangle\top$ by IH, and then it is finished. Or $\langle\sigma\rangle\top \in x$, and then $\langle\sigma\rangle\neg P_i^G\chi \in x$. Let us suppose it. Let ψ be a $\mathcal{L}_{pral}$-formula such that $\mathcal{M}^c \models [\sigma^\sim](K_i\psi \rightarrow K_i\chi)$, let us prove that $(x, \mathcal{R}_\sigma^c, \mathcal{R}_{\sigma\|_i^G\psi}^c) \notin \mathcal{P}_i^c$. By IH we have that $\vdash [\sigma^\sim](K_i\psi \rightarrow K_i\chi)$, which means with $\langle\sigma\rangle\neg P_i^G\chi \in x$ that $(x, \mathcal{R}_\sigma^c, \mathcal{R}_{\sigma\|_i^G\psi}^c) \notin \mathcal{P}_i^c$.

  ($\Leftarrow$) If $\langle\sigma\rangle P_i^G\chi \in x$, then for all $\psi \in \mathcal{L}_{pral}$ such that $\vdash [\sigma^\sim](K_i\chi \rightarrow K_i\psi)$ we have, by inference rule R, that $\langle\sigma\rangle P_i^G\psi \in x$ and thus $(x, \mathcal{R}_\sigma^c, \mathcal{R}_{\sigma\|_i^G\chi}^c) \in \mathcal{P}_i^c$. This proves that $\mathcal{M}^c, x \models \langle\sigma\rangle P_i^G\chi$.

- $\varphi = \langle\sigma\rangle\neg P_i^G\chi$:

  ($\Rightarrow$) Suppose that $\mathcal{M}^c, x \models \langle\sigma\rangle\neg P_i^G\chi$. Then $(x, \mathcal{R}_\sigma^c, \mathcal{R}_{\sigma\|_i^G\chi}^c) \notin \mathcal{P}_i^c$, i.e. there exists a $\psi \in \mathcal{L}_{pral}$ such that $\vdash [\sigma^\sim](K_i\chi \rightarrow K_i\psi)$ and $\langle\sigma\rangle\neg P_i^G\psi \in x$. Thus, by inference rule R, we obtain that $\langle\sigma\rangle\neg P_i^G\chi \in x$.

($\Leftarrow$) If $\langle\sigma\rangle\neg P^G_i\chi \in x$ then, by definition of $\mathcal{P}^c_i$, for all $\psi \in \mathcal{L}_{pral}$ such that $\vdash [\sigma^\sim](K_i\psi \rightarrow K_i\chi)$ we have $(x, \mathcal{R}^c_\sigma, \mathcal{R}^c_{\sigma||^G_i\psi}) \notin \mathcal{P}^c_i$. This is equivalent, by IH, to the fact that for all $\psi \in \mathcal{L}_{pral}$ such that $\mathcal{M}^c \models [\sigma^\sim](K_i\psi \rightarrow K_i\chi)$ we have $(x, \mathcal{R}^c_\sigma, \mathcal{R}^c_{\sigma||^G_i\psi}) \notin \mathcal{P}^c_i$. That means exactly that $\mathcal{M}^c, x \not\models \langle\sigma\rangle P^G_i\chi$. Using another IH we have that $\mathcal{M}^c, x \models \langle\sigma\rangle K_i\chi$, and then from $\mathcal{M}^c, x \models \neg\langle\sigma\rangle P^G_i\chi$ we obtain $\mathcal{M}^c, x \models \langle\sigma\rangle\neg P^G_i\chi$.

∎

Theorem 1.1. *PPrAL is sound and complete with respect to the class of all models.*

Proof. Soundness has been proved in Proposition 1.8. For the completeness part, let $\varphi \in \mathcal{L}_{ppral}$ be a valid formula. Thus we have: $\models \varphi$ only if $\models tr(\varphi)$ only if $\mathcal{M}^c \models tr(\varphi)$ only if $\vdash tr(\varphi)$ (by Proposition 1.10) only if $\vdash \varphi$ (by Remark 1.2). ∎

2   Use of the Formalism in Special Cases

2.1   Case Study: AIDS

Let us recall the case of Michel, a patient that did an AIDS test, presented in the introduction. His case can be represented in the following way with individual permissions and transgressions (see Figure 1.1). Let us explain the visual primitives.

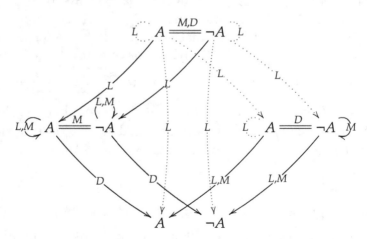

Figure 1.1: AIDS example

At the top, a two-state Kripke model where neither Michel nor the doctor can distinguish between a state where Michel has Aids (A) and a state where he has not ($\neg A$). Instead, the laboratory knows (there is no label L on the double links between A and $\neg A$). Note that reflexive arrows $\overset{L,M,D}{\text{(( ))}}$ for knowledge are omitted in every state, the reflexive arrows appearing represent the empty announcement as explained after. We see three more of such models in the figure, on the left is the situation where the uncertainty has been removed for the doctor but where Michel still is uncertain, on the right is the dual where the doctor is still uncertain, but Michel knows. For the record: this is the suicide-risk situation that we want to avoid! So getting there, should not be permitted. At the bottom, everybody knows.

The pointed arrows stand for the results of announcements. If they are dotted, they are not permitted, if they are plain, they are permitted. The reflexive (pointed) arrows labelled with L in the top Kripke model (information state) for the laboratory show that the empty announcement, *i.e.* the announcement of 'true', after which the same structure results, is not permitted for the laboratory: the laboratory is obliged to say something informative. In the top information state, it is permitted for the laboratory to announce the outcome of the test to the doctor. This action (whether A is true, or the different action for when A is false) brings us to the left state (plain arrows). Also, these are the *only* plain arrows from those states: the laboratory obliged to inform the doctor: $\mathcal{M}, A \models O_L^D A$ and $\mathcal{M}, \neg A \models O_L^D \neg A$.

Apart from the reflexive arrows, two more non-permitted actions on top are: informing Michel (go to right): $\mathcal{M}, A \models \neg P_L^M A$, and informing the doctor and Michel at the same time (straight to the bottom, where everybody knows): $\mathcal{M}, A \models \neg P_L^{\{D,M\}} A$. The other connections can be similarly explained. Finally, after the violation of the laboratory informing Michel, the laboratory is still obliged to inform the doctor, and also Michel is obliged to contact the doctor: $\mathcal{M}, A \models \langle !_L^M A \rangle (O_L^D A \wedge O_M^D A)$ — which we could now interpret that action will be undertaken if Michel has not contacted the doctor after the laboratory has improperly informed him directly of the outcome of the AIDS-test. Therefore, the plain arrows from the right to the bottom are labelled both with L and with M. Further intricacies in the reflexive arrows on the right-hand side are left to the imagination of the reader.

2.2 Dealing with Privacy Policies

In Aucher et al. (2010), the authors propose a formalism close to ours with the difference that in their proposal the 'right to say' can be derived from the 'right to know'. In other words, they assume that there is a list of permissions or obligations to know that have to be satisfied. This list defines whether an announcement is permitted or not: it is permitted if and only if it leads to a situation that satisfies these obligations/permissions. This condition does not allow to model every situation: two different announcements that lead to a same epistemic situation (then that satisfy the same permission to know) can be one permitted the other forbidden, as far as they are announced in different situations. The previous situation is such a counter-example: we have $\mathcal{M}, A \models \neg P_L^{\{D,M\}} A \wedge \langle !_L^M A \rangle P_L^D A$: the laboratory is not allowed to announce A to the doctor and Michel at the same time, but after having informed Michel he is allowed to announce it to the doctor. These two announcements are not permitted in the same way, and yet they lead to the same situation (the A-situation at the bottom of Figure 1.1) — but they did not come from the same one!

But in some situations, the restrictions on announcements is derivable from a Privacy Policy which says what each agent is allowed to know. Therefore, we present in this section an idea of how to adapt Aucher *et al.*'s notion of Privacy Policy, to model those multi-agent situations in which the right to know is the relevant notion, deriving the permission relation $\mathcal{P}$ from it. This proposition avoids another limit of their work, that it is limited to a single 2-agents situation, in which a *sender* gives information to a *receiver*, the latter having a perfect knowledge of the epistemic state of the former.

Let us see a compelling example, cited from Aucher et al. (2010):

> Consider the information about websites contacted by a user (U), which are available on a server logfile. The list of websites for each user is clearly a sensitive information which he would not like to disclose. However, knowing which websites have been visited is a valuable information, for example, for the configuration of a firewall, or to make statistics. Thus it has become anonym by replacing the names of the users with numbers by means of a hashcode (h). So even if one knows the list of users one cannot understand who contacted which website. However, from the association between users and numbers and between numbers

and websites the original information can be reconstructed. Therefore the mappings from the users to the numbers (c) and from the numbers to the websites (e) can be distributed individually but not altogether since their association would allow to reconstruct the mapping from the users to the websites they visited (v): $c \wedge e \rightarrow v$.

The last sentence says that the user u is permitted to know c and to know e but not to know v. The privacy policy being the set of what is (not) permitted to be known by the agent, it would be in this case $\{\neg P(K_U v)\}$: it is not permitted that U knows v. To construct our model, presented in Figure 1.2, we start from an initial epistemic model and we define $\mathcal{P}_S$ as the set of transitions such that $K_u v$ is wrong in the resulting state.

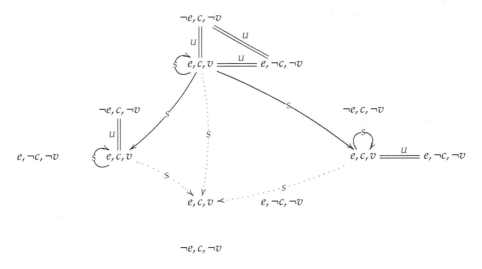

Figure 1.2: server example

In Figure 1.2, as in Figure 1.1, double arrows represent knowledge, dotted arrows represent non-permitted announcements and plain arrows permitted ones. At the top we see a three-state Kripke model where the user does not known neither c nor e, nor v. We see three more of such models in the figure, on the left is the situation where the uncertainty on c has been removed, on the right is the situation in which the uncertainty on e has been removed. At the bottom, v is known (epistemic situation we want to forbid). Once again, the pointed arrows stand for the results of announcements. If they are dotted, they are not permitted, if they are plain, they are permitted. To make the figure readable, we put only the pointed arrows for the e, c, v-states. Thus this model says that the server is allowed to say c or to say e to the user, but not to say v to her: $\mathcal{M}, (e, c, v) \models P_s^u c \land P_s^u e \land \neg P_s^u v$. After the announcement of one of the two informations e or c, the server is not allowed to say to the user the other one: $\mathcal{M}, (e, c, v) \models \langle !_s^u e \rangle \neg P_s^u c \land \langle !_s^u c \rangle \neg P_s^u e$.

Let us define more formally how we define a privacy policy and, from it and an epistemic model, the corresponding model. The notions we present here are slightly different from the ones in Aucher et al. (2010) as they capture multi-agent notions and preconditions to the permission. We define the following notion:

Privacy policy An *epistemic norm* is a construction of the form $pre \rightarrow P_i \psi$ or $pre \rightarrow \neg P_i \psi$ with $pre, \psi \in \mathcal{L}_{el}$ and $i \in AG$. A privacy policy is a finite set of epistemic norms.

We interpret $pre \rightarrow P_i \psi$ (resp. $pre \rightarrow \neg P_i \psi$) by "if pre is true then i is allowed (resp. not allowed) to get to a situation where ψ is true". We note $pre \rightarrow F_i \psi := pre \rightarrow O_i \neg \psi$.

We detail now how to construct a POPRAL model from an epistemic one and a privacy policy:

Let $\mathcal{M} = (S, V, \mathcal{R})$ be an epistemic model and PP be a privacy policy, we construct the liberal model $\mathcal{M}_{PP}^l = (S, V, \mathcal{R}, \mathcal{P}^l)$ and the dictatorial one $\mathcal{M}_{PP}^d = (S, V, \mathcal{R}, \mathcal{P}^d)$ in the following way: for all agent $i \in AG$,

$$\mathcal{P}_i^l = \{(s, \mathcal{R}_1, \mathcal{R}_2) \mid \forall (pre \rightarrow \neg P_i \psi) \in PP, \text{ if } \mathcal{M}_{\mathcal{R}_1}, s \models pre$$
$$\text{then } \mathcal{M}_{\mathcal{R}_2}, s \not\models \psi\}$$

$$\mathcal{P}_i^d = \{(s, \mathcal{R}_1, \mathcal{R}_2) \mid \exists (pre \rightarrow P_i \psi) \in PP, \mathcal{M}_{\mathcal{R}_1}, s \models pre$$
$$\text{and } \mathcal{M}_{\mathcal{R}_2}, s \models \psi\}$$

These notions give us a deterministic construction of a model starting from a privacy policy and an epistemic model. Following Aucher et al. (2010) we consider two situations: the liberal situation considers that every situation that is not explicitly forbidden is permitted, the dictatorial one considers that every situation that is not explicitly permitted is forbidden.

3   Conclusion and perspectives

We proposed a logic for the permission and obligation to say something to somebody (or to a group of persons). We axiomatized the logic and proved completeness of the axiomatization for the fragment of the language without obligation operators, and we illustrated the logic with two main examples. This logic can be used in situations in which every private communication have a public part: the topic of the message and the agents involved in the communication are public. The first further step in this work would thus be to avoid this limit by considering permission over other kinds of private communication. In this sense, having a general framework for permission and obligation over every epistemic action (Baltag et al. (1998)) would be a final step.

We also consider to expand the framework with changing permissions, as in Pucella et al. Pucella and Weissman (2004). In this context, as in the example of Section 2.1, it would mean to define an operation that defines or modifies the permission relation $\mathcal{P}$ of a given model.

Bibliography

Aucher, G., Boella, G., and van der Torre, L., 2010. Privacy policies with modal logic: The dynamic turn. In *DEON*, pages 196–213.

Balbiani, P. and Seban, P., 2011. Reasoning about permitted announcement. *Journal of Philosophical Logic*. Published Online First. http://www.springerlink.com/content/g215033h036441v5/.

Baltag, A. and Moss, L., 2004. Logics for epistemic programs. *Synthese*, 139:165–224. Knowledge, Rationality & Action 1–60.

Baltag, A., Moss, L., and Solecki, S., 1998. The logic of public announcements, common knowledge, and private suspicions. In Gilboa, I. (ed.), *Proceedings of the 7th Conference on Theoretical Aspects of Rationality and Knowledge (TARK 98)*, pages 43–56.

Blackburn, P., de Rijke, M., and Venema, Y., 2001. *Modal Logic*. Cambridge University Press, Cambridge. Cambridge Tracts in Theoretical Computer Science 53.

Fagin, R., Halpern, J., Moses, Y., and Vardi, M., 1995. *Reasoning about Knowledge*. MIT Press, Cambridge MA.

Groenendijk, J. and Stokhof, M., 1997. Questions. In van Benthem, J. and ter Meulen, A. (ed.), *Handbook of Logic and Language*, pages 1055–1124. Elsevier.

Plaza, J., 1989. Logics of public communications. In Emrich, M., Pfeifer, M., Hadzikadic, M., and Ras, Z. (ed.), *Proceedings of the 4th International Symposium on Methodologies for Intelligent Systems: Poster Session Program*, pages 201–216. Oak Ridge National Laboratory.

Pucella, R. and Weissman, V., 2004. Reasoning about dynamic policies. In Walukiewicz, I. (ed.), *FOSSACS 2004*, pages 453–467. Springer. LNCS 2987.

van Benthem, J., Gerbrandy, J., Hoshi, T., and Pacuit, E., 2009. Merging frameworks for interaction. *Journal of Philosophical Logic*, 38:491–526.

van der Meyden, R., 1996. The dynamic logic of permission. *Journal of Logic and Computation*, 6(3):465–479.

van Ditmarsch, H., van der Hoek, W., and Kooi, B., 2007. *Dynamic Epistemic Logic*, volume 337 of *Synthese Library*. Springer.

Adaptive Logics and the Solution of Abductive Problems Triggered by Anomaly

Laura LEONIDES*

ABSTRACT. Abductive problems are triggered by a surprising fact that the background theory cannot explain. The surprising fact can be a novelty or an anomaly. The former refers to a fact that is completely new to the theory, that is, the theory accounts nor for it, neither for its negation; the latter refers to a fact whose negation is explained by the theory. To solve an abductive problem triggered by novelty, an expansion of the theory is needed; whereas for the solution of an abductive problem triggered by anomaly, it is necessary to carry out a revision of the theory. We will analyse how adaptive logics can help us with the solution of abductive problems triggered by anomaly and we will present a new adaptive logic that serves this purpose: LATA^r. LATA^r, together with an abductive procedure, which we also describe, can assist us in the revision of the theory as well as in the generation of abductive explanations.

Introduction

When we search for an explanation, the quintessential kind of reasoning we use, is abductive. Abduction is a kind of reasoning in which premises are inferred from a set of conclusions in a given background theory (Aliseda, 2006).

Several procedures that deal with the problem of finding an abductive solution exist in the literature, mainly when the fact that needs an explanation is a completely new fact. The aim of this paper is to present a method, based on adaptive logics, that aids in the solution of abductive problems with special attention on those problems where the previous knowledge not only does not account for the surprising fact, but it explains its negation.

*Universidad Nacional Autónoma de México.

Overview

In the second section of this paper we present the basic concepts and definitions related to abduction. In the third section we introduce adaptive logics and exhibit two different adaptive logics: one that can deal with inconsistent theories and another one capable of solving abductive problems triggered by an anomaly. In Section 4 we present a new adaptive logic (LATA′), which serves as starting point for an abductive procedure based on its dynamic proofs. Finally, we present our conclusions and open lines for future research.

1   Preliminaries

According to Peirce (Peirce, 1932), an abductive reasoning is triggered by a surprising fact that requires an explanation, although it should be noted that other approaches have been considered as well (D'Agostino et al., 2008). Aliseda (Aliseda, 2006) distinguishes between two kinds of abductive triggers:

Abductive novelty. Happens when the surprising fact φ is completely new, in other words, when the previous knowledge Θ accounts neither for it, nor for its negation.

$$\Theta \not\models \varphi \quad \Theta \not\models \neg\varphi$$

Abductive anomaly. Occurs when the surprising fact φ is anomalous, that is, when the previous knowledge Θ explains its negation.

$$\Theta \models \neg\varphi$$

We will denote by $\langle \Theta, \varphi \rangle$ the abductive problem triggered by the surprising fact φ (new or anomalous) with the background theory Θ. According to the traditional characterization of an abductive solution (Aliseda, 2006), given an abductive problem $\langle \Theta, \varphi \rangle$, α is a solution if:

1. $\Theta \cup \alpha \models \varphi$.
2. α is consistent with Θ.
3. α is minimal.[1]
4. α has a syntactical restriction.[2]

---

[1]The criterion for minimality can change depending on the specific abductive problem that is treated. It may refer to the weakest explanation or to the preferred one.

[2]The syntactic restriction limits the kind of formulas that are considered as an explanation. For example, we may require them to be atomic or conjunctive.

We should notice that the previous characterization does not contemplate abductive problems triggered by anomaly. For this reason, we propose the following characterization of an abductive solution, which is a generalization of Aliseda's account, that takes into consideration abductive problems triggered by novelty as well as those triggered by anomaly:[3]

Definition 1.1 (Solution for an abductive problem). $\langle \Theta', \gamma \rangle$ is a solution for the abductive problem $\langle \Theta, \varphi \rangle$ if:

1. $\Theta' \subseteq \Theta$ and $\Theta' \nvDash \neg\varphi$.
2. $\Theta' \cup \{\gamma\} \vDash \varphi$.
3. γ is consistent with Θ'.
4. γ is minimal.
5. γ has a syntactic restriction.
6. Θ' is maximum, in the sense that it preserves as many formulas from Θ as possible.
7. The selection of Θ' is methodologically justified.[4]

We say that Θ' is the revised theory and that γ is the explanation.

2 Adaptive Logics

Adaptive logics can model defeasible reasoning processes, in other words, the reasoning processes in which a conclusion derived at a certain point can be revoked later and maybe reconsidered at a future stage. Unlike other logics that deal with dynamic reasoning processes, adaptive logics do not require the addition of new premises to revoke conclusions; all that is needed is the continuation of the proof, which leads to the acquisition of more insight on the premise set and allows for conclusions to be withdrawn.

An adaptive logic adapts itself to the premise set to which it is applied; that is, the premises determine which inferences are correct. The aim of adaptive logics is to interpret a premise set as normally as possible, according to a specific standard of normality (Batens, 2002).

2.1 The standard format

An adaptive logic AL is fully defined by a triple, which is called the standard format (Batens, 2002):

---

[3]If the abductive problem is triggered by a novelty, then the revised theory Θ' is exactly the same theory Θ.

[4]Different criteria that can be used for the election of the appropriate revised theory Θ' are presented in Section 3.3.

Lower Limit Logic (LLL). Any logic with static proofs.
Set of abnormalities. Set of well formed formulas characterized by a
    logical form.
Adaptive strategy. Strategy that specifies what it means to interpret the
    premises as normally as possible.

The Lower Limit Logic is the stable part of the adaptive logic and it is
independent from the premise set. The set of abnormalities, which we
denote by Ω, contains the formulas that are considered as false unless
and until proven otherwise. These are the formulas that are presumed
to be false unless the theory prevents so.

It is important to notice that a premise set can imply a disjunction of
abnormalities (members of Ω) without being able to derive just one of
the disjuncts. It is in these cases where the adaptive strategies display
their power, because they are in charge of determining which formulas are *responsible* for the abnormality. We refer to the disjunctions of
abnormalities as *Dab–formulas*. If $\Delta \subseteq \Omega$, then the classical disjunction
of all the members of Δ is a *Dab–formula*, which we denote by $Dab(\Delta)$.
Likewise, the *Dab–formulas* that can be derived from a set Θ are called
Dab–consequences of Θ.

Since the disjunction of the *Dab–formulas* is classical, if $Dab(\Delta)$ is a
Dab–consequence of Θ, then so is $Dab(\Delta \cup \Gamma)$. For that reason it is of
interest to consider only the *minimal Dab–consequences of* Θ. $Dab(\Delta)$ is a
minimal Dab–consequence of Θ if and only if $\Theta \vdash_{LLL} Dab(\Delta)$ and there is
no $\Delta' \subset \Delta$ such that $\Theta \vdash_{LLL} Dab(\Delta')$.

Several adaptive strategies have been proposed so far; nevertheless,
in this work we focus on one of them: the *reliability* strategy (Batens,
1989).[5] This strategy will be detailed in the next section.

2.2   Proof theory

As we pointed out before, the dynamic nature of defeasible reasoning
processes leads to dynamic proofs, that is, conclusions derived at a
certain stage, could be revoked afterwards and reconsidered back again
at a later stage.

Static proofs — usual in other logics — are finite sequences of lines.
Three elements constitute each line: (a) a line number i, (b) the formula
α derived in that line and (c) the justification for the derivation of α.
Each of the formulas in a static proof is either a premise, an axiom or

---

[5]Besides the *reliability* strategy, another adaptive strategy widely used is *minimal
abnormality*, first presented by Batens (Batens, 1986).

the result of applying an inference rule to a subset of the formulas that were previously derived in the proof. Once a formula has been added to the proof, it cannot be revoked by any means.

Adaptive logics have a different kind of proofs. Because of its internal dynamics — which forces the imposition of conditions on the formulas derived at every stage of the proof — adaptive proofs require an additional element in every line of a proof: the conditions imposed in order for the derived formula α to be considered as a part of the proof.

A condition is a set of formulas, more specifically, a set of abnormalities. These formulas are considered as false unless and until proven otherwise. A dynamic proof for an adaptive logic has the following form:

Line number	Formula	Justification	Condition
1	α	R_1	$\emptyset$
2	β	$R_2(1)$	$\{\gamma, \eta\}$
3	η	$R_3(1,2)$	$\emptyset$

For example, we could read line 2 as follows: by applying rule R_2 to line 1, we derive β as long as γ and η are false. If at a later stage in the proof, γ or η were derived — as happens when line 3 is added — then line 2 would no longer be considered as a part of the proof. The means by which we will indicate that a line is no longer considered as a part of the proof are the line markings. This is another difference between dynamic adaptive proofs and static proofs: adaptive proofs not only have deduction rules, but also marking definitions, which make it possible to *remove* lines from the proof at a certain stage.

In Table 1.1 we present the generic deduction rules for adaptive logics. As we said before, we will focus on the *reliability* strategy, which is specified by a marking definition. In order to present the marking definition for *reliability*, we introduce the concept of *unreliable formulas*:

Definition 2.1 (Unreliable formulas). The set of unreliable formulas of Θ is:

$$U(\Theta) = \{A \mid A \in \Delta \text{ for some } minimal\ Dab\text{–}consequence\ Dab(\Delta) \text{ of } \Theta\}$$

The *reliability* strategy considers a formula as abnormal if and only if it is a member of $U(\Theta)$. Therefore, the marking definition for *reliability* is:

Definition 2.2 (Marking for reliability). Line i is marked on stage s if and only if, where Δ is its condition and U_s is the set of unreliable formulas of Θ at stage s, $\Delta \cap U_s(\Theta) \neq \emptyset$.

According to the tradition in the existing literature in adaptive logics, we indicate that a line i is marked by placing the symbol $\checkmark_k$ at the end of the line i, where k is the number of the line that causes line i it to be marked.

PREM	If A is a premise:	$\vdots$	$\vdots$
		A	$\emptyset$

RU	If $A_1, \ldots, A_n \vdash_{\text{LLL}} B$:	A_1	Δ_1
		$\vdots$	$\vdots$
		A_n	Δ_n
		B	$\Delta_1 \cup \ldots \cup \Delta_n$

RC	If $A_1, \ldots, A_n \vdash_{\text{LLL}} B \vee Dab(\Sigma)$	A_1	Δ_1
		$\vdots$	$\vdots$
		A_n	Δ_n
		B	$\Delta_1 \cup \ldots \cup \Delta_n \cup \Sigma$

Table 1.1: Generic rules for adaptive proofs.

2.3 CLuN^r: An adaptive logic for inconsistent theories

In this section we present an adaptive logic that can handle inconsistent theories: CLUN^r (Batens, 1999). CLUN^r interprets a theory as consistently as possible, in other words, it considers all the inconsistencies as false, except when the theory prevents so. Before we present CLUN^r through its standard format, we briefly introduce the ideas on which CLUN, a paraconsistent logic, is based.[6]

CLUN is a paraconsistent logic, that is, $A \wedge \neg A$ can be true without leading to triviality. CLUN preserves all positive classical logic, so if $A_1, \ldots A_n \vdash_{\text{CL}} B$ and no negation occurs in $A_1, \ldots A_n$, then

---

[6]CLUN should not be confused with CLUN^r. CLUN is a paraconsistent logic and CLUN^r is the adaptive logic that uses CLUN as its lower limit logic.

$A_1, \ldots A_n \vdash_{\text{CLUN}} B$. CLUN also preserves the *excluded middle*, but does not validate the *disjunctive syllogism*.[7]

As we saw before, every adaptive logic is completely characterized by its *standard format*. Now we present the standard format of CLUN[r]:

Lower Limit Logic. CLUN
Set of abnormalities. $\Omega = \{(\exists x)(A(x) \land \neg A(x))\}$
Adaptive strategy. Reliability.[8]

The dynamic proofs in CLUN[r] are governed by the generic rules presented in Table 1.1 and the marking rule for *reliability*. In CLUN[r]–proofs, the conditions imposed on every derived formula α, correspond to the set of formulas that must behave consistently in order to derive the formula α.

Example 2.1 (CLUN[r]–proof with the premise set Θ).

$$\Theta = \left\{ \begin{array}{c} (\forall x)(P(x) \lor \neg Q(x)), (\forall x)(R(x) \land S(x)), (\forall x)(\neg R(x) \lor T(x)), \\ \neg P(a), \neg R(a) \end{array} \right\}$$

First we add the premises to the proof:

1	$(\forall x)(P(x) \lor \neg Q(x))$	PREM	$\emptyset$
2	$(\forall x)(R(x) \land S(x))$	PREM	$\emptyset$
3	$(\forall x)(\neg R(x) \lor T(x))$	PREM	$\emptyset$
4	$\neg P(a)$	PREM	$\emptyset$
5	$\neg R(a)$	PREM	$\emptyset$

Then, by applying the conditional rule on lines 1 and 4, and 3 and 5 respectively, we derive lines 6 and 7. The reason we can apply the conditional rule to lines 1 and 4 is that

$$\neg P(a), (\forall x)(P(x) \lor \neg Q(x)) \vdash_{\text{CLUN}} \neg Q(a) \lor (P(a) \land \neg P(a))$$

An analogous justification applies for lines 3 and 5.

6	$\neg Q(a)$	RC(1,4)	$\{P(a) \land \neg P(a)\}$
7	$T(a)$	RC(3,5)	$\{R(a) \land \neg R(a)\}$

If the unconditional rule is applied to line 2, we obtain

---

[7]The logic is named CLUN because it is obtained from CL by allowing for glu*t*s with respect to *n*egation (Batens, 1999).
[8]CLUN[r] takes its name from CLUN and the reliability strategy.

$$8 \quad R(a) \quad \text{RU}(2) \quad \emptyset$$

If we now apply the unconditional rule to lines 5 and 8, we have

$$9 \quad R(a) \wedge \neg R(a) \quad \text{RU}(5,8) \quad \emptyset$$

We should now notice that the formula $R(a) \wedge \neg R(a)$ is a member of the set of abnormalities that must be false in order for line 7 to be considered as a part of the proof; according to the marking definition for reliability, line 7 is marked as no longer derived in the proof.

$$7 \quad T(a) \quad \text{RC}(3,5) \quad \{R(a) \wedge \neg R(a)\} \quad \checkmark_9$$

2.4 LA_s^r: An adaptive logic for abduction

We now present an adaptive logic that can be used for solving abductive problems triggered by novelty: LA_s^r. As any adaptive logic, LA_s^r interprets the premises as normally as possible, according to some specific standard of normality, which is determined by the set of abnormalities Ω and the adaptive strategy. In the specific case of LA_s^r, the standard of normality consists of applying the abductive format[9] as frequently as possible (Meheus, 2010).

The first attempt for dealing with abductive problems through the utilization of adaptive logics resulted in the logics LA and LA^k (Meheus, 2005); nevertheless, these logics were not presented in the standard format for adaptive logics. Subsequently, Meheus and Batens (Meheus and Batens, 2006) presented the adaptive logic LA^r; this logic, although given in the standard format, requires that one defines the set of formulas that constitute possible explanations for the formula that needs to be explained.

The most recent proposal by Meheus (Meheus, 2010), consists of a new adaptive logic — LA_s^r— that does not require to have in advance the set of formulas that constitute possible explanations.

The standard format of LA_s^r is:

Lower Limit Logic. CL

---

[9]We call *abductive format* the following rule:

$$\frac{(\forall x)(A(x) \rightarrow B(x)), B(c)}{A(c)}$$

known as the *Fallacy of Affirming the Consequent* in the classical tradition.

Set of abnormalities.

$$\Omega = \{(\forall x)\,(A\,(x) \to B\,(x)) \wedge (B\,(c) \wedge \neg A\,(c))\ |$$
no predicate which occurs in $B(c)$ occurs in $A(c)\}$

Adaptive strategy. Reliability.[10]

The dynamic proofs in LA_s^r are used for solving abductive problems triggered by novelty. Given an abductive problem $\langle \Theta, \varphi \rangle$, we construct a proof in LA_s^r by first including as premises all the formulas in Θ. We also add the formula φ as premise. Then, we carry out a proof as in any adaptive logic, taking into account that any application of the conditional rule RC leads to a formula that may be an abductive solution for the problem $\langle \Theta, \varphi \rangle$. As CLUN^r–proofs, LA_s^r–proofs are governed by the generic rules presented in Table 1.1.

Example 2.2 (LA_s^r–proof). Given the abductive problem $\langle \Theta, \varphi \rangle$ with

$$\Theta = \left\{ \begin{array}{c} (\forall x)(P(x) \to Q(x)), (\forall x)(P(x) \to R(x)), \\ (\forall x)(S(x) \to \neg P(x)), Q(a) \wedge S(a) \end{array} \right\}$$

and

$$\varphi = Q(b)$$

we perform a proof in which the premises are the elements of Θ and, as a distinguished premise, φ. The proof begins as follows:

1	$(\forall x)(P(x) \to Q(x))$	PREM	$\emptyset$
2	$(\forall x)(P(x) \to R(x))$	PREM	$\emptyset$
3	$(\forall x)(S(x) \to \neg P(x))$	PREM	$\emptyset$
4	$Q(a) \wedge S(a)$	PREM	$\emptyset$
5	$Q(b)$	PREM	$\emptyset$

If we now apply the conditional rule RC to lines 1 and 4, we can add the line:

6	$P(a)$	RC(1,4)	$\{(\forall x)(P(x) \to Q(x)) \wedge (Q(a) \wedge \neg P(a))\}$

By applying the unconditional rule RU to lines 2 and 6 and 3 and 4, we add lines 7 and 8, respectively.

7	$R(a)$	RU(2,6)	$\{(\forall x)(P(x) \to Q(x)) \wedge (Q(a) \wedge \neg P(a))\}$
8	$\neg P(a)$	RU(3,4)	$\emptyset$

---

[10]LA_s^r takes its name from **L**ogic for the **A**bduction of **S**ingular Hypothesis and the reliability strategy.

If we now consider lines 1, 4 and 8 and we apply the unconditional rule, we add the line:

$$9 \quad (\forall x)(P(x) \to Q(x)) \wedge (Q(a) \wedge \neg P(a)) \quad \text{RU}(1,4,8) \quad \emptyset$$

The formula derived in line 9 is a member of the sets of abnormalities in the conditions for lines 6 and 7. According to our marking definition for reliability, lines 6 and 7 are marked as no longer derived in the proof.

$$6 \quad P(a) \quad \text{RC}(1,4) \quad \{(\forall x)(P(x) \to Q(x)) \wedge (Q(a) \wedge \neg P(a))\} \quad \checkmark_9$$
$$7 \quad R(a) \quad \text{RU}(2,6) \quad \{(\forall x)(P(x) \to Q(x)) \wedge (Q(a) \wedge \neg P(a))\} \quad \checkmark_9$$

If we now apply the conditional rule to lines 1 and 5, we add the line

$$10 \quad P(b) \quad \text{RC}(1,5) \quad \{(\forall x)(P(x) \to Q(x)) \wedge (Q(b) \wedge \neg P(b))\}$$

Since $P(b)$ is derived when we apply the conditional rule, $P(b)$ a is possible explanation for the abductive problem $\langle \Theta, \varphi \rangle$.

2.5   Combined adaptive logics

It is possible to combine two adaptive logics if we know their standard formats.[11] By combining adaptive logics we can join, integrate and increase their power in order to deal with problems that each one of them could not solve independently.

The simplest way to combine two adaptive logics AL_1 and AL_2 that share both their LLL and their adaptive strategies, but not their sets of abnormalities Ω_1 and Ω_2, is to take the union of Ω_1 and Ω_2 as the set of abnormalities for the new combined adaptive logic and keep the same LLL and the same strategy.

An advantage of this kind of combination, known as *unions of sets of abnormalities* is that, aside from obtaining an adaptive logic, the resulting adaptive logic is already in its standard format. That important characteristic does not occur with other combinations, such as the *sequential superpositions* and the *closed unions of consequence sets* (Batens, 2002).

3   LATA^r: An adaptive logic for anomaly–triggered abductive problems

We now present a new adaptive logic: LATA^r. First we describe the ideas in which LATA^r is based and then we show how the two previously

---

[11] For the sake of presentation, we introduce combined adaptive logics that result from the combination of two plain adaptive logics, but the same concept can be extended to three or more adaptive logics.

presented adaptive logics (CLUN^r and LA$_s^r$) can be combined for the definition of LATA^r. At the end, we provide an example of a dynamic proof in this logic.

The main objective of CLUN^r is to interpret a theory as consistently as possible and the prime goal of LA$_s^r$ is to apply the abductive format as frequently as possible. If we take into account that, for solving abductive problems triggered by an anomaly, it is necessary to handle an inconsistent theory (the original theory together with the anomalous fact) as well as to determine which formulas should be added so that the revised theory can account for the observed fact, it should be clear that CLUN^r and LA$_s^r$ are ideal candidates to aid in the task of solving abductive problems triggered by an anomalous fact.

LATA^r combines CLUN^r and LA$_s^r$ in order to interpret a theory as consistently as possible while seeking for an explanation for the surprising anomalous fact. There is a detail worth mentioning: unlike the combination presented before, these two adaptive logics do not share their LLL, so we have to determine which LLL to use for the combined adaptive logic. CL is not a good candidate for being the LLL, because it cannot deal with inconsistent theories. In contrast to CL, CLUN— being a more *permissive* logic than CL— allows for the interpretation of the inconsistent premise set without leading to triviality. The abductive explanations may be derived from the CLUN^r–interpretation of the premise set in the same way as they are derived form the LA$_s^r$–interpretation of a consistent premise set.

3.1 The standard format

The standard format of LATA^r is the following:

Lower Limit Logic. CLUN

Set of abnormalities. $\Omega = \Omega_{\text{CLUN}^r} \cup \Omega_{\text{LA}_s^r}$, where

$\Omega_{\text{CLUN}^r} = \{(\exists x)(A(x) \wedge \neg A(x))\}$ and

$\Omega_{\text{LA}_s^r} = \{(\forall x)(A(x) \rightarrow B(x)) \wedge (B(a) \wedge \neg A(a)) \mid$

no predicate that occurs in $B(a)$ occurs in $A(a)\}$

Adaptive strategy. Reliability.[12]

---

[12]LATA^r takes its name from **L**ogic for **A**nomaly–**T**riggered **A**bduction and the reliability strategy.

3.2 Dynamic proofs in LATA^r

Combined adaptive logics obtained through the *union of sets of abnor-malities* also follow the generic rules presented in Table 1.1. With this in consideration, we can see that LATA^r–proofs have the same form and rules as CLUN^r–proofs and LA^r_s–proofs, the only change resides in the set of abnormalities.

Example 3.1 (LATA^r–proof). Given the abductive problem $\langle \Theta, \varphi \rangle$, where

$$\Theta = \left\{ \begin{array}{c} (\forall x)(P(x) \to Q(x)), (\forall x)(R(x) \to \neg Q(x)), \\ (\forall x)(P(x) \to S(x)), P(a), S(a) \lor R(a) \end{array} \right\}$$

and

$$\varphi = \neg Q(a)$$

we perform a proof in LATA^r in which the premise set is $\Theta \cup \{\varphi\}$. Since $\langle \Theta, \varphi \rangle$ is an anomaly triggered abductive problem, $\Theta \cup \{\varphi\}$ is necessarily an inconsistent set. Through its treatment with LATA^r, it is interpreted as consistently as possible while seeking for an explanation for the surprising fact φ.

First, all the elements in $\Theta \cup \{\varphi\}$ are added to the proof as premises. A special mark is added to the fact that requires an explanation.

1	$(\forall x)(P(x) \to Q(x))$	PREM	$\emptyset$
2	$(\forall x)(R(x) \to \neg Q(x))$	PREM	$\emptyset$
3	$(\forall x)(P(x) \to S(x))$	PREM	$\emptyset$
4	$P(a)$	PREM	$\emptyset$
5	$S(a) \lor R(a)$	PREM	$\emptyset$
6	$\neg Q(a)$	PREM★	$\emptyset$

Consider now lines 1 and 4; due to the fact that

$$(\forall x)(P(x) \to Q(x)), P(a) \vdash_{\text{CLUN}} Q(a)$$

we add the line

$$7 \quad Q(a) \quad \text{RU}(1,4) \quad \emptyset$$

If we consider lines 6 and 7, the following line can be added:

$$8 \quad \neg Q(a) \land Q(a) \quad \text{RU}(6,7) \quad \emptyset$$

Now, if we consider lines 2 and 6, the following line may be added:

$$9 \quad R(a) \quad \text{RC}(2,6) \quad \left\{ \begin{array}{c} (\forall x)(R(x) \to \neg Q(x)) \land \\ (\neg Q(a) \land \neg R(a)) \end{array} \right\}$$

3.3 Abductive process

LATA^r proofs alone are not enough to solve anomaly triggered abductive problems. We need an abductive procedure that is able to *extract* the relevant information from the proof. The process of finding a solution for an anomaly–triggered abductive problem is constituted by two stages: (a) the construction of the adaptive proof and; (b) the application of the abductive procedure.

Once we construct the proof in LATA^r, it goes through an abductive process that finds the formulas that should be removed from the theory to get rid of the inconsistencies that arose when the anomalous fact was added. That process is also in charge of determining the formulas that should be added to the theory in order to account for the surprising fact.

The abductive procedure comprises two subprocedures:

Backtracking for revision. This procedure carries out a revision of the theory to eliminate the formulas that contradict the fact that needs an explanation. It identifies the inconsistencies and then removes from the theory some of the formulas involved in the generation of such inconsistencies.

Generation of explanations. Once the backtracking is done, we generate the abductive explanations that account for the surprising fact, with the certainty that no inconsistencies occur in the revised theory.

Let ℓ_φ be the line that has the special mark ★, that is, the one where the surprising anomalous fact is added to the proof. Let ℓ_c be the line where the formula $\varphi \wedge \neg\varphi$ is derived, where φ is the surprising fact. The backtracking procedure for the revision of the theory begins by considering line ℓ_c. The procedure inspects the third element (justification) of this line to determine which lines are responsible for the derivation of the formula in line ℓ_c. Let $\ell_1 \ldots \ell_2$ be the lines that allowed the derivation of $\varphi \wedge \neg\varphi$. We now inspect the third element of each ℓ_i in order to detect the lines that permitted the generation of each one of them. We apply the same procedure recursively to each new line that we encounter, unless it is the line ℓ_φ or the justification of that line is PREM (in this case there are no formulas responsible for the derivation).

When the procedure finds the rule PREM as justification, it adds the formula derived in that line to a set Υ. By the end of the procedure, Υ

contains the formulas that might be held responsible for the inconsistencies in the theory when the fact φ was added.

It is worth noticing that not every element in Υ should be removed from the theory in order to avoid the inconsistencies. It is enough to eliminate a set $\Upsilon' \subseteq \Upsilon$ from Θ. Clearly, there could exist several Υ' which, when removed from the original theory, would leave a revised consistent theory. Choosing the appropriate Υ' is a pragmatic issue, whose solution will depend on the context of the abductive problem that is being treated. We now present some criteria that may help in the selection of such set; nevertheless, this does not does not conform an exhaustive list, other criteria may be used and incorporated with an adaptive framework:[13]

Slightest impact. Eliminate the formulas that involve the smallest number of different predicates as possible.
Confidence in the theory. Rule out the observed facts (because of the low reliability of the observations). In this case, the formulas without variables would be chosen for removal.
Confidence in the observations. Favor the observed facts. In this case, the quantified formulas would be chosen for removal.[14]
Subformulas. Remove subformulas of those contained in Υ. For example, for conjunctions, it may not be necessary to remove the whole conjunction, but just the part of it that is inconsistent with the observed fact.

Let us now return to the proof presented in Example 3.1. In Table 1.2 we show the complete proof together with a graphical representation of the backtracking procedure.

When the recursive procedure is over, it returns the set

$$\Upsilon = \{(\forall x)(P(x) \rightarrow Q(x)), P(a)\}$$

If we now apply the criterion of *confidence in the theory*, then the revised theory Θ' is

$$\Theta' = \left\{ \begin{array}{c} (\forall x)(P(x) \rightarrow Q(x)), (\forall x)(R(x) \rightarrow \neg Q(x)), \\ (\forall x)(P(x) \rightarrow S(x)), S(a) \vee R(a), S(a) \end{array} \right\}$$

---

[13]Another possible criterion for the selection of formulas to be removed is the assignment of priorities to each of the formulas in the theory. The formula with the lowest priority in the set Υ would be the one chosen for removal.

[14]Gärdenfors uses the concept of *epistemic entrenchment* for determining which elements of the theory are more valuable than others (Gärdenfors, 2003).

$$
\begin{array}{llll}
1 & (\forall x)(P(x) \rightarrow Q(x)) & \text{PREM} & \emptyset \\
2 & (\forall x)(R(x) \rightarrow \neg Q(x)) & \text{PREM} & \emptyset \\
3 & (\forall x)(P(x) \rightarrow S(x)) & \text{PREM} & \emptyset \\
4 & P(a) & \text{PREM} & \emptyset \\
5 & S(a) \vee R(a) & \text{PREM} & \emptyset \\
6 & \neg Q(a) & \text{PREM} \bigstar & \emptyset \\
7 & Q(a) & \text{RU}(1,4) & \emptyset \\
8 & \neg Q(a) \wedge Q(a) & \text{RU}(6,7) & \emptyset \\
9 & R(a) & \text{RC}(2,6) & \left\{ \begin{array}{l} (\forall x)(R(x) \rightarrow \neg Q(x)) \\ \wedge(\neg Q(a) \wedge \neg R(a)) \end{array} \right\}
\end{array}
$$

Table 1.2: Backtracking procedure for a proof in LATA^r.

The generation of abductive explanations also uses the proof in LATA^r. As with LA$_s^r$, we focus on the applications of the conditional rule RC and consider formulas derived with this rule as candidates for becoming abductive explanations. If we consider only the formulas derived by the applications of the conditional rule directly to the line that contains the fact which needs to be explained, we can assure it is an abductive solution. In the proof shown as example, we only have one direct application of the conditional rule to the distinguished line that contains the surprising fact. This occurs on line 9, where the formula $R(a)$ is derived. Therefore, $R(a)$ is the formula that needs to be added to the revised theory in order to solve the abductive problem.

The solution to the anomaly triggered abductive problem $\langle \Theta, \varphi \rangle$, using the criterion of confidence in the theory, is $\langle \Theta', \gamma \rangle$ with

$$
\Theta' = \left\{ \begin{array}{l} (\forall x)(P(x) \rightarrow Q(x)), (\forall x)(R(x) \rightarrow \neg Q(x)), \\ (\forall x)(P(x) \rightarrow S(x)), S(a) \vee R(a) \end{array} \right\}
$$

and

$$
\gamma = R(a)
$$

4   Conclusions and further work

We have presented a new adaptive logic that brings together the power of two previously existing adaptive logics: CLUN^r and LA$_s^r$. This new adaptive logic, LATA^r, is capable of solving abductive problems triggered by an anomaly as well as those triggered by novelty. It accomplishes that task by interpreting the theory as consistently as possible while seeking for an explanation for the surprising anomalous fact.

Due to the combination used to put together CLUN^r and LA_s^r, we introduced LATA^r by means of its standard format and its dynamic proofs. We also described an abductive procedure that utilizes the LATA^r–proofs to solve abductive problems triggered by an anomaly. The procedure comprises two stages: the backtracking procedure for the theory revision and the procedure for the generation of abductive explanations. Clearly, if the abductive problem was triggered by a novelty, the backtracking procedure is unnecessary, because we do not need a new revised theory: the original theory is already consistent with the surprising fact.

Together with the backtracking procedure for the revision of the theory, we exposed some criteria that can serve as a guide during the selection of the formulas that should be removed from the theory in order to get a new revised theory that is consistent with the surprising fact. These criteria are only examples of the different possibilities that could be considered for the revision of the theory and that could be incorporated with an adaptive framework. The application of other criteria may be possible as long as they are justified by methodological means.

The procedure for generating explanations takes into account the formulas that were derived by means of the application of rule RC to the line where the surprising fact φ appears in the proof. Nonetheless, other abductive explanations could be found if we consider not only formulas derived by the direct application of rule RC to φ. Suppose, for example, that a formula α was derived by the application of rule RC and that, thanks to α, it is possible to derive φ unconditionally. In that case, the formula α would be an abductive explanation for our fact φ. The exact procedure that would allow us to detect such formulas is still pending, although strategies like the ones used in goal oriented–proofs could be considered.

A study of the advantages of using a different adaptive strategy is needed, as well as the detailed specification of the algorithms proposed and their complexity analysis.

Acknowledgements. Research for this paper was supported by the National Council of Science and Technology (CONACYT) under grant number 268447, for master studies at the National Autonomous University of Mexico (UNAM) within the project *Abducción y lógicas no clásicas*, under the supervision of Atocha Aliseda. The author is indebted to the anonymous referees for their valuable suggestions and comments, which helped improving this paper.

Bibliography

Aliseda, A., 2006. *Abductive Reasoning. Logical investigations into Discovery and Explanation*, volume 330. Synthese Library. Springer. ISBN 978-1-4020-3906-5.

Batens, D., 1986. Dialectical dynamics within formal logics. *Logique et Analyse*, 114: 161–173.

Batens, D., 1989. Dynamic dialectical logics. In Gabbay (ed.), *Paraconsistent Logic. Essays on the Inconsistent*, pages 187–217. Philosophia Verlag.

Batens, D., 1999. Inconsistency-adaptive logics. In Orłowska, E. (ed.), *Logic at Work. Essays Dedicated to the Memory of Helena Rasiowa*, pages 445–472. Physica Verlag (Springer), Heidelberg, New York.

Batens, D., 2002. A General Characterization of Adaptive Logics. *Logique et analyse*, 173–175:45–68.

D'Agostino, M., Finger, M., and Gabbay, D., 2008. Cut-Based Abduction. *Logic Journal of the IGPL*, 16(6):431–451. ISSN 1367-0751. doi: 10.1093/jigpal/jzn020.

Gärdenfors, P., 2003. Belief revision: An introduction. In Gärdenfors, P. (ed.), *Belief revision*, Cambridge Tracts in Theoretical Computer Science. Cambridge University Press.

Meheus, J., 2005. Empirical progress and ampliative adaptive logics. *Confirmation, Empirical Progress and Truth Approximation (Poznań Studies in the Philosophy of Sciences and the Humanities)*, 83:193–217.

Meheus, J., 2010. A Formal Logic for the Abduction of Singular Hypotheses. *To appear*.

Meheus, J. and Batens, D., March 2006. A formal logic for abductive reasoning. *Logic Journal of the IGPL*, 14(2):221–236.

Peirce, C., 01 1932. Collected Papers of Charles Sanders Peirce. *Volumes 1-6 edited by C. Hartshorne y P. Weiss. Cambride, Harvard University Press. 1931-1935; and volumes 7.8 edited by A.W. Burks. Cambridge, Harvard University Press. 1958.*

A Dynamic-Epistemic Approach to Abductive Reasoning

FERNANDO SOLER-TOSCANO* & FERNANDO RAYMUNDO
VELÁZQUEZ-QUESADA†

ABSTRACT. We discuss what an abstract abductive problem means in terms of an agent, her information and the way the latter changes due to informational actions. Then, by using examples of abductive situations, we argue that different assumptions about the agent's reasoning abilities and her information give rise to different kinds of abductive problems, and therefore different kinds of solutions. Finally, following recent *dynamic epistemic logic* developments, we present a semantic model that allows us to represent certain forms of abductive reasoning.

1   Abductive reasoning

Beyond the obvious facts that he has at some time done manual labour, that he takes snuff, that he is a Freemason, that he has been in China, and that he has done a considerable amount of writing lately, I can [get] nothing else.

Sherlock Holmes
The Red-Headed League

Among the non-monotonic reasoning processes, abduction (Aliseda, 2006) is one of the most important. The concept, introduced into modern logic by Charles S. Peirce, is usually described as the process of *searching for an explanation*, and it has been recognized as one of the most commonly used in our daily activities. Observing that Mr. Wilson's right cuff is very shiny for five inches and that the left one has a smooth patch near the elbow, Holmes assumes that Mr. Wilson has done a

---

*Grupo de Lógica, Lenguaje e Información, Universidad de Sevilla, Spain.
†Institute for Logic, Language and Computation, Universiteit van Amsterdam, The Netherlands.

considerable amount of writing lately. In classical mechanics, rules are introduced in order to explain macroscopical movements. Karen knows that the grass gets wet when it rains and that the grass is wet right now, so she suspects that it has rained. In Peirce's own words (Hartshorne and Weiss, 1934), abduction can be described in the following way:

> The surprising fact χ is observed.
> But if γ were true, χ would be a matter of course.
> Hence, there is reason to suspect that γ is true.

Though traditional examples of abductive reasoning are given in terms of an agent's information and its changes, classical definitions of an abductive problem and its solutions are given in terms of theories and formulas, without mentioning the agent's information and how it is modified.

The present work proposes a study of abductive reasoning from an epistemic and dynamic perspective. We propose straightforward translations that, following the *epistemic logic* (Hintikka, 1962) and *dynamic epistemic logic* (van Ditmarsch et al., 2007) philosophy, redefine abductive problems and abductive solutions in terms of the agent's information and the actions that modify it. Then we discuss how different examples of abductive reasoning can be classified according to the assumptions about the agent's reasoning abilities and the properties of her information. Finally, we show how we can represent certain forms of abductive reasoning with an extension of the *awareness logic* of Fagin and Halpern (1988).

Remark We recall that abductive reasoning is very often seen as a two-stage process: find possible explanations for the abductive problem, and then select the best one(s) according to some suitable criteria (Hintikka, 1998). Our work focusses only in defining what an abductive problem and an abductive solution are from a dynamic epistemic perspective, leaving the 'selecting the best explanation' issue for further work.

2   From a classical to a dynamic epistemic approach

Traditionally, it is said that an abductive problem arises when there is a formula χ in $\mathcal{L}$ that does not follow from a theory (i.e., a set of formulas) Φ under a given consequence (inference) relation $\vdash$. The intuitive idea is that Φ represents the current information about the world, and observing a situation χ that is not entailed by Φ under $\vdash$ shows that there is a gap.

With this idea in mind, in order for the tuple $(\Phi, \chi, \vdash)$ to be an abductive problem, χ should not follow from Φ under $\vdash$. Note that there is no constraint on the theory's opinion about $\neg\chi$: it may be the case that Φ entails neither χ nor $\neg\chi$, the case abductive reasoning has typically focussed on, but it may also be the case that Φ not only does not entail χ but, moreover, it entails $\neg\chi$.[1]

In a few words, the key ingredient for an abductive problem is the existence of a χ that is not entailed by the current information Φ, given an inference relation $\vdash$. This situation generates two basic forms of abductive problems, according to what the information predicts about $\neg\chi$ (Aliseda, 2006).

Definition 2.1 (Abductive problem). Let Φ and χ be a theory (a set of formulas) and a formula, respectively, in some language $\mathcal{L}$. Let $\vdash$ be an inference relation on $\mathcal{L}$.

- The tuple $(\Phi, \chi, \vdash)$ is a *novel abductive problem* when neither χ nor $\neg\chi$ are consequences of Φ under $\vdash$, i.e., when

$$\Phi \nvdash \chi \quad \text{and} \quad \Phi \nvdash \neg\chi$$

- The tuple $(\Phi, \chi, \vdash)$ is an *anomalous abductive problem* when, though χ is not a consequence of Φ under $\vdash$, $\neg\chi$ is, i.e., when

$$\Phi \nvdash \chi \quad \text{and} \quad \Phi \vdash \neg\chi$$

We will assume through the whole paper, as it is typically done, that $\vdash$ is the *logical consequence* relation, that is, a truth-preserving inference relation satisfying *reflexivity, contraction, permutation, cut* and, more importantly, *monotonicity*. Hence, we will not mention it when presenting an abductive problem. At this stage, we will also assume that a theory is closed under the inference relation (though we will drop this assumption later; see Section 3).

So suppose we have an abductive problem; how can it be solved? Consider the novel case. The observation of a χ that is not entailed by the theory Φ under the inference relation $\vdash$ shows that something is *incomplete*. Since we are assuming that $\vdash$ is fixed, the only possibility to solve the problem is to modify the theory to make it entail χ;[2] since

---

[1]This second case has been extensively studied in *belief revision* (Gärdenfors, 1992; Williams and Rott, 2001).

[2]If we do not fix $\vdash$, then another possibility is to look for a different inference relation under which Φ does entail χ, as suggested in (Soler-Toscano et al., 2010).

we are assuming that ⊢ is the logical consequence relation, the only possibility is to look for extra information that, together with the theory, entails χ.[3] This solves the problem because now the theory is strong enough to *explain* χ. Consider now the anomalous case. The observation of a χ whose negation is entailed by the theory shows that something is *incorrect*. Again, given that ⊢ is fixed as the logical consequence relation, there is only one way to solve the problem: perform a *theory revision*,[4] that is, remove some formulas of the theory so that ¬χ is no longer entailed,[5] and then look for extra information that, together with the modified theory, entails χ.

Definition 2.2 (Abductive solution).

- Given a *novel* abductive problem (Φ, χ), the formula γ is an *abductive solution* if

$$\Phi \cup \{\gamma\} \vdash \chi$$

- Given an *anomalous* abductive problem (Φ, χ), the formula γ is an *abductive solution* if it is possible to perform a theory revision to get a *novel* problem (Φ', χ) for which γ is a solution.

Definition 2.2 is often considered as too weak: since ⊢ represents logical consequence, a solution γ can take many 'trivial' forms. For example, anything that contradicts Φ is a solution, and also is χ itself. Further conditions can be imposed in order get more satisfactory results. Following Aliseda (2006), here are some of them.

Definition 2.3 (Classification of abductive solutions). Let (Φ, χ) be an abductive problem. An abductive solution γ is

consistent if	$\Phi \cup \{\gamma\} \nvdash \bot$
explanatory if	$\gamma \nvdash \chi$
minimal if, for every other abductive solution γ',	$\gamma \vdash \gamma'$ implies $\gamma' \vdash \gamma$

---

[3]If we deal with a different inference relation (e.g., a non-monotonic one), it could be possible to make Φ to entail χ by *removing* formulas from it.

[4]Some authors use the concept *revision* in a different way: a contraction of the theory (removing some formulas) followed by an extension (adding others). We separate these steps into two different process and reserve the word *revision* for just the first one.

[5]With a different inference relation, it could be possible to *add* formulas to the theory to make it not to entail ¬χ.

The *consistency* requirement discards those γ inconsistent with Φ, since a reasonable explanation should not be in contradiction with the theory. In a similar way, the *explanatory* requirement discards those explanations that would justify χ by themselves, since it is preferred that the explanation only complements the current theory. Finally, the *minimality* requirement works as Occam's razor, searching for the simplest explanation: a solution γ is minimal if it is actually equivalent under $\vdash$ to any other solution it implies.

2.1 From an agent's perspective

Abduction, like other forms of non-monotonic reasoning (e.g., belief revision, default reasoning), is classified as common-sense reasoning rather than mathematical one, and most of its classical examples involve 'real' agents and their information. It is Holmes who observes that Mr. Wilson's right cuff is very shiny; it is the scientific community which incorporates rules to explain the movement of objects; it is Karen who observes that the grass is wet. Thus, the notion of an abductive problem is not objective: it is relative to an agent, and what is an abductive problem for an agent may not be so for a different one. More importantly, an abductive solution is defined in terms of actions that change the agent's information: *removing* pieces from the agent's information so that it does not entail the negation of the observation, and then *incorporating* new pieces so that the observation is entailed. These two observations suggest that we can look for representations of abductive reasoning in a different framework: one in which we can represent and reason about not only the information of diverse agents, but also the actions that modify this information. One of such frameworks is the dynamic extension of epistemic logic, *dynamic epistemic logic*.

Epistemic logic (*EL*) deals with agents, their information, and properties of this information. *Dynamic epistemic logic* (*DEL*), allows us additionally to reason about the way the agents' information changes as consequence of several informational actions. The *DEL* methodology offers to us three important advantages. First, it allows us to talk about the information of different agents. Second, it allows us to talk about different informational attitudes, useful because abduction, as a non-monotonic form of reasoning, involves not only what the agent knows, but also what she believes.[6] Third, it allows us to talk about the effect that diverse informational actions have over the agents' information.

For these reasons, our work proposes a dynamic epistemic approach to abductive reasoning. We present definitions of abductive problem and abductive solution in terms of an agent's information and the way it changes. We emphasize that, though we will use formulas in *DEL* style, we will use them just to indicate properties of the agents' information and the involved informational actions, without committing ourselves to any semantic model or any semantic interpretation unless is explicitly stated (see Section 5).

Our first step is to state what an abductive problem is in terms of the agent's information. When we put an agent in the picture, the theory Φ becomes *the agent's information*. Then, the key ingredient for an abductive problem, a formula χ that does not follow from the theory Φ, becomes a formula *that is not part of the agent's information*. Since in the classical case we assumed that a theory is closed under the inference (logical consequence) relation, here we will assume the same for the agent's information. Hence, "χ is *(not) part of the agent's information*" is equivalent to "χ does *(not) follow from the agent's information*". The following definitions use formulas in *EL* style, with Inf ψ read as *"the agent is informed about ψ"*.

Definition 2.4 (Subjective abductive problems). Let $\mathcal{L}$ be a formal language, and let χ be a formula in it.

- An agent has a *novel χ-abductive problem* when neither χ nor $\neg\chi$ are part of her information, i.e., when the following formula holds:

$$\neg\text{Inf}\,\chi \ \wedge \ \neg\text{Inf}\,\neg\chi$$

- An agent has an *anomalous χ-abductive problem* when χ is not part of her information but $\neg\chi$ is, i.e., when the following formula holds:

$$\neg\text{Inf}\,\chi \ \wedge \ \ \text{Inf}\,\neg\chi$$

Our second step is to state what an abductive solution is in terms of the agent's information and the actions that change it. From the

---

[6] And even inside each one of these notions we can make further refinements, like distinctions between *implicit* and *explicit* forms of knowledge and belief, giving us the possibility of dealing with logically non-omniscient agents, as we will discuss in Section 3.

classical definition of an abductive solution (Definition 2.2), we can see that there are two important actions involved: add some formula to the agent's information, and remove some formula from it.

We will express changes in the agent's information by using formulas in *DEL* style. In particular, we will use formulas of the form $\langle \text{Add}_\psi \rangle \varphi$ ("*ψ can be added to the agent's information and, after that, φ is the case*") and formulas of the form $\langle \text{Rem}_\psi \rangle \varphi$ ("*ψ can be removed from the agent's information and, after that, φ is the case*"). Dual modalities $[\text{Add}_\psi] \varphi$ ("*if ψ is added to the agent's information, then after the action φ is the case*") and $[\text{Rem}_\psi] \varphi$ ("*if ψ is removed from the agent's information, then after the action φ is the case*") are defined as $\neg \langle \text{Add}_{\neg\psi} \rangle \neg\varphi$ and $\neg \langle \text{Rem}_\psi \rangle \neg\varphi$, respectively.

Properties of the actions Here it is important to be precise about the intended behaviour of the actions. The following are the most important questions about each one of them: (1) Can the action be executed in any situation? (2) Is it deterministic in the sense that it can be executed in just one way? (3) How does it affect the agent's information?

Consider the Add action. Since we are assuming that ⊢ is the logical consequence relation, then it is reasonable to assume that we can always add any formula to an agent's information (keeping in mind that this will make the information inconsistent if the new piece contradicts it), and that adding a piece of information can be done in a unique way. The modal notation (box and diamond), which in general assumes that a modality is a partial relation, allow us to specify this particular behaviour: while the property of Add being executable at any time for any formula ψ (i.e., the *total* property) is specified by asking for $[\text{Add}_\psi] \varphi \rightarrow \langle \text{Add}_\psi \rangle \varphi$ to be always true for every ψ, the property of the action being deterministic (i.e., a *function*) is specified by asking for $\langle \text{Add}_\psi \rangle \varphi \rightarrow [\text{Add}_\psi] \varphi$ to be always true for every ψ. More importantly, we expect for the action to satisfy the the following property, for any formula ψ:

$$[\text{Add}_\psi] \text{Inf } \psi \quad \text{"After adding } \psi \text{, the agent is informed about it."}$$

In the case of the Rem action, our assumptions about ⊢ makes the answer to the first two questions different. The action may not be executable in every situation (e.g., if the formula to be removed is a tautology), and even if it is executable, there may be different ways to do it (if we want to remove a conjunction, we can choose to remove any of the two conjuncts, or even both). Here the modal notation is adequate. But again, what is important, is that if a given formula can be removed at all, then any of its possible executions will produce an agent that is not informed about it:

[Rem$_\psi$] ¬Inf ψ *"After removing ψ, the agent is not informed about it."*

Note that, given our assumption that the theory is closed under ⊢, the Rem operation should remove the formula so it is no longer derivable from the agent's information.

Though these two requirements might seem obvious, we state them because, in general, they do not need to be the case. In *DEL*, the action of "adding ψ to the agent's information" can be understood as a *public announcement "ψ!"* (Plaza, 1989; Gerbrandy, 1999); however, there are some formulas ψ that do not become part of the agent's information after being announced, that is, formulas for which [ψ!] Inf ψ is not the case (see Holliday and Icard (2010)).

With the behaviour of the operations specified, we can now present our definitions of what a formula should satisfy in order to be an abductive solution.

Definition 2.5 (Subjective abductive solution). Suppose an agent has a *novel* χ-abductive problem, that is, ¬Inf χ ∧ ¬Inf ¬χ holds. A formula γ is an *abductive solution* to this problem if, when added to the agent's information, the agent becomes informed about χ. In a formula,

$$[Add_\gamma] \, Inf \, \chi$$

Now suppose the agent has an *anomalous* χ-abductive problem, that is, ¬Inf χ ∧ Inf ¬χ holds. A formula γ is an *abductive solution* to this problem if the agent can revise her information to remove ¬χ from it, producing in this form a novel abductive problem for which γ is a solution. In a formula,

$$\langle Rem_{\neg\chi} \rangle \, [Add_\gamma] \, Inf \, \chi$$

Observe the requirements we have stated for the solution of a novel abductive problem: [Add$_\gamma$] Inf χ. Since we are assuming that the Add operation is a total function, the requirement is equivalent to $\langle Add_\gamma \rangle$ Inf χ. The case of an anomalous abductive problem is different. Though we have asked for γ to satisfy $\langle Rem_{\neg\chi} \rangle$ [Add$_\gamma$] Inf χ, a formula γ satisfying [Rem$_{\neg\chi}$] [Add$_\gamma$] Inf χ could be consider as a solution. The two requirements are not equivalent because the Rem is not a total function, but a partial relation. We will leave the analysis of these additional solutions for further work.

We can also provide formulas that characterize further properties of abductive solutions.

Definition 2.6 (Classification of subjective abductive solutions). Suppose an agent has a χ-abductive problem and that γ is a solution for it. Then,

- The solution γ is *consistent* if it can be added to the agent's information without making it inconsistent, that is, if it additionally satisfies

$$[\text{Add}_\gamma] \neg \text{Inf} \perp$$

- The solution γ is *explanatory* if it does not imply χ by itself, that is, there are some formulas in the agent's information such that, if they were removed, γ would not be a solution anymore. In symbols, γ is explanatory if it additionally satisfies

$$\text{there are } \beta_1, \dots, \beta_n \text{ such that } \langle \text{Rem}_{\beta_1} \rangle \cdots \langle \text{Rem}_{\beta_n} \rangle [\text{Add}_\gamma] \neg \text{Inf} \chi$$

If such β's do not exist, then though γ is a solution, it is not explanatory since it does not require the agent's information to make her informed about χ.

- The solution γ is *minimal* if, for any other solution γ', if γ' is incorporated into the agent's information after γ is added, then γ is also incorporated into the agent's information after γ' is added. In symbols, γ is minimal if it additionally satisfies

$$\left([\text{Add}_{\gamma'}] \text{Inf} \chi \wedge [\text{Add}_\gamma] \text{Inf} \gamma' \right) \rightarrow [\text{Add}_{\gamma'}] \text{Inf} \gamma$$

3 Different problems for different kinds of agents

In the classical definition of an abductive problem, we have understood the set of formulas Φ as closed under $\vdash$, the logical consequence relation. Then, we have defined abductive problem and abductive solutions for *logically omniscient* agents, that is, agents that have already everything they can derive.

But, of course, agents without this ideal assumption can also face abductive problems. For example, while in the Holmes' example what Sherlock is missing is a premise that would allow him to derive Mr. Wilson's cuffs' status, in the mechanics one what is missing is a relation between facts (that is, a *rule*). And we can even think of situations in which what is missing is not some piece of information, but rather an epistemic action: you are surprised to see smoke in the kitchen, until you understand that the chicken you started to cook has burnt.

Different kinds of abductive problems arise when we consider agents with different abilities, and even more appear when we combine different notions of information. Here we will discuss some examples, showing how they correspond to different kinds of agents.[7]

3.1   Adding reasoning to the picture

Suppose that Karl is in his dinning room and sees smoke going out of the kitchen. This is unjustified at first, but then he realizes that the chicken he put on the fire has been there for a long time, and it should be burnt by now. Though initially Karl did not have any explanation about the smoke, he did not need any additional information in order to find a reason for the fire: reasoning was more than enough.

But this case does not seem to fit in any of the abductive problems described before (Definition 2.4). Indeed, this case is not one of them. The difference is that Karl is not an omniscient agent: he does not have all logical consequences of his information, and therefore he did not realize that the information he had before seeing the smoke was enough to predict it (i.e, to infer that there would be smoke). This shows that non-omniscient agents can face at least a new kind of abductive problem. Are there more?

To provide formal definitions for the abductive problems and solutions that involve non-omniscient agents, we need a setting in which we can distinguish between the information the agent actually has, her *explicit* information (Inf_{Ex}), and what follows logically from it, her *implicit information* (Inf_{Im}) (Levesque, 1984; Lakemeyer, 1986; Vardi, 1986). Note that in general explicit information is not closed under logical consequence. It is a typical feature of non-omniscient agents like Karl. Based on this distinction, we say that a non-omniscient agent has a χ-abductive problem whenever χ is not part of her *explicit* information. Combinato-

---

[7]A systematic revision of the different cases that arise can be found in Soler-Toscano and Velázquez-Quesada (2010).

rially, this gives us eight different cases, according to whether the agent has explicit information about $\neg\chi$ or not, and whether she has implicit information about χ and $\neg\chi$ or not. However, not all these cases are possible: given the mentioned intuitive definition, explicit information should be implicit information too, that is,

$$\text{Inf}_{\text{Ex}}\,\psi \rightarrow \text{Inf}_{\text{Im}}\,\psi$$

Then we can discard the cases in which this formula does not hold.[8]

Definition 3.1 (Non-omniscient abductive problems). A non-omniscient faces a χ-abductive when χ is not part of her *explicit* information. This and the restriction $\text{Inf}_{\text{Ex}}\,\psi \rightarrow \text{Inf}_{\text{Im}}\,\psi$ gives us the six different abductive problems shown in Table 1.1.

	$\neg\text{Inf}_{\text{Im}}\,\chi \;\wedge\; \neg\text{Inf}_{\text{Im}}\,\neg\chi$	**(1.1)**
	$\text{Inf}_{\text{Im}}\,\chi \;\wedge\; \neg\text{Inf}_{\text{Im}}\,\neg\chi$	**(1.2)**
$\neg\text{Inf}_{\text{Ex}}\,\chi \;\wedge\; \neg\text{Inf}_{\text{Ex}}\,\neg\chi \;\wedge$	$\neg\text{Inf}_{\text{Im}}\,\chi \;\wedge\; \text{Inf}_{\text{Im}}\,\neg\chi$	**(1.3)**
	$\text{Inf}_{\text{Im}}\,\chi \;\wedge\; \text{Inf}_{\text{Im}}\,\neg\chi$	**(1.4)**
$\neg\text{Inf}_{\text{Ex}}\,\chi \;\wedge\; \text{Inf}_{\text{Ex}}\,\neg\chi \;\wedge$	$\neg\text{Inf}_{\text{Im}}\,\chi \;\wedge\; \text{Inf}_{\text{Im}}\,\neg\chi$	**(2.3)**
	$\text{Inf}_{\text{Im}}\,\chi \;\wedge\; \text{Inf}_{\text{Im}}\,\neg\chi$	**(2.4)**

Table 1.1: Abductive problems for non-omniscient agents.

The smoke example corresponds to the case **(1.2)**. Though the observation is surprising because before it the agent is not explicitly informed about the smoke in the kitchen, she had this information implicitly, and she could have predicted it by the proper reasoning step.

If the agent is omniscient, implicit information is always explicit, and hence the abductive problems in Table 1.1 are reduced to **(1.1)** and **(2.3)**: precisely the problems in Definition 2.4.

Abductive solutions A solution for a χ-abductive problem has now as a goal to make the agent *explicitly* informed about χ, without having either implicit or explicit information about $\neg\chi$. Each one of the different cases admits different kinds of solutions; let us briefly revise the possibilities for the consistent cases, leaving **(1.4)** and **(2.4)** for further discussion.

---

[8]More cases can be eliminated with further assumptions about the agent's information, like truth or consistency; see Section 4.

In case **(1.1)**, the agent needs more information because χ is not even implicit. If the extra information γ gives her also explicit information about χ, nothing else is needed; otherwise the agent will need to perform a further reasoning step. In case **(1.2)**, the one of our example, reasoning is enough and extra information is not essential. In cases **(1.3)** and **(2.3)** we have an anomalous problem. In the first, the anomaly is implicit and the agent needs to make it explicit before solving it; in the second, the agent should solve the anomaly, and then she will be in case **(1.1)**. In each case there is more than one strategy (i.e., more than one sequence of actions) that solves the abductive problem; for simplicity we will focus on the most representative one for each one of them.

In the following definition, formulas of the form $\langle \alpha \rangle \varphi$ indicate that the agent can perform some reasoning step α after which φ is the case. In particular, with respect to the agent's information, this operation is such that

$$\text{Inf}_{\text{Im}} \psi \leftrightarrow \langle \alpha_\psi \rangle \text{Inf}_{\text{Ex}} \psi$$

where α_ψ represents some reasoning step that makes ψ explicit information.

We have now a distinction between implicit and explicit information, so we restate the requirements of the Add and Rem operations: while the first adds the formula to the *explicit* information, the second removes the formula from the *implicit* information.

$$[\text{Add}_\psi] \text{Inf}_{\text{Ex}} \psi \qquad\qquad [\text{Rem}_\psi] \neg\text{Inf}_{\text{Im}} \psi$$

Definition 3.2 (Non-omniscient abductive solutions). Solutions for consistent non-omniscient abductive problems are provided in Table 1.2.

Classification of abductive solutions The extra requirements of Definition 2.6 can be adapted to this non-omniscient case. The *consistency* and the *explanatory* requirements do not have important changes (now, we ask that γ is consistent or explanatory at the level of implicit information, that is, we replace Inf with Inf_{Im}). The minimality requirement now gives us more options. We can define it over the action $[\text{Add}_\gamma]$, looking for the weakest formula γ, but it can also be defined over the action $\langle \text{Rem}_{\neg\chi} \rangle$, looking for the revision that removes the smallest amount of information. It can even be defined over the action $\langle \alpha \rangle$, looking for the shortest reasoning chain.

Case	Solution
(1.1)	A formula γ such that $[\text{Add}_\gamma]\,\text{Inf}_{\text{Ex}}\,\chi$
(1.2)	A reasoning α such that $\langle\alpha\rangle\,\text{Inf}_{\text{Ex}}\,\chi$
(1.3)	A reasoning α and a formula γ such that $\langle\alpha\rangle\left(\text{Inf}_{\text{Ex}}\,\neg\chi \wedge \langle\text{Rem}_{\neg\chi}\rangle\,[\text{Add}_\gamma]\,\text{Inf}_{\text{Ex}}\,\chi\right)$
(2.3)	A formula γ such that $\langle\text{Rem}_{\neg\chi}\rangle\,[\text{Add}_\gamma]\,\text{Inf}_{\text{Ex}}\,\chi$

Table 1.2: Solutions for consistent non-omniscient abductive problems.

3.2 Not only formulas but also rules

Consider now the mechanics example. At some stage in history, the scientific community observed the trajectory described by cannonballs, and become interested in explaining this and other related phenomena. But rather than a plain piece of information, the found explanation was an equation that relates initial speed, initial angle and gravity with the described trajectory. In other words, the found explanation was a *rule* that allows us to derive the movement of the projectile, given the initial conditions.

Again, this case does not fit any of the abductive problems described before. The difference is that the agent is not only non-omniscient in the sense that she does not have automatically all logical consequences of her information; she also lacks of the necessary reasoning tools that would allow her to infer more information. To put it in other words, besides not having all the logical consequences of her explicit information automatically, the agent might not be able to even derive them. This gives us another kind of agent, and therefore a new and finer classification of abductive problems and abductive solutions.

In order to classify the new abductive problems, we need to make a further distinction: we need to distinguish between what follows logically from the agent's explicit information, the *objective* implicit information (Inf_{Im}), and what the agent can actually derive, the *subjective* implicit information (Inf_{Der}). With this refinement, each one of the six abductive problems of Table 1.1 turns into four cases, according to whether the agent can derive or not what follows logically from her explicit information, that is, according to whether $\mathrm{Inf_{Der}}\,\chi$ and $\mathrm{Inf_{Der}}\,\neg\chi$ hold or not. However, we can also make further reasonable assumptions: explicit information is derivable and derivable information is also implicit

$$\mathrm{Inf_{Ex}}\,\psi \to \mathrm{Inf_{Der}}\,\psi \qquad\qquad \mathrm{Inf_{Der}}\,\psi \to \mathrm{Inf_{Im}}\,\psi$$

Definition 3.3 (Extended abductive problems). A non-omniscient agent with limited reasoning abilities can face eleven different abductive problems, each one of them characterized by a formula in Table 1.3.

$\neg\mathrm{Inf_{Ex}}\,\chi \wedge \neg\mathrm{Inf_{Ex}}\,\neg\chi \wedge$	$\big\{\; \neg\mathrm{Inf_{Der}}\,\chi \wedge \neg\mathrm{Inf_{Der}}\,\neg\chi \;\big\}$	$\wedge\; \neg\mathrm{Inf_{Im}}\,\chi \wedge \neg\mathrm{Inf_{Im}}\,\neg\chi$	**(1.1.a)**
$\neg\mathrm{Inf_{Ex}}\,\chi \wedge \neg\mathrm{Inf_{Ex}}\,\neg\chi \wedge$	$\left\{\begin{array}{l}\neg\mathrm{Inf_{Der}}\,\chi \wedge \neg\mathrm{Inf_{Der}}\,\neg\chi \\ \mathrm{Inf_{Der}}\,\chi \wedge \neg\mathrm{Inf_{Der}}\,\neg\chi\end{array}\right\}$	$\wedge\; \mathrm{Inf_{Im}}\,\chi \wedge \neg\mathrm{Inf_{Im}}\,\neg\chi$	**(1.2.a)** **(1.2.b)**
$\neg\mathrm{Inf_{Ex}}\,\chi \wedge \neg\mathrm{Inf_{Ex}}\,\neg\chi \wedge$	$\left\{\begin{array}{l}\neg\mathrm{Inf_{Der}}\,\chi \wedge \neg\mathrm{Inf_{Der}}\,\neg\chi \\ \neg\mathrm{Inf_{Der}}\,\chi \wedge \mathrm{Inf_{Der}}\,\neg\chi\end{array}\right\}$	$\wedge\; \neg\mathrm{Inf_{Im}}\,\chi \wedge \mathrm{Inf_{Im}}\,\neg\chi$	**(1.3.a)** **(1.3.c)**
$\neg\mathrm{Inf_{Ex}}\,\chi \wedge \neg\mathrm{Inf_{Ex}}\,\neg\chi \wedge$	$\left\{\begin{array}{l}\neg\mathrm{Inf_{Der}}\,\chi \wedge \neg\mathrm{Inf_{Der}}\,\neg\chi \\ \mathrm{Inf_{Der}}\,\chi \wedge \neg\mathrm{Inf_{Der}}\,\neg\chi \\ \neg\mathrm{Inf_{Der}}\,\chi \wedge \mathrm{Inf_{Der}}\,\neg\chi \\ \mathrm{Inf_{Der}}\,\chi \wedge \mathrm{Inf_{Der}}\,\neg\chi\end{array}\right\}$	$\wedge\; \mathrm{Inf_{Im}}\,\chi \wedge \mathrm{Inf_{Im}}\,\neg\chi$	**(1.4.a)** **(1.4.b)** **(1.4.c)** **(1.4.d)**
$\neg\mathrm{Inf_{Ex}}\,\chi \wedge \mathrm{Inf_{Ex}}\,\neg\chi \wedge$	$\big\{\; \neg\mathrm{Inf_{Der}}\,\chi \wedge \mathrm{Inf_{Der}}\,\neg\chi \;\big\}$	$\wedge\; \neg\mathrm{Inf_{Im}}\,\chi \wedge \mathrm{Inf_{Im}}\,\neg\chi$	**(2.3.c)**
$\neg\mathrm{Inf_{Ex}}\,\chi \wedge \mathrm{Inf_{Ex}}\,\neg\chi \wedge$	$\big\{\; \mathrm{Inf_{Der}}\,\chi \wedge \mathrm{Inf_{Der}}\,\neg\chi \;\big\}$	$\wedge\; \mathrm{Inf_{Im}}\,\chi \wedge \mathrm{Inf_{Im}}\,\neg\chi$	**(2.4.d)**

Table 1.3: Abductive problems with subjective/objective implicit information.

The mechanics example corresponds to the case **(1.2.a)**. The trajectory of a projectile is fixed (that is, it is implicit information) once the initial conditions are given; nevertheless, the scientific community could not predict (i.e., derive) the trajectory without knowing the relevant equations.

Abductive solutions Recall that some of the abductive problems of Subsection 3.1 can be solved in the same way. For example, though abductive problem **(1.2)** can be solved by means of reasoning steps (see Table 1.2), it can also be solved like case **(1.1)**. But the further refinement we have just done really makes them different. In case **(1.2.b)**, χ is subjective implicit information, so the agent can derive it and solve the problem by only reasoning. Nevertheless, this is not possible in **(1.2.a)** since χ is objective but not subjective implicit information. The agent cannot derive χ; she needs a formula that, when added to her explicit information, makes χ explicit; or, more interesting, she can *extend her reasoning abilities* with a formula/rule that allows her to derive χ. The same happens with other cases.

Just like actions of reasoning, revision and addition can take us from one abductive problem of Table 1.1 to another, they also allow us to move between the abductive problems of Table 1.3. Again, we will focus on the consistent cases, discarding **(1.4.∗)** and **(2.4.d)**. In Table 1.4, the action $\text{Add}_{\sigma_1 \cdots \sigma_n}$ extends the previous action Add_ψ: it now adds inference resources (formulas γ, but also rules α) that make derivable information that was only objectively implicit before. This new operation can be characterized as

$$\text{Inf}_{\text{Im}} \, \psi \leftrightarrow \langle \text{Add}_{\sigma_1^\psi \cdots \sigma_n^\psi} \rangle \, \text{Inf}_{\text{Der}} \, \psi$$

where $\sigma_1^\psi, \ldots, \sigma_n^\psi$ are inference resources that allow the agent to derive ψ whenever ψ is implicit, and depend on the agent's current information and ψ itself.

Also, note how in this case in which implicit information does not need to be derivable, the reasoning action α only needs to fulfil one direction of the equivalence stated in 58, that is, we only need that

$$\langle \alpha_\psi \rangle \, \text{Inf}_{\text{Ex}} \, \psi \rightarrow \text{Inf}_{\text{Im}} \, \psi$$

Definition 3.4 (Extended abductive solutions). Solutions for consistent extended abductive problems are provided in Table 1.4. It should be read as a transition table that provides actions and conditions that should hold in order to move from one abductive problem to another.

Table 1.4 establishes a natural path to solve the new abductive problems. The longest path corresponds to case **(1.3.a)** in which the agent does not have explicit information about either χ or $\neg\chi$ and, though $\neg\chi$ follows logically from her explicit information, she cannot derive it. In this case, the agent should first get enough information to derive $\neg\chi$, then going into case **(1.3.c)**. Then, after reasoning to derive $\neg\chi$, she will have an explicit anomaly, case **(2.3.c)**. From here she needs to revise her information to remove $\neg\chi$ from it and, once she has done this (case **(1.1.a)**), she needs to extend her information with some γ that will make her be explicitly informed about χ.

Case	(1.1.a)	(1.2.a)	(1.2.b)	(1.3.a)	(1.3.c)	(2.3.c)
$[\mathrm{Add}_\gamma]\,\mathrm{Inf}_{\mathrm{Ex}}\,\chi$	Solved	—	—	—	—	—
$[\mathrm{Add}_{\sigma_1^\chi\cdots\sigma_n^\chi}]\,\mathrm{Inf}_{\mathrm{Der}}\,\chi$	—	(1.2.b)	—	—	—	—
$\langle\alpha\rangle\,\mathrm{Inf}_{\mathrm{Ex}}\,\chi$	—	—	Solved	—	—	—
$[\mathrm{Add}_{\sigma_1^{\neg\chi}\cdots\sigma_n^{\neg\chi}}]\,\mathrm{Inf}_{\mathrm{Der}}\,\neg\chi$	—	—	—	(1.3.c)	—	—
$\langle\alpha\rangle\,\mathrm{Inf}_{\mathrm{Ex}}\,\neg\chi$	—	—	—	—	(2.3.c)	—
$\langle\mathrm{Rem}_{\neg\chi}\rangle\,\neg\mathrm{Inf}_{\mathrm{Im}}\,\neg\chi$	—	—	—	—	—	(1.1.a)

Table 1.4: Solutions for consistent extended abductive problems.

Reducing the cases From a subjective point of view, the agent does not need to solve an anomaly that she cannot detect. What guides the process of solving an abductive problem is the explicit information and what she can derive from it. In other words, unaccessible anomalies should not matter!

Following this observation, we can notice that some problems in Table 1.3 are in fact indistinguishable for the agent. Without further external interaction, she can only access her explicit information and eventually what she can derive from it; the rest, the implicit information that is not derivable, is also not relevant. For example, abductive problems **(1.{1,2,3,4}.a)** are in fact the same from the agent's perspective. Then, by grouping indistinguishable problems, we get the following.

$$\neg\mathrm{Inf}_{\mathrm{Ex}}\,\chi \;\wedge\; \neg\mathrm{Inf}_{\mathrm{Ex}}\,\neg\chi \;\wedge\; \left\{ \begin{array}{ll} \neg\mathrm{Inf}_{\mathrm{Der}}\,\chi \;\wedge\; \neg\mathrm{Inf}_{\mathrm{Der}}\,\neg\chi & \textbf{(1.\{1,2,3,4\}.a)} \\ \mathrm{Inf}_{\mathrm{Der}}\,\chi \;\wedge\; \neg\mathrm{Inf}_{\mathrm{Der}}\,\neg\chi & \textbf{(1.\{2,\,4\}.b)} \\ \neg\mathrm{Inf}_{\mathrm{Der}}\,\chi \;\wedge\; \mathrm{Inf}_{\mathrm{Der}}\,\neg\chi & \textbf{(1.\{3,\,4\}.c)} \\ \mathrm{Inf}_{\mathrm{Der}}\,\chi \;\wedge\; \mathrm{Inf}_{\mathrm{Der}}\,\neg\chi & \textbf{(1.4.d)} \end{array} \right.$$

$$\neg\mathrm{Inf}_{\mathrm{Ex}}\,\chi \;\wedge\; \mathrm{Inf}_{\mathrm{Ex}}\,\neg\chi \;\wedge\; \left\{ \begin{array}{ll} \neg\mathrm{Inf}_{\mathrm{Der}}\,\chi \;\wedge\; \mathrm{Inf}_{\mathrm{Der}}\,\neg\chi & \textbf{(2.3.c)} \\ \mathrm{Inf}_{\mathrm{Der}}\,\chi \;\wedge\; \mathrm{Inf}_{\mathrm{Der}}\,\neg\chi & \textbf{(2.4.d)} \end{array} \right.$$

Note how these classes correspond to abductive problems in Table 1.1 in which $\mathrm{Inf}_{\mathrm{Der}}$ appears in place of $\mathrm{Inf}_{\mathrm{Im}}$.

3.3 Explaining explicit information

Abduction is usually defined as the problem of explaining a surprising observation. Novelty is an important characteristic of the fact to explain. So, what is the purpose of explaining explicit information? This information (knowledge or belief) is not supposed to be surprising at all.

But, from another perspective, when we make a (truthful) observation, as surprising as it can be, it automatically becomes part of our explicit information. After observing Mr. Wilson's cuffs, Holmes knows that while one is very shiny on some area, the other one has a smooth patch; after observing the grass, Karen knows it is wet.

What makes this explicit information special (that is, what makes the agent look for an explanation) is that it cannot be justified with the rest of the explicit information the agent possesses. For example, the *fifth postulate* is an obvious piece of explicit information in Euclidean geometry. But, can it be proved from the first four postulates?[9] This generates a variant of an abductive problem that does not depend of recent observations, but rather from unjustified information. The agent identifies a piece of explicit information she has and, when she realizes that it cannot be supported by the rest of her information, she tries to find an explanation for it.

To state this abductive problem formally, we introduce the operation Dis_ψ of discarding formula ψ. When executable, discarding ψ makes it go from being explicit information to being only *implicit*:

$$\text{Inf}_{\text{Ex}}\, \psi \rightarrow [\text{Dis}_\psi]\,(\text{Inf}_{\text{Im}}\, \psi \wedge \neg\text{Inf}_{\text{Ex}}\, \psi)$$

Note how Dis_ψ does not have the same effect that Rem_ψ, which aims to remove ψ *completely* from the agent's information, that is, from both explicit *and* implicit information. The idea is that, by making ψ only implicit, we can verify whether it can actually be derived with the rest of the agent's information or not.

Now we make a further distinction in the agent's explicit information, splitting it in what she knows and can actually justify (if no one provides us the quadratic formula, we can still derive it by using the method of completing squares), and what she knows but cannot derive if she would have not observed it (if Holmes had not seen Mr. Wilson, he had not known the status of his cuffs). More precisely, we say that ψ is *observed explicit information* if, after being discarded, becomes not derivable, that is, if:

$$\text{Inf}_{\text{Ex}}\, \psi \wedge [\text{Dis}_\psi]\, \neg\text{Inf}_{\text{Der}}\, \psi$$

---

[9]In fact, non-Euclidean geometries originated when going in depth into this question.

On the other hand, we say that ψ is *entailed explicit information* if, after being discarded, the agent can still derive it:

$$\text{Inf}_{\text{Ex}}\, \psi \wedge [\text{Dis}_\psi]\, \text{Inf}_{\text{Der}}\, \psi$$

Abductive problems of Table 1.3 in which $\neg\text{Inf}_{\text{Der}}\, \chi$ is the case (that is, all the abductive problems of types (∗.∗.{a,c})) can be adapted for observed explicit information. If Ω is the formula that represents the abductive problem labelled as **n**, then:

$$\text{Inf}_{\text{Ex}}\, \chi \wedge [\text{Dis}_\chi]\, \Omega$$

is the formula that represents the version of abductive problem **n** for observed explicit information. The solutions of these problems start with $[\text{Dis}_\chi]$ and then proceed as in Table 1.4.

4   Knowledge and belief

So far we have talked about the agent's information, without making any specific assumption about it, and even allowing cases when it is inconsistent.

Here we briefly explore two assumptions that define certain notions of information; then we will argue why cases that involve more than one notion are the most natural to describe abductive problems.

4.1   Restrictions on the agent's information

In the mechanics example, the information in the theory of mechanics is information that has been confirmed (via experiments) as true. On the other hand, consider Natalia, who is truthfully informed that Chilly Willy is a bird and then assumes it flies, a situation that does not need to be the case.

There are two main constrains that we can impose on the agent's information. The strongest one is to assume that the information is *knowledge*, and therefore satisfies the property of being *true*. A weaker assumption is to assume the information as *beliefs*, and ask for it to be simply *consistent*.[10]

The first assumption, *true* information, corresponds syntactically to assuming $\text{Inf}\, \psi \rightarrow \psi$ in the case of omniscient agents, and $\text{Inf}_{\text{Im}}\, \psi \rightarrow \psi$ in the case of non-omniscient ones.

Under this assumption, the agent can face *novel* abductive problems, simply because she does not need to have complete information about

---

[10]In the most general case, beliefs do not need to be consistent.

the real situation, and therefore there may be a fact χ that is not part of her information. Solutions in these cases should satisfy the further requirement of preserving the information's properties, so a solution γ for a χ-abductive problem needs to be *true*. This implies that all solutions are consistent. But *anomalous* abductive problems are not possible. The agent's information is true, so if she faces a χ contradicting it, she can be sure that χ is not true, and therefore can simply discard it.

The second assumption, *consistent* information, corresponds syntactically to assuming the formula $\neg \text{Inf} \perp$ in the case of omniscient agents, and $\neg \text{Inf}_{\text{Im}} \perp$ in the case of non-omniscient ones.

With this assumption, novel abductive problems are possible, but also anomalous ones since the agent's information does not need to be true. Like in the previous cases, a solution should preserve the relevant property of the agent's information, that is, the solution should not create an inconsistency when added to the agent's information. This makes all solutions consistent.

4.2   Agents with different kinds of information

Specific assumptions about the agent's information, like the mentioned *truth* and *consistency*, restrict the kind of abductive problems the agent can face, and also impose further restrictions in the possible solutions. Still, one can argue that some abductive problems involve not one single notion of information, but several of them. For example, Natalie is certain about Chilly Willy being a bird, but she only assumes it flies.

But, by looking with more detail to the whole abductive process, we can see that there is a stronger reason why abductive problems are better handled in a framework that allows us to represent different notions of information. Abduction is a *non-monotonic* reasoning process: what the agent chooses as the explanation for the observation does not need to be true, even if the other pieces of information are definitely the case. Karen knows for sure that when it rains, the grass gets wet, and she also knows for a fact that the grass is wet right now. She has a very good reason to suspect that it has rained, but she cannot claim she knows that, because there are many other hypotheses that, though less plausible, can also explain the observed fact. In other words, and from the agent-related perspective, abductive reasoning does not generate knowledge, but *beliefs*.

So far we have discussed important facts that need to be taken into account when studying abductive reasoning from an agent's point of view: her omniscient/non-omniscient characteristics, the notions of information she can handle, and the actions that modify this information. We will now show that a framework that puts all these ingredients together allows us to represent certain forms of abductive reasoning.

5   A semantic model

We have discussed the different abductive problems and abductive solutions that arise when we put into the picture the agent's information and the actions that modify it. So far our discussion has been purely syntactic, presenting formulas that characterize abductive problems and abductive solutions. In this final section we make a step towards a concrete proposal by discussing a semantic structure in which we can model some of our definitions. In order to simplify the analysis, we will focus in our initial example: Sherlock Holmes' observation and explanation for the status of Mr. Wilson's cuffs.

Let us revise Holmes' reasoning. The first step is the irrefutable observation about the status of Mr. Wilson's cuffs, which gives him a piece of true information. This observation is now part of Holmes' knowledge, but it is knowledge that is not justified (i.e., supported) by the rest of his information. In other words, before the observation, Holmes did not have any piece of information that would have allowed him to expect the status of Mr. Wilson's cuffs. Nevertheless, he knows that a lot of writing will make one cuff very shiny and will tear apart the other. Then, after observing the cuffs, it is reasonable for Holmes to assume that Mr. Wilson indeed has done a considerable amount of writing lately because, if he had known that before, he would have expected the cuffs' status. More precisely, Holmes *knows* a piece of information (the status of Mr. Wilson's cuffs) and he also *knows* how he could have predicted it (if Mr. Wilson has been writing a lot, then his cuffs will have such status). Then, Holmes has reasons to suspect that what he would have needed to make the prediction is actually the case: he *believes* that Mr. Wilson has written a lot lately.

This brief analysis shows us the needed ingredients for a semantic representation of this kind of abductive reasoning. We need a framework in which we can represent not only an agent's knowledge but also her beliefs. Moreover, the framework should allow us to represent the tools the agent has to perform inferences, since these tools are precisely the ones that provide the agent with the possible explanations for her observation. From this perspective, this case of abductive reasoning can be seen as a particular form of belief revision driven by the agent's inferential abilities; she knows γ and also knows that from certain φ she can derive γ, so she will revise her beliefs in order to believe φ.

The framework of Velázquez-Quesada (2010) provides us with the needed tools to represent this form of abductive reasoning. It extends the plausibility models (which are themselves a particular case of possible worlds models) developed in van Benthem (2007) and Baltag and Smets (2008) with ideas for representing non-omniscient agents presented in Fagin and Halpern (1988) and Jago (2006). The intuition is that the standard *epistemic logic* notions of knowledge and beliefs should not be considered as real 'full-blooded' information, but just as an *implicit* form of it: the best the agent can do. In order for them to be considered *explicit* information, they should satisfy an extra property in all the possible worlds relevant for the notion (the indistinguishable worlds for the case of knowledge, the most plausible ones for the case of beliefs). The resulting models, *plausibility access* models, allow us to represent the agent's implicit and explicit knowledge/beliefs about not only formulas, but also about rules.

5.1 Representing knowledge and beliefs

Definition 5.1 (Plausibility-access language). Given a set of atomic propositions P, formulas φ, ψ and rules σ of the *plausibility-access (PA)* language $\mathcal{L}$ are given, respectively, by

$$\varphi ::= p \mid A\,\varphi \mid R\,\sigma \mid \neg\varphi \mid \varphi \vee \psi \mid \langle \simeq \rangle\,\varphi \mid \langle \leq \rangle\,\varphi$$
$$\sigma ::= (\{\psi_1, \ldots, \psi_{n_\sigma}\}, \varphi)$$

where $p \in \mathrm{P}$. Formulas of the form $A\,\varphi$ are read as *"the agent has acknowledged (accepted) that formula φ is true"*, and formulas of the form $R\,\sigma$ as *"the agent has acknowledged (accepted) that rule σ is truth-preserving"*. For the modalities, $\langle \leq \rangle\,\varphi$ is read as *"there is a world at least as plausible where φ holds"*, and $\langle \simeq \rangle\,\varphi$ as *"there is an epistemically indistinguishable world where φ holds"*. Other boolean connectives as well as the universal modalities $[\simeq]$, $[\leq]$ are defined as usual.

On the other side, a rule σ is a pair $(\{\psi_1, \ldots, \psi_{n_\sigma}\}, \varphi)$, sometimes represented as $\{\psi_1, \ldots, \psi_{n_\sigma}\} \Rightarrow \varphi$, where $\{\psi_1, \ldots, \psi_{n_\sigma}\}$ is a *finite* set of formulas, the rule's *premises* PREM(σ), and φ is a formula, the rule's *conclusion* cn(σ).[11]

We denote by $\mathcal{L}_f$ the set of formulas of $\mathcal{L}$, and by $\mathcal{L}_r$ its set of rules.

---

[11]Note how this definition of what a rule is is not as general as one might wish. In particular, it is not possible to represent rules that allow us to introduce assumptions,

For the semantic model, plausibility models are extended with two functions, indicating the formulas and the rules the agent has acknowledged as true and truth-preserving, respectively, at each possible world.

Definition 5.2 (Plausibility-access model). Let P be a set of atomic propositions. A *plausibility-access (PA) model* is a tuple $M = \langle W, \leq, V, \mathsf{A}, \mathsf{R} \rangle$ where

- W is a non-empty set of *possible worlds*,

- $\leq \subseteq (W \times W)$ is a *plausibility relation* (a locally connected and a conversely well-founded preorder) representing the plausibility order of the worlds from the agent's point of view ($u \leq v$ is read as v *is at least as plausible as* u),

- $V : W \to \wp(\mathrm{P})$ is an *atomic valuation function*, indicating the atomic propositions in P that are true at each possible world,

- $\mathsf{A} : W \to \wp(\mathscr{L}_f)$ is the *access set function*, indicating the set of formulas the agent has acknowledged as true at each possible world,

- $\mathsf{R} : W \to \wp(\mathscr{L}_r)$ is the *rule set function*, indicating the set of rules the agent has acknowledged as truth-preserving at each possible world.

A *pointed PA model* (M, w) is a PA model with a distinguished world $w \in W$.

The plausibility relation $\leq$ will allow us to define the agent's beliefs as what is true in the most plausible worlds (Grove, 1988; Segerberg, 2001), but for defining the agent's knowledge, an *indistinguishability* relation is needed. The approach is to assume that the agent cannot distinguish between two worlds if and only if she considers one of them more plausible than the other. Then, the indistinguishability relation $\simeq$ is defined as the union of $\leq$ and its converse, that is, $\simeq := \leq \cup \geq$.

For the semantic interpretation, the two modalities $\langle \leq \rangle$ and $\langle \simeq \rangle$ are interpreted with the help of their respective relations in the standard

---

like the rules for introducing an implication or eliminating a disjunction in natural deduction. Nevertheless, they are enough for our goal here: showing how a semantic model that involves knowledge, beliefs and the agent's inferential powers allows us to represent certain forms of abductive reasoning.

way, and the two 'acknowledgement' formulas $A\,\varphi$ and $R\,\sigma$ simply look at the A- and R-set of the evaluation point. Formally,

Definition 5.3 (Semantic interpretation). Let (M, w) be a pointed *PA* model with $M = \langle W, \leq, V, A, R \rangle$. Atomic propositions and boolean operators are interpreted as usual. For the remaining cases,

$$(M, w) \Vdash A\,\varphi \quad \text{iff} \quad \varphi \in A(w)$$
$$(M, w) \Vdash R\,\sigma \quad \text{iff} \quad \sigma \in R(w)$$
$$(M, w) \Vdash \langle \leq \rangle\,\varphi \quad \text{iff} \quad \text{there is a } u \in W \text{ such that } w \leq u \text{ and } (M, u) \Vdash \varphi$$
$$(M, w) \Vdash \langle \simeq \rangle\,\varphi \quad \text{iff} \quad \text{there is a } u \in W \text{ such that } w \simeq u \text{ and } (M, u) \Vdash \varphi$$

Defining the notions The key part now is the definition of the notions of implicit/explicit knowledge and beliefs. For *implicit* knowledge, the classical *EL* approach is used: the agent knows φ implicitly iff φ is true in all the worlds she considers possible; for φ to be *explicitly* known, the agent needs to acknowledge this in all such worlds:

The agent knows *implicitly* the *formula* φ	$K_{\text{Im}}\varphi := [\simeq]\,\varphi$
The agent knows *explicitly* the *formula* φ	$K_{\text{Ex}}\varphi := [\simeq]\,(\varphi \wedge A\,\varphi)$

For defining beliefs, the idea of the cited papers is that we can define notions weaker than knowledge if, instead of looking at all the epistemically possible worlds, we look only at a subset of them. In particular, we say than an agent believes φ *implicitly* if and only if φ is true *in the worlds she considers the most plausible ones*. Given the properties of the plausibility relation, φ is true in the most plausible worlds if and only if, by following the $\leq$ ordering, from some moment on we only find worlds that satisfy φ. For the *explicit* counterpart, we ask for the agent to additionally acknowledge φ in these most plausible worlds.

The agent believes *implicitly* the *formula* φ	$B_{\text{Im}}\varphi := \langle \leq \rangle\,[\leq]\,\varphi$
The agent believes *explicitly* the *formula* φ	$B_{\text{Ex}}\varphi := \langle \leq \rangle\,[\leq]\,(\varphi \wedge A\,\varphi)$

We have defined the notions of implicit/explicit knowledge/beliefs for *formulas*. For the case of *rules*, in the implicit case, we translate a rule σ into an implication $\text{tr}(\sigma)$ whose antecedent is the (finite) conjunction of the rule's premises and whose consequent is the rule's conclusion; in the *explicit* case, we use the 'acknowledgement of rule' formulas:

The agent knows *implicitly* the *rule* σ	$K_{\mathrm{Im}}\sigma := [\approx]\,\mathrm{tr}(\sigma)$
The agent knows *explicitly* the *rule* σ	$K_{\mathrm{Ex}}\sigma := [\approx]\big(\mathrm{tr}(\sigma) \wedge R\,\sigma\big)$
The agent believes *implicitly* the *rule* σ	$B_{\mathrm{Im}}\sigma := \langle\leq\rangle\,[\leq]\,\mathrm{tr}(\sigma)$
The agent believes *explicitly* the *rule* σ	$B_{\mathrm{Ex}}\sigma := \langle\leq\rangle\,[\leq]\big(\mathrm{tr}(\sigma) \wedge R\,\sigma\big)$

Consider now the three notions of information we have discussed in Section 3, explicit, derivable and implicit, and how they relate to each other in this framework.

From the just given definitions, it is clear that *explicit* information (knowledge/beliefs) is also *implicit* information. Moreover, as we will discuss below, the information the agent can derive by using the rules in the deductive way (from the rule and the premises to the conclusion) is also implicit information. This gives us the two implications that we asked for in Section 3.2.

Note also how in this setting these implications are strict. Since the A-sets do not need to satisfy any particular property, this framework allow us to represent agents whose implicit information (knowledge/beliefs) does not need to be explicit, that is, non-omniscient agents.[12] Moreover, since the R-sets do not need to satisfy any particular property, the framework allows us to represent agents whose implicit information (knowledge/beliefs) does not need to be derivable.

This framework satisfies our 'static' requirements. We now move on to the 'dynamic' part: actions that change the agent's information.

5.2   Some actions definable in this framework

Here we make a brief recap of some actions that can be defined in this framework and that are useful for our purposes. First, an action that adds a given ψ to the agent's knowledge.

Definition 5.4 (Adding ψ to knowledge). The act of *adding* a formula ψ to the agent's knowledge can be represented by a small modification of the so-called public announcement in *public announcement logic* (Plaza, 1989; Gerbrandy, 1999). The idea is that after ψ is publicly announced, the agent will discard those possibilities she recognizes as not satisfying ψ, acknowledging that ψ should be the case in the remaining ones.

---

[12]It is also worthwhile to observe that, in this framework, implicit knowledge/beliefs are not the closure under logical consequence of explicit knowledge/beliefs. This happens when the A-sets contain the valuation of the corresponding world, that is, when for every $p \in P$, $p \in A(w)$ if $p \in V(w)$ and $\neg p \in A(w)$ if $p \notin V(w)$.

Technically, given the model $M = \langle W, \leq, V, \mathsf{A}, \mathsf{R} \rangle$, a public announcement of ψ removes the worlds where $\neg \psi \wedge \mathsf{A} \neg \psi$ is the case, adding ψ to the A-sets of these surviving worlds.

In general, this operation does not satisfy our requirement for Add (page 53): after adding ψ, the agent does not need know ψ.[13] Nevertheless, if ψ is a propositional formula (without epistemic operators) we do have $[\mathrm{Add}_\psi] \, \mathrm{Inf} \, \psi$.

We now present an action that represents the application of a rule.

Definition 5.5 (A reasoning step). The act of *applying* a rule σ in a truth-preserving way can be represented by an operation that adds the rule's conclusion to the A-sets of every epistemically possible world, provided that the agent knows explicitly both the rule and its premises (Grossi and Velázquez-Quesada, 2009).

Note how this action satisfies the requirement on page 61, $\langle \alpha_\psi \rangle \, \mathrm{Inf}_{\mathrm{Ex}} \, \psi \; \to \; \mathrm{Inf}_{\mathrm{Im}} \, \psi$. This is because we have defined a reasoning step that makes ψ explicit knowledge as the application of a rule that has ψ as its conclusion. But a rule can be applied only when the agent knows explicitly both the rule and its premises. Then, the rule is truth-preserving and the premises are true in all epistemically possible worlds. Hence, the conclusion ψ is also true in such worlds, and therefore is implicitly known.

5.3   An action representing abductive reasoning

In the presented framework, the agent's beliefs are given by the plausibility relation. Then, changes in beliefs can be represented by changes in this order (van Ditmarsch, 2005; van Benthem, 2007; Baltag and Smets, 2008). In particular, the act of *revising* beliefs with the aim to believe a given χ can be seen as a change that puts χ-worlds at the top of the plausibility order. Of course, there are several ways in which such a new order can be defined, but each one of them can be seen as a different policy for *revising* beliefs. Here is one of the many possibilities.

Definition 5.6 (Upgrade operation). Let $M = \langle W, \leq, V, \mathsf{A}, \mathsf{R} \rangle$ be a *PA* model and let ψ be a formula in $\mathscr{L}_f$. The *upgrade* operation produces the *PA* model $M_{\psi + \Uparrow} = \langle W, \leq', V, \mathsf{A}, \mathsf{R} \rangle$, differing from M just in the plausibility relation, which is given in the following way. After an upgrade with

---

[13]The typical example are formulas expressing (lack of) knowledge about something, like the Moore sentence *"p is the case but the agent does not know it"*; after this is announced, the agent does not know it because she knows *p* now. See Holliday and Icard (2010).

ψ, *"all G_ψ-worlds become more plausible than all $\neg G_\psi$-worlds, and within the two zones the old ordering remains"* (van Benthem, 2007). More precisely, we will have $w \leq' u$ iff (1) $w \leq u$ and u is a G_ψ-world, or (2) w is a $\neg G_\psi$-world and $w \leq u$, or (3) w and u are already comparable (i.e., $w \simeq u$), w is a $\neg G_\psi$-world and u is a G_ψ-world.[14]

In this definition, G_ψ indicates what the worlds should satisfy in order for the agent to put them at the top of the ordering. In the case of an omniscient agent, G_ψ is given directly by ψ, but a non-omniscient agent may not recognize whether ψ holds in a given world or not. In such case, G_ψ is given by $\psi \wedge A \psi$.

The key observation of the discussed Holmes' example is that the described form of abductive reasoning can be seen as a form of belief revision guided by the agent's inferential abilities: if the agent knows a rule and its conclusion, then it is reasonable for her to believe that all the rule's premises are the case. With this idea in mind, here is our proposal for an action representing this form of abductive reasoning.

Syntactically, we introduce a new modality that allows us to build formulas of the form $\langle \text{Abd}_\sigma \rangle \, \varphi$, read as *"the agent can perform an abductive step with rule σ after which φ is the case"*. This new modality has the following semantic interpretation.

$$(M, w) \Vdash \langle \text{Abd}_\sigma \rangle \, \varphi \quad \text{iff} \quad (M, w) \Vdash K_{\text{Ex}}\sigma \wedge K_{\text{Ex}}\text{cn}(\sigma) \quad \text{and} \quad (M_{\text{PM}_\sigma {}^{+}\Uparrow}, w) \Vdash \varphi$$

where the formula PM_σ, identifying the worlds that the agent recognizes as satisfying all σ's premises, is defined as

$$\text{PM}_\sigma := \bigwedge_{\gamma \in \text{PREM}(\sigma)} (\gamma \wedge A \gamma)$$

Let us spell out the definition. The agent can perform an abductive step with rule σ after which φ is the case, $(M, w) \Vdash \langle \text{Abd}_\sigma \rangle \, \varphi$, if and only if she knows explicitly the rule and its conclusion, $(M, w) \Vdash K_{\text{Ex}}\sigma \wedge K_{\text{Ex}}\text{cn}(\sigma)$, and, after putting on top of her plausibility order those worlds she identifies as satisfying all σ's premises, φ is the case, $(M_{\text{PM}_\sigma {}^{+}\Uparrow}, w) \Vdash \varphi$.

---

[14]Using *propositional dynamic logic* notation, the given definition corresponds to

$$\leq' := (\leq; G_\psi?) \cup (\neg G_\psi?; \leq) \cup (\neg G_\psi?; \simeq; G_\psi?)$$

5.4   An example

Consider the *PA* model below. In it our agent, Sherlock Holmes, knows explicitly the status of Mr. Wilson's cuffs (c), and also knows explicitly that if Mr. Wilson has been doing a considerable amount of writing lately (r), then the status of his cuffs would follow. Nevertheless, Holmes does not believe, either explicitly or implicitly, that Mr. Wilson has been writing lately. The formulas on the right of the diagram express all this.

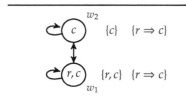

- $K_{Ex} c \wedge K_{Ex}(r \Rightarrow c)$
- $\neg B_{Ex} r$
- $\neg B_{Im} r$

In this situation Holmes has an abductive problem of the kind described in Section 3.3: c is observed explicit information because Holmes knows c explicitly but he cannot justify it with the rest of his information: $K_{Ex} c \wedge [Dis_c] \neg Inf_{Der} c$. More precisely, the problem corresponds to the case **1.2.a** of Table 1.3 with the adaptation described in Section 3.3: Holmes knows c explicitly but, if he discards it (in this setting, by simply removing c from the A-sets), then he does not know either c or $\neg c$ explicitly, he cannot derive either c or $\neg c$, and though he does not know implicitly $\neg c$, he does know implicitly c.

Now Holmes decides to apply abductive reasoning in order to explain the particularities of Mr. Wilson's cuffs. According to Table 1.4, r is an abductive solution for this case **1.2.a**: by adding r to Holmes' information (in the style of the public announcement of 5.4), c becomes derivable, and an inference step with the rule $r \Rightarrow c$ (in the style of the truth-preserving inference of 5.5) will give Holmes explicit knowledge of c. In a formula,

$$[Add_r]\left(Inf_{Der} c \wedge \langle r \Rightarrow c \rangle K_{Ex} c\right)$$

In other words, Holmes knows that if he knew that Mr. Wilson has being doing a considerable amount of writing lately, he would have been able to conclude the observed state of his cuffs. Then r is an abductive solution for this problem. Moreover, it is consistent as it does not contradict Holmes' knowledge, and it is also explanatory as by itself it does not imply c (the previously known rule $r \Rightarrow c$ is also needed).

Once an abductive solution has been identified, it is time for Holmes to incorporate it to his information. Since an abductive solution has a 'tentative' status, it should not be incorporated as knowledge but rather as belief, and we can do that with the upgrade operation (Definition 5.6). The model that results from this operation appears on the right.

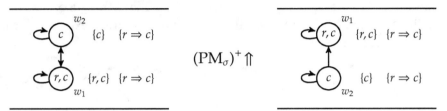

What has changed in the new model is the ordering of the worlds: now the unique world that Holmes recognizes as a r-world, w_1, has become more plausible than the other. In this resulting model Holmes still knows explicitly the status of Mr. Wilson's cuffs, and still knows explicitly the rule that links that with a considerable amount of writing ($K_{Ex} c \wedge K_{Ex}(r \Rightarrow c)$). But, as a result of abductive reasoning, Holmes now believes (both implicitly and explicitly) that the high amount of writing is indeed the case.

5.5   Some remarks

There are two important observations about the proposed system. First, note how we have suggested that, when trying to explain an explicitly known χ, the candidates can be found in the premises of those rules that would allow us to derive χ. This agrees with syntactic approaches to abductive reasoning in which explanations are generated based on the agent's inferential tools (tableaux: Reyes-Cabello et al. (2006); sequent calculi: Mayer and Pirri (1993); logic programming: Denecker and Kakas (2002)).

Second, the proposed operation only deals with the effect of incorporating the agent's chosen explanation to her information, but not with the process of *choosing* the explanation. In general, the agent may have several ways in which she could have derived the observed fact, which in this rule-based setting corresponds to the agent having several rules that allow her to derive the observation. Some of the possible solutions can be trivial or inconsistent with the agent's information and in some cases none of them may fulfil any of the requirements in Definition 2.6. When looking for a criterion to decide which one(s) of these possible explanations is (are) 'the best', our framework provides us with some options. We cannot rely on how plausible is the rule that provides the explanation because our precondition is that the rule is explicitly *known* and therefore recognized as true in all the worlds the agent considers possible. One possibility is to rely on the plausibility of the rule's premises: if the agent already believes in some of them, then it is reasonable to believe in the rest.

All in all, the example shows how, by using a framework for representing knowledge and beliefs of a non-omniscient agent, we can represent some forms of abductive reasoning.

6 Summary and future work

We have presented definitions of abductive problem and abductive solution in terms of an agent's information and the way it changes. Then we have shown how different examples of abductive reasoning correspond to different kinds of agents, like those whose information is not closed under logical consequence and whose reasoning abilities are not complete. We have discussed particular interpretations of the agent's information, and argued that a setting involving an agent's knowledge and beliefs is more adequate for representing the abductive process. Finally, we have shown how a syntactic extension of the possible worlds model allows us to represent certain forms of abductive reasoning.

Our work is just an initial exploration of abductive reasoning in a dynamic epistemic logic setting, and there are many aspects yet to be studied. The most important one is the semantic representation of abductive reasoning, and though we have shown that certain forms can be represented, a deep study of the diverse types that can be described is still pending. In order to achieve this, we first should provide a proper semantic definition for the actions we have sketched through the work: $Add_{\varphi/\alpha}$, Rem_{φ}, α and Dis_{φ}. Natural candidates can be found in the current *DEL* literature (Plaza, 1989; Gerbrandy, 1999; van Benthem, 2007; Baltag and Smets, 2008; Velázquez-Quesada, 2010). Once a full *DEL* setting has been formally defined, the next step is a proper comparison between it and other approaches to abductive reasoning, in order to identify strengths and weaknesses and, more importantly, in order to obtain a better picture of the abductive process.

Acknowledgements. We thank Johan van Benthem and Ángel Nepomuceno-Fernández for their valuable comments and suggestions on preliminary versions of this paper, and two anonymous referees for pointing out problems and providing useful suggestions for improving this work. Fernando Soler-Toscano also thanks the Centro de Filosofia das Ciências da Universidade de Lisboa for the stay he carried out there during the research and writing of this paper.

Bibliography

Aliseda, A., 2006. *Abductive Reasoning. Logical Investigations into Discovery and Explanation*, volume 330 of *Synthese Library Series*. Springer.

Baltag, A. and Smets, S., 2008. A qualitative theory of dynamic interactive belief revision. In Bonanno, G., van der Hoek, W., and Wooldridge, M. (ed.), *Logic and the Foundations of Game and Decision Theory (LOFT7)*, volume 3 of *Texts in Logic and Games*, pages 13–60. Amsterdam University Press.

Boissier, O., Seghrouchni, A. E. F., Hassas, S., and Maudet, N. (ed.), August 2010. *Proceedings of The Multi-Agent Logics, Languages, and Organisations Federated Workshops (MALLOW 2010)*, volume 627, Lyon, France. CEUR Workshop Proceedings. URL http://ceur-ws.org/Vol-627.

Denecker, M. and Kakas, A. C., 2002. Abduction in logic programming. In Kakas, A. C. and Sadri, F. (ed.), *Computational Logic: Logic Programming and Beyond*, volume 2407 of *Lecture Notes in Computer Science*, pages 402–436. Springer. ISBN 3-540-43959-5. doi: 10.1007/3-540-45628-7_16. URL http://link.springer.de/link/service/series/0558/bibs/2407/24070402.htm.

Fagin, R. and Halpern, J. Y., 1988. Belief, awareness, and limited reasoning. *Artificial Intelligence*, 34(1):39–76. ISSN 0004-3702. doi: 10.1016/0004-3702(87)90003-8.

Gärdenfors, P. (ed.), 1992. *Belief Revision*. Number 29 in Cambridge Tracts in Theoretical Computer Science. Cambridge Press.

Gerbrandy, J., 1999. *Bisimulations on Planet Kripke*. PhD thesis, Institute for Logic, Language and Computation, Universiteit van Amsterdam, Amsterdam, The Netherlands. ILLC Dissertation Series DS-1999-01.

Grossi, D. and Velázquez-Quesada, F. R., 2009. *Twelve Angry Men*: A study on the fine-grain of announcements. In He, X., Horty, J. F., and Pacuit, E. (ed.), *LORI*, volume 5834 of *Lecture Notes in Computer Science*, pages 147–160. Springer. ISBN 978-3-642-04892-0. doi: http://dx.doi.org/10.1007/978-3-642-04893-7. URL http://dx.doi.org/10.1007/978-3-642-04893-7_12.

Grove, A., May 1988. Two modellings for theory change. *Journal of Philosophical Logic*, 17(2):157–170. ISSN 0022-3611. doi: 10.1007/BF00247909.

Halpern, J. Y. (ed.), 1986. *Proceedings of the 1st Conference on Theoretical Aspects of Reasoning about Knowledge, Monterey, CA, March 1986*, San Francisco, CA, USA. Morgan Kaufmann Publishers Inc. ISBN 0-934613-04-4.

Hartshorne, C. and Weiss, P. (ed.), 1934. *Collected Papers of Charles S. Peirce*, volume V: Pragmatism and Pramaticism. Harvard Universit Press, Cambridge. ISBN 9780674138001.

Hintikka, J., 1962. *Knowledge and Belief: An Introduction to the Logic of the Two Notions*. Cornell University Press, Ithaca, N.Y.

Hintikka, J., 1998. What is abduction? The fundamental problem of contemporary epistemology. *Transactions of the Charles S. Peirce Society*, 34(3):503–533.

Holliday, W. H. and Icard, T. F., 2010. Moorean phenomena in epistemic logic. In Beklemishev, L., Goranko, V., and Shehtman, V. (ed.), *Advances in Modal Logic*, pages 178–199. College Publications. ISBN 978-1-84890-013-4. URL http://www.aiml.net/volumes/volume8/Holliday-Icard.pdf.

Jago, M., August 2006. Rule-based and resource-bounded: A new look at epistemic logic. In Ågotnes, T. and Alechina, N. (ed.), *Proceedings of the Workshop on Logics for Resource-Bounded Agents, organized as part of the 18th European Summer School on Logic, Language and Information (ESSLLI)*, pages 63–77, Malaga, Spain.

Lakemeyer, G., 1986. Steps towards a first-order logic of explicit and implicit belief. In Halpern (1986), pages 325–340. ISBN 0-934613-04-4.

Levesque, H. J., 1984. A logic of implicit and explicit belief. In *Proc. of AAAI-84*, pages 198–202, Austin, TX.

Mayer, M. C. and Pirri, F., 1993. First order abduction via tableau and sequent calculi. *Logic Journal of the IGPL*, 1(1):99–117. doi: 10.1093/jigpal/1.1.99.

Plaza, J. A., 1989. Logics of public communications. In Emrich, M. L., Pfeifer, M. S., Hadzikadic, M., and Ras, Z. W. (ed.), *Proceedings of the 4th International Symposium on Methodologies for Intelligent Systems*, pages 201–216, Tennessee, USA. Oak Ridge National Laboratory, ORNL/DSRD-24.

Reyes-Cabello, A. L., Aliseda-Llera, A., and Nepomuceno-Fernández, Á., March 2006. Towards abductive reasoning in first-order logic. *Logic Journal of the IGPL*, 14(2):287–304. ISSN 1367-0751. doi: 10.1093/jigpal/jzk019.

Segerberg, K., 2001. The basic dynamic doxastic logic of AGM. In Williams and Rott (2001), pages 57–84. ISBN 978-0-7923-7021-5. URL http://www.springer.com/computer/artificial/book/978-0-7923-7021-5.

Soler-Toscano, F. and Velázquez-Quesada, F. R., August 2010. Abduction for (non-omniscient) agents. In Boissier et al. (2010). URL http://ceur-ws.org/Vol-627.

Soler-Toscano, F., Fernández-Duque, D., and Nepomuceno-Fernández, Á., 2010. A modal framework for modeling abductive reasoning. *Logic Journal of the IGPL*. ISSN 1367-0751. doi: 10.1093/jigpal/jzq059. To appear.

van Benthem, J., 2007. Dynamic logic for belief revision. *Journal of Applied Non-Classical Logics*, 17(2):129–155.

van Ditmarsch, H., 2005. Prolegomena to dynamic logic for belief revision. *Synthese*, 147(2):229–275. ISSN 0039-7857. doi: 10.1007/s11229-005-1349-7.

van Ditmarsch, H., van der Hoek, W., and Kooi, B., 2007. *Dynamic Epistemic Logic*, volume 337 of *Synthese Library Series*. Springer.

Vardi, M. Y., 1986. On epistemic logic and logical omniscience. In Halpern (1986), pages 293–305. ISBN 0-934613-04-9.

Velázquez-Quesada, F. R., August 2010. Dynamic epistemic logic for implicit and explicit beliefs. In Boissier et al. (2010). URL http://ceur-ws.org/Vol-627.

Williams, M.-A. and Rott, H. (ed.), 2001. *Frontiers in Belief Revision*. Number 22 in Applied Logic Series. Kluwer Academic Publishers. ISBN 978-0-7923-7021-5. URL http://www.springer.com/computer/artificial/book/978-0-7923-7021-5.

Logic of Time Division on Intervals of Finite Size

Tero TULENHEIMO[*]

ABSTRACT. Logic of time division (or **TD**) was formulated in (Tulenheimo, 2008). It is syntactically like basic modal logic with an additional unary operator but it has an interval-based semantics. The formula $\Box\psi$ is interpreted as meaning 'the current interval has a finite partition of size at least two such that all its members are non-empty and satisfy ψ.' In the present paper the expressive power of **TD** is studied on the class $\mathcal{K}_{fin}$ of all intervals of *finite* size. This logic is characterized from the viewpoint of formal language theory by using certain regular-like operators. We prove that **TD** is not translatable into first-order logic over $\mathcal{K}_{fin}$. An extension **TDN** of **TD** is considered, obtained by making the additional operator 'and next' available. The logic **TDN** is characterized in terms of regular operators and it is seen to coincide for its expressive power with monadic second-order logic over $\mathcal{K}_{fin}$. We also study some closure properties of definable classes of intervals in connection with certain fragments of **TDN**.

1   Introduction

Logic of time division or **TD** was introduced and studied in (Tulenheimo, 2008). Conceptually this logic was motivated by G. H. von Wright's discussion of 'real contradictions' (von Wright, 1969). In his terminology, an interval exemplifies a real contradiction if at least one part of any division of this interval involves the presence of contradictorily related (though non-simultaneous) states. Now, von Wright used a modal-logical formalism to explicate this notion. However, as spelled out in (Tulenheimo, 2011), his characterization of real contradictions was mistaken: in his formulation he used negation in an ambiguous way, without distinguishing the two negations 'does not hold at an interval' and 'fails throughout an interval.' The logic **TD** is an interval-based modal logic in which those two negations are distinguished and

---

[*]STL-CNRS / University of Lille 3, France.

whose modal operators are so interpreted that the logic can be used to describe *divisibility properties* of temporal intervals. In computer scientist's jargon, then, **TD** is a tool for reasoning about divisibility. In philosophical discussions on the nature of time, considerations related to divisibility have had a role at least since Zeno of Elea (5th c. BC). The logic **TD** identifies a simple framework to study properties of temporal flows describable in terms of divisibility statements. The general semantics of **TD** is defined on intervals of any cardinality and any order type. In the present paper we take up one of the questions left open in (Tulenheimo, 2008), namely looking into the behavior of this logic on intervals of finite size.

1.1 Basic notions

Given a fixed finite set π of propositional atoms, temporal flows are represented as triples $(T, <, V)$, where T is a finite set, $<$ is an irreflexive linear order on T, and V is a valuation function which associates every element t of T with a subset $V(t)$ of π. These triples $(T, <, V)$ are termed *intervals*. If $\mathbf{i} = (T, <, V)$, the set T is the *domain* of $\mathbf{i}$, denoted *dom*($\mathbf{i}$). Intuitively, T is a set of instants and $<$ is an *earlier than* relation on T. The function V specifies how the events represented by propositional atoms are distributed over the abstract time structure $(T, <)$. Note that because the set T is assumed to be finite, it has automatically both a minimum and a maximum relative to the relation $<$. Also, the relation $<$ is automatically discrete in the sense that every instant $t \in T$ distinct from $\max(T)$ has an immediate successor, and every instant $t \in T$ distinct from $\min(T)$ has an immediate predecessor. If $\mathbf{i} = (T, <, V)$ is an interval, the structure $(T', <', V')$ is its *subinterval* provided that $T' \subseteq T$, and $<'$ and V' are the restrictions of $<$ and V, respectively, to the set T'. The structure $(T', <', V')$ is itself an interval, and we say more specifically that it is the *subinterval of* $\mathbf{i}$ *determined by the set* T', denoted $\mathbf{i}_{T'}$. If an interval $\mathbf{i} = (T, <, V)$ is clear from the context and $t, t' \in T$, we write $[\![t, t']\!]$ for the subinterval $\mathbf{i}_{[t,t']}$ and $(\!(t, t']\!]$ for the subinterval $\mathbf{i}_{(t,t']}$, where $[t, t'] := \{x : t \leq x \leq t'\}$ and $(t, t'] := \{x : t < x \leq t'\}$. If $t = t'$, the domain of the subinterval $[\![t, t']\!]$ is the singleton $\{t\}$; we denote this interval simply by $[\![t]\!]$.

Note 1.1. In the terminology of the present paper, intervals are structures with a built-in order and a built-in valuation. By contrast, in the common mathematical usage, an interval I is simply a set, specified relative to a fixed linear order $<$ on some set T in terms of bounds $a, b \in T$ with $a \leq b$. For example, the sets $[a, b] := \{x : a \leq x \leq b\}$ and

$(a, b] := \{x : a < x \leq b\}$ are such intervals. This common usage could be generalized by defining an interval I as any *inwards-closed* subset of T: if $t_1, t_2 \in I$ and x is any element of T with $t_1 < x < t_2$, then $x \in I$. In this generalized sense for instance the set $\{x \in \mathbb{Q} : 2 < x^2 < 5\}$ would be an interval relative to the set of rational numbers ordered by magnitude, although the set in question could not be expressed in terms of bounds: the relevant infimum and supremum do not exist in $\mathbb{Q}$. Regarding intervals construed as structures (as opposed to sets), an external and an internal viewpoint may be distinguished. If some structure $(T, <, V)$ has been fixed, an interval in the *external* sense is any substructure $(T', <', V')$ of $(T, <, V)$ such that the set T' is inwards-closed. In the present paper we speak of intervals in the *internal* sense. Intervals of this kind are not defined with reference to any larger structures. For example, if $[0, 1]$ and $[2, 3]$ are inwards-closed sets of rational numbers ('rational intervals' in the sense of the common usage), $<$ is the order of rationals by magnitude, and V is any valuation, then the substructure of $(\mathbb{Q}, <, V)$ determined by the set $[0, 1] \cup [2, 3]$ is an interval in the internal sense. But it is not an interval in the external sense relative to $(\mathbb{Q}, <, V)$, as its domain $[0, 1] \cup [2, 3]$ is not inwards-closed.

We allow the domain of an interval to be empty. There is exactly one empty interval, namely the structure $(\varnothing, \varnothing, \varnothing)$ which will be denoted by Λ. If S is a set, we denote by $|S|$ its cardinality. The *size* of an interval $\mathbf{i}$ is denoted by $|\mathbf{i}|$; by definition $|\mathbf{i}| := |dom(\mathbf{i})|$. We write $t \in \mathbf{i}$ to indicate that t belongs to the domain of $\mathbf{i}$. We let $\mathcal{K}_{\text{fin}}$ stand for the class of all intervals — which by definition are of finite size. Further, we write $\mathcal{K}_{\text{fin}}(\pi)$ for the class of *those* intervals $(T, <, V)$ whose associated valuation is of type $T \to \mathcal{P}(\pi)$.[1]

The notion of division is crucial throughout the paper. We think of divisions as triggered by *division points*. Because the temporal flows considered are finite, *a fortiori* the sets of division points are finite as well. The *division* of an interval $\mathbf{i}$ is a tuple $\langle \mathbf{i}_1, \ldots, \mathbf{i}_n \rangle$ of intervals such that (*a*) it has at least two members (the division is proper, so to say), (*b*) the set $\{dom(\mathbf{i}_1), \ldots, dom(\mathbf{i}_n)\}$ is a partition of the set $dom(\mathbf{i})$, (*c*) no set $dom(\mathbf{i}_j)$ is empty, (*d*) if $j < k$, $t \in dom(\mathbf{i}_j)$ and $t' \in dom(\mathbf{i}_k)$, then t precedes t' in the order of the interval $\mathbf{i}$, and (*e*) the members of the partition are determined by the correlated set of division points. For simplicity, we will apply the following specific definition. If $\mathbf{i}$ is an interval and $\min(\mathbf{i}) \leq t_1 < \ldots < t_n < \max(\mathbf{i})$, we take the division $\mathbb{D}_{\mathbf{i}}(t_1, \ldots, t_n)$ of $\mathbf{i}$ by

---

[1] If S is a set, $\mathcal{P}(S)$ stands for its power set.

the points $t_1, \ldots, t_n$ to be the tuple

$$\langle [\![\min(\mathbf{i}), t_1]\!], (\!(t_1, t_2)\!], \ldots, (\!(t_{n-1}, t_n)\!], (\!(t_n, \max(\mathbf{i})]\!] \rangle.$$

The members of a division are called its *parts*. We write $\mathbf{j} \in \mathbb{D}_{\mathbf{i}}(t_1, \ldots, t_n)$ to indicate that $\mathbf{j}$ is a part of the division $\mathbb{D}_{\mathbf{i}}(t_1, \ldots, t_n)$ of the interval $\mathbf{i}$.

If $\mathcal{K}$ is a class of intervals and $\mathcal{L}$ and $\mathcal{L}'$ are logics whose semantics are defined over intervals, $\mathcal{L}$ is *translatable into* $\mathcal{L}'$ *over* $\mathcal{K}$ (written $\mathcal{L} \leq_{\mathcal{K}} \mathcal{L}'$) if for every $\varphi \in \mathcal{L}$, there is $\psi_\varphi \in \mathcal{L}'$ such that for all $\mathbf{i} \in \mathcal{K}$: $\mathbf{i} \models \varphi$ iff $\mathbf{i} \models \psi_\varphi$. This is the standard definition of a logic being at most as expressive as another one; cf., e.g., (Ebbinghaus and Flum, 1999, Def. 7.1.3). It is *not* required that there be a computable function providing the translation. Below we indeed comment on the computability aspect in connection with certain translations, but it is not a part of the definition. We say that $\mathcal{L}'$ is *more expressive than* $\mathcal{L}$ *over* $\mathcal{K}$ (denoted $\mathcal{L} <_{\mathcal{K}} \mathcal{L}'$) if $\mathcal{L} \leq_{\mathcal{K}} \mathcal{L}'$ but $\mathcal{L}' \not\leq_{\mathcal{K}} \mathcal{L}$. The logics $\mathcal{L}$ and $\mathcal{L}'$ are said to *have the same expressive power over* $\mathcal{K}$ (in symbols $\mathcal{L} =_{\mathcal{K}} \mathcal{L}'$) if $\mathcal{L} \leq_{\mathcal{K}} \mathcal{L}'$ and $\mathcal{L}' \leq_{\mathcal{K}} \mathcal{L}$. Finally, $\mathcal{L}$ and $\mathcal{L}'$ are *incomparable over* $\mathcal{K}$ (written $\mathcal{L} \|_{\mathcal{K}} \mathcal{L}'$) if $\mathcal{L} \not\leq_{\mathcal{K}} \mathcal{L}'$ and $\mathcal{L}' \not\leq_{\mathcal{K}} \mathcal{L}$. In this paper we will speak in a generalized sense of translatability even between logics and certain classes of expressions other than logical formulas.

It is assumed that the reader is familiar with the standard formulation of first-order logic (**FO**), when the semantic relation $\mathcal{M}, \gamma \models \varphi$ is defined for all models $\mathcal{M}$ with a non-empty domain M, first-order formulas φ and variable assignments $\gamma : Free(\varphi) \to M$, where $Free(\varphi)$ is the set of free individual variables of φ. We restrict attention to vocabularies which contain only relation symbols (no constant or function symbols). In the present paper we allow the case that the domain of a model is *empty*.[2] Strictly speaking there is one such 'empty model' for every vocabulary; in each case every relation symbol of the vocabulary is interpreted by the empty set. For every vocabulary τ, the relation $\mathcal{M}, \gamma \models \varphi$ is defined in this generalized setting for all models $\mathcal{M}$ of vocabulary τ (including the empty ones), first-order formulas φ of vocabulary τ, and

---

[2]Formulations of **FO** allowing empty domains are well known in the literature; see e.g. Mostowski (1951); Hailperin (1953); Hintikka (1953); Quine (1954); Williamson (1999). There are various subtleties involved in the formulation; the choices one makes will affect the metalogical properties of the resulting language (e.g., formulas equivalent over non-empty domains may fail to be so when empty models are accepted, cf. vacuous quantification). For the purposes of the present paper it suffices that we have a semantics agreeing with the standard one on non-empty models and rendering all *sentences* of the form $\forall x \varphi$ (respectively $\exists x \varphi$) true (false) over empty models.

assignments $\gamma : Free(\varphi) \to M$. It should be noted that if M is empty, *there are no* assignments of type $Free(\varphi) \to M$ unless also the set $Free(\varphi)$ is empty, i.e., unless φ is a sentence (formula whose all occurrences of variables are bound). If indeed $Free(\varphi) = \varnothing$, there is exactly one assignment of type $Free(\varphi) \to \varnothing$, namely the empty assignment, which set-theoretically speaking equals the empty set. The semantic clauses for quantifiers are kept intact. If $\mathcal{M}$ is an empty model and $Q \in \{\forall, \exists\}$, the condition $\mathcal{M}, \gamma \models Qx\psi$ is defined iff γ is the empty assignment and the only free variable of ψ is x. If $Q = \forall$, the condition holds trivially and if $Q = \exists$, it fails trivially. In the former case this is because for every $a \in \varnothing$, we have $\mathcal{M}, \gamma \cup \{(x, a)\} \models \psi$; in the latter case, again, because for every $a \in \varnothing$, we have $\mathcal{M}, \gamma \cup \{(x, a)\} \not\models \psi$. Both conditions hold because there are no elements a in $\varnothing$. The *quantifier rank* of an **FO** formula is its maximum number of nested quantifiers. For the technique of using Ehrenfeucht-Fraïssé games to prove the elementary equivalence of two structures up to a given quantifier rank, see (Ebbinghaus and Flum, 1999). *Monadic second-order logic* (**MSO**) is obtained from **FO** by allowing atomic formulas Xy and complex formulas $\forall X\varphi$ and $\exists X\varphi$, where X is a unary relation variable and y is an individual variable; see e.g. (Ebbinghaus et al., 1994). The unary relation variables range over arbitrary subsets of the domain. Here the relation $\mathcal{M}, \gamma \models \varphi$ is defined for **MSO** formulas φ and assignments $\gamma : Free(\varphi) \cup Free_2(\varphi) \to M$, where $Free_2(\varphi)$ is the set of free relation variables of φ, by extending the corresponding definition for **FO** sketched above. Note that if $M = \varnothing$, the condition $\mathcal{M}, \gamma \models \varphi$ is defined iff the set $Free(\varphi)$ is empty; the condition is indeed defined even if the formula φ contains free *relation* variables, because the power set of M is non-empty even if M is empty. We will write **FO**$[\tau]$ (respectively **MSO**$[\tau]$) for the set of all *sentences* of first-order logic (monadic-second order logic) of vocabulary τ.

2 Logic of time division

Let us begin by recalling the syntax and semantics of the logic of time division or **TD**, here formulated with an eye on our present interests, i.e., assuming that the relevant intervals of evaluation are finite. Basic semantic properties of this logic are then briefly discussed before we proceed, from Section 3 on, to a more systematic study of the expressive power of this logic.

2.1 Syntax and semantics of TD

Syntactically, the logic of time division is simply basic modal logic (**ML**) with an additional unary operator ($\sim$). Let π be a finite (possibly empty) set of atoms. The syntax of the logic **TD**$[\pi]$ is given by the grammar

$$\varphi ::= p \mid \perp \mid \top \mid \sim\!\varphi \mid \neg\varphi \mid (\varphi \vee \varphi) \mid (\varphi \wedge \varphi) \mid \Diamond\varphi \mid \Box\varphi,$$

with $p \in \pi$. When making claims which hold for every set of atoms π, we simply write **TD**. In this case, then, we speak of the logic of time division generically.

The way in which the symbols $\Box$ and $\Diamond$ are interpreted is totally unrelated to **ML**. Here we use these operators to speak of divisibility properties of intervals relative to which the formulas are evaluated. Both $\neg$ and $\sim$ are negation symbols, to be referred to as the 'contradictory negation' and 'universal negation,' respectively. The formula $\neg\varphi$ denies what φ affirms: $\neg\varphi$ is true at an interval iff φ is not true at it. By contrast, $\sim\!\varphi$ states that φ *fails throughout* the interval of evaluation: $\sim\!\varphi$ is true at **i** iff φ is false separately at every time point that belongs to **i**.[3] We may construe the symbols $\perp$ and $\top$ as nullary connectives.

The semantics of **TD**$[\pi]$ is specified by defining recursively the relation '$\mathbf{i} \models \varphi$' for all intervals $\mathbf{i} = (T, <, V)$ in the class $\mathcal{K}_{\text{fin}}(\pi)$ and for all formulas φ of **TD**$[\pi]$:

- $\mathbf{i} \models p$ iff $p \in V(t)$ for all $t \in \mathbf{i}$
- $\mathbf{i} \models \perp$ iff $t \neq t$ for all $t \in \mathbf{i}$
- $\mathbf{i} \models \top$ iff $t = t$ for all $t \in \mathbf{i}$
- $\mathbf{i} \models \sim\!\psi$ iff $[\![t]\!] \not\models \psi$ for all $t \in \mathbf{i}$
- $\mathbf{i} \models \neg\psi$ iff $\mathbf{i} \not\models \psi$
- $\mathbf{i} \models (\psi \wedge \chi)$ iff $\mathbf{i} \models \psi$ and $\mathbf{i} \models \chi$
- $\mathbf{i} \models (\psi \vee \chi)$ iff $\mathbf{i} \models \psi$ or $\mathbf{i} \models \chi$
- $\mathbf{i} \models \Box\psi$ iff for some positive integer n there are instants $t_1, \ldots, t_n$ with $\min(\mathbf{i}) \leq t_1 < \ldots < t_n < \max(\mathbf{i})$ such that for each part $\mathbf{j}$ of the division $\mathbb{D}_{\mathbf{i}}(t_1, \ldots, t_n)$, we have $\mathbf{j} \models \psi$
- $\mathbf{i} \models \Diamond\psi$ iff for all positive integers n and all instants $t_1, \ldots, t_n$ with $\min(\mathbf{i}) \leq t_1 < \ldots < t_n < \max(\mathbf{i})$, there is a part $\mathbf{j}$ of the division $\mathbb{D}_{\mathbf{i}}(t_1, \ldots, t_n)$ such that $\mathbf{j} \models \psi$.

---

[3]Strictly speaking we wish the evaluation to be always relative to intervals. When saying that a formula holds (fails) at an instant t, what we mean is that it holds (fails) at the singleton interval $[\![t]\!]$.

Seen as a generalized quantifier, the unary operator $\Box$ involves semantically second-order existential and first-order universal quantification. To make this explicit, note that the truth-condition of $\Box\varphi$ relative to the interval $\mathbf{i}$ is as follows: there exists a non-empty set $\{t_1, \ldots, t_n\}$ of division points (existential quantification over sets), φ holds at the interval $[\![\min(\mathbf{i}), t_1]\!]$, and for all t_i and t_j which are successive in the set $\{t_1, \ldots, t_n, \max(\mathbf{i})\}$, the formula φ holds at the interval $(\!(t_i, t_j]\!]$ (here we have first-order universal quantification). Dually, $\Diamond\varphi$ asserts at $\mathbf{i}$ that for any division of $\mathbf{i}$, at least one of its parts makes φ true.[4]

2.2 Examples of definable properties

If φ is a formula of $\mathbf{TD}[\pi]$, we write $\mathrm{Mod}(\varphi)$ for the set $\{\mathbf{i} \in \mathcal{K}_{\mathrm{fin}}(\pi) : \mathbf{i} \models \varphi\}$. A formula φ is said to *define* a class $\mathcal{K}$ of intervals, if $\mathcal{K} = \mathrm{Mod}(\varphi)$. By the above semantics, the empty interval Λ belongs to the set $\mathrm{Mod}(p)$ for every $p \in \pi$. Regarding the nullary connectives $\top$ and $\bot$, we may note the following:

$$\mathrm{Mod}(\top) = \mathcal{K}_{\mathrm{fin}}, \quad \mathrm{Mod}(\bot) = \{\Lambda\},$$
$$\mathrm{Mod}(\neg\bot) = \mathcal{K}_{\mathrm{fin}} \setminus \{\Lambda\}, \quad \mathrm{Mod}(\neg\top) = \varnothing.$$

In the present setting, then, due to the availability of the empty interval, $\bot$ cannot be defined as $\neg\top$, nor can $\top$ be defined as $\neg\bot$. In particular, $\neg\bot$ has existential force: it states that in the interval considered there is at least one time point. The formula $\top$, again, lacks existential force. It is also worth noting that $\bot$ is not equivalent to the formula $(p \wedge \neg p)$ for any $p \in \pi$. Namely, the formula $\neg p$ has existential force (it states that there is at least one point at which p fails), while $\bot$ does not have. On the other hand, $\top$ is indeed equivalent to $(p \vee \neg p)$, for any $p \in \pi$.

The operator $\Box$ has a limited capacity to speak of the size of the interval of evaluation: it is a necessary condition for the truth of the formula $\Box\varphi$ at $\mathbf{i}$ that $\mathbf{i}$ be of size at least 2. This is because divisions by definition have at least 2 parts. The following are examples of conditions on the size of the interval of evaluation that can be expressed.

---

[4]It might be possible to formulate the truth-conditions of **TD** formulas in the framework of neighborhood semantics. Our general viewpoint on modal semantics does not lead us in that direction, however. We see no problem in allowing the use of any abstract logic (not necessarily **FO**) for the specification of truth-conditions. Accordingly, the semantics of $\Box$ and $\Diamond$ is in effect in terms of **MSO**. For a general formulation of this perspective, see (Hella and Tulenheimo, 2012); for the special case in which **FO** suffices for phrasing the semantics, see e.g. (Gabbay et al., 1994).

Example 2.1. If $n \geq 1$, write $\square^n$ for the string consisting of n occurrences of $\square$; define $\lozenge^n$ similarly.

(*i*) $\mathrm{Mod}(\square^n \top) = \{\mathbf{i} \in \mathcal{K}_{\mathrm{fin}} : |\mathbf{i}| \geq 2^n\}$

(*ii*) $\mathrm{Mod}(\lozenge^n \bot) = \{\mathbf{i} \in \mathcal{K}_{\mathrm{fin}} : |\mathbf{i}| \leq 2^n - 1\}$

(*iii*) $\mathrm{Mod}(\neg\bot \wedge \lozenge\bot) = \{\mathbf{i} \in \mathcal{K}_{\mathrm{fin}} : |\mathbf{i}| = 1\}$.

In particular, then, the condition 'being of size 1' is definable in **TD**: the defining formula $(\neg\bot \wedge \lozenge\bot)$ simply says of its interval of evaluation that it is non-empty (the left conjunct) but is not of size at least 2 (the right conjunct). The formula $\lozenge\bot$ cannot be true at any interval of size at least two, since those intervals do have divisions into at least two non-empty parts, while no non-empty part can make $\bot$ true. Conversely, the formula $\lozenge\bot$ is clearly trivially true at any interval of size at most 1.

If p is atomic, then $\neg p$ holds at $\mathbf{i}$ iff there is at least one instant in $\mathbf{i}$ at which p does not hold. By the combined use of the two negations, using the formula $\neg \sim p$, it can be positively stated that at some instant of $\mathbf{i}$, the atom p holds. Moving to complex formulas, note that for example $\neg\lozenge q$ does not state that there is an instant at which $\lozenge q$ fails (there is, of course, no such instant); instead the formula states that the interval has a division such that q fails at all parts of the division. Observe also that a complex formula may hold at $\mathbf{i}$ without holding at all instants of this interval. Here is a strong counterexample: a formula which is true at a certain interval while *failing at all* of its instants. Let $\mathbf{i}_0$ be an interval consisting of just two instants, one making p true and q false, the other making q true and p false. Consider the formula $\varphi := \neg(p \vee q)$. Then clearly $\mathbf{i}_0 \models \varphi$, while $\mathbf{i}_0 \models \sim\varphi$. The latter condition prevails due to the fact that both instants in $\mathbf{i}_0$ indeed fail to satisfy φ, because both of them do satisfy $(p \vee q)$.

To illustrate why the distinction between the two negations is of interest in the setting of arbitrary intervals, and specifically why this distinction was useful when critically discussing von Wright's notion of real contradiction in (Tulenheimo, 2011), let us allow for the sake of example the use of intervals with an infinite domain; recall the notion of real contradiction from the beginning of Section 1. Von Wright correctly noted that an interval $\mathbf{i}$ manifests in his sense a real contradiction iff the formula $\square(p \vee \sim p)$ does *not* hold at $\mathbf{i}$,[5] for some atom p. (He

---

[5] Suppose $\mathbf{i}$ is an arbitrary interval and $t_1, \ldots, t_n$ are elements of $\mathbf{i}$ such that $t_1 < \ldots < t_n$ and t_n is not the last element (if any) of $\mathbf{i}$. Then the division *determined by* these points is

considered atoms as representing the sorts of states of the world that he was interested in.) However, operating with a single negation, he took this negative condition to be positively expressible by the formula $\sim\Box(p \lor \sim p)$, which he furthermore also took to be expressed by the formula $\Diamond(p \land \sim p)$. Thus, von Wright thought $\sim$ to be capable of representing the contradictory negation 'does not hold at an interval.' Yet he was also committed to $\sim p$ being true of an interval iff p fails throughout the interval. But if $\sim$ is the contradictory negation, $\sim p$ means something less: that somewhere within the interval p fails. If $\sim$ has the force 'does not hold at an interval,' it cannot also have the force 'fails throughout an interval.' In fact, the notion of real contradiction is correctly captured by making joint use of the two negations of **TD**: the relevant condition is expressed by the formula $\neg\Box(p \lor \sim p)$ or, equivalently, by $\Diamond(\neg p \land \neg \sim p)$.

Example 2.2. Let T be the set of all integers. Write $<$ for their usual order (order by magnitude). Define an order $\prec$ on T as follows: $z \prec z'$ iff $(0 \leq z < z')$ or $(z < z' \leq -1)$ or $(z \geq 0$ and $z' \leq -1)$. The order type of the order $(T, \prec)$ is, then, $\omega + \omega^*$. The minimum of T w.r.t. $\prec$ is 0 and its maximum is -1. Let V be a valuation satisfying $p \in V(z)$ iff the absolute value of z is even. Then the interval $\mathbf{i} = (T, \prec, V)$ exemplifies a real contradiction. Namely, let the points $t_1, \ldots, t_n$ with $0 \leq t_1 \prec \ldots \prec t_n \prec -1$ be arbitrary, and consider the division $\mathcal{D}$ determined by these points. Let s be the greatest non-negative integer in the set $\{0, t_1, \ldots, t_n, -1\}$ w.r.t. the order $\prec$, and let s' be the smallest negative integer of this set w.r.t. the same order. Thus, one of the parts of $\mathcal{D}$ is the interval $(\!(s, s']\!]$. Now, there are infinitely many integers z with $s \prec z \prec s'$. Among them there are points making p true and points making p false. Therefore the interval $(\!(s, s']\!]$ satisfies neither p nor $\sim p$. As the division $\mathcal{D}$ was assumed to be arbitrary, it follows that $\mathbf{i} \not\models \Box(p \lor \sim p)$.

It is not difficult to see that when attention is restricted to *finite* intervals of size at least 2, real contradictions may not occur. At any interval of size at most 1, all formulas of the form $\Box\varphi$ fail. Under the above definition they exemplify, then, a real contradiction, but they do not do so because of the way in which their constituent states are distributed over the interval (which is where the interest lies in connection with real contradictions), but because they are 'too small.'

---

the tuple whose members are the subintervals of $\mathbf{i}$ determined by the sets $\{x : x \in \mathbf{i}$ and $x \leq t_1\}, (t_1, t_2], \ldots, (t_{n-1}, t_n], \{x : x \in \mathbf{i}$ and $x > t_n\}$, in this order. The general condition for the truth of $\Box\varphi$ at $\mathbf{i}$ is simply this: there is a finite set of division points in $\mathbf{i}$ such that every part of the division determined by these points makes φ true.

Fact 2.1. If **i** is a finite interval with $|\mathbf{i}| \geq 2$ and p is an atom, then $\mathbf{i} \models \Box(p \vee \sim p)$.

Proof. Let **i** be a finite interval of size at least 2. If its domain is $\{t_1, \ldots, t_n\}$ with $t_1 < \ldots < t_n$, consider its division by the points $t_1, \ldots, t_{n-1}$. The parts of the division are the singleton intervals $[\![t_j]\!]$ with $1 \leq j \leq n$. Since every point t_j either satisfies p or does not satisfy it, it follows that this division witnesses the claim $\mathbf{i} \models \Box(p \vee \sim p)$. ∎

We may note that in the general formulation of **TD**, infinity and finiteness are definable properties of intervals.

Example 2.3. We have that $\mathbf{i} \models (\Box\top \wedge \Diamond\Box\top)$ iff **i** is infinite. The left conjunct states that the interval of evaluation can be divided (is at least of size 2) and the right conjunct adds that an arbitrary division of the interval has at least one part which can be further divided. Together these conditions evidently exclude all finite intervals. Conversely, the formula is plainly true at every infinite interval. It follows, then, that $\mathbf{i} \models (\Diamond\bot \vee \Box\Diamond\bot)$ iff **i** is finite. (Note that while $\bot$ is not equivalent to $\neg\top$, still $\Diamond\bot$ is equivalent to $\Diamond\neg\top$.) Thus, relative to the class $\mathcal{K}_{\text{fin}}$, $(\Diamond\bot \vee \Box\Diamond\bot)$ is valid and $(\Box\top \wedge \Diamond\Box\top)$ is contradictory.

2.3 Dropping superfluous operators

Often in logics certain syntactically given operators may be defined in terms of other syntactically given operators. It is clear that if we are exclusively interested in the expressive power of the logic **TD**, not all of its operators are needed. Obviously $\wedge$ may be (contextually) defined in terms of $\vee$ and $\neg$, and $\Diamond$ may be (contextually) defined using $\Box$ and $\neg$: for any formulas φ and ψ, we have that $(\varphi \wedge \psi)$ is equivalent to $(\neg\varphi \vee \neg\psi)$, while $\Diamond\varphi$ is equivalent to $\neg\Box\neg\varphi$. Further, $\top$ may be defined in terms of $\bot$, $\vee$ and $\neg$: indeed $\top$ is equivalent to $(\bot \vee \neg\bot)$. From now on we will freely use the operators $\wedge$, $\Diamond$ and $\top$ — construing the expressions in which they appear as abbreviations of expressions in which they do not appear. More interestingly, since we are considering *finite* intervals, even the universal negation $\sim$ becomes superfluous: it is definable from $\Box$, $\neg$ and $\bot$. In fact, over the class $\mathcal{K}_{\text{fin}}$ any formula $\sim\varphi$ is equivalent to the formula

$$(\bot \vee \psi_\varphi \vee \Box\psi_\varphi),$$

where $\psi_\varphi := ((\neg\bot \wedge \Diamond\bot) \wedge \neg\varphi)$. To see this, recall from Example 2.1 that the subformula $(\neg\bot \wedge \Diamond\bot)$ is true at all and only intervals of size

1. Therefore, $\Box\psi_\varphi$ states that the interval of evaluation is of size at least 2 and has a division all of whose parts are singletons, each singleton making φ false. The remaining two disjuncts of $(\bot \lor \psi_\varphi \lor \Box\psi_\varphi)$ cover the case that the interval is empty (in which case $\sim\varphi$ is trivially true), and the case that the interval itself is a singleton and makes φ false.

From now on, in this paper we will take the 'official syntax' of **TD**$[\pi]$ to be the one specified by the grammar $\varphi ::= p \mid \bot \mid \neg\varphi \mid (\varphi \lor \varphi) \mid \Box\varphi$, with $p \in \pi$.

3   Characterization of the expressive power of TD

We will next present a characterization of the expressive power of **TD** on certain intervals (to be termed 'word intervals') using an independent tool from formal language theory, namely regular-like expressions.

3.1   Regular-like expressions

Let us define some basic notions. An *alphabet* is a finite (possibly empty) set $\Sigma = \{s_1, \ldots, s_k\}$. Any finite string $w = a_1 \ldots a_n$ of symbols a_i from Σ is a *word* over Σ. The empty string (corresponding to the case that $n = 0$) is denoted by λ. We write Σ^* for the set of all words over the alphabet Σ, and we write $\Sigma^+ = \Sigma^* \setminus \{\lambda\}$ for the set of all non-empty words over Σ. A *(formal) language* over Σ is any subset of Σ^*, i.e., any set of words over Σ. If $w = a_1 \ldots a_n$ and $w' = b_1 \ldots b_m$, their *catenation* ww' is the word $ww' = c_1 \ldots c_{n+m}$, where $c_i = a_i$ ($1 \le i \le n$) and $c_{n+j} = b_j$ ($1 \le j \le m$). We note that $\lambda w = w = w\lambda$ for all $w \in \Sigma^*$. We say that v is a *subword* of w if there are $u_1, u_2 \in \Sigma^*$ such that $w = u_1 v u_2$. A *factorization* of a word w is any tuple $\langle w_1, \ldots, w_n \rangle$ of words such that $w = w_1 \ldots w_n$; a *division* of a word is its factorization into at least two factors all of which are non-empty. The *length* of a word w, in symbols $|w|$, is the number of symbols in w, when each symbol is counted as many times as it occurs. Given an alphabet Σ, the relative *complement* L^c of L is the set $\{w \in \Sigma^* : w \notin L\}$. The *catenation* of languages L_1 and L_2 is the set $L_1 \cdot L_2 := \{ww' : w \in L_1 \text{ and } w' \in L_2\}$, the *catenation closure* of the language L is the set $L^* := \{w_1 \ldots w_n : w_i \in L \text{ and } n \ge 0\}$, while the *positive catenation closure* of L is the set $L^+ := \{w_1 \ldots w_n : w_i \in L \text{ and } n \ge 1\}$. Note that $\lambda \in L^+$ iff $\lambda \in L$. Finally, we define a unary operation $^\circ$ on languages by setting $L^\circ = \{w_1 \ldots w_n : w_i \in L \text{ and } w_i \ne \lambda \text{ and } n \ge 2\}$. In the absence of better terminology, we refer to L° as the *2-positive catenation closure* of L; every element of L° has a division whose all parts belong to L. Note that while $L^* \setminus (\{\lambda\} \cup L)$ is included in L°, the converse need not hold: a word in L° may belong to L as well. For instance if $L = \{a, b, ab\}$, then $ab \in (L^\circ \cap L)$.

Let an alphabet Σ be fixed, and let $\emptyset$ and $\mathbf{1}$ be symbols not in Σ. For the purposes of the present paper, the set $\mathsf{RLE}(\Sigma)$ of *regular-like expressions* over Σ is the smallest set containing all symbols from the set $\Sigma \cup \{\emptyset, \mathbf{1}\}$ and closed under the following rules:[6]

- If r and s are in $\mathsf{RLE}(\Sigma)$, then so are $(r \cup s)$ and $(r \cap s)$ and $(r \cdot s)$.

- If r is in $\mathsf{RLE}(\Sigma)$, then so are r^c and r^* and r°.

The *denotations* $[r]$ of regular-like expressions r are defined recursively as follows:

- $[\emptyset] = \varnothing$ and $[\mathbf{1}] = \{\lambda\}$.

- $[a] = \{a\}$ for all $a \in \Sigma$.

- $[r \cup s] = [r] \cup [s]$ and $[r \cap s] = [r] \cap [s]$ and $[r \cdot s] = [r] \cdot [s]$.

- $[r^c] = [r]^c$ and $[r^*] = [r]^*$ and $[r^\circ] = [r]^\circ$.

If r is a regular expression over Σ, the elements of the set $[r]$ are words over Σ; hence the denotations are languages over Σ. We refer to $\emptyset, \mathbf{1},{}^c,{}^*,$ $^\circ, \cup, \cap$ and $\cdot$ as *regular-like operators* and to the correlated operations on languages as *regular-like operations*. The operators $\emptyset$ and $\mathbf{1}$ are nullary. We note that $\emptyset$ behaves, so to say, as a zero element w.r.t. catenation, while $\mathbf{1}$ can be said to behave as a unit element: $[\emptyset \cdot r] = [\emptyset] \cdot [r] = [\emptyset] = [r] \cdot [\emptyset] = [r \cdot \emptyset]$ and $[\mathbf{1} \cdot r] = [\mathbf{1}] \cdot [r] = [r] = [r] \cdot [\mathbf{1}] = [r \cdot \mathbf{1}]$.

If $\mathcal{F}$ is any subset of $\{\emptyset, \mathbf{1}, \cup, \cap, \cdot,{}^c,{}^*,{}^\circ\}$ and Σ is an alphabet, we write $\mathsf{RLE}(\Sigma, \mathcal{F})$ for the smallest set of regular-like expressions generated from the alphabet Σ by closing it under the operators from $\mathcal{F}$. That is, $\mathsf{RLE}(\Sigma, \mathcal{F})$ consists of those regular-like expressions over the alphabet Σ in which no symbols from the set $\{\emptyset, \mathbf{1}, \cup, \cap, \cdot,{}^c,{}^*,{}^\circ\} \setminus \mathcal{F}$ occur. By definition, the set $\mathsf{RE}(\Sigma)$ of *regular expressions* over Σ is the set $\mathsf{RLE}(\Sigma, \{\emptyset, \cup, \cdot,{}^*\})$. A language $L \subseteq \Sigma^*$ is *regular*, if there is $r \in \mathsf{RE}(\Sigma)$ such that $L = [r]$.

As a matter of fact, $\mathsf{RLE}(\Sigma, \{\emptyset, \mathbf{1}, \cup, \cap, \cdot,{}^c,{}^*,{}^\circ\}) = \mathsf{RE}(\Sigma)$, that is, the set of all regular expressions over Σ is closed under the operations

---

[6]Nothing would prevent us from considering further operations on languages and letting them define further regular-like expressions; if this was done, the above definition of $\mathsf{RLE}(\Sigma)$ would of course be different.

1, ∩, ᶜ and °: for every regular-like expression r over Σ there is an expression $r' \in \mathsf{RE}(\Sigma)$ such that $[r] = [r']$. It is well known — though not absolutely immediate — that the set $\mathsf{RE}(\Sigma)$ is closed under relative complement. This is easiest proven by making use of the connection of regular expressions to finite automata; cf., e.g., (Salomaa, 1981, Thm. 2.7). Intersection is, then, obviously definable from ᶜ and ∪. Further, $[\mathbf{1}] = [\emptyset^*]$. Finally, let $r^+ := (\mathbf{1}^{\mathsf{c}} \cap r^*)$. Thus, $[r^+] = \Sigma^+ \cap [r^*] = [r]^+$. We observe that $[r°] = [r]° = [r^+] \cdot [r^+] = [r^+ \cdot r^+]$. Although the operators **1, ∩, ᶜ** and ° need not be separately given when considering regular expressions, there are sets $\mathcal{F}$ of regular-like operators for which the fragment $\mathsf{RLE}(\Sigma, \mathcal{F})$ is not closed under the operations expressed by some or all of the remaining regular-like operators. In what follows, we encounter some such sets.

3.2 Characterizing TD with regular-like operators

Let us agree on some definitions which enable us to make precise the connection between words and certain sorts of intervals; this connection is needed in order to formulate a characterization of **TD** in terms of certain regular-like expressions.

Given an alphabet Σ, we write π_Σ for the set $\{p_a : a \in \Sigma\}$ of propositional atoms. By definition a *word interval* (relative to Σ) is an interval $\mathbf{i} = (T, <, V)$ of finite size satisfying the following three conditions: (i) $\mathbf{i}$ belongs to the class $\mathcal{K}_{\mathrm{fin}}(\pi_\Sigma)$; (ii) for every $t \in T$ there is $a \in \Sigma$ such that $p_a \in V(t)$; and (iii) for any distinct a and b in Σ, there is no $t \in T$ such that $\{p_a, p_b\} \subseteq V(t)$. There is a straightforward correspondence between words and word intervals. On the one hand, every word interval $(T, <, V)$ induces a word $w = a_1 \ldots a_n$ such that $n = |T|$, and if t_i denotes the i-th element of T w.r.t. the order $<$, then a_i is the unique $a \in \Sigma$ such that $p_a \in V(t_i)$. The word w may be termed the *word induced by* $\mathbf{i}$ and denoted by $w_{\mathbf{i}}$. Conversely, for every word $w = a_1 \ldots a_n$ over Σ, there is a unique associated word interval $(T, <, V)$ such that $T = \{1, \ldots, n\}$, $<$ is the relation 'strictly smaller than' among the elements of T, and for every $1 \le i \le n$, we have $p_a \in V(t_i)$ iff $a = a_i$. The word interval $(T, <, V)$ is called the *word interval induced by* the word w and denoted $\mathbf{i}_w$. We will denote by $\mathcal{K}_{\mathrm{word}}$ the class $\{\mathbf{i} :$ there is an alphabet Σ and a word $w \in \Sigma^*$ such that $\mathbf{i}$ is isomorphic to $\mathbf{i}_w\}$ consisting of intervals isomorphic to intervals induced by words. Evidently $\mathcal{K}_{\mathrm{word}}$ is a proper subset of $\mathcal{K}_{\mathrm{fin}}$. We write $\mathcal{K}_{\mathrm{word}}(\pi)$ for the class $\mathcal{K}_{\mathrm{word}} \cap \mathcal{K}_{\mathrm{fin}}(\pi)$. In what follows, for simplicity we allow writing $w \models \varphi$ when what we mean is $\mathbf{i}_w \models \varphi$.

No confusion should be possible, given the immediate correspondence between a word w and its induced word interval $\mathbf{i}_w$.

We will apply the following notion of translation to compare a logic defined on (structures encoding) words and a fragment of the set of all regular-like expressions.

Definition 3.1 (Translation, characterization). Let $\mathcal{L}$ be a logic evaluated on (structures encoding) words. Given an alphabet Σ and a set $\mathcal{F}$ of regular-like operators, let $\mathsf{R} = \mathsf{RLE}(\Sigma, \mathcal{F})$. **(a)** We say that $\mathcal{L}$ is *translatable* into R, in symbols $\mathcal{L} \leq \mathsf{R}$, if there is a (possibly non-computable) function $f : \mathcal{L} \to \mathsf{R}$ such that for all formulas $\varphi \in \mathbf{TD}$ and words $w \in \Sigma^*$, we have: $w \models \varphi$ iff $w \in [f(\varphi)]$. **(b)** Conversely, we say that R is *translatable* into $\mathcal{L}$, symbolically $\mathsf{R} \leq \mathcal{L}$, if there is a (possibly non-computable) function $g : \mathsf{R} \to \mathcal{L}$ such that for all regular-like expressions $r \in \mathsf{R}$ and words $w \in \Sigma^*$, we have: $w \in [r]$ iff $w \models g(r)$. **(c)** If $\mathcal{L} \leq \mathsf{R}$ and $\mathsf{R} \leq \mathcal{L}$, we write $\mathcal{L} = \mathsf{R}$ and say that R *characterizes* $\mathcal{L}$ on the class of all (structures encoding) words.

We note that if $\mathsf{R} \leq \mathcal{L}$, then every subset of Σ^* denoted by an expression $r \in \mathsf{R}$ is definable by a formula φ of $\mathcal{L}$ in the sense that $[r] = \mathrm{Mod}(\varphi) \cap \mathcal{K}_{\mathrm{word}}(\pi_\Sigma)$. And if $\mathcal{L} \leq \mathsf{R}$, then every subset of Σ^* defined by some formula of $\mathcal{L}$ relative to the class $\mathcal{K}_{\mathrm{word}}$ is denoted by some expression of R.

We will now show that over word intervals, the logic $\mathbf{TD}$ is characterized by the set $\mathsf{RLE}(\Sigma, \{\mathbf{1}, \cup, ^\circ, ^c\})$. For simplicity, we will refer to this set of regular-like expressions as $\mathsf{R}_0(\Sigma)$. Note that the operation * is definable in $\mathsf{R}_0(\Sigma)$: for any expression $r \in \mathsf{R}_0(\Sigma)$, we have $[r^*] = [\mathbf{1} \cup r \cup r^\circ]$.

Theorem 3.1. *Let Σ be an alphabet. Then $\mathbf{TD}[\pi_\Sigma] = \mathsf{R}_0(\Sigma)$.*

Proof. We will first prove that $\mathsf{R}_0(\Sigma) \leq \mathbf{TD}[\pi_\Sigma]$. Define a map $T : \mathsf{R}_0(\Sigma) \to \mathbf{TD}[\pi_\Sigma]$ as follows: $T(\mathbf{1}) = \bot$, $T(a) = ((\neg\bot \wedge \Diamond\bot) \wedge p_a)$, $T(r^c) = \neg T(r)$, $T(r \cup s) = (T(r) \vee T(s))$, $T(r^\circ) = \Box T(r)$. We proceed to show that for all words $w \in \Sigma^*$ and all $r \in \mathsf{R}_0(\Sigma)$, we have $w \in [r]$ iff $w \models T(r)$. Now, $w \in [\mathbf{1}]$ iff $w = \lambda$ iff $w \models \bot$. Further, $w \in [a]$ iff $w = a$ iff (w is of size 1 and $w \models p_a$) iff $w \models ((\neg\bot \wedge \Diamond\bot) \wedge p_a)$. Assume, then, inductively that if $u \in \{r, s\}$ is an expression in $\mathsf{R}_0(\Sigma)$, then for all words $w \in \Sigma^*$ we have: $w \in [u]$ iff $w \models T(u)$. Clearly the claim holds for the expressions r^c and $(r \cup s)$. Let us still consider the expression r°. Suppose $w \in [r^\circ]$. Then for some $n \geq 2$ there are words $w_i \neq \lambda$ such that $w_i \in [r]$ (with $1 \leq i \leq n$) and $w = w_1 \ldots w_n$. By the inductive hypothesis, then, $w_i \models T(r)$ for every i. Since $n \geq 2$, it follows that $w \models \Box T(r)$, where $\Box T(r) = T(r^\circ)$. The converse direction is proven similarly.

It remains to show that conversely, $\mathbf{TD}[\pi_\Sigma] \leq \mathsf{R}_0(\Sigma)$. Let a map $S : \mathbf{TD}[\pi_\Sigma] \to \mathsf{R}_0(\Sigma)$ be defined in the following way: $S(\bot) = \mathbf{1}$, $S(p_a) = (\mathbf{1} \cup a \cup a^\circ)$, $S(\neg\varphi) = S(\varphi)^\mathbf{c}$, $S(\varphi \vee \psi) = (S(\varphi) \cup S(\psi))$, $S(\Box\varphi) = S(\varphi)^\circ$. We claim that for all words $w \in \Sigma^*$ and all formulas φ of $\mathbf{TD}[\pi_\Sigma]$, we have $w \models \varphi$ iff $w \in [S(\varphi)]$. Note that $w \models p_a$ iff $p_a \in V(t)$ for all $t \in \mathbf{i}_w$ iff for some $n \geq 0$, we have that $w = a_1 \ldots a_n$, where $a_i = a$ for all $1 \leq i \leq n$ iff $w \in [a^*]$, where $[a^*] = [\mathbf{1} \cup a \cup a^\circ]$. It is obvious that the claim holds for $\bot$, as well as for negations, disjunctions, and formulas of the form $\Box\varphi$. ∎

By Theorem 3.1, instead of asking whether a formula $\varphi \in \mathbf{TD}[\pi_\Sigma]$ is true at an interval $\mathbf{i} \in \mathcal{K}_{\mathrm{word}}(\pi_\Sigma)$, we may equivalently ask whether the word $w_\mathbf{i} \in \Sigma^*$ induced by the word interval $\mathbf{i}$ is an element of the language $[S(\varphi)]$, where S is the map defined in the above proof. The size of the expression $S(\varphi)$ is linearly bounded by the size of the input formula φ (i.e., by the number of occurrences of symbols it contains). Therefore, the model-checking problem of $\mathbf{TD}$ over word intervals can be reduced in linear time to the membership problem for R_0. Since $[r^\circ] = [(\mathbf{1}^\mathbf{c} \cap r^*) \cdot (\mathbf{1}^\mathbf{c} \cap r^*)]$, it is possible to translate $\mathsf{R}_0(\Sigma) = \mathsf{RLE}(\Sigma, \{\mathbf{1}, \cup, {}^\circ, {}^\mathbf{c}\})$ into $\mathsf{RLE}(\Sigma, \{\mathbf{1}, \cup, \cdot, {}^\mathbf{c}, {}^*\})$ in exponential time. As the membership problem for $\mathsf{RLE}(\Sigma, \{\mathbf{1}, \cup, \cdot, {}^\mathbf{c}, {}^*\})$ is contained in PTIME (Stockmeyer and Meyer, 1973), we may conclude that the model-checking problem for $\mathbf{TD}$ over word intervals is solvable in EXPTIME.

Observe that we have not characterized the expressive power of $\mathbf{TD}$ on the full class $\mathcal{K}_{\mathrm{fin}}$, only on its subclass consisting of word intervals. We will later see how our result can be utilized to prove general facts about the expressivity of $\mathbf{TD}$ on all intervals (Theorem 5.1). Further, the proof of Fact 6.2 will tell us that actually word intervals are in a precise sense representative of arbitrary intervals in connection with the logic $\mathbf{TD}$.

4 Properties of TD

To illustrate features of $\mathbf{TD}$, let us turn attention to two closure properties of definable classes of intervals: closure under 'multiplication' and closure under 'mirror images.' The logic $\mathbf{TD}$ lacks the former property but enjoys the latter.

4.1   Contradictory negation is not superfluous

It was seen above that the universal negation $\sim$ is superfluous as an operator of the logic **TD** when attention is restricted to the class $\mathcal{K}_{\text{fin}}$. We will now show that the contradictory negation $\neg$ is *not* superfluous: it cannot be defined from the other operators of this logic.[7] This fact can be proven in a variety of ways. One way would be to work at the level of regular-like languages and show that $\mathsf{RLE}(\Sigma, \{\mathbf{1}, \vee, ^\circ, ^{\mathsf{c}}\}) \neq \mathsf{RLE}(\Sigma, \{\mathbf{1}, \vee, ^\circ\})$. Then, making use of (the proof of) Theorem 3.1 which states that $\mathbf{TD}[\pi_\Sigma] = \mathsf{RLE}(\Sigma, \{\mathbf{1}, \vee, ^\circ, ^{\mathsf{c}}\})$, it could be shown that if negation was definable from the other connectives of **TD**, then also complementation could be defined using the operators $\mathbf{1}$, $\vee$ and $^\circ$, which precisely is not possible. However, we will present a model-theoretic proof for the indispensability of negation.

Let us define the notion of multiplication of an interval. First, consider intervals $\mathbf{i}_1 = (T_1, <_1, V_1)$ and $\mathbf{i}_2 = (T_2, <_2, V_2)$, supposing their domains are disjoint. Their *ordered sum* is by definition the interval $\mathbf{i}_1 \oplus \mathbf{i}_2 = (T, <, V)$, where $T := T_1 \cup T_2$, $< := <_1 \cup <_2 \cup (T_1 \times T_2)$ and $V := V_1 \cup V_2$. If the intersection of the domains T_1 and T_2 is non-empty, some standard operation is used to produce isomorphic copies $\mathbf{i}_1'$ of $\mathbf{i}_1$ and $\mathbf{i}_2'$ of $\mathbf{i}_2$ with disjoint domains, and we define $\mathbf{i}_1 \oplus \mathbf{i}_2 := \mathbf{i}_1' \oplus \mathbf{i}_2'$. Recall from Note 1.1 that in the present paper we consider intervals in the 'internal sense.' The structure $\mathbf{i}_1 \oplus \mathbf{i}_2$ as defined above is indeed an interval according to the definition provided at the beginning of Subsection 1.1. Thus, if for instance $[\![0, 1]\!]$ and $[\![2, 3]\!]$ are subintervals of an interval whose domain is the set of rational numbers and whose order is the order of rationals by magnitude, indeed $[\![0, 1]\!] \oplus [\![2, 3]\!]$ is an interval in the sense of the present paper, although it is not an interval in the external sense, since its domain $[0, 1] \cup [2, 3]$ of course is not inwards-closed.

If $\mathbf{i}$ is an interval, we define recursively the multiplication of an interval by a positive integer as follows: $1 \otimes \mathbf{i} := \mathbf{i}$ and $(n + 1) \otimes \mathbf{i} := (n \otimes \mathbf{i}) \oplus \mathbf{i}$. We observe that $n \otimes \mathbf{i}$ is an interval which results from having 'concatenated' the interval $\mathbf{i}$ with itself n times: $\mathbf{i} \oplus \ldots \oplus \mathbf{i}$ (n times). Note that $n \otimes \Lambda = \Lambda$ for all n. The intervals $n \otimes \mathbf{i}$ are called *multiples* of the interval $\mathbf{i}$ and the operation of producing these intervals *multiplication*. Now, write $\mathbf{TD}(\bot, \vee, \square)$ for the fragment of **TD** generated without negation. We show that any class defined by a formula of $\mathbf{TD}(\bot, \vee, \square)$ is actually

---

[7]The question of being superfluous is of course not absolute: here our considerations are relative to the operators $\bot, \neg, \vee, \square$ taken as primitive.

closed under arbitrary multiplications. Then we point out that not all classes definable in **TD** are closed in this way.

Lemma 4.1. *Let* φ *be a formula of* $\mathbf{TDN}(\bot, \vee, \square)$. *If* $\mathbf{i} \in \mathrm{Mod}(\varphi)$, *then* $(n \otimes \mathbf{i}) \in \mathrm{Mod}(\varphi)$ *for all* $n \geq 1$.

Proof. The claim holds evidently for $\bot$ and for atomic formulas $p \in \pi$. Assume, then, inductively that for all $\chi \in \{\varphi, \psi\}$ and all intervals $\mathbf{j}$ we have: if $\mathbf{j} \models \varphi$, then $(k \otimes \mathbf{j}) \models \varphi$ for all positive integers k. The claim holds for the formula $(\varphi \vee \psi)$. For, suppose $\mathbf{i} \models (\varphi \vee \psi)$. So $\mathbf{i} \models \varphi$ or $\mathbf{i} \models \psi$. By the inductive hypothesis, $(n \otimes \mathbf{i}) \models \varphi$ for all $n \geq 1$, or $(n \otimes \mathbf{i}) \models \psi$ for all $n \geq 1$. Thus, $(n \otimes \mathbf{i}) \models (\varphi \vee \psi)$ for all $n \geq 1$. Suppose, then, that $\mathbf{i} \models \square\varphi$, whence there is a division $\mathcal{D} = \langle \mathbf{j}^1, \ldots, \mathbf{j}^r \rangle$ with $r \geq 2$ such that $\mathbf{j}^m \models \varphi$ for all m. Let $n \geq 1$ be arbitrary and consider the interval $(n \otimes \mathbf{i})$. This interval has by construction a partition into n subintervals $\mathbf{i}_1, \ldots, \mathbf{i}_n$ each of which is isomorphic to the interval $\mathbf{i}$. Therefore the division $\mathcal{D}$ of $\mathbf{i}$ induces on each of these subintervals $\mathbf{i}_j$ a division $\langle \mathbf{i}_j^1, \ldots, \mathbf{i}_j^r \rangle$ such that every $\mathbf{i}_j^m$ is isomorphic to $\mathbf{i}^m$. Since φ holds at every $\mathbf{i}^m$, this formula also holds at every $\mathbf{i}_j^m$. But then $\langle \mathbf{i}_1^1, \ldots, \mathbf{i}_1^r, \ldots, \mathbf{i}_n^1, \ldots, \mathbf{i}_n^r \rangle$ is a division of the interval $(n \otimes \mathbf{i})$ each of whose parts makes φ true. This means, again, that $(n \otimes \mathbf{i}) \models \square\varphi$. (Note that the inductive hypothesis is not needed in the case of formulas of the form $\square\varphi$.) ∎

Theorem 4.1. $\mathbf{TD}(\bot, \vee, \square) <_{\mathcal{K}_{\mathrm{fin}}} \mathbf{TD}$.

Proof. Trivially $\mathbf{TD}(\bot, \vee, \square) \leq_{\mathcal{K}_{\mathrm{fin}}} \mathbf{TD}$. To see that the translatability does not hold in the converse direction, observe that using negation, the class of all intervals of size exactly 1 can be defined in **TD**: $\mathrm{Mod}(\neg\bot \wedge \Diamond\bot) = \{\mathbf{i} \in \mathcal{K}_{\mathrm{fin}} : |\mathbf{i}| = 1\}$. Obviously this class is not closed under multiplication. By Lemma 4.1, then, this class cannot be defined in $\mathbf{TD}(\bot, \vee, \square)$. So **TD** cannot be translated into $\mathbf{TD}(\bot, \vee, \square)$. ∎

While the result of Theorem 4.1 might appear obvious, in some logics negation is actually not needed as a syntactically given connective, but can be expressed in terms of other operators. An example is furnished by the interval-based modal logic **MLR** (modal logic of regular expressions) studied in (Hella and Tulenheimo, 2012).[8]

---

[8]The logic **MLR** is defined so that it has an even more straightforward connection to regular expressions than the logic **TDN** to be discussed in Section 6 of the present paper. Over finite intervals, **MLR** has the same expressive power as **TDN**. Yet it turns out that in **TDN** negation is not superfluous. This difference stems from the different ways in which the two logics interpret atomic formulas.

4.2   Mirror images

We just saw that while the $\mathbf{TD}(\bot, \vee, \Box)$ definable classes of intervals are closed under multiplication, this is not so for all $\mathbf{TD}$ definable classes. We will now discern a closure property that $\mathbf{TD}$ has; it will be useful later in connection with certain expressivity considerations. If $w = a_1 \ldots a_n$ is a word over an alphabet Σ, also the string $a_n \ldots a_1$ is a word over Σ, known as the *mirror image* of w and denoted $\mathrm{mi}(w)$. The empty word is its own mirror image.[9] More generally, if $\mathbf{i} = (T, <, V)$ is any interval, we define its mirror image $\mathrm{mi}(\mathbf{i})$ to be the interval $(T, <^{-1}, V)$, where $<^{-1}$ is the converse of the relation $<$. Note that $\mathrm{mi}(\mathrm{mi}(\mathbf{i})) = \mathbf{i}$ for all $\mathbf{i}$. Let us show that if a class $\mathcal{K}$ is defined by a $\mathbf{TD}$ formula, then it is closed under taking mirror images.

Lemma 4.2. *Let $\varphi \in \mathbf{TD}$ and $\mathbf{i} \in \mathcal{K}_{\mathrm{fin}}$ be arbitrary. If $\mathbf{i} \in \mathrm{Mod}(\varphi)$, then $\mathrm{mi}(\mathbf{i}) \in \mathrm{Mod}(\varphi)$.*

Proof. We prove by induction on the formula φ of $\mathbf{TD}[\pi]$ the following more general claim: $\mathbf{i} \in \mathrm{Mod}(\varphi)$ iff $\mathrm{mi}(\mathbf{i}) \in \mathrm{Mod}(\varphi)$, for all intervals $\mathbf{i}$. (The more specific claim appearing in the statement of the lemma could not be proven by induction on φ for negated formulas.) The base case of formulas $\varphi \in \{\bot\} \cup \pi$ holds trivially. Suppose, then, inductively that for all $\chi \in \{\varphi, \psi\}$ and for all intervals $\mathbf{j}$, we have: $\mathbf{j} \models \chi$ iff $\mathrm{mi}(\mathbf{j}) \models \chi$. It is immediate that the claim holds for formulas $\neg\varphi$ and $(\varphi \vee \psi)$. In particular, $\mathbf{i} \models \neg\varphi$ iff $\mathbf{i} \not\models \varphi$ iff (ind. hyp.) $\mathrm{mi}(\mathbf{i}) \not\models \varphi$ iff $\mathrm{mi}(\mathbf{i}) \models \neg\varphi$. Let us, then, consider the formula $\Box\varphi$. Suppose first that $\mathbf{i} \models \Box\varphi$. So there is a division $\langle \mathbf{j}_1, \ldots, \mathbf{j}_n \rangle$ of $\mathbf{i}$ with $n \geq 2$ such that every part $\mathbf{j}_i$ of the division satisfies: $\mathbf{j}_i \models \varphi$. By the inductive hypothesis, we have for every i that $\mathrm{mi}(\mathbf{j}_i) \models \varphi$. But then $\langle \mathrm{mi}(\mathbf{j}_n), \ldots, \mathrm{mi}(\mathbf{j}_1) \rangle$ is a division of the interval $\mathrm{mi}(\mathbf{i})$ whose every part satisfies the formula φ. Therefore, we have $\mathrm{mi}(\mathbf{i}) \models \Box\varphi$. The direction from $\mathrm{mi}(\mathbf{i}) \models \Box\varphi$ to $\mathbf{i} \models \Box\varphi$ can be proven similarly.   ∎

Lemma 4.2 marks an obvious limitation of $\mathbf{TD}$ as a temporal logic: it is characteristic of time that it has a 'direction', but by the lemma, the logic $\mathbf{TD}$ does not capture this feature of time. Whenever a statement made using $\mathbf{TD}$ is true of an interval, it is also true of its mirror image. However, this does not diminish the interest of $\mathbf{TD}$, since it is not even meant to be first and foremost a temporal logic, but a logic applicable when reasoning about durations and their divisions. And neither the

---

[9]So is any *palindrome*, i.e., any word w satisfying $a_1 \ldots a_n = w = a_n \ldots a_1$.

notion of duration nor the notion of divisibility appears conceptually dependent on the direction of time. In Section 6 we will formulate an extension of **TD** in which direction of time can indeed be discussed.

5   Comparing TD with first-order logic

Next we wish to settle the question of how **TD** is related to first-order logic. Many instant-based modal logics are semantically fragments of **FO**. Relative to arbitrary modal structures, for example basic modal logic equals the bisimulation invariant fragment of **FO**. And relative to Dedekind-complete linear orders, the logic of *Until* and *Since* simply coincides with first-order logic.[10] In these cases the first-order translation of a modal formula φ is an **FO** formula $\psi_\varphi(x)$ of one free variable, x, such that $\psi_\varphi(x)$ uses in its vocabulary one binary predicate symbol, interpreted as the modal accessibility relation, and unary predicate symbols corresponding to the propositional atoms appearing in the modal formula. The question of translatability that interests us in the present paper in connection with our interval-based logic **TD** (and its extensions) is formulated in terms of **FO** *sentences* (instead of formulas with free variables), as follows.[11]

An interval $\mathbf{i} = (T, <, V)$ with V of type $T \to \mathcal{P}(\{p_1, \ldots, p_n\})$ induces in a straightforward manner a first-order structure, namely the structure $\mathcal{M}_\mathbf{i} = (T, <^{\mathcal{M}_\mathbf{i}}, P_1^{\mathcal{M}_\mathbf{i}}, \ldots, P_n^{\mathcal{M}_\mathbf{i}})$ of vocabulary $\{<, P_1, \ldots, P_n\}$ such that $<^{\mathcal{M}_\mathbf{i}} :=\; <$ and $P_i^{\mathcal{M}_\mathbf{i}} := \{t : p_i \in V(t)\}$. Note that if $\mathbf{i}$ is empty, the induced first-order structure is the $(n + 2)$-tuple each member of which is the empty set. From now on, when considering abstract logics $\mathcal{L}$ (such as **FO** or **MSO**), we will write $\mathbf{i} \models \psi$ to indicate that the sentence ψ of $\mathcal{L}$ is true in the model $\mathcal{M}_\mathbf{i}$. That is, we do not notationally distinguish intervals from their corresponding first-order structures. We proceed to pose the following question of translatability related to **FO**: is there for every formula $\varphi \in$ **TD** a *sentence* $\psi_\varphi \in$ **FO** such that for all intervals $\mathbf{i} \in \mathcal{K}_{\text{fin}}$,

---

[10]These two expressivity results are due to J. van Benthem (1976) and H. Kamp (1968), respectively. For nice presentations of the respective results, see, e.g., (Blackburn et al., 2002, Sect. 2.6) and (Gabbay et al., 1994, Sect. 10.3).

[11]For an approach in which k-dimensional modal formulas (formulas evaluated relative to k-tuples of points) are translated by formulas of some abstract logic using k free variables, see (Hella and Tulenheimo, 2012). If we agree to confine attention to intervals defined in terms of bounds, like $[\![t, t']\!]$ or $(\!(t, t']\!]$, then interval-based modal logics can be understood as 2-dimensional modal logics. However, if we allow any inwards-closed set to determine an interval, this is no longer the case. For example, the subinterval of an interval $(\mathbb{Q}, <, V)$ determined by the set $\{x : 2 < x^2 < 5\}$ cannot be defined in terms of bounds.

we have $\mathbf{i} \models \varphi$ iff $\mathbf{i} \models \psi_\varphi$? This question is shown to receive a negative answer.

Henceforth, if an alphabet Σ is given, we write τ_Σ for the vocabulary $\{P_a : a \in \Sigma\} \cup \{<\}$, where the P_a are unary and $<$ is binary. Taking advantage of our characterization result (Theorem 3.1), we take a detour via the fragment R_0 of regular-like expressions and prove that not all languages denoted by expressions in $\mathsf{R}_0(\Sigma)$ are first-order definable, given that the size of the alphabet Σ is at least 2. By Theorem 3.1 it then follows that $\mathbf{TD}[\pi_\Sigma]$ cannot be translated into $\mathbf{FO}[\tau_\Sigma]$ whenever $|\Sigma| \geq 2$.

The idea of proof is as follows. Given that $\{a, b\} \subseteq \Sigma$, we find a certain expression r_0 of $\mathsf{R}_0(\Sigma)$ whose denotation contains in particular all words of the form $(aabbaabbaabb)^n$ with $n \geq 1$, but no word of the form $(aabbaabbaabb)^n aabb$ with $n \geq 1$. Then we show, using a simple Ehrenfeucht-Fraïssé game argument, that for any natural number n there is $k_n \geq 1$ such that the words $(aabbaabbaabb)^{k_n}$ and $(aabbaabbaabb)^{k_n} aabb$ cannot be distinguished by any $\mathbf{FO}$ sentence of quantifier rank at most n. It follows that the expression r_0 cannot be translated into $\mathbf{FO}$. For if it could, let n_0 be the quantifier rank of its translation χ. Since χ translates r_0, we have $(aabbaabbaabb)^{k_{n_0}} \models \chi$ while $(aabbaabbaabb)^{k_{n_0}} aabb \not\models \chi$. Still the two words $(aabbaabbaabb)^{k_{n_0}}$ and $(aabbaabbaabb)^{k_{n_0}} aabb$ cannot be distinguished by any formula of quantifier rank at most n_0 and therefore not by χ. This is a contradiction, and we may conclude that indeed r_0 cannot be translated into $\mathbf{FO}$.

In the proof presented below a specific regular-like expression r_0 is constructed; therefore the proof offers us (via a translation of R_0 into $\mathbf{TD}$) a concrete example of a $\mathbf{TD}$ formula not translatable into $\mathbf{FO}$. We take this to be a sufficient motivation for formulating the proof as we do. In Section 7 we will note that the result could be alternatively approached with reference to certain results known from the literature that characterize $\mathbf{FO}$ in terms of regular-like expressions.

We recall that $[r^*]$ is definable as $[\mathbf{1} \cup r \cup r^\circ]$, for any r in R_0. To facilitate the discussion, let us agree on writing r_* for the 'dual' of the expression r^*, that is, for the expression r^{c*c}. Hence the set $[r_*]$ contains exactly those words whose every factorization has at least one factor that belongs to the denotation of r.

Lemma 5.1. *Let $|\Sigma| \geq 2$. There is no map $f : \mathsf{R}_0(\Sigma) \to \mathbf{FO}[\tau_\Sigma]$ such that for all expressions $r \in \mathsf{R}_0(\Sigma)$ and all words $w \in \Sigma^*$, we have: $w \in [r]$ iff $w \models f(r)$.*

Proof. We single out an expression r_0 witnessing that no translation of $R_0(\Sigma)$ into $\mathbf{FO}[\tau_\Sigma]$ exists. First, define the expressions r_1, r_2, r_3 and r_4 as follows:

- $r_1 := ((a^\circ \cup b)^* \cap a^{*c} \cap b^{*c})$ and $r_2 := ((b^\circ \cup a)^* \cap a^{*c} \cap b^{*c})$;

- $r_3 := ((a \cup b \cup r_1)_* \cap a^c \cap b^c \cap \mathbf{1}^c \cap (a \cup b)^*)$ and
  $r_4 := ((a \cup b \cup r_2)_* \cap a^c \cap b^c \cap \mathbf{1}^c \cap (a \cup b)^*)$.

We observe that $[r_1]$ consists of those words over the alphabet $\{a, b\}$ which contain as a subword at least one of the words *aab* or *baa*. So there are no words of size less then 3 in $[r_1]$, and the only words of size 3 in it are *aab* and *baa*. Similarly, $[r_2]$ consists of the words over $\{a, b\}$ containing *bba* or *abb* as a subword, and the shortest words in $[r_2]$ are *bba* and *abb*. Let us, then, consider the expressions r_3 and r_4. First, we note that in $[(a \cup b \cup r_1)]$ there are no words whose size equals 2. For, in $[a]$ and in $[b]$ there are only words of size 1, and in $[r_1]$ only words of size at least 3. Similarly, in $[(a \cup b \cup r_2)]$ there are no words of size 2. Which are the words in the denotation of $[r_3]$, then? It is explicitly said that $[r_3] \subseteq \{a, b\}^* \setminus \{\lambda, a, b\}$. In addition it is said that *every* factorization of a word in $[r_3]$ has *some* part belonging to the denotation of $(a \cup b \cup r_1)$. This rather strong condition excludes a whole lot of words. Indeed, it excludes all words of even size: any such word has a factorization each of whose parts is of size exactly 2, but there is no word of size 2 in $[(a \cup b \cup r_1)]$. What about words of odd size, then? In particular, each word of size $2n + 3$ has $n + 1$ factorizations into factors of which exactly one is of size 3 and the rest are of size 2. For each of those factorizations the factor of size 3 must be in $[r_1]$, i.e., must either equal *aab* or else equal *baa*. This again imposes a rather strong restriction on what sort of words of odd size are accepted by the expression $(a \cup b \cup r_1)_*$. A moment's reflection reveals that — apart from a and b which are excluded from $[r_3]$ anyway — the odd words in $[(a \cup b \cup r_1)_*]$ are as follows: *aab, baa; aabaa, baaab; aabaaab, baaabaa; aabaaabaa, baaabaaab*; etc. Similarly we may observe that the set $[r_4]$ consists of the words *bba, abb; bbabb, abbba; bbabbba, abbbabb; bbabbbabb, abbbabbba*; etc.

Consider, then, words w satisfying the following three conditions: (1) w is the result of concatenating some finite number of words in $[r_3]$, (2) w has a factorization each of whose factors belongs to $[a^\circ]$ or to $[b^\circ]$, and (3) w cannot be factored into at least 4 factors each of which belongs to $[a^\circ]$ or to $[b^\circ]$. By conditions (1) and (2), the set of words considered is actually a subset of $\{aab, baa, baaab\}^*$. Namely, all words in $[r_3]$ except for *aab*, *baa* and *baaab* contain at least one occurrence of *b* which is neither immediately followed nor immediately preceded by another occurrence of *b*, and which is neither in the beginning nor in the end of the word in question. Therefore, no word which contains as a subword a word from the set $[r_3] \setminus \{aab, baa, baaab\}$ may satisfy condition (2). Now, in the set $\{aab, baa, baaab\}^*$, there is only one word which satisfies both conditions (2) and (3), namely *aabbaa*. In particular, the shortest word satisfying these conditions and containing the word *baaab* as a subword, namely *aabbaaabbaa* can be divided into 5 parts each belonging to $[a^\circ]$ or to $[b^\circ]$ (hence *a fortiori* the number of such parts is at least 4). Write, then, $r_5 := r_3^* \cap (a^\circ \cup b^\circ)^* \cap (a^\circ \cup b^\circ)^{\circ\circ c}$. So we note that $[r_5] = \{aabbaa\}$. Similarly, letting $r_6 := r_4^* \cap (a^\circ \cup b^\circ)^* \cap (a^\circ \cup b^\circ)^{\circ\circ c}$, we have that $[r_6] = \{bbaabb\}$. Finally, put $r_0 := (r_5 \cup r_6)^*$. We observe that the language $[r_0]$ contains in particular all words of the form $(aabbaabbaabb)^n$ with $n \geq 1$, but it contains no word of the form $(aabbaabbaabb)^n aabb$.

Given $n \geq 1$, let m and k_n be the unique numbers such that $m \in \{4, 8\}$ and $4 \cdot 2^{n-1} + m = 12 \cdot k_n$. Further, let $k_0 := k_1$. We proceed to show that for every $n < \omega$, (the first-order structures encoding) the words $(aabbaabbaabb)^{k_n}$ and $(aabbaabbaabb)^{k_n} aabb$ are **FO** equivalent up to quantifier rank n.[12] Consider the longer (shorter) word as factored into $3 \cdot k_n + 1$ (respectively, $3 \cdot k_n$) blocks *aabb* of 4 symbols. Now, a moment's reflection shows that in the n-round Ehrenfeucht-Fraïssé game played relative to the words $(aabbaabbaabb)^{k_n}$ and $(aabbaabbaabb)^{k_n} aabb$, an optimal strategy for Spoiler consists of letting him choose successively the following elements of the longer word: the last symbol of block 2^0, the last symbol of block 2^1, and so on, until the last symbol of block 2^{n-1}. A strategy allowing Duplicator to win against this strategy of Spoiler's in the relevant Ehrenfeucht-Fraïssé game consists simply of choosing successively the last symbol of block 2^0, the last symbol of block 2^1, and so on, until the last symbol of block 2^{n-1}. Since Spoiler's strategy is optimal, this strategy is winning for Duplicator. If the $(n + 1)$-th move was

---

[12]In order to make sure that Duplicator will be able to make at least n moves in the Ehrenfeucht-Fraïssé game of n rounds, we want that there are at least 2^{n-1} blocks *aabb* of 4 symbols in the longer word. Further, since we also want the word to belong to $[(r_5 \cup r_6)^*]$, we must make sure its size is divisible by 12. As a matter of fact the only relevant numbers to add to the quantity $4 \cdot 2^{n-1}$ are indeed 4 and 8. The number $4 \cdot 2^{n-1} + 0$ is not divisible by 3 and so not by 12. Also, no odd number added to $4 \cdot 2^{n-1}$ can yield a number divisible by 12. Finally, out of the non-negative integers less than 12 the remaining candidates — besides 4 and 8 — namely 2, 6, and 10 are not possible since $2 \cdot 2^{n-1} + 1$ and $2 \cdot 2^{n-1} + 3$ and $2 \cdot 2^{n-1} + 5$ are odd and therefore not divisible by 6.

still available, Spoiler could choose the last symbol of the block $3 \cdot k_n + 1$ from the longer word and to this move Duplicator could not respond without immediately losing, given that she would have already chosen the last symbol of the block 2^{n-1} from the shorter word before. (If Duplicator applied a different strategy against Spoiler's first n moves, she might survive even for more than n rounds. What is relevant here is only that there is a strategy for her to survive at least n rounds.) ∎

We are in a position to prove that the expressive powers of the logics **TD** and **FO** are incomparable. If π is a set of atoms, let us write τ_π for the vocabulary $\{P_q : q \in \pi\} \cup \{<\}$, where the P_q are unary.

Theorem 5.1. *Let* $|\pi| \geq 2$. *Over the class* $\mathcal{K}_{\mathrm{fin}}$, **TD**$[\pi]$ $\|_{\mathcal{K}_{\mathrm{fin}}}$ **FO**$[\tau_\pi]$.

Proof. Fix a set π of atoms with $\{p_a, p_b\} \subseteq \pi$ and let Σ be the corresponding alphabet, with $\{a, b\} \subseteq \Sigma$. Let us first show that **TD**$[\pi]$ $\not\leq_{\mathcal{K}_{\mathrm{fin}}(\pi)}$ **FO**$[\tau_\pi]$. Suppose for contradiction that **TD**$[\pi]$ $\leq_{\mathcal{K}_{\mathrm{fin}}(\pi)}$ **FO**$[\tau_\pi]$, i.e., that there is a function $f :$ **TD**$[\pi] \to$ **FO**$[\tau_\pi]$ such that for all $\mathbf{i} \in \mathcal{K}_{\mathrm{fin}}(\pi)$ and all $\varphi \in$ **TD**$[\tau_\pi]$, we have $\mathbf{i} \models \varphi$ iff $\mathbf{i} \models f(\varphi)$. Consider the expression r_0 of alphabet Σ singled out in the proof of Lemma 5.1, and let $\varphi := T(r_0)$ be the translation of r_0 into **TD**$[\pi]$ with T as specified in the proof of Theorem 3.1. Hence $w \in [r_0]$ iff $w \models \varphi$, for all words w over Σ. Let ψ_φ be a first-order translation of φ, existing by the assumption that **TD**$[\pi]$ $\leq_{\mathcal{K}_{\mathrm{fin}}}$ **FO**$[\tau_\pi]$. So for all words w over Σ, we have $w \models \varphi$ iff $w \models \psi_\varphi$. Therefore, $w \in [r_0]$ iff $w \models \psi_\varphi$. It follows that the language $[r_0]$ is first-order definable, which is impossible in view of Lemma 5.1.

It remains to show that conversely, **FO**$[\tau_\pi]$ $\not\leq_{\mathcal{K}_{\mathrm{fin}}(\pi)}$ **TD**$[\pi]$. This rather obvious fact can be proven as follows. Let χ be the following **FO** sentence: $\exists x \exists y (P_a x \wedge P_b y \wedge x < y)$. Consider the two simple words ab and ba over the alphabet Σ. Now, $ab \models \chi$ but $ba \not\models \chi$. Yet $ba = \mathrm{mi}(ab)$, so if **FO**$[\tau_\pi]$ was translatable into **TD**$[\pi]$, by Lemma 4.2 we would have in particular that either χ is true at both words ab and ba, or else χ is false at both of them. It follows that χ has no translation into **TD**$[\pi]$. ∎

6 Extending TD: and next

We have seen that **TD** is not able to describe order-related properties of temporal flows. In order to make it possible to speak of properties of intervals which are not 'direction invariant', we introduce a new connective **and next** and extend the syntax of the logic **TD** by this connective, obtaining a logic to be dubbed **TDN**.

6.1   Syntax and semantics of TDN

The syntax of **TDN**$[\pi]$ is given by the following grammar:

$$\varphi ::= p \mid \bot \mid \neg\varphi \mid (\varphi \vee \varphi) \mid \Box\varphi \mid (\varphi \text{ and next } \varphi),$$

with $p \in \pi$. The semantics of the novel binary connective and next is given by the following clause: $\mathbf{i} \models (\varphi \text{ and next } \psi)$ iff there are intervals $\mathbf{i}_1$ and $\mathbf{i}_2$ such that $\mathbf{i} = \mathbf{i}_1 \oplus \mathbf{i}_2$ and $\mathbf{i}_1 \models \varphi$ and $\mathbf{i}_2 \models \psi$. Observe that this definition allows the case that one or both of the intervals $\mathbf{i}_1$ and $\mathbf{i}_2$ are empty. For example, if $\Lambda \models \varphi$ and $\mathbf{i} \models \psi$, then $\mathbf{i} \models (\varphi \text{ and next } \psi)$, where $\mathbf{i} = \Lambda \oplus \mathbf{i}$. So, $(\varphi \text{ and next } \psi)$ is true at $\mathbf{i}$ iff one of the following conditions hold: $\mathbf{i}$ can be split into two non-empty pieces of which the earlier one makes φ true while the later one makes ψ true, or exactly one of φ and ψ is true at the empty interval while the other is true at $\mathbf{i}$, or $\mathbf{i}$ itself is empty and both φ and ψ are true at it.

The semantic relationship between the operators $\Box$ and and next can be explicated as follows. Given a formula ψ of **TDN**, let us define: $(\psi \text{ and next } \psi)^0 := (\psi \text{ and next } \psi)$ and $(\psi \text{ and next } \psi)^{n+1} := ((\psi \text{ and next } \psi)^n \text{ and next } \psi)$. The operator $\Box$ is the 'closure' of and next in the following sense: $\mathbf{i} \models \Box\varphi$ iff there is $n \geq 0$ such that $\mathbf{i} \models ((\varphi \wedge \neg\bot) \text{ and next } (\varphi \wedge \neg\bot))^n$. (We recall that the semantics of $\Box$ calls for splitting the interval of evaluation into *non-empty* pieces, hence the conjunct $\neg\bot$.) This does not mean, of course, that we can dispense with $\Box$ as soon as and next is available in our language. Indeed we cannot express $\Box$ in terms of the other connectives of **TDN**. This fact may appear rather obvious; we will see a proof later (Corollary 7.1). It is even easier to get convinced of the fact that the availability of and next indeed adds to the expressive power of **TD**.

Theorem 6.1. *Let* $|\pi| \geq 2$. *Then* **TD**$[\pi] <$ **TDN**$[\pi]$.

Proof. Let π be any set of atoms. Trivially we have **TD**$[\pi] \leq$ **TDN**$[\pi]$. So it suffices to show that **TDN**$[\pi] \nleq$ **TD**$[\pi]$. Consider the word ab. By Lemma 4.2, any **TD**$[\pi]$ formula true at ab is also true at its mirror image ba. Yet the **TDN**$[\pi]$ formula $(p_a \text{ and next } p_b)$ is true at ab but not at ba. So **TDN**$[\pi]$ is not translatable into **TD**$[\pi]$. $\blacksquare$

Actually we can drop the restriction on the size of the set π in the statement of Theorem 6.1. In Section 7 we discern a certain formula (u and next u) of **TDN**$[\pi]$ with $|\pi| = 0$; this formula is true at all and only intervals of size 2. From Fact 7.1 it will follow that the formula in question cannot be translated into **TD**.

6.2 Characterizing TDN

In Theorem 3.1 we characterized the expressive power of **TD** on the class $\mathcal{K}_{word}$ by using the regular-like operators **1**, $\vee$, ° and ^{c}. Now, **TDN** can actually be characterized by *regular* operators. We recall that by definition the set $RE(\Sigma)$ of regular expressions over Σ equals $RLE(\Sigma, \{\emptyset, \vee, ^*, \cdot\})$. Note that in this case the operator for relative complement (viz. ^{c}) is not among the given operators.

Theorem 6.2. *Let Σ be an alphabet. Then* **TDN**$[\pi_\Sigma] = RE(\Sigma)$.

Proof. The proof proceeds like that of Theorem 3.1. For the direction from right to left, define a map $T : RE(\Sigma) \rightarrow$ **TDN**$[\pi_\Sigma]$ as follows: $T(\emptyset) = \neg\top$, $T(a) = ((\neg\bot \wedge \diamondsuit\bot) \wedge p_a)$, $T(r \cup s) = (T(r) \vee T(s))$, $T(r^*) = (\bot \vee T(r) \vee \Box T(r))$, $T(r \cdot s) = (T(r)$ and next $T(s))$. Plainly the map T satisfies $w \in [r]$ iff $w \models T(r)$, for all words $w \in \Sigma^*$ and all expressions $r \in RE(\Sigma)$. As regards the converse direction, recall that in $RE(\Sigma)$ we may define the operation $^+$ satisfying $[r^+] = [r] \setminus \{\lambda\}$ and use it to define the operation °, because $[r°] = [r^+ \cdot r^+]$. Recall also that $RE(\Sigma)$ is closed under relative complement. Now, define a map $S :$ **TDN**$[\pi_\Sigma] \rightarrow RE(\Sigma)$ by setting $S(\bot) = \emptyset^*$, $S(p_a) = a^*$, $S(\neg\varphi) = S(\varphi)^c$, $S(\varphi \vee \psi) = (S(\varphi) \cup S(\psi))$, $S(\Box\varphi) = S(\varphi)°$, $S(\varphi$ and next $\psi) = (S(\varphi) \cdot S(\psi))$. Clearly we have $w \models \varphi$ iff $w \in [S(\varphi)]$, for all words $w \in \Sigma^*$ and all formulas φ of **TDN**$[\pi_\Sigma]$. ∎

We may note that in the above proof the size of the expression $S(\varphi)$ is linear in the size of the input formula φ. Therefore there exists a linear time reduction of the model-checking problem of **TDN** over word intervals into the membership problem for regular expressions; the latter problem is NLOGSPACE complete (Jiang and Ravikumar, 1991).

6.3 Comparing TDN with MSO

In Section 5 we saw that **TD** cannot be translated into **FO**. Because **TD** is a fragment of **TDN**, it of course follows that neither can **TDN**. On the other hand, by inspecting the clauses defining the semantics of **TDN** we see that it can be translated into monadic second-order logic. After explaining how this translation works (the proof of Fact 6.1), we will pose the question: which fragment of **MSO** does **TDN** capture?

Let us first agree on some abbreviations. Given a vocabulary containing the binary relation symbol $<$ interpreted as an irreflexive linear order, we write $x \leq y$ for $(x < y \vee x = y)$, $\mathsf{min}(x)$ for $\forall y(x \leq y)$ and $\mathsf{max}(x)$ for $\forall y(y \leq x)$. We abbreviate by $\mathsf{not\text{-}betw}(x, y, X)$ the sentence

$\neg\exists z(Xz \wedge x < z \wedge z < y)$, saying that there is no element of X between x and y. Observe that this is the case in particular when $x = y$, and likewise when $x < y$ and $y = min(X)$. We write $\mathsf{succ}(x, y, X)$ for the sentence $(Xx \wedge Xy \wedge x < y \wedge \mathsf{not\text{-}betw}(x, y, X))$, stating that x and y are successive elements of X, i.e., elements of X between which there is no further element of X (though there might be elements between them which are not in X). Finally, if Φ is an **MSO** sentence, let $\Phi^{[x,y]}$ and $\Phi^{(x,y]}$ be the results of relativizing all first-order quantifiers of Φ to the set $[x, y] := \{z : x \leq z \leq y\}$ and to the set $(x, y] := \{z : x < z \leq y\}$, respectively. Such relativizations may be defined recursively. For example, $(\exists z\Psi)^{[x,y]} := \exists z(x \leq z \wedge z \leq y \wedge \Psi^{[x,y]})$.

Fact 6.1. TDN $\leq_{\mathcal{K}_{\mathrm{fin}}}$ **MSO.**

Proof. Let π be any set of atoms. Let us define a map $F : \mathbf{TDN}[\pi] \to \mathbf{MSO}[\tau_\pi]$ recursively as follows. Put $F(\bot) := \forall x(x \neq x)$ and $F(p_i) := \forall x P_i x$. Assume, then, that F has already been defined on φ and on ψ. Let $F(\neg\varphi) = \neg F(\varphi)$ and $F(\varphi \vee \psi) = (F(\varphi) \vee F(\psi))$. Finally, define $F(\Box\varphi)$ and $F(\varphi \text{ and next } \psi)$ by putting

- $F(\Box\varphi) := \exists X \exists x(Xx \wedge \mathsf{max}(x) \wedge$
$$\exists y \exists z(\mathsf{min}(y) \wedge Xz \wedge z \neq x \wedge (Xy \to y = z) \wedge$$
$$\mathsf{not\text{-}betw}(y, z, X) \wedge F(\varphi)^{[x,y]}) \wedge$$
$$\forall x \forall y(\mathsf{succ}(x, y, X) \to F(\varphi)^{(x,y]}));$$

- $F(\varphi \text{ and next } \psi) = (\chi_0 \vee \exists x \exists y \exists z(\mathsf{min}(x) \wedge y \leq z \wedge \mathsf{max}(z) \wedge$
$$(\chi_1 \vee \chi_2))),$$

where $\chi_0 := \forall x(x \neq x) \wedge F(\varphi) \wedge F(\psi)$; $\chi_1 := F(\varphi)^{(x,x]} \wedge F(\psi)^{[x,z]}$; and $\chi_2 := F(\varphi)^{[x,y]} \wedge F(\psi)^{(y,z]}$. Here the subformula χ_0 corresponds to the case that the relevant factorization $\langle \mathbf{i}_1, \mathbf{i}_2 \rangle$ of the interval $\mathbf{i}$ of evaluation satisfies $\mathbf{i}_1 = \Lambda = \mathbf{i}_2$, the formula χ_1 corresponds to the case that $\mathbf{i}_1 = \Lambda$ and $\mathbf{i}_2 = \mathbf{i}$, while χ_2 covers the remaining two cases. It is straightforward to prove by induction on the structure of the $\mathbf{TDN}[\pi]$ formula φ that indeed F provides a translation: for every interval $\mathbf{i} \in \mathcal{K}_{\mathrm{fin}}(\pi)$, we have that $F(\varphi)$ is an $\mathbf{MSO}[\tau_\pi]$ sentence satisfying $\mathbf{i} \models \varphi$ iff $\mathbf{i} \models F(\varphi)$. ∎

We wish to identify the fragment of **MSO** captured by **TDN** relative to the class $\mathcal{K}_{\mathrm{fin}}$. Let us first think of word intervals (rather than arbitrary intervals). We will utilize the following well-known result which ties together regular languages, word intervals and monadic second-order logic.

Proposition 6.1 (Büchi 1960). *Let Σ be an alphabet and let $L \subseteq \Sigma^*$. The language L is regular if and only if there is an* **MSO**$[\tau_\Sigma]$ *sentence Φ such that $L = \{i \in \mathcal{K}_{\text{word}}(\pi_\Sigma) : i \models \Phi\}$. That is, over $\mathcal{K}_{\text{word}}$ we have* RE = MSO.[13]

Precisely those languages are denoted by a regular expression, then, that are defined by some **MSO** sentence. It turns out that on the class $\mathcal{K}_{\text{word}}$, **TDN** is very expressive. Actually it captures the whole of **MSO**. Given a set π of atoms, write Σ_π for the alphabet $\{a_p : p \in \pi\}$.

Lemma 6.1. TDN $=_{\mathcal{K}_{\text{word}}}$ **MSO**.

Proof. Let π be any set of atoms. By Theorem 6.2, we have that **TDN**$[\pi] = $ RE(Σ_π). By Proposition 6.1, RE$(\Sigma_\pi) = $ **MSO**$[\tau_\pi]$. It follows that over the class $\mathcal{K}_{\text{word}}(\pi)$, we have **TDN**$[\pi] = $ **MSO**$[\tau_\pi]$.   ∎

As a matter of fact, the expressive powers of the logics **TDN** and **MSO** coincide on the whole class $\mathcal{K}_{\text{fin}}$, not only on $\mathcal{K}_{\text{word}}$. To see this, we prove the following fact. If π is the set $\{p_i : 1 \le i \le n\}$, let $w(\pi)$ be the set $\{q_f : f \in \{0,1\}^n\}$. Now, every interval $i = (T, <, V)$ with V of type $T \to \mathcal{P}(\pi)$ can be turned into a word interval $w(i) = (T, <, U)$ with U of type $T \to \mathcal{P}(w(\pi))$ by setting, for every function $f : \{1,\ldots,n\} \to \{0,1\}$: $q_f \in U(t)$ iff for all $1 \le i \le n$, we have $\big(p_i \in V(t)$ if $f(i) = 1$ and $p_i \in \pi \setminus V(t)$ if $f(i) = 0\big)$.

Fact 6.2. Let π be a set of atoms. **(1.a)** For every formula $\varphi \in $ **TDN**$[\pi]$, there is a formula $\psi_\varphi \in $ **TDN**$[w(\pi)]$ such that for all $i \in \mathcal{K}_{\text{fin}}(\pi)$, we have: $i \models \varphi$ if and only if $w(i) \models \psi_\varphi$. **(1.b)** Conversely, for every formula $\chi \in $ **TDN**$[w(\pi)]$ we can find a formula $\theta_\chi \in $ **TDN**$[\pi]$ such that $w(i) \models \chi$ if and only if $i \models \theta_\chi$, for all $i \in \mathcal{K}_{\text{fin}}(\pi)$. **(2)** If in the statements (1.a) and (1.b) concerning **TDN** we replace **TDN**$[\pi]$ by **MSO**$[\tau_\pi]$ and **TDN**$[w(\pi)]$ by **MSO**$[w(\tau_\pi)]$, we obtain corresponding statements concerning **MSO**.

Proof. Consider item (1); the proof of item (2) is entirely analogous. Let π be any set of atoms. For the case (a), if φ is any **TDN**$[\pi]$ formula, let

---

[13]Typically this result is formulated for languages L not containing the empty word; this is because usually first-order structures are taken to have a non-empty domain, while the first-order structure induced by the empty word has an empty domain. It is not difficult to show that Proposition 6.1 follows from the usual formulation of Büchi's theorem.

ψ_φ be the formula of $\textbf{TDN}[w(\pi)]$ obtained from φ by replacing in φ all occurrences of p_i by the disjunction of all atomic formulas q_f for which $f(i) = 1$. Clearly $\mathbf{i} \models \varphi$ iff $w(\mathbf{i}) \models \psi_\varphi$, for all $\mathbf{i} \in \mathcal{K}_{\text{fin}}(\pi)$. As regards the case (b), if χ is a formula of $\textbf{TDN}[w(\pi)]$, obtain the formula θ_χ of $\textbf{TDN}[\pi]$ from χ by replacing all occurrences of $\acute{q}_f$ by the formula

$$\bigwedge_{1 \leq i \leq n} p_i^{f(i)},$$

where $p_i^1 = p_i$ and $p_i^0 = \neg p_i$. Obviously $w(\mathbf{i}) \models \chi$ iff $\mathbf{i} \models \theta_\chi$, for all $\mathbf{i} \in \mathcal{K}_{\text{fin}}(\pi)$.   ∎

Fact 6.2 means, in particular, that in connection with both logics **TDN** and **MSO**, word intervals are representative of the whole class $\mathcal{K}_{\text{fin}}$: instead of asking whether a formula φ of **TDN** (respectively, of **MSO**) is true at an interval $\mathbf{i}$, we may equivalently ask whether ψ_φ is true at the word interval $w(\mathbf{i})$. Using Fact 6.2, we are in a position to generalize Lemma 6.1 to the entire class $\mathcal{K}_{\text{fin}}$.

Theorem 6.3. TDN $=_{\mathcal{K}_{\text{fin}}}$ MSO.

Proof. Let π be any set of atoms. Directly by Fact 6.1, we have that $\textbf{TDN}[\pi] \leq \textbf{MSO}[\tau_\pi]$ over $\mathcal{K}_{\text{fin}}(\pi)$. For the converse direction, let $\Psi \in \textbf{MSO}[\tau_\pi]$ be arbitrary. By Fact 6.2(2.a) we find a formula $\Phi_\Psi \in \textbf{MSO}[\tau_{w(\pi)}]$ such that $\mathbf{i} \models \Psi$ iff $w(\mathbf{i}) \models \Phi_\Psi$ for all $\mathbf{i} \in \mathcal{K}_{\text{fin}}(\pi)$. Further, by Lemma 6.1 and the fact that for every $\mathbf{j} \in \mathcal{K}_{\text{word}}(w(\pi))$ there is $\mathbf{i} \in \mathcal{K}_{\text{fin}}(\pi)$ such that $\mathbf{j} = w(\mathbf{i})$, we know that there is a formula $\chi \in \textbf{TDN}[w(\pi)]$ such that $w(\mathbf{i}) \models \Phi_\Psi$ iff $w(\mathbf{i}) \models \chi$, for all $\mathbf{i} \in \mathcal{K}_{\text{fin}}(\pi)$. Finally, applying Fact 6.2(1.b) we may conclude that there is a formula $\theta_\chi \in \textbf{TDN}[\pi]$ such that $w(\mathbf{i}) \models \chi$ iff $\mathbf{i} \models \theta_\chi$, for all $\mathbf{i} \in \mathcal{K}_{\text{fin}}(\pi)$. It follows, then, that for all $\mathbf{i} \in \mathcal{K}_{\text{fin}}(\pi)$ we have: $\mathbf{i} \models \Psi$ iff $\mathbf{i} \models \theta_\chi$, that is, θ_χ is a translation of Ψ in $\textbf{TDN}[\pi]$ relative to the class $\mathcal{K}_{\text{fin}}(\pi)$.   ∎

6.4 Negation in TDN

We saw in Subsection 4.1 that in **TD**, the contradictory negation $\neg$ could not be dispensed with without loss of expressive power. Is $\neg$ perhaps superfluous in **TDN**? Given the fact that **TDN** is characterized by regular expressions in which the operation of relative complement is indeed superfluous, one might surmise that the answer is in the affirmative. However, the situation is more nuanced. Write $\textbf{TDN}(\bot, \vee, \Box, \text{and next})$ for the logic resulting from not allowing the use of $\neg$ in **TDN**. We may first observe that in any case the proof of Theorem 6.2 does not allow inferring that **TDN** can be translated into **TDN**($\bot, \vee, \square$, and next) over $\mathcal{K}_{\text{word}}$. This would be possible if in the formulas belonging to the image of the map $T : \mathsf{RE}(\Sigma) \to \mathbf{TDN}[\pi_\Sigma]$, there appeared no negation signs. However, negation has been used to translate $\emptyset$ and to translate the symbol a of the alphabet Σ. Of course, this does not yet prove that we could not have avoided using negation in the translation. Could we? That the answer is negative is entailed by the following closure result pertaining to **TDN**($\bot, \vee, \square$, and next). The result is a weakened version of Lemma 4.1, which was shown to hold for **TD**($\bot, \vee, \square$). This lemma cannot as such be extended to **TDN**($\bot, \vee, \square$, and next). If, for example, i_0 is an interval consisting of two instants, the earlier making p true but q false and the later making q true but p false, the formula (p and next q) holds at i_0, but does not hold at any multiple ($n \otimes i_0$) of i_0 with $n \geq 2$.

Lemma 6.2. *Let φ be a formula of* **TDN**($\bot, \vee, \square$, and next). *If* $\mathrm{Mod}(\varphi) \cap \{\Lambda\} \neq \varnothing$, *then for every* $k < \omega$ *there is in* $\mathrm{Mod}(\varphi)$ *an interval of size greater than* k.

Proof. There is nothing to prove if $\varphi = \bot$, since in that case $\mathrm{Mod}(\varphi) = \{\Lambda\}$. If φ is an atom, the claim holds trivially: then $\mathrm{Mod}(\varphi)$ contains an interval of every finite size. Suppose, then, inductively that if $\chi \in \{\varphi, \psi\}$ and $\mathrm{Mod}(\chi) \cap \{\Lambda\} \neq \varnothing$, then in $\mathrm{Mod}(\chi)$ there is no interval with a maximal size. We consider cases. (1) If $\mathbf{i} \neq \Lambda$ and $\mathbf{i} \models (\varphi \vee \psi)$, there is $\chi \in \{\varphi, \psi\}$ such that $\mathbf{i} \models \chi$. For every $k < \omega$ there is by the inductive hypothesis an interval $\mathbf{j}$ with $|\mathbf{j}| > k$ such that $\mathbf{j} \models \chi$. So $\mathbf{j} \models (\varphi \vee \psi)$. (2) If $\mathbf{i} \neq \Lambda$ and $\mathbf{i} \models (\varphi$ and next $\psi)$, there are intervals $\mathbf{i}_1$ and $\mathbf{i}_2$ such that $\mathbf{i}_1 \oplus \mathbf{i}_2 = \mathbf{i}$ and $\mathbf{i}_1 \models \varphi$ and $\mathbf{i}_2 \models \psi$, and at least one of $\mathbf{i}_1$ and $\mathbf{i}_2$ is distinct from Λ. Suppose $\mathbf{i}_1 \neq \Lambda$ (the case that $\mathbf{i}_2 \neq \Lambda$ can be dealt with similarly). Let $k < \omega$ be arbitrary. Then by the inductive hypothesis there is an interval $\mathbf{j}$ with $|\mathbf{j}| > k$ such that $\mathbf{j} \models \varphi$. Thus, the formula ($\varphi$ and next ψ) is true at $(\mathbf{j} \oplus \mathbf{i}_2)$, where $|(\mathbf{j} \oplus \mathbf{i}_2)| > k$. (3) Finally, if $\mathbf{i} \models \square\varphi$, there is a division $\langle \mathbf{i}_1, \dots, \mathbf{i}_n \rangle$ with $n \geq 2$ such that $\mathbf{i}_m \neq \Lambda$ and $\mathbf{i}_m \models \varphi$ for all $1 \leq m \leq n$. Let $k < \omega$ be arbitrary. Define $\mathbf{j} := (k+1) \otimes \mathbf{i}_1$, whence $\mathbf{j}$ is an ordered sum of $k + 1$ of intervals each of which is isomorphic to $\mathbf{i}_1$. The terms of the ordered sum induce a division $\langle \mathbf{j}_1, \dots, \mathbf{j}_{k+1} \rangle$ of $\mathbf{j}$. Since $\mathbf{i}_1 \models \varphi$ and every $\mathbf{j}_i$ is isomorphic to $\mathbf{i}_1$, we have $\mathbf{j}_i \models \varphi$ for all $1 \leq i \leq k+1$. Further, $|\mathbf{j}| > k$ since $\mathbf{i}_1 \neq \Lambda$. Now, evidently $\mathbf{j} \models \square\varphi$. (Observe that in the case for $\square$ the inductive hypothesis was not needed.) ∎

Call a formula φ *strongly satisfiable* if there is at least one interval $\mathbf{i} \neq \Lambda$ such that $\mathbf{i} \models \varphi$. Call a set S of non-negative integers a *spectrum* of a formula φ if $S = \{|\mathbf{i}| : \mathbf{i} \in \mathrm{Mod}(\varphi)\}$. By Lemma 6.2, every strongly satisfiable formula φ of $\mathbf{TDN}(\perp, \vee, \square, \text{and next})$ has an infinite spectrum. We are in a position to see that $\mathbf{TDN}(\perp, \vee, \square, \text{and next})$ is not closed under negation.

Corollary 6.1. $\mathbf{TDN}(\perp, \vee, \square, \text{and next}) <_{\mathcal{K}_{\mathrm{fin}}} \mathbf{TDN}$.

Proof. Trivially $\mathbf{TDN}(\perp, \vee, \square, \text{and next}) \leq_{\mathcal{K}_{\mathrm{fin}}} \mathbf{TDN}$. To see that the converse does not hold, let π be a set of atoms and suppose for contradiction that $\mathbf{TDN}[\pi] \leq_{\mathcal{K}_{\mathrm{fin}}(\pi)} \mathbf{TDN}(\perp, \vee, \square, \text{and next})[\pi]$. Recall that the spectrum of the $\mathbf{TDN}$ formula $(\neg\perp \wedge \Diamond\perp)$ is $\{1\}$. *A fortiori* its spectrum is finite. By assumption this formula has a translation into $\mathbf{TDN}(\perp, \vee, \square, \text{and next})[\pi]$, call it χ. From Lemma 6.2 it follows that the spectrum of χ is infinite. This is a contradiction in view of χ being a translation of $(\neg\perp \wedge \Diamond\perp)$. $\blacksquare$

So it has turned out that negation is not superfluous in $\mathbf{TDN}$. On the other hand, as witnessed by the proof of Theorem 6.2 (combined with Fact 6.2), only a very limited use of negation is needed to reach the full expressive power of $\mathbf{TDN}$ over the class $\mathcal{K}_{\mathrm{fin}}$. Let us formulate this observation precisely. Let a set $\pi = \{p_1, \ldots, p_n\}$ of atoms be fixed. A *Boolean combination* of the atoms $p_1, \ldots, p_n$ is any conjunction $p_1^{f(1)} \wedge \ldots \wedge p_n^{f(n)}$, where f is a function of type $\{1, \ldots, n\} \to \{0, 1\}$ and $p_i^1 = p_i$ and $p_i^0 = \neg p_i$. Write $\mathbf{TDN}_0[\pi]$ for the fragment of $\mathbf{TDN}[\pi]$ syntactically generated by the following grammar:

$$\varphi ::= \perp \mid \mathbf{L} \mid (\mathbf{u} \wedge \beta) \mid (\varphi \vee \varphi) \mid (\varphi \text{ and next } \varphi) \mid \square\varphi,$$

where β is a Boolean combination of atoms in π, $\mathbf{L}$ is short for $(\neg\perp \wedge \perp)$, and $\mathbf{u}$ abbreviates $(\neg\perp \wedge \Diamond\perp)$. The letter 'u' is reminiscent of the fact that the formula in question is true precisely at unit intervals (i.e., intervals of size 1). In $\mathbf{TDN}_0$, the occurrences of $\neg$ are very restricted indeed: they only appear in formulas of the forms $\neg\perp$ and $((\neg\perp \wedge \Diamond\perp) \wedge \bigwedge_{1 \leq i \leq n} p_i^{f(i)})$; recall here that $\Diamond$ and $\wedge$ are abbreviations, themselves defined using negation.

Theorem 6.4. *Over the class $\mathcal{K}_{\mathrm{fin}}$, $\mathbf{TDN}_0 = \mathbf{TDN} = \mathbf{MSO}$.*

Proof. Let $\pi = \{p_1, \ldots, p_n\}$ be a set of atoms. Let us show that over the class $\mathcal{K}_{\mathrm{fin}}(\pi)$, we have $\mathbf{TDN}_0[\pi] \leq \mathbf{TDN}[\pi] \leq \mathbf{MSO}[\tau_\pi] \leq \mathbf{TDN}_0[\pi]$.

Now, the first inclusion is trivial and the second holds by Fact 6.1. For the third inclusion, let Ψ be any $\mathbf{MSO}[\tau_\pi]$ sentence. Applying Fact 6.2(2.a) we obtain a sentence $\Phi_\Psi \in \mathbf{MSO}[\tau_{w(\pi)}]$ such that $\mathbf{i} \models \Psi$ iff $w(\mathbf{i}) \models \Phi_\Psi$, for all $\mathbf{i} \in \mathcal{K}_{\mathrm{fin}}(\pi)$. By the *proof* of Theorem 6.2 (and applying Proposition 6.1), there is a formula χ of $\mathbf{TDN}[w(\pi)]$ which is generated from formulas of the forms $\bot$, $\mathbb{L}$ and $(\mathbf{u} \wedge p)$ by using the connectives $\vee$, $\square$ and **and next**, and which satisfies $w(\mathbf{i}) \models \Phi_\Psi$ iff $w(\mathbf{i}) \models \chi$, for all $\mathbf{i} \in \mathcal{K}_{\mathrm{fin}}(\pi)$. Then, utilizing Fact 6.2(1.b), we may conclude that there is a formula θ_χ of $\mathbf{TDN}[\pi]$ which satisfies $w(\mathbf{i}) \models \chi$ iff $\mathbf{i} \models \theta_\chi$, for all $\mathbf{i} \in \mathcal{K}_{\mathrm{fin}}(\pi)$, and which differs from χ only in that in place of the atoms of χ there appear in θ_χ Boolean combinations of atoms from the set π. But this means that θ_χ is actually a formula of $\mathbf{TDN}_0[\pi]$. To summarize, for all $\mathbf{i} \in \mathcal{K}_{\mathrm{fin}}(\pi)$ we have $\mathbf{i} \models \Psi$ iff $\mathbf{i} \models \theta_\chi$. Since $\Psi \in \mathbf{MSO}[\tau_\pi]$ was assumed to be arbitrary, we may conclude that $\mathbf{MSO}[\tau_\pi] \leq_{\mathcal{K}_{\mathrm{fin}}(\pi)} \mathbf{TDN}_0[\pi]$. ∎

7 Conclusion

We have studied the logic of time division (**TD**) on intervals of finite size. This logic was characterized over the class $\mathcal{K}_{\mathrm{word}}$ by using the regular-like operators $\mathbf{1}$, $\vee$, $^\circ$ and ^{c}. Some of its model-theoretic properties were discussed. This logic was shown to be incomparable with first-order logic for its expressive power. The logic **TD** was extended to the logic **TDN** by making available the additional connective **and next**. It turned out that **TDN** is very expressive: it has the full expressive power of monadic-second order logic over the class $\mathcal{K}_{\mathrm{fin}}$. We remarked that negation ($\neg$) cannot be dropped from the syntax of **TDN** without loss in expressivity. However, it was observed that a very limited use of negation suffices. This observation was made explicit by discerning the expressively equivalent fragment **TDN**$_0$ of **TDN**. Let us conclude with a couple of remarks and systematic observations.

7.1 FO as a fragment of TDN

We already mentioned Büchi's result which establishes a connection between regular expressions and **MSO**. There is a corresponding result about **FO**. The set $\mathsf{SFRE}(\Sigma)$ of *star-free regular expressions* over an alphabet Σ is by definition the set $\mathsf{RLE}(\Sigma, \{\emptyset, \cup, \cdot,^{\mathsf{c}} \})$.

Proposition 7.1 (McNaughton and Papert 1971). *Let Σ be an alphabet and let $L \subseteq \Sigma^*$. The language L is denoted by a star-free regular expression if and* *only if there is an* $\mathbf{FO}[\tau_\Sigma]$ *sentence* φ *such that* $L = \{\mathbf{i} \in \mathcal{K}_{\text{word}}(\pi_\Sigma) : \mathbf{i} \models \varphi\}$. *That is,* SFRE = FO.[14]

Write $\mathbf{TDN}(\bot, \vee, \text{and next}, \neg)$ for the logic resulting from $\mathbf{TDN}$ when the use of $\Box$ is disallowed. Making use of Proposition 7.1, it can be seen that this logic coincides in expressive power with $\mathbf{FO}$ over $\mathcal{K}_{\text{fin}}$. Observe that in $\mathbf{TDN}(\bot, \vee, \text{and next}, \neg)$ the formula $(\neg\bot \wedge \neg(\neg\bot \text{ and next } \neg\bot))$ defines the class of all intervals of size 1. In particular the subformula $\neg(\neg\bot \text{ and next } \neg\bot))$ says that the interval cannot be divided into two non-empty parts; the only intervals meeting this condition are those whose size is at most 1. Here we obviously cannot make use of the formula $\Diamond\bot$ which is indeed equivalent to the formula $\neg(\neg\bot \text{ and next } \neg\bot)$, since $\Diamond$ is not syntactically available.

Theorem 7.1. $\mathbf{TDN}(\bot, \vee, \text{and next}, \neg) =_{\mathcal{K}_{\text{fin}}} \mathbf{FO}$.

Proof. Let π be any set of atoms. It is immediate that the logic $\mathbf{TDN}(\bot, \vee, \text{and next}, \neg)[\pi]$ can be translated into $\mathbf{FO}[\tau_\pi]$, cf. the proof of Fact 6.1. For the converse direction, let us first define a map T : $\mathbf{SFRE}(\Sigma_\pi) \to \mathbf{TDN}(\bot, \vee, \text{and next}, \neg)[\pi]$ recursively as follows: $T(\emptyset) = \neg\top$, $T(a_p) = ((\neg\bot \wedge \neg(\neg\bot \text{ and next } \neg\bot)) \wedge p)$, $T(r \cup s) = (T(r) \vee T(s))$, $T(r \cdot s) = (T(r) \text{ and next } T(s))$, $T(r^c) = \neg T(r)$. Clearly the map T satisfies $\mathbf{i} \in [r]$ iff $\mathbf{i} \models T(r)$, for all $\mathbf{i} \in \mathcal{K}_{\text{word}}(\pi)$ and all expressions $r \in \mathbf{SFRE}(\Sigma_\pi)$. Applying first Fact 6.2(2.a), then Proposition 7.1, then using the translation T, and then applying Fact 6.2(1.b), we find for every $\varphi \in \mathbf{FO}[\tau_\pi]$ a formula $\chi \in \mathbf{TDN}(\bot, \vee, \text{and next}, \neg)[\pi]$ such that for every $\mathbf{i} \in \mathcal{K}_{\text{fin}}(\pi)$, we have $\mathbf{i} \models \varphi$ iff $\mathbf{i} \models \chi$.   ∎

It is worth noting that Proposition 7.1 suggests an alternative way of proving that $\mathbf{TD} \not\leq \mathbf{FO}$ (cf. Theorem 5.1). This negative result was established above by first proving that R_0 cannot be translated into $\mathbf{FO}$ (Lemma 5.1) and then resorting to the fact that $\mathbf{TD} = \mathsf{R}_0$. Instead, we could attempt to prove — remaining at the level of regular-like expressions — that there is an expression $r \in \mathsf{R}_0$ such that $[r]$ is not denoted by any expression of SFRE. By Proposition 7.1 and Theorem 3.1 it would then follow that $\mathbf{TD}$ cannot be translated into $\mathbf{FO}$ over the class $\mathcal{K}_{\text{word}}$ and therefore not, *a fortiori*, over $\mathcal{K}_{\text{fin}}$.

Corollary 7.1. *Over the class* $\mathcal{K}_{\text{fin}}$, *we have:*

---

[14]Like Büchi's result about **MSO**, also this result is typically formulated for languages L not containing the empty word. It is not difficult to show that Proposition 7.1 follows from the usual formulation of McNaughton & Papert's theorem.

(a) **TDN**($\bot$, $\vee$, and next, $\neg$) < **TDN**;

(b) *If* $|\pi| \geq 2$, *then* **TDN**($\bot$, $\vee$, and next, $\neg$)$[\pi]$ $\|$ **TD**$[\pi]$.

Proof. For (a), we note that over $\mathcal{K}_{\text{fin}}$, **TDN**($\bot$, $\vee$, and next, $\neg$) = **FO** < **MSO** = **TDN**. The statement (b) follows immediately from Theorems 5.1 and 7.1. ∎

7.2 Open questions

Concerning the expressive power of the logic of time division, we have seen that semantically it determines, relative to $\mathcal{K}_{\text{fin}}$, a fragment of **MSO** which does not cover **FO** but which is also not included in **FO**. We leave it as a question for future research to characterize the fragment of **MSO** determined by the logic **TD** in model-theoretic terms. As a first guess, one might be tempted to think, wrongly, that **TD** coincides semantically with the fragment of **MSO** consisting of sentences Φ that are *invariant under mirror images*, i.e., that satisfy the following: if $\mathbf{i} \models \text{Mod}(\Phi)$, then $\text{mi}(\mathbf{i}) \in \text{Mod}(\Phi)$. By Lemma 4.2 we do know that all **MSO** translations of **TD** formulas are indeed invariant under mirror images, but as a matter of fact it is not the case that conversely, every **MSO** sentence (or even every **FO** sentence) invariant under mirror images is equivalent to a **TD** formula. For a counterexample, consider the **TDN**[$\varnothing$] formula $\varphi := (\mathbf{u} \text{ and next } \mathbf{u})$, satisfying $\text{Mod}(\varphi) = \{\mathbf{i} \in \mathcal{K}_{\text{fin}} : |\mathbf{i}| = 2\}$; recall that by definition $\mathbf{u}$ is the formula $(\neg\bot \wedge \Diamond\bot)$. The **MSO** translations of this formula are obviously invariant under mirror images: the mirror image of any interval of size 2 is likewise an interval of size 2. The following fact implies that φ is not translatable into **TD**.[15]

Fact 7.1. Let π be any set of atoms. There is no formula $\chi \in \textbf{TD}[\pi]$ such that $\text{Mod}(\chi) \cap \mathcal{K}_{\text{fin}}(\pi) = \{\mathbf{i} \in \mathcal{K}_{\text{fin}}(\pi) : |\mathbf{i}| = 2\}$.

Proof. We will first prove the claim in the case $\pi = \varnothing$ and then generalize it to pertain to all sets of atoms. For convenience, let us use the syntax where $\Diamond$ and $\wedge$ are available as primitives. Consider **TD**[$\varnothing$] formulas in negation normal form, i.e., suppose they are written in a form in which the negation symbol may only appear in front of $\bot$. We prove the following claim: if a formula χ of **TD**[$\varnothing$] is true at an interval of size 2,

---

[15]If φ had a translation into **TD**, this translation would be in **TD**[$\varnothing$]. Fact 7.1 establishes the stronger result that for every set π of atoms, there is no formula χ of **TD**[π] such that $\text{Mod}(\varphi) \cap \mathcal{K}_{\text{fin}}(\pi) = \text{Mod}(\chi) \cap \mathcal{K}_{\text{fin}}(\pi)$.

then it is true at an interval of size 3. Once this is shown, it immediately follows that the statement of the Fact holds in the case $\pi = \varnothing$. If $n < \omega$, write $\mathcal{K}_n(\pi)$ for the set $\{\mathbf{i} \in \mathcal{K}_{\mathrm{fin}}(\pi) : |\mathbf{i}| = n\}$.

Now, the spectra of the formulas $\perp$ and $\neg\perp$ are $\{0\}$ and $\omega \setminus \{0\}$, respectively, so they satisfy the claim. Note that for every n, the set $\mathcal{K}_n(\varnothing)$ contains, up to isomorphism, only one interval. If $\Box\psi$ is true at an interval $\mathbf{i} \in \mathcal{K}_2(\varnothing)$, then there are $\mathbf{i}_1, \mathbf{i}_2 \in \mathcal{K}_1(\varnothing)$ with $\mathbf{i}_1 \oplus \mathbf{i}_2 = \mathbf{i}$ such that $\mathbf{i}_j \models \psi$ for $j := 1, 2$. But then the interval $\mathbf{i}_1 \oplus \mathbf{i}_2 \oplus \mathbf{i}_2$ belongs to $\mathcal{K}_3(\varnothing)$ and makes $\Box\psi$ true. Further, if $\Diamond\psi$ is true at an interval $\mathbf{i} \in \mathcal{K}_2(\varnothing)$ and $\mathbf{i} = \mathbf{i}_1 \oplus \mathbf{i}_2$ with $\mathbf{i}_1, \mathbf{i}_2 \in \mathcal{K}_1(\varnothing)$, there is, by the semantics of $\Diamond$, a number $l \in \{1, 2\}$ such that $\mathbf{i}_l \models \psi$. Let $\mathbf{j} := \mathbf{i}_1 \oplus \mathbf{i}_2 \oplus \mathbf{i}_1$ if $l = 1$ and let $\mathbf{j} := \mathbf{i}_2 \oplus \mathbf{i}_1 \oplus \mathbf{i}_2$ if $l = 2$. By the construction of $\mathbf{j}$ we have that $\mathbf{j} \in \mathcal{K}_3(\varnothing)$ and $\mathbf{j} \models \Diamond\psi$. We will need the inductive hypothesis only to deal with disjunctions and conjunctions: indeed, suppose inductively that for $\theta \in \{\psi, \chi\}$ we have: if θ is true at some $\mathbf{i} \in \mathcal{K}_2(\varnothing)$, then θ is true at some $\mathbf{j} \in \mathcal{K}_3(\varnothing)$. The claim follows trivially for disjunction. Suppose, then, that $\mathbf{i} \models (\psi \wedge \chi)$ with $\mathbf{i} \in \mathcal{K}_2(\varnothing)$. By the inductive hypothesis there are intervals $\mathbf{j}_1$ and $\mathbf{j}_2$ in $\mathcal{K}_3(\varnothing)$ such that $\mathbf{j}_1 \models \psi$ and $\mathbf{j}_2 \models \chi$. Since the intervals in $\mathcal{K}_3(\varnothing)$ are pairwise isomorphic, it follows in particular that $\mathbf{j}_1 \models \chi$ and so $\mathbf{j}_1 \models (\psi \wedge \chi)$.

Having proven the statement of the Fact for the empty set of atoms, let $\pi \neq \varnothing$ be arbitrary. Suppose for contradiction that there is a formula $\theta \in \mathbf{TD}[\pi]$ in which at least one atom appears and which satisfies: $\mathrm{Mod}(\theta) \cap \mathcal{K}_{\mathrm{fin}}(\pi) = \mathcal{K}_2(\pi)$. Let us say that $(T, <, V)$ is an f-interval if $V(t) = \varnothing$ for every $t \in T$, i.e., it renders all atoms false at every instant. For every n there is, up to isomorphism, exactly one f-interval in $\mathcal{K}_n(\pi)$. Let θ' be the result of replacing in θ every atom by the formula $\perp$. If $\mathbf{i}$ is an f-interval and $\mathbf{i} \in \mathcal{K}_n(\pi)$, we clearly have that $\mathbf{i} \models \theta'$ iff $n = 2$. Since θ' contains no atoms, its truth-value must be the same at any two intervals which differ only in their valuations. Therefore we have for *all* intervals $\mathbf{i}$ in $\mathcal{K}_n(\pi)$: $\mathbf{i} \models \theta'$ iff $n = 2$. But this means that we have found a formula of $\mathbf{TD}[\varnothing]$, namely θ', which satisfies $\mathrm{Mod}(\theta') = \{\mathbf{i} \in \mathcal{K}_{\mathrm{fin}} : |\mathbf{i}| = 2\}$. This is a contradiction in view of what already proven.   ∎

By Fact 7.1, then, closure under mirror images does not suffice to yield a model-theoretic characterization of the fragment of **MSO** captured by **TD**. This characterization issue remains open. Among further questions for future research we can mention the following. The satisfiability problem of the logic **TD** is decidable over $\mathcal{K}_{\mathrm{fin}}$, since **MSO**-SAT is decidable over $\mathcal{K}_{\mathrm{fin}}$ and there is a translation of **TD** into **MSO** (which can actually be computed in exponential time). On the other hand, as regards **MSO**, its decision algorithms are far from feasible. Actually, already the satisfiability problem for **FO** over $\mathcal{K}_{fin}$ is non-elementary: neither its time nor its space complexity is bounded above by any tower of exponentials of a fixed height; cf. (Stockmeyer, 1974, Fact 5.1, p. 162). Now, it appears to be a most reasonable conjecture that **TD**-SAT is non-elementary. This remains to be proven, however. Further, it might be of interest to find a fragment $\mathcal{L}$ of **TD** (not obtained by syntactically banning $\neg$ or $\square$) whose satisfiability problem would indeed be elementarily decidable and which would be capable of describing independently occurring decision problems.

Acknowledgements. The author wishes to thank Lauri Hella for helpful discussions on formal languages and modal logics, and the anonymous referee for useful comments.

Bibliography

Blackburn, P., de Rijke, M., and Venema, Y., 2002. *Modal Logic*. Cambridge University Press, Cambridge.

Büchi, J., 1960. Weak second-order arithmetic and finite automata. *Zeitschrift für Matematische Logik und Grundlagen der Mathematik*, 6(1-6):66–92.

Ebbinghaus, H. and Flum, J., 1999. *Finite Model Theory*. Springer, Berlin.

Ebbinghaus, H., Flum, J., and Thomas, W., 1994. *Mathematical Logic*. Springer, New York.

Gabbay, D., Hodkinson, I., and Reynolds, M., 1994. *Temporal Logic, volume 1*. Oxford University Press, Oxford.

Hailperin, T., 1953. Quantification theory and empty individual-domains. *The Journal of Symbolic Logic*, 18(3):197–200.

Hella, L. and Tulenheimo, T., 2012. On the existence of a modal-logical basis for monadic second-order logic. To appear in *Journal of Logic and Computation*.

Hintikka, J., 1953. *Distributive Normal Forms in the Calculus of Predicates*. PhD thesis, University of Helsinki. Volume 6 of *Acta Philosophica Fennica*.

Jiang, T. and Ravikumar, B., 1991. A note on the space complexity of some decision problems for finite automata. *Information Processing Letters*, 40(1):25–31.

Kamp, H., 1968. *Tense Logic and the Theory of Linear Order*. PhD thesis, UCLA.

McNaughton, R. and Papert, S., 1971. *Counter-Free Automata*. The MIT press, Cambridge, Mass.

Mostowski, A., 1951. On the rules of proof in the pure functional calculus of the first order. *The Journal of Symbolic Logic*, 16(2):107–111.

114   *T. Tulenheimo*

Quine, W. V., 1954. Quantification and the empty domain. *The Journal of Symbolic Logic*, 19(3):177–179.

Salomaa, A., 1981. *Jewels of Formal Language Theory*. Computer Science Press, Rockville, Maryland.

Stockmeyer, L. J., 1974. *The Complexity of Decision Problems in Automata Theory and Logic*. PhD thesis, MIT.

Stockmeyer, L. J. and Meyer, A. R., 1973. Word problems requiring exponential time. In *Proc. 5th ACM Symp. on the Theory of Computing*, pages 1–9.

Tulenheimo, T., 2008. Modal logic of time division. In *Advances in Modal Logic vol. 7*, pages 363–387. College Publications, London.

Tulenheimo, T., 2011. Negation and temporal ontology. *Australasian Journal of Philosophy*, 89(1):101–114.

van Benthem, J., 1976. *Modal Correspondence Theory*. PhD thesis, University of Amsterdam.

von Wright, G. H., 1969. *Time, Change and Contradiction*. Cambridge University Press, Cambridge. Reprinted in von Wright (1983) pp. 115–131.

von Wright, G. H., 1983. *Philosophical Logic. Philosophical Papers vol. II*. Basil Blackwell, Oxford.

Williamson, T., 1999. A note on truth, satisfaction and the empty domain. *Analysis*, 59 (1):3–8.

PART II

ARGUMENTATION IN INTENSIONAL CONTEXTS

The Dialogic of Actually

NICOLAS CLERBOUT*

ABSTRACT.   We present and discuss four dialogical semantics for the propositional modal language with an Actuality operator. We take the occasion to recall the main features of the dialogical approach to modal logic in general. We make brief conceptual comparisons between the dialogical and the main-stream model theoretical approaches to meaning (with respect to the propositional modal language).

Introduction

The main purpose of this work is to delve into the dialogical approach of (propositional) Modal Logic with an Actuality operator, focusing on the specificities of the dialogical approach to meaning. In this respect, we shall be more concerned with giving a clear presentation of the dialogical framework (when applied to modal languages) than with systematically proving results. As was argued elsewhere — Rahman and Keiff (2005) or more recently Rahman (2010) — the dialogical framework provides a pragmatist theory of meaning alternative to the main-stream model-theoretical semantics.

This claim motivates the first detour we shall make in this work: we shall briefly recall the model-theoretical semantics for the basic modal language and the modal language with actuality operator. In both cases, we shall assume that the underlying logic is **S5**. There are various reasons why we make this detour. The main one is that part of this work studies the interrelations we can establish, and the differences we can highlight, between the dialogical approach and the better known model-theoretical approach.

We shall also use the occasion to make a second detour, namely to recall the main underlying ideas of the dialogical semantics for the basic

*Univ Lille Nord de France, F-59000 Lille France;
UdL3, STL, F-59653 Villeneuve d'Ascq France;
CNRS UMR8163.

modal language although this has been done previously.[1] Indeed our study partly consists of presenting the changes triggered by adding the Actuality operator to the language. Thus we give first the standard setting and then discuss the possible dialogical approaches to this operator. As a matter of fact we shall not only recall the standard dialogical semantics for **S5**: we shall also present a second, alternative, dialogical semantics for **S5**.

Moreover a large part of the features of the dialogical approach to Modal Logic underlies the dialogical approach to epistemic logics. For example, at the end of the day, the dialogical approaches to Public Announcement Logic and to Bonanno's Logic which are presented elsewhere in this volume[2] apply and extend some of the ideas which we present in Section 2.

From these remarks the paper is organized as follows:

In the first section we set the preliminaries of our study, recall the model-theoretical semantics for the logics we are interested in, and provide a general presentation of the dialogical framework. Section 2 is devoted to the presentation of our two alternative dialogical semantics for **S5**. Finally the third section delves into the various possible dialogical semantics for Modal Logic with an Actuality operator.

1   Preliminaries

In this section we give the basic definitions for our study. We also make some recalls on the well-known model-theoretical semantics for the languages we are interested in, so that we have benchmarks for a comparison with the dialogical approach.

Definition 1.1 (The Languages $\mathcal{L}$ and $\mathcal{L}_A$). The language $\mathcal{L}$ is simply the basic (propositional) modal language. It is built upon: (i) a denumerable set At of propositional variables; (ii) the connectives $\{\vee, \wedge, \rightarrow, \neg\}$; (iii) the unary operators $\{\Box, \Diamond\}$ and (iv) parentheses.

The set of formulas of $\mathcal{L}$ is given by:

$$\varphi ::= p \mid (\varphi \vee \psi) \mid (\varphi \wedge \psi) \mid (\varphi \rightarrow \psi) \mid \neg\varphi \mid \Box\varphi \mid \Diamond\varphi,$$

where $p \in At$.

The modal language $\mathcal{L}_A$ is obtained from $\mathcal{L}$ by adding the unary operator A to the primitives. The set of formulas of $\mathcal{L}_A$ is then given by:

---

[1]Rahman and Rückert (1999), Keiff (2009).
[2]See respectively Magnier's and Fiutek's papers in this volume.

$$\varphi ::= p \mid (\varphi \lor \psi) \mid (\varphi \land \psi) \mid (\varphi \rightarrow \psi) \mid \neg\varphi \mid \Box\varphi \mid \Diamond\varphi \mid \mathcal{A}\varphi,$$

where $p \in At$.

1.1 Model-Theoretical Semantics

We first recall that there are two possible, equivalent, ways to define **S5**-validity for the basic modal language. We then describe how the two different semantics apply to the language $\mathcal{L}_{\mathcal{A}}$.

Two Definitions of validity for **S5**

First we recall the usual Kripke semantics for **S5**.

Definition 1.2 (S5 Models). An **S5** *model* $\mathcal{M}$ is a triple (W, R, V) where W is a non-empty set of points or *worlds*, $R \subseteq W \times W$ is an equivalence relation on W (i.e., R is reflexive, symmetric and transitive) and $V :$ $At \longrightarrow \mathcal{P}(W)$ is a function which assigns a subset of W to each $p \in At$. The model $\mathcal{M}$ is said to be based on the *frame* $\mathcal{F} = (W, R)$.

Definition 1.3 (Satisfaction and Validity). The notion for a formula φ to be satisfied at world w in an **S5** model $\mathcal{M}$ is defined as follows:

(i) $\mathcal{M}, w \models p$ $\Leftrightarrow$ $w \in V(p)$

(ii) $\mathcal{M}, w \models \neg\varphi$ $\Leftrightarrow$ $\mathcal{M}, w \not\models \varphi$

(iii) $\mathcal{M}, w \models \varphi \lor \psi$ $\Leftrightarrow$ $\mathcal{M}, w \models \varphi$ or $\mathcal{M}, w \models \psi$

       $\mathcal{M}, w \models \varphi \land \psi$ $\Leftrightarrow$ $\mathcal{M}, w \models \varphi$ and $\mathcal{M}, w \models \psi$

       $\mathcal{M}, w \models \varphi \rightarrow \psi$ $\Leftrightarrow$ $\mathcal{M}, w \not\models \varphi$ or $\mathcal{M}, w \models \psi$

(iv) $\mathcal{M}, w \models \Box\varphi$ $\Leftrightarrow$ $\mathcal{M}, w' \models \varphi$ for every $w' \in W$

                                              such that wRw'.

       $\mathcal{M}, w \models \Diamond\varphi$ $\Leftrightarrow$ $\mathcal{M}, w' \models \varphi$ for some $w' \in W$

                                              such that wRw'.

     A formula $\varphi \in \mathcal{L}$ is **S5**-valid if for every w in every **S5** model $\mathcal{M}$, we have: $\mathcal{M}, w \models \varphi$.

     In the case of the basic modal language, there is a different but equivalent way to define satisfaction and validity in the sense of the logic **S5**. The point is that since R is an equivalence relation in **S5** models, we can as well think of each such model as a collection of models where every world is accessible from every world. In other words we could equally consider R to be a universal relation holding between any pair of worlds.[3] Another way to put this observation is that accessibility does

---

[3]See e.g. (Hughes and Cresswell, 1996, Chapter 3).

not really matter. Thus we can work with another semantics which we shall call **L**-semantics.

Definition 1.4 (L-Semantics). An **L** model for $\mathcal{L}$ is a pair (W, V) where W and V are the same as in Definition 1.2.

The notion for a formula to be satisfied at world w in an **L** model $\mathcal{M}$ is defined as in Definition 1.3 except for clause (iv) which becomes:

(iv) $\mathcal{M}, w \models_L \Box\varphi \quad \Leftrightarrow \quad \mathcal{M}, w' \models_L \varphi$ for every $w' \in W$

$\mathcal{M}, w \models_L \Diamond\varphi \quad \Leftrightarrow \quad \mathcal{M}, w' \models_L \varphi$ for some $w' \in W$

A formula $\varphi \in \mathcal{L}$ is **L**-valid if for every w in every **L** model $\mathcal{M}$, we have: $\mathcal{M}, w \models_L \varphi$.

Adding the Actuality Operator: semantics for $\mathcal{L}_A$

We see the semantic clause for the actuality operator in **S5** and **L** semantics. We shall see that the actuality operator introduces a difference between the two semantics: contrary to the case of $\mathcal{L}$, the two semantics are no longer equivalent in the case of $\mathcal{L}_A$.

Definition 1.5. An **S5A** model is a tuple $(W, @, R, V)$ where W, R and V are as in Definition 1.2 and @ is a designated member of W called the *actual world*.

The notion for a formula φ to be satisfied at w in an **S5A** model $\mathcal{M}$ is defined by extending Definition 1.3 with the following clause:

(v) $\mathcal{M}, w \models \mathcal{A}\varphi \quad \Leftrightarrow \quad \mathcal{M}, @ \models \varphi$

A formula $\varphi \in \mathcal{L}_A$ is **S5A**-valid if for every w in every **S5A** model $\mathcal{M}$, we have: $\mathcal{M}, w \models \varphi$.

Definition 1.6. An **LA** model is a triple $(W, @, V)$ where W, @ and V are the same as in Definition 1.5.

The notion for a formula φ to be satisfied at w in an **LA** model $\mathcal{M}$ is defined as in Definition 1.5 except for clause (iv) which becomes:

(iv) $\mathcal{M}, w \models_L \Box\varphi \quad \Leftrightarrow \quad \mathcal{M}, w' \models_L \varphi$ for every $w' \in W$

$\mathcal{M}, w \models_L \Diamond\varphi \quad \Leftrightarrow \quad \mathcal{M}, w' \models_L \varphi$ for some $w' \in W$

A formula $\varphi \in \mathcal{L}_A$ is **LA**-valid if for every w in every **LA** model $\mathcal{M}$, we have: $\mathcal{M}, w \models_L \varphi$.

Contrary to the case of $\mathcal{L}$, accessibility *does* matter in the case of $\mathcal{L}_A$. The semantics for the operator $\mathcal{A}$ leads to a difference between **S5A** and **LA** semantics in the following way: it is not the case that for any formula φ of $\mathcal{L}_A$, φ is **S5A**-valid if and only if φ is **LA**-valid. To prove this, it is enough to exhibit a formula which is valid in one of our semantics but not valid in the other one. Take $\Box p \to Ap$.[4]

On the one hand it is **LA**-valid. Indeed suppose $\mathcal{M}, w \models_L \Box p$, for arbitrary **LA** model $\mathcal{M}$ and $w \in \mathcal{M}$. Then for any $w' \in \mathcal{M}$, we have: $\mathcal{M}, w' \models_L p$. In particular, $\mathcal{M}, @ \models_L p$. Now suppose $\mathcal{M}, w \not\models_L Ap$. Then $\mathcal{M}, @ \not\models_L p$. This is a contradiction.

On the other hand, it is not **S5A**-valid. We construct a counter-model. Consider $\mathcal{M}' = (W, @, R, V)$ such that:

- $W = \{@, w_1\}$
- $R = \{\langle @, @ \rangle, \langle w_1, w_1 \rangle\}$
- $V(p) = \{w_1\}$

By Definition 1.5 we have $\mathcal{M}', w_1 \models \Box p$ but $\mathcal{M}', w_1 \not\models Ap$ because $@ \notin V(p)$.

In semantics such as **S5A** and **LA**, it is possible to introduce a distinct, less general, notion of validity often called "real-world" validity.[5] In fact, some would argue that such an introduction is not only possible but *desirable*.[6] We shall not commit ourselves with respect to the desirability of such a notion, and restrict ourselves to formulating it (and to further study it from the dialogical perspective).

Definition 1.7 (Real-World Validity). A formula $\varphi \in \mathcal{L}_A$ is @-valid if for every **S5A** model $\mathcal{M}$, we have: $\mathcal{M}, @ \models \varphi$ (or equivalently if for every **LA** model $\mathcal{M}$ we have: $\mathcal{M}, @ \models_L \varphi$).

Now that we have recalled the model-theoretical notions that we are interested in, let us move to a general introduction to the dialogical approach.

1.2 The Dialogical Approach (Generalities)

For the dialogical approach, we need to extend the language in the following way:

Definition 1.8. The language $\mathcal{L}^{\mathcal{D}}$ (respectively $\mathcal{L}_A^{\mathcal{D}}$) is obtained by extending $\mathcal{L}$ (respectively $\mathcal{L}_A$) with:

- Two labels **P** and **O** standing for two *players*, respectively the Proponent and the Opponent.

---

[4]This example is from Crossley and Humberstone (1977).
[5]Crossley and Humberstone (1977).
[6]For example, Williamson in Williamson (2007).

- A non-empty (denumerable) set $\mathbb{C}$ of *dialogical contexts* c_i, with $i \in \mathbb{N}$.

An *expression* of $\mathcal{L}^{\mathcal{D}}$ is either a formula of $\mathcal{L}$ or one of the following seven strings:

$$?_L \, ; \, ?_R \, ; \, ?_\vee \, ; \, ?_\diamond \, ; \, ?_{\square/c_i} \, ; \, n := j \, ; \, m := k,$$

where $c_i \in \mathbb{C}$ and j, k are symbols for (not necessarily distinct) positive integers that are assigned to the variables n and m respectively. The positive integers j and k denote what we will call later *repetition ranks*.[7]

An expression of $\mathcal{L}_A^{\mathcal{D}}$ is either an expression of $\mathcal{L}^{\mathcal{D}}$ or one of the following two strings:

$$?_A \, ; \, \eta := c_i.$$

The string $\eta := c_i$ stands for the possibility to set a certain dialogical context c_i to have a special status in a play. We will give more details in Section 3.

Comments. There are two differences between dialogical contexts and model-theoretical worlds. First, the dialogical semantics never assumes a given accessibility relation between contexts, while in the case of at least some normal modal logics, models necessarily feature such a relation between worlds. The dialogical framework rather stresses the *use* of contexts in terms of choices by the player (see Section 2.3). In addition to the accessibility relation, model-theoretical worlds are also characterized by the contingent information given by the valuation function. Therefore, worlds are at the heart of the definition of meaning in terms of truth and falsity. Dialogical contexts, on the other hand, are nothing more than labels which occur as parts of players' moves and which use is governed by game rules. Their role in the dialogical theory of meaning is thus independent from the notion of truth.

Definition 1.9 (Moves). Every *move* is an expression of the form $X\text{-}e\text{-}c_i$ where $X \in \{O, P\}$, e is an expression and $c_i \in \mathbb{C}$.

A *play* is a legal sequence of moves. A *dialogue* is a terminal play (in the sense of *SR4* below). Finally, the dialogical game for φ, written $\mathcal{D}(\varphi)$, is the set of all plays with φ as the thesis (see the starting rule *SR0*). The game rules specify if a given sequence of moves is legal or not, i.e., if it is a play. There are two kinds of game rules: *particle rules* and *structural rules*. Particle rules define the *local* meaning of logical constants and

---

[7]See Rules *SR0* and *SR1* below.

structural rules extend the semantics. We say that the rules govern the *play level*. We shall see that the notion of satisfaction (truth) has no role at the play level. However we can relate the dialogical approach to the model-theoretical one by working at the *strategic level*: the existence of a winning strategy for one of the players in a given dialogical game coincides with a certain notion of validity. We now delve into details by studying the dialogical approach to **S5**.

2 Standard Modal Dialogical Logic (for S5)

In this section, we present standard modal dialogical logic, and in particular the dialogical semantics for **S5** and **L**. The seminal paper on modal dialogics is Rahman and Rückert (1999). Other presentations can be found, e.g., in Keiff (2009) and Fontaine and Redmond (2008). Compared with these publications, this section use different formulations for the structural rules in order to formulate the dialogical semantics exclusively in terms of the interaction between the two players.[8] Moreover, we use *repetition ranks* which allow a simpler formulation of the structural rules and have an important role for the metatheory of dialogical games.[9] Finally, contrary to the quoted works, we present and discuss two dialogical semantics for the modal logic **S5**. The reason why we present both alternatives is that we want to compare the strategic levels of both systems with **S5** and **L** validity as introduced in Section 1.

2.1 Particle Rules

Particle rules give an abstract description of how the game may proceed *locally* (i.e., independently of any particular game situation) depending only upon the logical form of formulas. In the following tables, we use **X** and **Y** as variables for **P** and **O**, assuming $X \neq Y$.

(Utterance)	$X\text{-}\varphi \vee \psi\text{-}c_i$	$X\text{-}\varphi \wedge \psi\text{-}c_i$	$X\text{-}\varphi \to \psi\text{-}c_i$	$X\text{-}\neg\varphi\text{-}c_i$
(Challenge)	$Y\text{-}?_\vee\text{-}c_i$	$Y\text{-}?_{\wedge_1}\text{-}c_i$ or $Y\text{-}?_{\wedge_2}\text{-}c_i$	$Y\text{-}\varphi\text{-}\psi$	$Y\text{-}\varphi\text{-}c_i$
(Defence)	$X\text{-}\varphi\text{-}c_i$ or $X\text{-}\psi\text{-}c_i$	$X\text{-}\varphi\text{-}c_i$ or $X\text{-}\psi\text{-}c_i$	$X\text{-}\psi\text{-}c_i$	$--$

---

[8] As opposed to Fontaine and Redmond (2008) in which the model-theoretical notion of accessibility between worlds is introduced in the rules.

[9] See Clerbout (2012).

(Utterance)	$X\text{-}\Diamond\varphi\text{-}c_i$	$X\text{-}\Box\varphi\text{-}c_i$
(Challenge)	$Y\text{-}?_\Diamond\text{-}c_i$	$Y\text{-}?_{\Box/c_j}\text{-}c_i$
(Defence)	$X\text{-}\varphi\text{-}c_j$	$X\text{-}\varphi\text{-}c_j$

Comments. Particle rules are triples of moves. Following the standard dialogical terminology, the second and third members are respectively called "Challenge" and "Defence". But, as Rahman (2010) has discussed, no strategical underpinning should be associated with this terminology.

Particle rules are player-independent or symmetric (hence the use of the variables X and Y): that is one of the reasons why we say that these rules are abstract, and constitutes an important feature of the dialogical framework. See Rahman et al. (2009) and especially Rahman (2010) for discussions on this topic.

Particle rules for disjunction and conjunction involve an alternative for one of the players. We say that it is X's (respectively Y's) *choice* to play according to one or the other alternative: in the case of the disjunction X chooses which disjunct he asserts while in the case of the conjunction Y chooses which conjunct he asks for. Similarly, particle rules for $\Box$ and $\Diamond$ involve a choice of a context by one of the players: Y chooses which context he asks for in the case of $\Box$ and X chooses the context in the case of $\Diamond$. We say that a player "chooses c_j at c_i".

2.2 Structural Rules

Structural rules govern the general organization of plays by describing how they begin, how they end and how the winner of the play is decided. They also put additional constraints on legality of moves. Thus they define the conditions under which a play is legal and belongs to a dialogical game.

SR0 (Starting Rule): Any play for φ starts with P uttering φ at context c_1 (if possible). The formula φ is called the *thesis* and $c_1 \in \mathbb{C}$ is called the initial context. Then first O and next P each choose a positive integer as the value of n and m respectively, called their *repetition rank*. The game then goes on with O and P playing alternately in accordance with the other rules.

Comments. The first part of the rule establishes that the player who utters the thesis is the Proponent. The proviso "if possible" is motivated by the Formal Rule *SR2* below: if φ is atomic then the Proponent cannot utter it. Repetition ranks are the reason why we defined 'n := j' and 'm := k' as expressions in Definition 1.8. Their role is given by the next structural rule.

SR1 (Game-playing Rule): Let r be **X**'s repetition rank. Whenever he has a turn to play, **X** can challenge any previous **Y**-move, or defend against any previous **Y**-challenge, at most r times.

Comments. Repetition ranks thus ensure that every play in a dialogical game is of finite length. It is important because the rule *SR*4 defines victory in terms of the end of a play. The study of repetition ranks is important for the meta-theory of Dialogical Logic but in this work we shall not go into details on this topic. The rule *SR*1 deals with more than the length of plays, since it also sets the general conditions under which a player can perform a challenge or a defence.[10]

SR2 (Formal Rule): Only **O** can introduce atomic formulas. If e is an atomic formula then for any context c, **P** can utter e at context c only if **O** uttered it previously.

Comments. The Formal Rule introduces an asymmetry in the game rules. It governs the use, and thus the meaning, of atomic formulas. The crucial point here is that this meaning is completely independent from the notion of satisfaction (truth). Neither the rights of **O** nor the obligations of **P** are defined with respect to the truth value of the atomic formulas at stake.[11]

We say that a context is *new* if it never occurred previously in the play.

SR3 (Choice of Context Rule): When defending a ◇ or challenging a □, **O** can choose any c_j at c_i. **P** can choose any c_j at c_i provided c_j is not new.

Rule SR3 establishes **P**'s rights with respect to the choice of a dialogical context. Again there are (many) other possible versions for this rule.[12] In fact we shall also deal with the following rule in this article:

SR3': When defending a ◇ or challenging a □, **O** can choose any c_j at c_i. The set of dialogical contexts which **P** can choose at an arbitrary context c_i is given by:

---

[10]The point is that there can be various versions for the Game-playing Rule, the most well-known other option being the intuitionistic version:

SR1i (Intuitionistic Game-playing Rule): Let r be **X**'s repetition rank. Whenever he has a turn to play, **X** can challenge any previous **Y**-move at most r times, or he can defend against **Y**'s *last non answered* challenge.

[11]Notice that it is possible to design dialogical systems in which truth values are assumed. See Rahman and Keiff (2005), Rahman and Tulenheimo (2009).

[12]Rahman and Rückert (1999), Keiff (2009).

(*a*) If **O** chose c_j from c_i beforehand then **P** can choose c_j at c_i.
(*b*) **P** can choose c_i at c_i.
(*c*) If **O** chose c_i at c_j beforehand then **P** can choose c_j at c_i.
(*d*) If **P** can choose c_k at c_j and c_j at c_i then **P** can choose c_k at c_i.
(*e*) **P** can choose no other dialogical context at c_i.

Comments. These clauses are the obvious dialogical counterparts of the frame conditions in model-theoretical semantics. Once again, our formulation is a bit different from previous works. In Rahman and Rückert (1999) and Keiff (2009), an implicit relation "successor of" is encoded in the syntax of dialogical contexts, and the 'Choice of context' rule is formulated in terms of this relation. We prefer to make explicit the fact that the use of contexts is determined by the interaction between the players: legal choices of contexts for **P** are mostly determined by the choices **O** previously made.

SR4 (Winning Rule): **X** wins the current play iff it is **Y**'s turn to move and he cannot play (he has no further allowed move). We say that the play is **X**-terminal.

Comments. This situation can occur for **Y** in various cases triggered by the other structural rules and/or by the fact that there is no defence for a negation. We will give examples in Section 2.3.

It is quite easy to adapt or extend the semantics we presented to give an account of various epistemic logics. Briefly, epistemic operators get their meaning in a way similar to that of the modal operators of our language. In fact, as long as we assume the standard notion of knowledge (**S5**), we obtain the dialogical semantics for the (mono-agent) logic of knowledge just by reading □ as the knowledge operator K. For the multi-agent case, see Magnier's article in this volume. In the case of languages featuring several different kinds of modality, the basic idea is that different structural rules define **P**'s rights for each kind of operator. For an application related to epistemic logic, see Fiutek's paper in this volume.

2.3 The strategic level and validity

Let *Part* denote the set of particle rules presented in Section 2.1. With the structural rules we just presented, we can define the following two dialogical systems:

$$\mathcal{D}_{\mathbf{S5}(1)} = \quad Part \cup \{\text{SR0, SR1, SR2, SR3, SR4}\}$$
$$\mathcal{D}_{\mathbf{S5}(2)} = \quad Part \cup \{\text{SR0, SR1, SR2, SR3', SR4}\}$$

We shall see that, when studied at the level of strategies, the two dialogical semantics meet the model-theoretical semantics of Section 1 and in particular the notion of **S5**-validity (or **L**-validity, since the two are equivalent). Before that let us give two examples.

Example 2.1. Consider the following play for $\Diamond p \to \Box \Diamond p$ with rules of $\mathcal{D}_{\mathbf{S5}(1)}$:

		O				**P**		
					$\Diamond p \to \Box \Diamond p$	c_1	(0)
(1)	c_1	$n := 1$			$m := 2$	c_1	(2)
(3)	c_1	$\Diamond p$	(0)		$\Box \Diamond p$	c_1	(4)
(5)	c_1	$?_{\Box / c_2}$	(4)		$\Diamond p$	c_2	(6)
(7)	c_2	$?_\Diamond$	(6)		p	c_3	(10)
(9)	c_3	p		(3)	$?_\Diamond$	c_1	(8)

Comments. The play starts by **P** uttering the thesis at the initial dialogical context. The external columns keep track of the order of the moves.[13] When players perform challenges, the inner columns keep track of the challenged move. Defences are written on the same line as the corresponding challenges, hence the position of move (10).

Once the players have chosen their repetition ranks, **O** challenges the thesis according to the particle rule for material implication. Player **P** defends with move (4).[14] The play proceeds according to the rules of $\mathcal{D}_{\mathbf{S5}(1)}$. The important point here is that **P** cannot defend himself immediately against **O**'s move (7) because of the formal rule SR2. Thus he counterattacks with move (8). Since he is allowed to do so by rule SR3, he chooses the very context **O** chose at move (9) for his own move (10). Player **P** wins the play because **O** has no further possible move: given her repetition rank, there are no remaining challenges to do or to answer for **O**.

This figure is also a play for φ in $\mathcal{D}_{\mathbf{S5}(2)}$. But the reason why **P** is allowed to choose c_3 at move 10 is a bit less straightforward. First, we notice that **O** made the following choices of contexts: c_2 at c_1 (move 5), c_3 at c_1 (move 9). Thus **P** is allowed to make the same choices. Now

---

[13]By convention, the thesis is numbered 0, and since choices of repetition ranks are moves we assign them a number in the order of moves.

[14]Notice that he could as well postpone the defence and counter-attack, i.e., he could challenge **O**'s move (3).

because of clause (c) of SR3', **P** is allowed to choose c_1 at c_2. Thus **P** can choose c_3 at c_1 and c_1 at c_2. Hence, by clause (d), **P** can choose c_3 at c_2 at move 10 and wins the play. This case is quite simple, but it is not difficult to find examples where applying rule $SR3'$ is even less straightforward. It may be helpful to keep explicitly track of **P**'s rights during the course of a play, as in Keiff (2007) or Magnier's paper in this volume.

We previously made some brief comparisons with model-theoretical semantics, mostly to stress the specificities of the dialogical approach to meaning and in particular the fact that the notion of truth has no role in it. Despite these specificities, there is a point at which the two kinds of semantics coincide, namely the notion of validity. We mentioned that this connexion occurs at the strategic level and we now give more details.

Definition 2.1 (Strategy). A *strategy* for player **X** in $\mathcal{D}(\varphi)$, or **X**-strategy for short, is a function which yields a legal move — if any — for each play at which it is **X**'s turn to move.

A strategy is in fact a complete plan of action: it tells to player **X** how to play against any sequence of moves by **Y**. We are mainly interested in a particular kind of strategy:

Definition 2.2 (Winning Strategy). An **X**-strategy is *winning* if following it leads to a win for **X** — in the sense of SR4 — no matter how **Y** plays.

The level of winning strategies is the one where dialogical semantics meet model-theoretical semantics. The relation between the two approaches is given by the following Theorem:

Theorem 2.1. There is a winning **P**-strategy for φ in $\mathcal{D}_{\mathbf{S5}(1)}(\varphi)$ if and only if φ is **L**-valid.

We only give the outlines of the proof. Suppose first that there is a winning **P**-strategy S in $\mathcal{D}_{\mathbf{S5}(1)}(\varphi)$. We take the extensive form $\mathfrak{S}$ of S from the extensive form $\mathfrak{E}(\varphi)$ of $\mathcal{D}_{\mathbf{S5}(1)}(\varphi)$. Relevant definitions are given in the appendix. We then define a model-theoretical interpretation of the branches of this tree.[15] In this interpretation, the Opponent's moves are understood as attempts to build a counter-model to the thesis and

---

[15]Similar to what is done in the case of modal tableaux: see, e.g., Fitting and Mendelsohn (1998), chapter 2.

the fact that the Proponent can win against every attempt means that there is no such counter-model.

In order to prove the other direction of Theorem 2.1, we prove the contrapositive. Suppose then that there is no winning **P**-strategy in $\mathcal{D}_{\mathbf{S5}(1)}(\varphi)$. Then there is a winning **O**-strategy in the game.[16] Under the model-theoretical interpretation, such a strategy is understood as establishing the existence of a counter-model to the thesis, hence φ is not valid.

Further results can be proven from Theorem 2.1 by means of the following Lemma:

Lemma 2.1. There is a winning **P**-strategy in $\mathcal{D}_{\mathbf{S5}(1)}(\varphi)$ if and only if there is a winning **P**-strategy for φ in $\mathcal{D}_{\mathbf{S5}(2)}(\varphi)$.

Since $\mathcal{D}_{\mathbf{S5}(1)}$ and $\mathcal{D}_{\mathbf{S5}(2)}$ differ only in terms of SR3, it is enough to show that SR3 and SR3' are equivalent. In other words: we have to show that a context is not new if and only if it obeys one of the clauses of SR3', which is routine (especially the left-to-right part). Thus we do not go into more details.

Now since **S5**-validity and **L**-validity coincide, we immediately get from Theorem 2.1 and Lemma 2.1:

- There is a winning **P**-strategy for φ in $\mathcal{D}_{\mathbf{S5}(1)}$ if and only if φ is **S5**-valid.

- There is a winning **P**-strategy for φ in $\mathcal{D}_{\mathbf{S5}(2)}$ if and only if φ is **S5**-valid.

- There is a winning **P**-strategy for φ in $\mathcal{D}_{\mathbf{S5}(2)}$ if and only if φ is **L**-valid.

As a last remark on standard modal dialogical logic, let us recall that variants of rule SR3 can establish other (combinations of) permissions for **P** with respect to choice of contexts. Suitable other versions for normal modal logics **K**, **T**, **B**, **S4** and **D** are presented in Rahman and Rückert (1999) and Keiff (2009). The dialogical approach to some non-normal logics is presented in Rahman (2009).

---

[16]Since dialogical games are zero-sum games without tie and where each play terminates after a finite number of moves, the Gale-Stewart Theorem (Gale and Stewart, 1953) applies and we have: **X** has a winning strategy in $\mathcal{D}_{\mathbf{S5}(1)}(\varphi)$ if and only if **Y** does not have a winning strategy in $\mathcal{D}_{\mathbf{S5}(1)}(\varphi)$. That is, Dialogical Games are *determined*.

3   Dialogical semantics for $\mathcal{L}_A$

We move to the dialogical outlook on (modal language with) the actuality operator $\mathcal{A}$. We still assume that the underlying logic is **S5**, thus
most of the rules are the same as in the systems we have presented so
far. In order to give a dialogical semantics for $\mathcal{L}_A$, we need to carry out
two tasks. First, since $\mathcal{A}$ is a logical constant, we need to give its local
semantics, which we do by providing a particle rule for it. Second, we
need to think of the possible structural influence of this operator. In
fact we shall present two kinds of semantics which rely on two possible
particle rules for $\mathcal{A}$.

3.1   The particle rule for $\mathcal{A}$

We shall discuss the following two particle rules for the Actuality operator:

(Utterance)	**X**-$\mathcal{A}\varphi$-c
(Challenge)	**Y**-?$_A$-c
(Defence)	**X**-φ-c_1

PR$\mathcal{A}$1

(Utterance)	**X**-$\mathcal{A}\varphi$-c
(Challenge)	**Y**-?$_A$-c
(Defence)	**X**-φ-η

PR$\mathcal{A}$2

where η is the designated dialogical context.[17]

The basic idea is the same in both rules: no matter which context
occurs in the first utterance, the defence consists in uttering φ at a
precise, designated context. The two rules differ in the context which
is the designated one. In the first rule it is set to be the initial context
c_1 of the play, while in the second rule the designated context, though
constant through a play, is not necessarily c_1. Thus PR$\mathcal{A}$1 is a special
case of PR$\mathcal{A}$2. Notice that contrary to the particle rules for □ and ◇ the
change of context in PR$\mathcal{A}$i does not involve any choice by the players at
the local level.

Actually the second rule PR$\mathcal{A}$2 *is* related to the notion of choice, but
not as part of the local meaning of $\mathcal{A}$. The point is that the value of η
must be decided: it is done by means of a choice by one of the players at
the beginning of the play — see SR0(η) below. Furthermore the one to
choose it must be **O** so that **P** cannot make the game conditions easier
for himself. Since this is an asymmetric argument, it is clear that the
choice of the designated context must be governed by a structural rule.

---

[17] As introduced when defining expressions of $\mathcal{L}_A^{\mathcal{D}}$.

We shall go into more details in Section 3.3. Before that let us start with the dialogical semantics based on PRA1.

3.2 Dialogical semantics with Rule PRA1

As we have discussed in Section 1, adding the operator A makes an important difference with respect to the question of validity. Hence it shall make a difference in terms of winning strategies in dialogical games. Thus we shall be quite careful and consider the two cases we presented in Section 2. Our first two dialogical semantics, $\mathcal{D}_{A(1)}$ and $\mathcal{D}_{A(2)}$, are therefore obtained by adding PRA1 to $\mathcal{D}_{\mathbf{S5}(1)}$ and $\mathcal{D}_{\mathbf{S5}(2)}$ respectively. Hence:

$$\mathcal{D}_{A(1)} = \mathcal{D}_{\mathbf{S5}(1)} \cup \{\text{PR}A1\}.$$
$$\mathcal{D}_{A(2)} = \mathcal{D}_{\mathbf{S5}(2)} \cup \{\text{PR}A1\}.$$

Example 3.1. A play for $A(Ap \to p)$ with rules of $\mathcal{D}_{A(1)}$.

		O				P		
						$A(Ap \to p)$	c_1	(0)
(1)	c_1	n := 1				m := 2	c_1	(2)
(3)	c_1	?$_A$	(0)			$Ap \to p$	c_1	(4)
(5)	c_1	Ap	(4)			p	c_1	(8)
(7)	c_1	p		(5)		?$_A$	c_1	(6)

$\mathcal{D}_{A(1)}$ *and* $\mathcal{D}_{A(2)}$: *the strategic level*

First, let us observe that it is not the case that there is a winning **P**-strategy for φ in $\mathcal{D}_{A(1)}$ iff φ is **LA**-valid. Consider for example $Ap \to p$. On the one hand it is straightforward from Definition 1.6 that it is not **LA**-valid. On the other hand, there is a winning **P** strategy in $\mathcal{D}_{A(1)}(Ap \to p)$, as can be seen from an obvious generalization of the following play:

		O				P		
						$Ap \to p$	c_1	(0)
(1)	c_1	n := 1				m := 2	c_1	(2)
(3)	c_1	Ap	(0)			p	c_1	(6)
(5)	c_1	p		(3)		?$_A$	c_1	(4)

Similarly, it is not the case that there is a winning **P**-strategy for φ in $\mathcal{D}_{A(2)}$ iff φ is **S5A**-valid. The formula $Ap \to p$ illustrates this too, but let us take an example where the accessibility relation has a role.

Consider $A\Box p \to \Box p$. On the one hand, it is straightforward from Definition 1.5 that it is not **S5A**-valid. On the other hand, an obvious generalization of the following play shows that there is a winning **P**-strategy in $\mathcal{D}_{A(2)}(A\Box p \to \Box p)$:

		O			P		
					$A\Box p \to \Box p$	c_1	(0)
(1)	c_1	n := 1			m := 2	c_1	(2)
(3)	c_1	$A\Box p$	(0)		$\Box p$	c_1	(4)
(5)	c_1	$?_{\Box/c_2}$	(4)		p	c_2	(10)
(7)	c_1	$\Box p$		(3)	$?_A$	c_1	(6)
(9)	c_2	p		(7)	$?_{\Box/c_2}$	c_1	(8)

Comments. Since **O** herself chose c_2 from c_1 with her move (5), **P** can do the same with his move (9) and wins the play.

Even if it is not with **LA** or **S5A**-validity, the strategic level of $\mathcal{D}_{A(1)}$ and $\mathcal{D}_{A(2)}$ still can be related to the model-theoretical semantics presented in section 1. But in this case the connexion occurs at the level of real-world validity (Definition 1.7).

Theorem 3.1. There is a winning **P**-strategy for φ in $\mathcal{D}_{A(1)}$ iff φ is @-valid.

The proof is similar to the case of Theorem 2.1. There is one crucial difference, though: in the model-theoretical interpretation of strategies, the initial context is no longer arbitrary within $\mathcal{D}_{A(1)}$ (or $\mathcal{D}_{A(2)}$). The point is that when associating dialogical contexts with model-theoretical worlds, we always have to assign the actual world to the initial context, because of our local rule for A. The immediate consequence is that we are no longer ensured that the thesis is always satisfied at any world, but only at the actual one, which is the very definition of @-validity. We can prove in a similar way:

Theorem 3.2. There is a winning **P**-strategy for φ in $\mathcal{D}_{A(2)}$ iff φ is @-valid.

3.3   Dialogical semantics with Rule $PRA2$

The second possible local meaning for A takes it that the designated context need not to be the initial one. As we mentioned, there is no choice of context to be made by the players on the local level in $PRA2$. On the other hand the value of η is needed so that players can actually apply $PRA2$ during a play. This value must be fixed as early as possible in a play and we have argued it must be chosen by **O**. Thus we introduce the following slightly different Starting Rule:

SR0(η): Any play for φ starts with **P** uttering φ at context c_1 (if possible). The formula φ is called the *thesis* and $c_1 \in \mathbb{C}$ is called the initial context. Then **O** chooses the value of η and her repetition rank. After that, **P** choose his repetition rank and the game goes on with **O** and **P** playing alternately in accordance with the other rules.

The dialogical systems $\mathcal{D}_{A(3)}$ and $\mathcal{D}_{A(4)}$ are similar respectively to $\mathcal{D}_{A(1)}$ and $\mathcal{D}_{A(2)}$ except that $PRA1$ is replaced by $PRA2$ and $SR0$ is replaced by $SR0(\eta)$.

Example 3.2. Consider the following play for $A(Ap \rightarrow p)$ in $\mathcal{D}_{A(3)}$:

		O				**P**		
						$A(Ap \rightarrow p)$	c_1	(0)
(1)	c_1	$\eta = c_2$ n := 1				m := 2	c_1	(2)
(3)	c_1	$?_A$	(0)			$Ap \rightarrow p$	c_2	(4)
(5)	c_2	Ap	(4)			p	c_2	(8)
(7)	c_2	p			(5)	$?_A$	c_2	(6)

Comments. The play is won by **P**. This example differs from Example 3.1 insofar as the designated context is no longer c_1 but the one chosen by **O**, namely c_2.

$\mathcal{D}_{A(3)}$ and $\mathcal{D}_{A(4)}$: the strategic level

The idea of $PRA2$ is that the designated context is not necessarily the initial context. Hence the initial context c_1 shall be associated with an arbitrary world when applying our model-theoretical interpretation. This suggests that we can restore a connexion with general validity.

Theorem 3.3. There is a winning **P**-strategy for φ in $\mathcal{D}_{A(3)}$ if and only if φ is **LA**-valid.

The proof follows the same ideas as in the cases of the previous theorems. In this case, the initial context is associated with an arbitrary world again. Then we simply set that η is associated with the world designated to be the actual one. Similarly we have:

Theorem 3.4. There is a winning **P**-strategy for φ in $\mathcal{D}_{A(4)}$ if and only if φ is **S5A**-valid.

Notice that η is never new, but is not necessarily available for **P** by $SR3'$. In other words, it is not the case that there is a winning **P**-strategy for φ in $\mathcal{D}_{A(3)}$ iff there is one in $\mathcal{D}_{A(4)}$.

Example 3.3. To illustrate this, let us look at two plays for the same formula. The first is played with rules of $\mathcal{D}_{A(3)}$ and the second one with rules of $\mathcal{D}_{A(4)}$.

		O			**P**		
					$\Box p \to \mathcal{A}p$	c_1	(0)
(1)	c_1	$\eta = c_2$ n := 1			m := 2	c_1	(2)
(3)	c_1	$\Box p$	(0)		$\mathcal{A}p$	c_1	(4)
(5)	c_1	$?_A$	(4)		p	c_2	(8)
(7)	c_2	p		(3)	$?_{\Box/c_2}$	c_1	(6)

Comments. The play is won by **P**. Player **O** sets the designated context to be different from c_1. However, **P** is allowed to choose c_2 for his move (6) since it is not new.

		O			**P**		
					$\Box p \to \mathcal{A}p$	c_1	(0)
(1)	c_1	$\eta = c_2$ n := 1			m := 2	c_1	(2)
(3)	c_1	$\Box p$	(0)		$\mathcal{A}p$	c_1	(4)
(5)	c_1	$?_A$	(4)				
(7)	c_1	p		(3)	$?_{\Box/c_1}$	c_1	(6)

Comments. Since **O** did not choose c_2 from c_1 by means of a particle rule for a modal operator, **P** cannot choose c_2 from c_1. The best he can do is move (6). But it does not help him answering **O**'s move (5). Player **P** has no further allowed move: he loses the play.

The point is that **O** never chooses the value of η by applying a particle rule for a modal operator. In other words the choice of η does not interact with $SR3'$, i.e., the designated context can be totally unrelated to the other contexts involved in the play. When translated in model-theoretical terms, it is precisely the reason why some **LA**-valid formulas are not **S5A**-valid.

4   Concluding remarks and further developments

We discussed the general ideas guiding the dialogical approach to meaning with respect to modal languages. We mentioned how (some of) these ideas underlie the dialogical approach to epistemic logics (epistemic operators in multi-agent settings or for belief revision), without going into details. We rather focused on propositional modal logic with an actuality operator.

We presented various dialogical semantics and explained how they relate to various model-theoretical notions of validity. To sum up, we argued that the following coincidences hold:

Winning **P**-strategy	Model-Theoretical validity
$\mathcal{D}_{\mathbf{S5}(1)}$	**S5** and **S5R**-validity
$\mathcal{D}_{\mathbf{S5}(2)}$	**S5R** and **S5**-validity
$\mathcal{D}_{\mathcal{A}(1)}$	**@**-validity
$\mathcal{D}_{\mathcal{A}(2)}$	**@**-validity
$\mathcal{D}_{\mathcal{A}(3)}$	**S5A**-validity
$\mathcal{D}_{\mathcal{A}(4)}$	**S5AR**-validity

We presented two kinds of dialogical semantics for $\mathcal{L}_{\mathcal{A}}$ which are based on two different particle rules for $\mathcal{A}$. There is a question that one might be interested in which we did not mention: should we make a choice between the two types of semantics and, if so, which one should we choose? This question is important for example if one wants to decide which one between @-validity or validity, is the best (or the right) notion of validity to stand for *logical truth*. But this goes beyond the purpose of this work. We shall keep it for the future developments, which we now shortly discuss.

A Modal Logic with an actuality operator raises important philosophical questions about the notion of necessity — see Crossley and Humberstone (1977), Davies and Humberstone (1980). In particular, it leads to the question of the relation between necessity and validity.[18] In future work we shall study the dialogical approach to these problems and the way the dialogical outlook contributes to these issues:

1. Crossley and Humberstone (1977) and Davies and Humberstone (1980) argue that the interaction between $\mathcal{A}$ and $\square$ leads to questioning whether $\square$ is the best candidate to stand for necessity in $\mathcal{L}_{\mathcal{A}}$. From this they consider various alternatives, such as understanding *necessary* as *true at whichever world is the actual one*. It

---

[18]Zalta (1988).

would be interesting to see if a dialogical reconstruction of such approaches provides new insights into the matter.

2. The interest of introducing A to the language increases a lot when one considers the interactions of A, $\square$ and quantifiers. Another development thus consists in extending the study we performed in Section 3 to the first-order case. Of course the two developments are not mutually exclusive.

Acknowledgements. I am grateful to anonymous referees for their helpful comments. I am especially thankful to the participants in the Symposium *Argumentation in Intentional Contexts: Knowledge, Belief, Dialogues* (Sevilla, May 2010) for their comments and questions. Many thanks to Tero Tulenheimo for discussions after the Symposium.

A   Appendix. Some precisions about the proofs

In order to prove the various theorems stated in the article, we work with *extensive forms* of winning strategies. We give relevant definitions and the main ideas of the proof in the case of Theorem 2.1.

A.1   Extensive forms

Definition A.1 (Extensive Form of a Dialogical Game). The extensive form of the dialogical game for φ, written $\mathfrak{E}(\varphi)$, is the (smallest) tree such that:

E_1. Nodes are labelled with triples (l, α, k) where l denotes the level of the node in the branch (the place of the move in a play), α denotes a move and k denotes the level of the challenged move, in case α is a challenge. The root is labelled with $(0, \langle \mathbf{P}\text{-}\varphi\text{-} c_1 \rangle, \emptyset)$.

E_2. Each node labelled with an **X**-move is called a *decision node for* **Y**.

E_3. Splits occur when a player has a choice of any kind between several moves: a decision node for **X** has more than one immediate successor if there is more than one legal move for **X**.

A particular *branch* of such a tree represents a particular terminal play in the game, and the successor relation stands for the order in which moves are performed in this play. A *terminal node* is a node with no successor. By *SR4* we have: if the terminal node of a play is a decision node for **Y** (or, equivalently, is labelled with an **X**-move), then **X** wins this play.

Definition A.2 (Extensive form of Strategies). The extensive form of an **X**-strategy is the fragment $\mathfrak{S}_X$ of $\mathfrak{E}(\varphi)$ such that:

S_1 The root of $\mathfrak{S}_X$ is the root of $\mathfrak{E}(\varphi)$,

S_2 For each decision node n for **Y**, if m is a successor of n in $\mathfrak{E}(\varphi)$ then m is a successor of n in $\mathfrak{S}_X$,

S_3 Each decision node for **X** has at most one successor. If it has a successor, then it is labelled with the move prescribed by the **X**-strategy.

If the **X**-strategy is winning, then every terminal node in $\mathfrak{S}_X$ is a decision node for **Y** (or, equivalently, is labelled with an **X** move).

A.2 Model-Theoretical Interpretation

In order to prove Theorem 2.1 we need to define a model-theoretical interpretation of the extensive form of a **P**-strategy. The intuitive idea is that **O** tries to build a counter-model to the thesis. If **P** has a winning strategy, then every attempt by **O** fails and the thesis is valid. If it is **O** who has a winning strategy, on the other hand, then she will succeed in exhibiting a counter-model of the thesis. Let $\mathfrak{S}$ be the extensive form of a (winning) strategy for player **X**. We interpret each branch of $\mathfrak{S}$ in the following way:

- A function f arbitrarily assigns a world to each dialogical context occurring on the branch,

- If c_i and c_j occur on the branch, we set $f(c_i)Rf(c_j)$,[19]

- For every atomic formula p, we set:

  - $f(c_i) \in V(p)$ only if **O**-p-c_i occurs on the branch,
  - $f(c_i) \notin V(p)$ only if (i) **P**-p-c_i occurs as the winning move OR **O**-p-c_i does not occur on the branch.

---

[19]When working with *SR3'* instead of *SR3*, we replace this by a clause setting the reflexivity, transitivity and symmetry of the accessibility relation.

In order to prove the Left-to-Right part of Theorem 2.1, we focus on the case of winning **P** strategies. For any such strategy, every leaf of its extensive form is labelled with an atomic formula uttered by **P**. Indeed, on the one hand we know that every leaf is labelled with a **P** move (by definition of a winning strategy). Suppose, on the other hand, that one of these moves is not the utterance of an atomic formula: then it is either the utterance of a complex formula or a symbolic challenge (a question). But in such cases the move is not terminal, since **O** can always challenge a complex formula or answer a question. Therefore every leaf of the extensive form of a winning **P** strategy is labelled with a **P** atomic formula.

Now because of the formal rule it follows that every branch of the extensive form contains an occurrence of an atomic formula uttered by **P** (the winning move of the branch) and an occurrence of the same atomic formula uttered by **O**. Therefore the interpretation of each branch leads to a contradiction: for every branch, there is an atomic formula χ such that $f(c_i) \in V(\chi)$ and $f(c_i) \notin V(\chi)$. The assumption that the thesis is falsifiable thus leads to a contradiction.

The Right-to-Left part of Theorem 2.1 is proven by contrapositive. We suppose that there is no winning **P** strategy for the thesis. Then, as we pointed out in footnote 16, there is a winning **O** strategy for the thesis. We then give the model-theoretical interpretation of the extensive form of this strategy showing that the thesis is not valid.[20]

Bibliography

Clerbout, N., 2012. First-Order Dialogical Games and Tableaux. Submitted.

Crossley, J. N. and Humberstone, L., 1977. The Logic of Actually. *Reports on Mathematical Logic*, 8:11–29.

Davies, M. and Humberstone, L., 1980. Two Notions of Necessity. *Philosophical Studies*, 38:1–30.

Fitting, M. and Mendelsohn, R. L., 1998. *First-Order Modal Logic*, volume 277 of *Synthese Library*. Kluwer Academic Publishers.

Fontaine, M. and Redmond, J., 2008. *Logique Dialogique : Une Introduction. Volume I. Méthode de Dialogique : Règles et Exercices*, volume 5 of *Cahiers de Logique et d'Epistémologie*. College Publications, London.

---

[20]We leave the details for a future work. Another way to prove the Right-to-Left part is to use the well-known tableau method of proof, showing how the tableau proof for a formula can be transformed and generalized into the extensive form of a winning **P** strategy. For a detailed proof in the case of First-Order Logic, see Clerbout (2012).

Gale, D. and Stewart, F., 1953. Infinite Games with Perfect Information. In Kuhn, H. W. and Tucker, A. W. (ed.), *Contributions to the Theory of Games, volume II*, volume 28 of *Annals of Mathematics Studies*, pages 245–266. Princeton University Press, Princeton.

Hughes, G. E. and Cresswell, M. J., 1996. *A New Introduction to Modal Logic*. Routledge, London/New York.

Keiff, L., 2007. *Le Pluralisme Dialogique*. PhD thesis, Université Charles de Gaulle Lille 3.

Keiff, L., 2009. Dialogical Logic. *Stanford Encyclopedia of Philosophy*. URL http://plato.stanford.edu/entries/logic-Dialogical.

Rahman, S., 2009. A non normal dialogic for a wonderful world and more. In van Benthem et alii, J. (ed.), *The Age of Alternative Logics*, pages 311–334. Kluwer-Springer, Dordrecht. (reprint ed. 2006).

Rahman, S., 2010. Negation in the Logic of First Degree Entailment and Tonk: A Dialogical Study. In G. Primiero, M. M. e. a. (ed.), *(Anti)Realism. The Realism-Antirealism Debate in the Age of Alternative Logics*, pages 175–201. Springer, Dordrecht.

Rahman, S. and Keiff, L., 2005. On How to Be a Dialogician. In Vanderveken, D. (ed.), *Logic, Thought and Action*, pages 359–408. Springer, New York.

Rahman, S. and Rückert, H., 1999. Dialogische Modallogik (für T, B, S4 und S5). *Logique et Analyse*, 42(167–168):243–282.

Rahman, S. and Tulenheimo, T., 2009. From Games to Dialogues and Back. Towards a general frame for validity. In O. Majer, A.-V. Pietarinen, T. T. (ed.), *Games: Unifying Logic, Language, and Philosophy*, pages 153–208. Springer, Dordrecht.

Rahman, S., Clerbout, N., and Keiff, L., 2009. On Dialogues and Natural Deduction. In Primiero, G. and Rahman, S. (ed.), *Acts of Knowledge - History, Philosophy and Logic*, pages 301–336. College Publications, London.

Williamson, T., 2007. *The Philosophy of Philosophy*. Blackwell, Oxford.

Zalta, E. N., 1988. Logical and Analytic Truths that are not Necessary. *The Journal of Philosophy*, 85(2):57–74.

A Dialogical Approach of Iterated Belief Revision

Virginie FIUTEK*

ABSTRACT. In this paper, we study Bonanno's system of iterated belief revision in the context of dialogical logic. In particular we build further on the work presented in Fiutek et al. (2010) and integrate the latest logic for belief revision that was introduced in Bonanno (2010). We review the corresponding dialogical language and its rules, in particular we focus in detail on the particle rules and we provide new structural rules. We prove that the corresponding dialogical system captures all Bonanno's axioms.

Introduction

One of the foundational works dealing with belief revision is the contribution of Alchourrón et al. (1985). Their well-known theory is the so-called AGM theory. They give a list of minimal properties that a revision operator should satisfy in order for it to be considered rational by means of postulates. Over the last decades, these postulates have been cast in the setting of modal logics in a number of different ways van Ditmarsch (2005); Leitgeb and Segerberg (2007); Baltag and Smets (2006, 2008a,b); Bonanno (2009, 2010); van Benthem (2007). In this paper we are interested in Bonanno's setting. Bonanno proposes to combine the AGM approach with the notion of static belief introduced in the work of Hintikka (1962). This approach uses a belief operator B and a semantics which is based on Kripke structures. The intended interpretation of $B\varphi$ is "the agent believes that φ". Properties of belief operators are given by means of axioms. Bonanno's aim is to represent the AGM postulates as axioms in a modal language.

In Bonanno (2009), Bonanno presents a multimodal temporal logic. One of the original points of his work is the introduction of temporality

*Institute for Logic, Language and Computation, Universiteit van Amsterdam, The Netherlands.

in a modal logic for belief revision. His temporal logic uses a branching-time structure allowing to represent different possible changes of beliefs. Thus he introduces two temporal modal operators: the next-time operator F and its inverse P, as well as two epistemic modal operators: the belief operator B and the information operator I, and the "all state" operator A. This approach allows to provide an axiomatic characterization of the AGM theory. The logic called Logic of AGM is such a characterization Bonanno (2009).

Bonanno's logic of AGM is particularly well fit for a dialogical reconstruction. We have worked out a first setting for such a reconstruction in Fiutek et al. (2010), where we provided the corresponding particle and structural rules. At the basis of a dialogical reconstruction lies the idea that we can start from the dialogical framework introduced by Lorenzen (see Lorenzen and Lorenz (1978)) and extend it. In the early 1950's, Lorenzen worked on an operative approach of logic in Lorenzen (1957). However he encountered some problems and he gave up his operative theory to develop dialogical logic at the end of the 1950's. So the idea is to keep particle rules for standard connectives and standard structural rules and add first particle rules to capture the possible additional connectives of the logic under consideration (in Bonanno's case it is about modal operators), then structural rules to capture the properties of the corresponding frame and those of its relations.

In a working paper Bonanno (2010), Bonanno provides an axiomatic characterization of the AGM theory with a new set of axioms. Indeed he is interested in studying iterated belief revision and he wants to capture the qualitative notion of AGM-consistency. Thus Bonanno introduces the concept of rationalizable belief revision by means of a new axiom called PLS.[1] The introduction of this new axiom leads Bonanno to change some of his previous axioms (those of the Logic of AGM in Bonanno (2009)). Let the corresponding new logic be $\mathcal{L}_{PLS*}$.[2] The advantage of this logic is that it allows us to go beyond the logic of AGM and to capture iterated belief revision.

In this paper our aim is to provide a dialogical reconstruction of $\mathcal{L}_{PLS*}$. Indeed our former reconstruction Fiutek et al. (2010) does not capture the logic $\mathcal{L}_{PLS*}$ and so it does not capture iterated belief revision either. First we present the logic $\mathcal{L}_{PLS*}$. Then we give a general presentation

---

[1] PLS stands for Plausibility. Indeed in the branching-time belief revision frames, beliefs are now rationalized by a plausibility ordering.

[2] Bonanno does not give a name to this new logic.

of dialogical logic and we present the dialogical rules for $\mathcal{L}_{PLS*}$. We prove that the corresponding dialogical system captures all Bonanno's axioms.

1 The logic $\mathcal{L}_{PLS*}$

In this section we review the basic setting of $\mathcal{L}_{PLS*}$ and follow explicitly the presentation in Bonanno (2007, 2008, 2009).

1.1 Language

The language of $\mathcal{L}_{PLS*}$ is an extension of the propositional classical language. The formal language is built up from a countable set of propositional atoms (p, q, r...), the usual connectives ($\neg, \wedge, \vee, \rightarrow$) and five unary modal operators[3] (F, P, B, I, A) such that $I\varphi$ is a well formed formula if and only if φ is Boolean:

$$\varphi ::= p \mid \neg\varphi \mid \varphi \vee \psi \mid F\varphi \mid P\varphi \mid B\varphi \mid I\varphi \mid A\varphi$$

The intended interpretation of the operators is as follows:

1. $F\varphi$ at every next instant it will be the case that φ
2. $P\varphi$ at the previous instant it was the case that φ
3. $B\varphi$ the agent believes that φ
4. $I\varphi$ the agent is informed that φ
5. $A\varphi$ it is true at every world that φ

1.2 Semantics

A temporal belief revision frame is a tuple $< T, \leadsto, W, \{B_t, I_t\}_{t \in T} >$ where $< T, \leadsto >$ is a next-time branching frame and:

- T is a non-empty, countable set of instants

- $\leadsto$ is an "immediate successor" relation satisfying the following conditions:
  $\forall t_1, t_2, t_3,$

  1. If $t_1 \leadsto t_3$ and $t_2 \leadsto t_3$ then $t_1 = t_2$
  2. If $< t_1, ..., t_n >$ is a sequence in T with $t_i \leadsto t_{i+1}$, for every $i = 1, ..., n-1$, then $t_n \neq t_1$

---

[3]We slightly change the notation of Bonanno changing $\bigcirc$ by F and $\bigcirc^{-1}$ by P. Moreover in his working paper Bonanno does not introduce the P operator in the language anymore. We keep it for convenience because we explicitly state the basic axioms what Bonanno does not do in Bonanno (2010).

Condition 1 makes sure that each instant has a unique predecessor and condition 2 excludes cycles in the structure, giving it a tree-form. The intended interpretation of $t_1 \rightsquigarrow t_2$ is taken to be "t_2 is an immediate successor of t_1 or t_1 is the immediate predecessor of t_2". Each instant can have several immediate successors. Let $t^{\rightsquigarrow}$ denote the set of all immediate successors of t.

- W is a non-empty set of states

- B_t and I_t are binary relations on W for every instant t, respectively capturing the beliefs of an agent and modeling the information an agent can receive. These relations can be casted in terms of maps:

$$B_t(w) = \{w' \in W : wB_tw'\}$$

$$I_t(w) = \{w' \in W : wI_tw'\}$$

A branching-time belief revision model is obtained from a branching-time belief revision frame by adding a valuation $V : S \rightarrow 2^W$ assigning to each atomic sentence the set of states in which the sentence is true.

The truth of an arbitrary formula is defined recursively as standard for the Boolean formulas. For the modal operators it is defined recursively as:

$\mathcal{M}, (w_0, t_0) \models A\varphi$ iff $\mathcal{M}, (w_1, t_0) \models \varphi$ for all $w_1 \in W$

$\mathcal{M}, (w_0, t_0) \models F\varphi$ iff $\mathcal{M}, (w_0, t_1) \models \varphi$ for every t_1
such that $t_0 \rightsquigarrow t_1$

$\mathcal{M}, (w_0, t_0) \models P\varphi$ iff $\mathcal{M}, (w_0, t_1) \models \varphi$ for every t_1
such that $t_1 \rightsquigarrow t_0$

$\mathcal{M}, (w_0, t_0) \models B\varphi$ iff $\mathcal{M}, (w_1, t_0) \models \varphi$ for all w_1
such that $w_1 \in B_{t0}(w_0)$

$\mathcal{M}, (w_0, t_0) \models I\varphi$ iff $\mathcal{M}, (w_1, t_0) \models \varphi$ for all w_1
such that $w_1 \in I_{t0}(w_0)$
and $\mathcal{M}, (w_1, t_0) \models \varphi$ then $w_1 \in I_{t0}(w_0)$

The branching-time belief revision frames of the logic $\mathcal{L}_{PLS*}$ satisfy the following properties: for all $w \in W$, for all $t_2, t_3, \ldots, t_n \in t_1^{\rightsquigarrow}$ with $t_n = t_2$ and for all $k = 1, \ldots, n$:

1. if $t_1 \rightsquigarrow t_2$ and $B_{t1}(w) \cap I_{t2}(w) \neq \emptyset$ then $B_{t2}(w) = B_{t1}(w) \cap I_{t2}(w)$
2. $B_{t1}(w) \subseteq I_{t1}(w)$

3. if $t_1 \rightsquigarrow t_2$, $t_1 \rightsquigarrow t_3$ and $I_{t2}(w) = I_{t3}(w)$ then $B_{t2} = B_{t3}(w)$
4. $B_{t1}(w) \neq \emptyset$
5. if $I_{t_{k-1}} \cap B_{t_k} \neq \emptyset$, then $I_{t_{k-1}} \cap B_{t_k} = B_{t_{k-1}} \cap I_{t_k}$

The properties 3, 4 and 5 are the new ones and have been introduced in Bonanno (2010).

1.3 Axiomatics

The logic $\mathcal{L}_{PLS*}$ is defined by the following axioms and rules of inference:

Basic axioms

- All propositional tautologies
- Axiom K for F: $F(\varphi \rightarrow \psi) \rightarrow (F\varphi \rightarrow F\psi)$
- Axiom K for P: $P(\varphi \rightarrow \psi) \rightarrow (P\varphi \rightarrow P\psi)$
- Axiom K for B: $B(\varphi \rightarrow \psi) \rightarrow (B\varphi \rightarrow B\psi)$
- Axiom K for A: $A(\varphi \rightarrow \psi) \rightarrow (A\varphi \rightarrow A\psi)$
- Temporal axioms: $\varphi \rightarrow F(\neg P \neg \varphi)$

                                         $\varphi \rightarrow P(\neg F \neg \varphi)$
- Backward Uniqueness axiom: $\neg P \neg \varphi \rightarrow P\varphi$
- Axiom T for A: $A\varphi \rightarrow \varphi$
- Axiom 5 for A: $\neg A\varphi \rightarrow A \neg A\varphi$
- Inclusion axiom B: $A\varphi \rightarrow B\varphi$
- Axioms to capture $(I\varphi \wedge I\psi) \rightarrow A(\varphi \leftrightarrow \psi)$

    the non-standard semantics for I: $A(\varphi \leftrightarrow \psi) \rightarrow (I\varphi \leftrightarrow I\psi)$

These basic axioms state that the belief operator, the "all state" operator and the temporal operators are normal operators, whereas the information operator is a non-normal operator. Moreover they express that the branching-time structure is such that each instant has a unique immediate predecessor but can have several immediate successors.

Further axioms[4]

Let $\bigwedge_{j=1,\dots,n} \varphi_j$ denotes the formula $(\varphi_1 \wedge \dots \wedge \varphi_n)$ such that $\varphi_0 = \varphi_n$ and $\chi_0 = \chi_n$

---

[4]Bonanno does not give a name to some axioms: we have chosen to call them "Equivalence" and "Consistency".

- No Drop: $(\neg B\neg\varphi \wedge B\psi) \rightarrow F(I\varphi \rightarrow B\psi)$
- No Add: $\neg B\neg(\varphi \wedge \neg\psi) \rightarrow F(I\varphi \rightarrow \neg B\psi)$
- Acceptance: $I\varphi \rightarrow B\varphi$
- Equivalence: $\neg F\neg(I\psi \wedge B\varphi) \rightarrow F(I\psi \rightarrow B\varphi)$
- PLS: $\bigwedge_{j=1,\ldots,n} \neg F\neg(I\varphi_j \wedge \neg B\neg\varphi_{j-1} \wedge B\chi_j) \rightarrow$

  $\bigwedge_{j=1,\ldots,n} F((I\varphi_j \rightarrow B(\varphi_{j-1} \rightarrow \chi_{j-1}))$

  $\wedge(I\varphi_{j-1} \rightarrow B(\varphi_j \rightarrow \chi_j)))$
- Consistency: $B\varphi \rightarrow \neg B\neg\varphi$

The first axiom says that initial beliefs are not dropped when the new information received is not surprising. The second axiom says that beliefs about which there is no information are not added when the information received is not surprising. The third axiom says that the new information is believed. The fourth axiom says that differences in beliefs must be due to differences in information. The fifth axiom says that beliefs must be rationalized. The sixth axiom says that beliefs are consistent. The last three axioms are the new ones.

Rules of inference
- Modus Ponens: if φ and $\varphi \rightarrow \psi$ then ψ
- Necessitation for A: if φ then $A\varphi$
- Necessitation for F: if φ then $F\varphi$
- Necessitation for P: if φ then $P\varphi$

Note that from Modus ponens and Necessitation for A one can derive necessitation for B.

2 Dialogical logic

2.1 General presentation

Dialogical logic was first introduced by Paul Lorenzen in the 1950's and then developed by Kuno Lorenz.[5] Shahid Rahman, one of Lorenz's students, has further developed dialogical logic to allow for the development and the combination of different logics in this framework (free logic, normal modal logic, non normal modal logic and so on). The aim was to propose a semantics based on argumentation games as a new

---

[5]The most important early papers on Dialogical Logic are collected in Lorenzen and Lorenz (1978).

alternative to model theory and proof theory: dialogical logic builds a bridge between model theory and proof theory.[6]

In a dialogical game two players confront each other: on the one hand the Proponent defends a thesis, he utters that a formula is valid; on the other hand the Opponent attacks the thesis, he aims to prove that it is not valid. They interact by alternately choosing moves.[7] Each move is a speech act: either an utterance or an interrogation. If the Proponent manages to answer to all the attacks of the Opponent, he wins and proves the validity of his thesis. Otherwise the Opponent wins and proves it is not valid.[8] Thus validity is defined in terms of winning strategies.

The dialogue is a game which obeys some rules. There are two kinds of rules: particle rules and structural rules. Particle rules constitute the local semantics of a logic: it determines the dialogical meaning of each logical constant. Thus they define the way in which connectives are played such that the main connective is played first. These rules are symmetric that is, they are strictly the same for Opponent as well as Proponent. That's why we use X and Y as variables ranging on $\{O, P\}$, always assuming that $X \neq Y$. Structural rules determine the global semantics of a logic: they define the way in which the dialogue proceeds. Thus the notion of proof in a given dialogue system is determined by the structural rules.

A dialogical language for propositional logic is obtained from the standard propositional language by the addition of two metalogical symbols '?' and '!', standing for interrogation and utterance, and two labels O and P, standing for the players (Opponent, Proponent) of the dialogue.

Modal dialogues are developed in Rahman and Rückert (2001). First, the introduction of modal operators needs the introduction of labels in dialogical logic. Indeed modal dialogues must specify the contextual nature of the moves, i.e. the context in which the moves are made. Then a particle rule must be added for each modal operator to define the way in which it is played. Finally, some structural rules must be added to define what labels can be chosen by the players to attack or defend a modal operator (according to its corresponding particle rule).

---

[6] For a more detailed presentation we refer to the book Fontaine and Redmond (2008) that clearly presents dialogical logic.

[7] Note that both players are idealized agents. Each player always plays the best possible move.

[8] It means that at least one player has a winning strategy in a dialogue.

2.2 Dialogical system for $\mathcal{L}_{PLS*}$

Language

We further extend the dialogical propositional language by adding Bonanno's modal operators. Since Bonanno's logic is a multimodal logic, we introduce two labels: one indicating the context and the other indicating the instant in which the move is made. We use the notation w to indicate contexts and the notation t to indicate instants.

Particule rules

Note that the particle rules for Bonanno's operators are slightly different from those in Fiutek et al. (2010). Indeed we explicitly stated accessibility relations inside these particle rules. However as mentioned above, particle rules give a local meaning: that's why they must be very abstract to avoid any reference to a determined context of game. Thus abstract particle rules become universal. For example if two different logics use a belief operator, then the corresponding particle rules for both operators are the same. Differences are captured by structural rules that give a global meaning. It is one of the aim of dialogical logic and one of its advantage: given the universality of particle rules, changing some structural rules allows to capture another logic.

So we make our particle rules more abstract and we transfer the issue of accessibility relations on structural rules.[9] Hence our dialogical system could easily be reused to study another system of belief revision.[10]

Standard connectives	X Utterance	Y Attack	X Defence
$\neg$ there is no possible defence, only a counterattack is available	w,t: $\neg\,\varphi$	w,t: φ	$\otimes$
$\wedge$ the challenger has the choice, he attacks by choosing a conjunct	w,t: $\varphi \wedge \psi$	w,t: $?_{\wedge 1}$ or w,t: $?_{\wedge 2}$	w,t: φ respectively w,t: ψ
$\vee$ the defender has the choice, he defends himself by choosing to utter a disjunct	w,t: $\varphi \vee \psi$	w,t: $?_\vee$	w,t: φ or w,t: ψ
$\rightarrow$ the challenger utters the antecedent and the defender must utter the consequent	w,t: $\varphi \rightarrow \psi$	w,t: φ	w,t: ψ

Particle rules for standard connectives

[9]See the Formal rule for contexts below.
[10]Here again we refer to Fontaine and Redmond (2008) for more detailed explanation.

When **X** utters the negation of a formula, **Y** attacks by uttering the formula and must be able to defend this utterance. Note that in a dialogue, the symbol $\otimes$ means that there is no possible defence. When **X** utters a conjunction, he must be able to defend any of the conjuncts, and when he utters a disjunction he must only be able to defend one of the disjuncts. When **X** utters an implication, he must be able to defend the consequent providing **Y** has uttered the antecedent.

Bonanno's operators	**X** Utterance	**Y** Attack	**X** Defence
P the challenger has the choice, he attacks by choosing an instant	$w,t_n\colon P\varphi$	$w,t_n\colon ?P_{t_{n'}}$	$w,t_{n'}\colon \varphi$
F the challenger has the choice, he attacks by choosing an instant	$w,t_n\colon F\varphi$	$w,t_n\colon ?F_{t_{n'}}$	$w,t_{n'}\colon \varphi$
B the challenger has the choice, he attacks by choosing a context	$w_n,t\colon B\varphi$	$w_n,t\colon ?B_{w_{n'}}$	$w_{n'},t\colon \varphi$
A the challenger has the choice, he attacks by choosing a context	$w_n,t\colon A\varphi$	$w_n,t\colon ?A_{w_{n'}}$	$w_{n'},t\colon \varphi$
I the challenger has the choice between two attacks	$w_n,t\colon I\varphi$	$w_n,t\colon ?I_{w_{n'}}$	$w_{n'},t\colon \varphi$
		$w_{n'},t\colon \varphi$	$w_n,t\colon ?I_{w_{n'}}$

Particle rules for Bonanno's operators

When **X** utters a formula of the form $P\varphi$, he must be able to defend φ at any instant chosen by **Y** to attack the P operator. When **X** utters a formula of the form $F\varphi$, he must be able to defend φ at any instant chosen by **Y** to attack the F operator. When **X** utters a formula of the form $B\varphi$, he must be able to defend φ at any context chosen by **Y** to attack the B operator. When **X** utters a formula of the form $A\varphi$, he must be able to defend φ at any context chosen by **Y** to attack the A operator. When **X** utters a formula $I\varphi$ at a context w_n, **Y** has the choice between two attacks. He can choose the standard attack: he attacks by choosing a context, and then **X** must be able to defend φ at any context chosen by **Y**. Or he can choose the non-standard attack: he utters φ at a context $w_{n'}$ which has not been chosen to attack an I operator at w_n, and then **X** must be able to defend that the context $w_{n'}$ can be chosen at w_n to attack an I operator.

Structural rules

We present the structural rules distinguishing explicitly standard structural rules (those that hold in any dialogical system), the structural rules presented in Fiutek et al. (2010) that still hold and the new ones.

Standard structural rules

(SR-0) (Starting rule):

The thesis is uttered by **P** in an initial context and at an initial time. Then **O** and **P** respectively choose a natural number n and m allowing a number of repetitions (called repetition rank).[11] It defines how many times a player can perform his defence or his challenge.

(SR-1) (Game-playing rule):

Moves are made alternately by **O** and **P** according to the other rules. In any move each player may attack any complex formula uttered by the other player, or he may defend himself against any attack, in accordance with his repetition rank.

(SR-3) (Winning rule):

A player wins a play if and only if the other player cannot make a move.

Maintained structural rules

(SR-2) (Formal rule for atomic formulas):

P cannot utter atomic formulas in a context w. Any atomic formula must be uttered by **O** first in this context. Then **P** can reuse this atomic formula in this context at any time. There is no attack on atomic formulas.

(SR-4) (Formal rule for instants):

At a given instant, **O** may choose an instant to attack a F operator at every time that other rules allow him to do. At a given instant, **O** may choose an instant to attack a P operator provided that he has not introduced another one before. **P** cannot choose a new instant. Any instant must be chosen by **O** first. **P** can only reuse instants already chosen by **O** to attack the same kind of operator.[12]

But **P** can be allowed to reuse the initial instant to attack an operator P or F.

(SR-4.1) **P** is allowed to use the initial instant t_n to attack a F operator at an instant $t_{n'}$, such that $t_{n'}$ has been chosen to attack a P operator at t_n.

(SR-4.2) **P** is allowed to use the initial instant t_n to attack a P operator at an instant $t_{n'}$, such that $t_{n'}$ has been chosen to attack a F operator at t_n.

New structural rules

(SR-5) (Formal rule for contexts):

P cannot choose a new context. Any context must be chosen by **O** first. **P** can only reuse contexts already chosen by **O** at the instant in

---

[11]Note that we did not explicitly state the repetition ranks in Fiutek et al. (2010) but it is not a real novelty of our system.

[12]Note that the initial instant is not chosen by **O**.

which they have been chosen, to attack the same kind of operator or the operator A.[13]

But **P** can be allowed to reuse the initial context to attack an operator I or A.

(SR-5.1) P is allowed to use the initial context w_n to attack an I operator or a A operator.

Moreover **P** can be allowed to reuse contexts to attack a different kind of operator.

(SR-5.2): if **O** has chosen $w_{n'}$ to attack a B operator at t_n in w_n, then **P** can reuse $w_{n'}$ to attack an I operator at t_n in w_n.

Furthermore **P** can be allowed to reuse contexts at an instant different from the instant of their utterance.

(SR-5.3): if **O** has chosen $w_{n'}$ to attack a A operator at t_n in w_n, then **P** can reuse $w_{n'}$ to attack a A operator at any time.

Let three instants t_n, $t_{n'}$ and $t_{n''}$ be such that $t_{n'}$ and $t_{n''}$ have been chosen to attack a F operator at the instant t_n, and consider three contexts w_n, $w_{n'}$ and $w_{n''}$:

(SR-5.4): if **O** has chosen $w_{n''}$ to attack a B operator at t_n in w_n and to attack an I operator at $t_{n'}$ in w_n, and if he has chosen $w_{n'}$ to attack a B operator at $t_{n'}$ in w_n, then **P** can reuse $w_{n'}$ to attack a B operator in w_n but at t_n.

(SR-5.5): if **O** has chosen $w_{n'}$ to attack a B operator at t_n in w_n and to attack an I operator at $t_{n'}$ in w_n, then **P** can reuse $w_{n'}$ to attack a B operator in w_n but at $t_{n'}$.

(SR-5.6): if **O** has chosen $w_{n'}$ to attack a B operator at $t_{n'}$ in w_n and if he has uttered the same formula after a standard attack on an I operator in w_n at $t_{n'}$ and in w_n at $t_{n''}$, then **P** can reuse $w_{n'}$ to attack a B operator in w_n but at $t_{n''}$.

(SR-5.7): if **O** has chosen $w_{n'}$ to attack a B operator at $t_{n'}$ in w_n and to attack an I operator at $t_{n''}$ in w_n, then **P** can reuse $w_{n'}$ to attack a B operator in w_n but at $t_{n''}$.

(SR-5.8): if **O** has not chosen any context, then **P** can choose a context to attack a B operator.

Note that the rules SR-5.6, SR-5.7 and SR-5.8 are the rules that capture the new axioms of Bonanno.

---

[13]Note that the initial context is not chosen by **O**.

Dialogical system for $\mathcal{L}_{PLS*}$
Our dialogical system is defined as the set of particle rules (for standard connectives and Bonanno's operators) and the set of structural rules (standard, maintained and new structural rules).

3   Validity of axioms of $\mathcal{L}_{PLS*}$

Our system capture all Bonanno's axioms. For convenience (and a matter of space) we only present the proofs for the new axioms Equivalence and Consistency. The proofs for basic axioms and maintained axioms (No drop, No add and Acceptance) are rather easy to provide, given the example of the proofs for Equivalence and Consistency.[14] The proof for axiom PLS is not so complicated but is very long. We let them for the reader.

We just present one play, but one can easily check that the losing player could not have played in an essentially different way. If a player wins then this means that there also exists a winning strategy for that player in the respective dialogue.[15] Let us test the validity of the axiom Equivalence: $\neg F\neg(I\psi \wedge B\varphi) \rightarrow F(I\psi \rightarrow B\varphi)$.

The first column corresponds to the number of the **O** moves. The second column corresponds to the context in which the **O** moves have been made. The third column corresponds to the instant in which the **O** moves have been made. The fourth column corresponds to **O** moves. The fifth column corresponds to the number of the **P** moves attacked by **O**. The sixth column corresponds to the number of the **O** moves attacked by **P**. The seventh column corresponds to **P** moves. The eighth column corresponds to the instant in which the **P** moves have been made. The ninth column corresponds to the context in which the **P** moves have been made. The tenth column corresponds to the number of the **P** moves.

---

[14]One can refer to Fiutek et al. (2010) to have an idea of the proofs for maintained axioms since, even if the particle rules are different, the mechanism remains the same.

[15]Remember that players are here idealized agents that play the best possible move.

			O			P			
						$\neg F\neg(I\psi \wedge B\varphi)$ $\rightarrow F(I\psi \rightarrow B\varphi)$	t_0	w_0	0
			n=1			m=2			
1	w_0	t_0	$\neg F\neg(I\psi \wedge B\varphi)$	0		$F(I\psi \rightarrow B\varphi)$	t_0	w_0	2
3	w_0	t_0	$?F_{t_1}$	2		$I\psi \rightarrow B\varphi$	t_1	w_0	4
5	w_0	t_1	$I\psi$	4		$B\varphi$	t_1	w_0	6
7	w_0	t_1	$?B_{w_1}$	6		φ	t_1	w_1	22
			$\otimes$		1	$F\neg(I\psi \wedge B\varphi)$	t_0	w_0	8
9	w_0	t_0	$?F_{t_2}$	8		$\neg(I\psi \wedge B\varphi)$	t_2	w_0	10
11	w_0	t_2	$I\psi \wedge B\varphi$	10		$\otimes$			
13	w_0	t_2	$I\psi$		11	$?_{\wedge 1}$	t_2	w_0	12
15	w_0	t_2	$B\varphi$		11	$?_{\wedge 2}$	t_2	w_0	14
17	w_0	t_1	ψ		5	$?I_{w_0}$	t_1	w_0	16
19	w_0	t_2	ψ		13	$?I_{w_0}$	t_2	w_0	18
21	w_1	t_2	φ		15	$?B_{w_1}$	t_2	w_0	20

Explanation: according to the starting rule, moves are made alternately by **O** and **P**. The thesis is uttered by **P** in the initial context w_0 and at the initial instant t_0. **O** and **P** respectively choose a natural number allowing a number of repetition: **O** chooses 1 and **P** chooses 2.

Then **O** attacks the main connective of the thesis, that is the implication. According to the particle rule for implication, **O** attacks by uttering the antecedent. According to the game-playing rule, each player may attack any complex formula uttered by the other player, or he may defend himself against any attack, in accordance with his repetition rank. So **P** has the choice: he can defend himself against the attack of **O** or to attack the utterance of **O**. In this play **P** defends himself by uttering the consequent.[16]

Then according to the particle rule for the F operator, **O** attacks the F operator by choosing the instant t_1 and **P** defends himself by uttering $I\psi \rightarrow B\varphi$ at the chosen instant t_1.

In move 5 **O** attacks the implication by uttering the antecedent and **P** defends himself by uttering the consequent.

Then **O** attacks the B operator by choosing the context w_1. According to the formal rule for atomic formulas, **P** cannot utter atomic formulas

---

[16] One can see that it is the best strategy.

in a context w. Any atomic formula must be uttered by **O** first in this context: so he cannot defend himself.

But he has other possible moves: in move 8 he attacks the negation of the move 1. According to the particle rule for negation, **O** has no possible defence: he can only counterattack.

He attacks the F operator by choosing the instant t_2. **P** defends himself by uttering $\neg(I\psi \wedge B\varphi)$ at the chosen instant t_2.

Then **O** attacks the negation and **P** can only counterattack. In move 12 he attacks the conjunction and, according to the particle rule for the conjunction, he chooses the first conjunct. **O** defends himself by uttering $I\psi$ in w_0 at t_2. Once again **P** attacks the conjunction of the move 11 and chooses the second conjunct. **O** defends himself by uttering $B\varphi$ in w_0 at t_2.

According to the formal rule for contexts (**P** can only reuse contexts already chosen by **O** at the instant in which they have been chosen, to attack the same kind of operator or the operator A) **P** cannot attack the B operator of move 15 since the context w_1 has been chosen by **O** to attack a B operator at the instant t_1 and not at t_2.

But **P** has other possible moves. He attacks the I operator of the move 5 and, according to the particle rule for the I operator, he chooses the standard attack. According to SR-5.1 (**P** is allowed to use the initial context to attack an I operator) **P** attacks the I operator by choosing the context w_0. **O** defends himself by uttering ψ in the chosen context w_0 at the instant t_1. As there is no attack on atomic formulas, **P** can only attack the I operator of the move 13 and once again, he chooses the standard attack and chooses the context w_0. **O** defends himself by uttering ψ in the chosen context w_0 at the instant t_2.

According to SR-5.6, as **O** has chosen w_1 to attack a B operator at t_1 in w_0 and as he has uttered the same formula ψ after a standard attack on an I operator in w_0 at t_1 and in w_0 at t_2, then **P** can reuse w_1 to attack a B operator in w_0 at t_2. So he attacks the B operator of the move 15 choosing the context w_1. **O** defends himself by uttering φ in the chosen context w_1 at the instant t_2.

Then according to the formal rule for atomic formulas (**P** can reuse an atomic formula in the context of its utterance at any time), **P** can now defend himself against the attack of move 7 and he utters φ in the chosen context w_1 at t_1.

According to the winning rule, a player wins a play if and only if the other player cannot make a move. **O** has to make a move but he cannot. **P** wins: the thesis is valid.

Let us test the validity of the axiom Consistency: $B\varphi \rightarrow \neg B\neg\varphi$.

			O			**P**			
						$B\varphi \rightarrow \neg B\neg\varphi$	t_0	w_0	0
			n=1			m=2			
1	w_0	t_0	$B\varphi$	0		$\neg B\neg\varphi$	t_0	w_0	2
3	w_0	t_0	$B\neg\varphi$	2		$\otimes$			
5	w_1	t_0	φ		1	$?B_{w_1}$	t_0	w_0	4
7	w_1	t_0	$\neg\varphi$		3	$?B_{w_1}$	t_0	w_0	6
			$\otimes$		7	φ	t_0	w_1	8

Explanation: according to the starting rule, moves are made alternately by **O** and **P**. The thesis is uttered by **P** in the initial context w_0 and at the initial instant t_0. **O** and **P** respectively choose a natural number allowing a number of repetition: **O** chooses 1 and **P** chooses 2.

Then **O** attacks the main connective of the thesis, that is the implication by uttering the antecedent. **P** defends himself by uttering the consequent.

Then **O** attacks the negation of move 2. According to the particle rule for negation, **P** has no possible defence, he can only counterattack.

According to SR-5.8, since **O** has not chosen any context then **P** can choose a context to attack a B operator. He chooses the context w_1 and attacks the B operator of move 1. **O** defends himself by uttering φ in the chosen context w_1. Once again, **P** chooses the context w_1 and attacks the B operator of move 3. **O** defends himself by uttering $\neg\varphi$ in the chosen context w_1. Then **P** attacks the negation of move 7 and, according to the formal rule for atomic formulas, utters φ in the context w_1.

According to the winning rule, a player wins a play if and only if the other player cannot make a move. **O** has to make a move but he cannot. **P** wins: the thesis is valid.

4 Conclusion and further work

We have presented here a dialogical reconstruction of the logic $\mathcal{L}_{PLS*}$. This new logic is provided by Bonanno to capture AGM iterated belief revision. So our dialogical system allows now to deal with iterated belief revision. Our construction is based on a slight revision of the dialogical structure provided in Fiutek et al. (2010). Indeed we have improved it to get close to the precepts of dialogical logic. This allows our system to be able to easily capture other belief revision logics. This ability of dialogic systems to capture or even to mix different logics is the advantage of dialogical logic in general. The main point consists in some changes or additions of structural rules in these dialogical systems.

As the reader will have noticed, there are plenty of advantages of using a dialogical logic for belief revision. Indeed the process of acquiring and changing beliefs is a dynamic process. This dynamics is not really captured by a standard modal semantics or an axiomatics either. In a dialogue the argumentative exchange between the two players makes the dynamics become apparent. Dialogical logic provides us with a very natural and legitimate setting in which the argumentative dynamics in a system of belief revision can be made explicit.

The study of meta-logical properties such as soundness and completeness for the presented dialogical system reaches beyond the scope of the current paper and will be investigated in future work.

Acknowledgements. We thank Sonja Smets for her help and feedback. Moreover we thank the editors and the anonymous referees for their useful comments.

Bibliography

Alchourrón, C., Gärdenfors, P., and Makinson, D., 1985. On the logic of theory change: Partial meet contraction and revision functions. *Journal of symbolic logic*, 50(2):510–530.

Baltag, A. and Smets, S., 2006. Conditional doxastic models: A qualitative approach to dynamic belief revision. *Electronic Notes in Theoretical Computer Science*, 165:5–21.

Baltag, A. and Smets, S., 2008a. The logic of conditional doxastic actions. *New perspectives on games and interaction*, 4:9–31.

Baltag, A. and Smets, S., 2008b. A qualitative theory of dynamic interactive belief revision. *Logic and the Foundation of Game and Decision Theory (LOFT7)*, 3:13–60.

Bonanno, G., 2007. Axiomatic characterization of the AGM theory of belief revision in a temporal logic. *Artificial Intelligence*, 171(2-3):144–160.

Bonanno, G., 2008. A sound and complete temporal logic for belief revision. In Dégremont, C., Keiff, L., and Rückert, H. (ed.), *Essays in honour of Shahid Rahman, Tributes*, volume 7 of *Tributes*, pages 67–80. London: College Publications.

Bonanno, G., 2009. Belief revision in a temporal framework. *New Perspectives on Games and Interaction*, 4:45–80.

Bonanno, G., 2010. Belief change in branging time: AGM-consistency and iterated revision. *Journal of Philosophical Logic*. To appear. Available online.

Fiutek, V., Rückert, H., and Rahman, S., 2010. A Dialogical Semantics for Bonanno's System of Belief Revision. In Bour, P. E., Rebuschi, M., and Rollet, L. (ed.), *Construction. Festschrift for Gerhard Heinzmann*, volume 14 of *Tributes*. London: College Publications.

Fontaine, M. and Redmond, J., 2008. *Logique dialogique: une introduction. Méthode de dialogique règles et exercices*. London: College publications.

Hintikka, J., 1962. *Knowledge and belief*. Cornell Univ. Press.

Leitgeb, H. and Segerberg, K., 2007. Dynamic doxastic logic: why, how, and where to? *Synthese*, 155(2):167–190.

Lorenzen, P., 1957. Einführung in die operative logik und mathematik. *Bull. Amer. Math. Soc*, 63:316–320.

Lorenzen, P. and Lorenz, K., 1978. *Dialogische logik*. Wissenschaftliche Buchgesellschaft.

Rahman, S. and Rückert, H., 2001. *New perspectives in dialogical logic*, volume 127 of *Synthese*.

van Benthem, J., 2007. Dynamic logic for belief revision. *Journal of Applied Non-Classical Logics*, 17(2):129–155.

van Ditmarsch, H., 2005. Prolegomena to dynamic logic for belief revision. *Synthese*, 147(2):229–275.

PAC vs. DEMAL

A Dialogical Reconstruction of Public Announcement Logic with Common

Knowledge

Sébastien MAGNIER*

ABSTRACT. Since the work of Plaza (1989) about acts of public communication, a lot of dynamic epistemic logic systems have emerged. A general state of the art can be found in van Ditmarsch et al. (2007). Such logics model situations in which some announcements can be made and after an announcement, the situations which are incompatible with it are deleted from the model. In this paper we propose a reconstruction of the logic **PAC** (*Public Announcement logic with Common knowledge*, see van Ditmarsch et al. (2007)) through the dialogical framework. The idea of this work is to rediscover announcements as acts: acts of an arguer during an argumentative dialogue about knowledge change of agents instead of "model-modifiers". We name this reconstruction **DEMAL** for *Dialogical Epistemic Multi-Agent Logic*.

Introduction

Epistemic logics are often used to explore different philosophical problems in epistemic area. Thanks to Plaza (1989), epistemic logics became dynamic, but in the same time they got closer to artificial intelligence and computational sciences than 'traditional' philosophy. So, when we try to understand what the philosophical ground or the signification of epistemic operators (knowledge and announcement operators) is, answers are a bit evasive. Hendricks (2005) and Hendricks and Symons (2010) have shown the connection between these two traditions but not directly through the meaning of what knowledge operators are. To sum up, in model theory, epistemic operators allow some particular moves through accessibility relations between different states of a model and

*Univ Lille Nord de France, F-59000 Lille France;
UdL3, STL, F-59653 Villeneuve d'Ascq France;
CNRS UMR8163.

announcements are considered as *truthful* operations on the model. In that case, it is not the announcement itself which brings new information: knowledge of agents grows up with announcements because the model is restricted as a consequence of announcements. Agents' knowledge emerges because the announcement *cuts* some accessibilities. Moreover, each knowledge operator receives a semantic definition which represents particular conditions in terms of truth. Indeed, with the model theoretic approach of epistemic problems, every operator is defined in terms of truth value. The problem is that defining operators in such way does not allow us to understand their meaning behind their truth value. Moreover they can be subject to attacks of scepticism about the question of truth.

Through our dialogical approach, we want to propose another way to define the epistemic operators. Rebuschi and Lihoreau (2008) and Rebuschi (2009) already present some interesting works in dialogical logic in epistemic fields. In dialogical logic, operators are *playable-defined* instead of truth-defined.[1] It means that we leave aside the question of their truth in benefits of their meaning through their conditions of use during an argumentative process. Thanks to the dialogical framework, i.e. a game built around the interaction between two players, we can explore the signification of utterances of players about agents' change of knowledge in an argumentative debate. In that specific case, the signification of those operators follows from the debate itself, from the way to *challenge* and *defend* them. In the course of the debate, epistemic operators represent either a commitment or a choice (sometimes both). They are commitments insofar as when a player utters an argument which implies the knowledge of one agent (or more), the other player will challenge the utterance, and the first shall defend his argument. Consequently, uttering an argument based on the knowledge of one agent leads to defend agent's knowledge. Epistemic operators also represent choices because when a player challenges any form of knowledge uttered during the debate, he has to choose different parameters for his challenge. According to the operator at stake he must choose: labels, agents or sequences of agents. In fact thanks to the dialogical framework, we can take literally Mackenzie's remark and start dynamical studies of the meaning of all knowledge operators defined

---

[1]Playable-defined is an original way to understand the notion of validity independently of the truth. In that case, validity is defined in terms of winning strategies instead of truth.

by the interaction between the two players of the dialogue, that is in a communicative context.[2]

First, we present the epistemic operators and the announcement operators with their intended interpretations and their model theoretical semantics. After that, we expose our dialogical reconstruction of these operators and some examples.

1   Public Announcement Logic

But first of all, some lexical definitions are required to avoid confusions. As we have already begun, we will deal with *agents* and *players*. The term *agent* refers to the possessor of knowledge and the term *player* is used when we speak about the arguer of the dialogue. Arguer and player can be synonymously used, the latter standing for an abbreviation of the 'arguer of the dialogue'. But we must be careful not to confuse agents and players: agents belong to the level of the logical language whereas players belong to the argumentative level of the dialogue.

Let us start by briefly explaining what we have in mind when we speak about knowledge operators. In fact, there are three knowledge operators and we can consider that each of them expresses a higher level of complexity.

The first knowledge operator represents a weak degree of complexity because it involves only one agent: it is named *individual knowledge operator*. It is a kind of link between two different things: *an agent* and *a proposition*. Somehow, we can consider that the agent is the bearer of the knowledge and the proposition is the content of it. This operator represents a particular way in which the agent turns himself towards the proposition. For an agent, a proposition can be judged known if and only if certain properties are respected. It is that judgement (involved by the properties) which is expressed by the epistemic operator.

If we want to treat the knowledge of several agents, other operators are required. We need one operator which is able to express the knowledge of all agents and another one which allows us to express the knowledge that agents can have about their own knowledge and

---

[2]In Mackenzie (1985), the author claims that although "Robinson Crusoe may have constructed derivations or proofs for his own edification, he could not engage in argument until Man Friday joined him." Mackenzie points out the fact that logic becomes interesting and really dynamic when it is studied in an argumentative context, otherwise it is a computational game without consideration on meaning.

about other agent's knowledge. Those operators are already expressed in **PAC**.[3]

The second knowledge operator expresses a quantification on agents; that is, relatively to a determined proposition and a determined group of agents, all agents of the group know the proposition: it is named *sharing knowledge operator*.[4] Indeed the knowledge of the proposition is shared by all agents, that is: everybody in the group knows the proposition. Beware: the knowledge about the proposition is the only thing which is shared. They do not share the knowledge about this knowledge.

The last knowledge operator considered allow us to express such form of knowledge, i.e., sharing knowledge about sharing knowledge. Indeed, this operator expresses an infinite iteration of the sharing knowledge operator. In other words, it means that everybody knows that everybody knows that everybody knows and so on ad infinitum.

In addition to those epistemic operators, we also have public announcement operators. Public announcement operators differ from the preceding operators because they do not directly concern the agents or their knowledge but firstly affect the model. Indeed, this kind of operator restricts the model $\mathcal{M}$ in which the knowledge of agents is evaluated to a submodel $\mathcal{M}^{announcement}$ in which the announcement holds.[5] That is, all states in which the announcement does not hold must be removed from the model $\mathcal{M}$. It is in that sense that an announcement can modify the knowledge of agents because it can change the accessibility relations by deleting states which do not respect the announcement. Those states are said to be incompatible with the epistemic alternatives of agents.

1.1 The Syntax

Given a finite set of agents Ag and a countable set of atoms $\mathcal{P}$, the language $\mathcal{L}_{KC[\ ]}(Ag, \mathcal{P})$ is inductively defined by the BNF as follows:

$$\varphi ::= p \mid \neg\varphi \mid \varphi \wedge \varphi \mid K_a\varphi \mid E_G\varphi \mid C_G\varphi \mid [\varphi]\varphi$$

where $a \in Ag, G \subseteq Ag$, and $p \in \mathcal{P}$. We denote the dual of $[\varphi]\,\varphi$ by $\langle\varphi\rangle\varphi$; so we have $\langle\varphi\rangle\varphi$ as an abbreviation of $\neg[\varphi]\neg\varphi$.

---

[3]See van Ditmarsch et al. (2007) pp. 90-91 for a detailed presentation.

[4]Also well known as *Everybody knows operator*, see Fagin et al. (1995) ch. 2.

[5]For convenient reason, we will write $\mathcal{M}^A$ instead of $\mathcal{M}^{announcement}$.

1.2 Intended interpretations

◇ K_a: Individual Knowledge
The intended interpretation of a formula $K_a\varphi$ is: "agent a knows φ".

◇ E_G: Sharing Knowledge
The intended interpretation of a formula $E_G\varphi$ is: "all members of the group G know φ".

◇ C_G : Common Knowledge
The intended interpretation of a formula $C_G\varphi$ is: "all members of the group G know that all members of the group... know φ".[6]

◇ $[\varphi]\psi$: Public Announcement
The intended interpretation of a formula $[\varphi]\psi$ is: "after every announcement of φ, ψ holds".

◇ $\langle\varphi\rangle\psi$: Dual of an Announcement
The intended interpretation of a formula $\langle\varphi\rangle\psi$ is "after a possible announcement of φ, ψ holds".

1.3 Model Theoretic Semantics

An epistemic model is a triple $\mathcal{M} = \langle W, \mathcal{R}_{a\{a\in Ag\}}, \mathcal{V}\rangle$ such that W is a set of states w, each $\mathcal{R}_a$ is a binary equivalence relation over W, and $\mathcal{V}$ is a valuation function such that for every $p \in \mathcal{P}$ yields the set $\mathcal{V}(p) \subseteq W$ of states in which p is true. Standard connectives have the usual semantics definition; operators mentioned above receive the following ones:

◇ K_a *operator*:

$\mathcal{M}, w \models K_a\varphi$ iff $\mathcal{M}, w' \models \varphi$ for all $w' \in W$ such as $w\mathcal{R}_a w'$.

◇ E_G *operator*:

$\mathcal{M}, w \models E_G\,\varphi$ iff $\mathcal{M}, w \models K_a\varphi$ for all $a \in G$.

◇ C_G *operator*:

$\mathcal{M}, w \models C_G\varphi$ iff $\mathcal{M}, w \models K_{a_1}... K_{a_n}\varphi$ for each sequence of agents $\langle a_1 ... a_n\rangle \in G^*$.[7]

---

[6]There are different semantic definitions of common knowledge (see Gerbrandy (1999) ch. 3 and Fagin et al. (1995) ch. 11 for more details on that issue) but we choose to use the 'iterated approach'.

[7]G^* stands for the set $G0 \cup G1 \cup G2 \cup ...$

◇ $[\varphi]\,\psi$ *operator*:

   $\mathcal{M},w \models [\varphi]\,\psi$ iff $\mathcal{M},w \models \varphi$ implies $\mathcal{M}^{\varphi}, w \models \psi$.

◇ $\langle\varphi\rangle\psi$ *operator*:

   $\mathcal{M},w \models \langle\varphi\rangle\psi$ iff $\mathcal{M},w \models \varphi$ and $\mathcal{M}^{\varphi}, w \models \psi$.

where $\mathcal{M}^{\varphi} = \langle \mathcal{W}', \mathcal{R}'_{a\{a\in Ag\}}, \mathcal{V}'\rangle$, is defined as follows:
$\mathcal{W}' = \{w' \in \mathcal{W} \mid \mathcal{M}, w' \models \varphi\}$
$\mathcal{R}'_a = \mathcal{R}_a \cap (\mathcal{W}' \times \mathcal{W}')$
$\mathcal{V}'(p) = \mathcal{V}p \cap \mathcal{W}'$

The special feature of the two last operators is to modify the model by eliminating states in which the announcement does not hold. It is precisely in that sense that those operators are considered as dynamic because they are able to restrict the model to a submodel. The problem is that in dialogical logic we do not have any model, so obviously we cannot restrict the model. But, in dialogical logic, players have to do some choices; hence we can impose some constraints on them. That point is further develop in the next section.

2   DEMAL: A Dialogical Reconstruction of PAC

In Rahman and Keiff (2005), Fontaine and Redmond (2008) and in Keiff (2009), the reader can find a detailed presentation of what the dialogical logic is. Here we just succinctly expose the purpose of such framework. In dialogical logic two players confront each other around an argument. We note d_Δ the dialogue which starts with a thesis Δ (also named the initial argument). On the one hand we have the **Proponent** who defends the thesis Δ; and on the other hand the **Opponent** who tries to challenge Δ in accordance with of the rules.[8] The **Opponent's** aim is to invalidate the thesis uttered by the **Proponent** by building a counter-argument to Δ. If the **Opponent** does not succeed in that task, we can consider that the **Proponent** has a winning strategy for Δ because he manages to defend against all possible challenges of the **Opponent** (still in accordance with the rules). Then it means that the **Proponent** proves the validity of his initial argument.

The debate which follows after the thesis offers to dialogical logic the possibility to define the meaning of the logical constants via the notions

---

[8]The set of rules determines the dialogical system in which the thesis can be challenged and defended.

of commitment and choice during the argumentative process between the two players. It is that very point which allows us to explore and to provide an original theory of the meaning of the different epistemic operators based on the use of these logical constants during an exchange on the argument.

Our dialogical language is obtained from $\mathcal{L}_{KC[\,]}(Ag, \mathcal{P})$ by the addition of:

- two meta-logical symbols ? and !

- two labels **O** and **P** standing for the players.

- a label i which indicates the context of the utterance. Labels are finite sequences of positive integers such as 1_a1 and 1_a2 indicate (from the model-theoretic point of view) that contexts 1 and 2 are reachable from 1 for the agent a.

2.1 A new form of Labels

In standard dialogical logic, labels are finite sequences of positive integers. If the label i is a sequence of length > 1, the positive integers of the sequence will be separated by periods. But in our work, sequences are separated by the 'name' of agents $(a_1, ..., a_n)$. Thus, if i is a label and n is a positive integer, then i_an is also a label of the agent a, called an extension of i.

The problem is that we want to treat about a logic with public announcement, hence this formulation of labels is not sufficient and we must enrich it. The idea is to keep track of the announcement on labels. For this reason, we use another way to denote a label. A labelled formula is now defined as a triple:

$\mathcal{A}|n : \Sigma$, such that:

- $\mathcal{A} = \sigma_1\sigma_2...\sigma_n$ is a sequence of announced formulas. If there is no announced formula, the sequence remains empty and we denote the list by ϵ.[9]

- n is a sequence of labels such as $i_{a_1}i'_{a_2}...i''_{a_n}$,

- Σ is either a $\mathcal{L}_{KC[\,]}$ formula or a dialogical symbolic challenge.[10]

---

[9]The idea of the sequence of announcement is taken from Balbiani et al. (2010).

[10]Dialogical symbolic challenges are challenges of the form "?...", see particle rules column "Y's-Challenge" section 2.2-2.4.

For short, we add the new argument carried by the announcement to the list $\mathcal{A}$, but strictly speaking no new label appears. The label remains the same; we just add more information on it, adding announcements as a prefixed list to the label.

2.2 The standard Particle Rules

As every game, a dialogical game obeys some rules. Two kinds of rules are required: particle rules and structural rules. Particle rules define how to challenge and defend each logical constant during the dialogue whereas structural rules regulate the course of the dialogue itself. Consequently, the first ones provides the local meaning of logical constants and the second ones the global meaning of the game. The latter kind of rules will be exposed in section 2.6.

Particle rules are symmetric, that is, they are strictly the same for the **O**pponent and for the **P**roponent. For this reason, we use the notation **X** and **Y** in their formulation. Table for particle rules must be read as "*In the course of the dialogue if the player* **X** *does the utterance* φ (**X**-Utterance); *then the player* **Y** *challenges it with the corresponding attack* (**Y**-Challenge) *and* **X** *must produce the corresponding defence* (**X**-Defence)". The Particle rules for standard connectives are defined below:

Logical constants	X - Utterance	Y - Challenge ?	X - Defence !
$\neg$, no possible defence	$\mathcal{A}\|i: \neg\varphi$	$\mathcal{A}\|i : \varphi$	$\otimes$
$\wedge$, the challenger has the choice on the conjunct to challenge	$\mathcal{A}\|i : \varphi \wedge \psi$	$\mathcal{A}\|i : ?_{\wedge 1}$ or $\mathcal{A}\|i : ?_{\wedge 2}$	$\mathcal{A}\|i : \varphi$ respectively $\mathcal{A}\|i : \psi$
$\vee$, the defender has the choice on the disjunct to defend	$\mathcal{A}\|i : \varphi \vee \psi$	$\mathcal{A}\|i : ?$	$\mathcal{A}\|i : \varphi$ or $\mathcal{A}\|i : \psi$

Particle Rules for Standard Connectives (PR–SC)

There is no possible defence for the negation, which is symbolized by "$\otimes$". The play on the conjunction and the disjunction shows the difference between having the burden of the choice or not. In case of a conjunction, it is the challenger who chooses the conjunct and the defender is subjected to his choice, whereas the roles are reversed with the disjunction, it is the defender who has the burden of the choice.

2.3 Epistemic Operators

As we have already said, our aim is to reconstruct the epistemic operators in dialogical logic, using the notion of choice. This is easily done by the interaction between the two arguers of the dialogue. Let us take the semantics of the individual knowledge operator as an example.

1. Individual knowledge's semantics stipulates that in a model $\mathcal{M}$ and in a state w, a formula $K_a\varphi$ is satisfied provided φ is satisfied in every state w' of $\mathcal{M}$ reachable for the agent a from w.

2. Consider $\langle \mathcal{A}|i : K_a\varphi \rangle \in d_\Delta$. The player **X** who makes this utterance, utters in fact that φ must hold in any label reachable for a. So, if **Y** wants to challenge it, he can arbitrary choose a label i' reachable for a in which **X** would be able to utter φ. And then the label of **X**'s defence turns into $\mathcal{A}|i_a i'$.[11]

From a general point of view, in every case in which a player **X** utters something like *"for all things, something is the case"*, the player **X** exposes himself to the choice of the player **Y**. And after that **X** has to play taking into account **Y**'s choice. If he is not able to do this, his utterance fails and he will not be able to defend his utterance.

Operators of sharing knowledge and common knowledge behave in a similar way. A player **X** who utters that φ is a shared knowledge into the group G ($E_G\varphi$), utters in fact that any agent in G individually knows the proposition φ. In that case, **Y** has the choice and can arbitrarily choose any agent in G in order to challenge **X**'s utterance. Consequently, after **Y**'s challenge, **X** must utter φ in the scope of the individual knowledge operator of the corresponding agent chosen by **Y**.

A player **X**, who utters that a proposition φ is commonly known by the group G ($C_G\varphi$), utters in fact that for any possible sequence of agents the proposition φ holds. Hence, **Y** can choose any arbitrary sequence of agents in G; and **X** must defend φ in the scope of the corresponding sequence of agents chosen by **Y**. The particle rules giving the meaning of all these operators are given in the following table.

---

[11]Due to the list of announcement, this must be completed by a specific rule which ensures that i' respects the list, see section Structural Rules (SR-A.1) for more details on that point.

Logical constants	X-Utterance	Y-Challenge ?	X-Defence !
K_a, the challenger can choose any label i' for a	$\mathcal{A}\|i : K_a\varphi$	$\mathcal{A}\|i : ?^a_{i'}$	$\mathcal{A}\|i_a i' : \varphi$
E_G, the challenger can choose any agent $a \in G$	$\mathcal{A}\|i : E_G\varphi$	$\mathcal{A}\|i : ?a \in G$	$\mathcal{A}\|i : K_a\varphi$
C_G, the challenger can choose any sequence of agents, this sequence can be empty	$\mathcal{A}\|i : C_G\varphi$	$\mathcal{A}\|i : ?\langle a_1...a_n\rangle \in G^*$	$\mathcal{A}\|i : K_{a_1}...K_{a_n}\varphi$

Particle Rules for Epistemic Operators (PR–KO)

Through those rules, a noticeable thing appears: *eventually*, exchanges starting with $E_G\varphi$ or $C_G\varphi$ will proceed according to the rule for K_a. Moreover, thinking about the rules for epistemic operators in that way gives us a better understanding on how each of them are constructed from an individual knowledge operator. In fact, it is always the notion of choice which leads to φ from any epistemic operators. The type of the choice simply depends on the operator at stake.

Note: Since we are in a multi-agent setting some notational requirements must be clarified. Let us consider a formula $\varphi \in d_\Delta$ where φ stands for $i\colon K_{a_1}K_{a_2}\psi$. As the challenger will have to choose a label for each different individual knowledge operator, the latest label is noted "$i_{a_1}i'_{a_2}i''$". In this way, we are able to retrace the "story" of the formula at stake.[12] And indeed, it is easy to see that the labelled formula "$i_{a_1}i'_{a_2}i''\colon \psi$" follows from $i\colon K_{a_1}K_{a_2}\psi$ because each a_n between labels represents a choice of a challenger for a K_a operator.

2.4 Announcement & Dialogue

We are now ready to present dynamic operators of public announcements in the dialogical framework. Public announcement operators can also be understood through the notion of choice plus the notion of commitment. Indeed, as in dialogical logic we assume that we do not have any model, the eliminating path of an announcement must be on choices of players. It means that after a play on an announcement

---

[12]This point is important for the application of the rule **(SR-5*)**, see section 2.6 Structural Rules for DEMAL for more details.

operator, players must take into account the announcement. One interesting point here is to understand the idea of migration to a sub-model through a commitment of a player during the debate instead of an operation on a model. It works for public announcement operator as well as for its dual. The difference between the public announcement operator and its dual is captured by a difference in the possible defence (after the challenge on the announcement operator).

In the case of the public announcement operator the defender can choose to commit himself or not in the announced formula, but in case of its dual he has not the choice, he must commit himself in the announced formula. That public announcement operator represents, in the dialogical framework, a kind of commitment in terms of concession. And in fact it is: the player who challenges the announcement can be constraint to concede the announcement if the defender does not commit himself in its defence (by challenging the negation, see the rule below). Whereas the dual of public announcement operator represents a commitment in terms of assertion: the player who utters a dual of a public announcement must be able to take in charge the utterance of the announced formula. It means that he will be able to defend that proposition against any challenge (allowed by the set of rules) of his adversary.

Following Walton and Krabbe (1995), Yamada (2012) proposes a logic that also brings out a such distinction between concession commitment and assertion commitment. It would seem that there exists some interesting connexions between Yamada's approach and **DEMAL**, but it is not our purpose to further expose them here.

The meaning of announcement operator is given by the rules in the following table (the symbol "+" means that the right part is added to the left part of the list):

Logical constants	X Utterance	Y Challenge ?	X Defence !
$[\varphi]\,\psi$, the defender has the choice for his defence	$\mathcal{A}\|i : [\varphi]\,\psi$	$\mathcal{A}\|i : ?$	$\mathcal{A}\|i : \neg\varphi$ *or* $\mathcal{A} + \varphi\|i : \psi$
$\langle\varphi\rangle\psi$, the challenger has the choice for his challenge	$\mathcal{A}\|i : \langle\varphi\rangle\psi$	$\mathcal{A}\|i : ?_{(1)}$ *or* $\mathcal{A}\|i : ?_{(2)}$	$\mathcal{A}\|i : \varphi$ *respectively* $\mathcal{A} + \varphi\|i : \psi$

Particle Rules for Announcement Operators (PR–AO)

The particle rule for public announcement operator can be intuitively understood as the following exchange:

> in accordance to announcements in $\mathcal{A}$, the player **X** says: "in the situation i, if I commit myself in the defence of the argument φ, then I will utter ψ in accordance to φ". So, player **Y** asks him what he will do, hence **X** has the choice:
>
> - he can reply "No I don't want to commit myself in the utterance of the argument φ", *or*
> - he can utter ψ assuming φ.

The particle rule for the dual of a public announcement operator can be understood following the same exchange except on who has the burden of the choice:

> in accordance to announcements in $\mathcal{A}$, the player **X** says: "in the situation i, I commit myself in the defence of the argument φ and I will utter ψ in respect of φ". Hence, now **Y** has the choice, he can compel **X** to utter:
>
> - φ, *or*
> - ψ assuming φ.

And of course, **X** must answer following **Y**'s choice.

2.5 The set *PartRules*

All of the particle rules presented above (particle rules for standard connectives, for knowledge operators and for public announcement operators) are brought together in a set named *PartRules*:

$$PartRules := \text{PR-SC} \cup \text{PR-EO} \cup \text{PR-AO}$$

2.6 Structural Rules

As mentioned in section 2.2, there are two kinds of rules in dialogical logic. We have seen the particle rules which are the rules for the logical constants, now we must expose the rules which govern the dialogue itself: the structural rules. These rules concern the process of the dialogue, they deal with how to play the dialogue. Firstly, we begin by presenting what we can name the standard structural rules. They can be said *Standard* because those rules are the base of any dialogical system.

Standard Structural Rules

- **Starting Rule (SR-0)**: Any dialogue d_Δ starts with **P** uttering Δ (the thesis). After the thesis has been uttered, players alternately choose a *repetition rank n* and *m*. A repetition rank is a positive integer number which corresponds to the number of defences or challenges that a player can perform.

- **Game-playing (SR-1)**: Players act alternately. Whenever he has a turn to play, player **X** can challenge any previous **Y** move or defend against any previous **Y** challenge up to his repetition rank.

- **Formal Rule (SR-2)**: **P** is allowed to utter an atomic formula only if **O** has uttered it first.

- **Winning Rule (SR-3)**: Player **X** wins a dialogue if and only if it is **Y**'s to play but he cannot.

Those rules are for a basic dialogue on propositional logic. But epistemic logic requires a dialogical modal logic, so we need to complete these standard rules. Rahman and Rückert (1999) and Rahman and Keiff (2005) have developed dialogical modal systems. For **DEMAL** we propose the following two rules: one for the condition of the choice of labels and another for the announcement operators.

Structural Rules for DEMAL

- **(SR-5*) A chosen label for agent a:**[13] to challenge a K_a *operator* from a label $\mathcal{A}|i...i'$, **P** can choose for a any label i'' in the sequence $\mathcal{A}|i...i'$ such that:

  - $\mathcal{A}|i'' = \mathcal{A}|i'$ *or*
  - we have both:
    * **O** has already chosen the label $\mathcal{A}|i''$ for a, and
    * there is no b in the sequence $\mathcal{A}|i'...j_b...i''$ where $a \neq b$.

The first requirement stipulates that **P** can use the reflexivity for his choice whereas the two other requirements express the symmetric and transitive closure for the choice made on a's label.

---

[13]The rule **(SR-5*)** is a slight adaptation of the rule **(SR-ST9.2S5)** found in Rahman and Keiff (2005). The rule **(SR-ST9.2S5)** characterizes a S5 accessibility between dialogical labels, **(SR-5*)** privatises that access to each agent $a \in Ag$.

- **Announcement & Label (SR-A.1)**: If there is a move $\langle \mathbf{X} - \mathcal{A}|i : e \rangle$ such that the sequence $\mathcal{A}$ is non-empty, then $\mathbf{Y}$ can compel $\mathbf{X}$ to utter the last element of $\mathcal{A}$ in the label i or in a label j if $e = ?_j$.

- **Step back & Step forward (SR-A.2)**: After an utterance φ that follows from a play on an announcement $[\varphi]...$ (or $\langle \varphi \rangle...$) in label i, $\mathbf{P}$ can defend an atomic formula p in a label:

    - i if $\mathbf{O}$ has uttered p in $\varphi|i$ (SB), *or*

    - $\varphi|i$ if $\mathbf{O}$ has uttered φ and p in i (SF).

All of the structural rules that we have presented above are brought together in a set named *StrucRules*:

$$StrucRules = \text{SR-0} \cup \text{SR-1} \cup \text{SR-2} \cup \text{SR-3} \cup \text{SR-5}^* \cup \text{SR-A}$$

2.7 DEMAL

DEMAL is defined as being the set *PartRules* and the set *StrucRules*.

$$\mathbf{DEMAL} = PartRules \cup StrucRules$$

With respect to the rules of **DEMAL**, there is a winning strategy for the **Proponent** for all of the formulas in Table 1 which characterize the system **PAC**. A soundness and completeness proof of **DEMAL** has been presented at the XIVth CLMPS and it is to appear.[14]

3 Examples

Let us take some examples to illustrate how to play with **DEMAL**. The first one only deals with individual knowledge operator, the next one a group of agents and the last one a public announcement. In the following examples, with respect to (SR-0), **P** always utters the thesis at move 0; and as the arguers must play alternatively, **P**'s moves are even-numbered whereas **O**'s moves are odd-numbered (see external columns). Challenged moves are noted in the middle columns (middle left column for **O** and middle right column for **P**).

---

[14]See Magnier and de Lima (2012).

$K_a(\varphi \to \psi) \to (K_a\varphi \to K_a\psi)$	distribution K_a over $\to$
$K_a\varphi \to \varphi$	truth
$K_a\varphi \to K_a K_a \varphi$	introspection positive
$\neg K_a\varphi \to K_a\neg K_a\varphi$	introspection negative
$[\varphi]p \to (\varphi \to p)$	atomic permanence
$[\varphi]\neg\psi \leftrightarrow (\varphi \to \neg[\varphi]\psi)$	announcement and negation
$[\varphi](\varphi \wedge \chi) \leftrightarrow ([\varphi]\psi \wedge [\varphi]\chi)$	announcement and conjunction
$[\varphi]K_a\psi \leftrightarrow (\varphi \to K_a[\varphi]\psi)$	announcement and knowledge
$[\varphi][\psi]\chi \leftrightarrow [\varphi \wedge [\varphi]\psi]\chi$	announcement and composition
$C_G(\varphi \to \psi) \to (C_G\varphi \to C_G\psi)$	distribution C_G over $\to$
$C_G\varphi \to (\varphi \wedge E_G C_G\varphi)$	mix of common knowledge
$C_G(\varphi \to E_G\varphi) \to (\varphi \to C_G\varphi)$	induction of common knowledge

Table 1: Axioms of PAC

3.1   Example 1

First, we take the formula $\neg K_a p \vee K_a K_b K_a p$ in order to show how the rule (SR-5*) works.

	O			**P**	
				$\epsilon\lvert 0$: $\neg K_a p \vee K_a K_b K_a p$	0
	$n := 1$			$m := 2$	
1	$\epsilon\lvert 0$: $?_\vee$	0		$\epsilon\lvert 0$: $\neg K_a p$	2
3	$\epsilon\lvert 0$: $K_a p$	2		$\otimes$	
				$\epsilon\lvert 0$: $K_a K_b K_a p$	4
5	$\epsilon\lvert 0$: $?_1^a$	4		$\epsilon\lvert 0_a 1$: $K_b K_a p$	6
7	$\epsilon\lvert 0_a 1$: $?_2^b$	6		$\epsilon\lvert 0_a 1_b 2$: $K_a p$	8
9	$\epsilon\lvert 0_a 1_b 2$: $?_3^a$	8		$--$	
11	$\epsilon\lvert 0_a 1$: p		3	$\epsilon\lvert 0$: $?_1^a$	10

Explanations: at move 1, **O** challenges the disjunction that **P** defends move 2. Move 3: **O** challenges the negation from move 2. **P** has no defence but he can either challenge move 3 or thanks to his rank of repetition ($m := 2$), he can repeat his defence, which he does at move 4. Move 5: in order to challenge the K operator from move 4, **O** chooses the label 1 for the agent a, from this label he chooses the label 2 for the agent b (move 7); and at move 9, **O** chooses the label 3 for a. Consequently, **P** should utter his defence in the label $\epsilon\lvert 0_a 1_b 2_a 3$.

Owing to (SR-2), **P** cannot answer for the moment, he only can counter-attack move 3 to have p in the appropriate label. The problem is that the rule (SR-5*) forbids this path. From the label $\epsilon|0$, **P** can choose for the agent a any label in the sequence $0_a1_b2_a3$ if and only if the label is not new for a (that is the case here for the label 3 introduced move 9) and if there is no b between the label where the choice is produced and the chosen label, that is between 0 and 3 such that $a \neq b$. But there is a b between 1 and 2 which breaks off the sequence 0...3 for a. So, **P** cannot reuse it and due to (SR-3) **O** wins the dialogue at move 11.

Thanks to this example, it clearly appears that in order to win **P** must violate the S5 closure of the agent a to mix it up with S5 closure of agent b.

3.2 Example 2

The next example presents the axiom called *mix of common knowledge* $C_Gp \rightarrow (p \wedge E_GC_Gp)$. We choose that axiom because it requires to use all epistemic particle rules of **DEMAL**. This axiom is translated in its disjunctive form: $\neg C_Gp \vee (p \wedge E_GC_Gp)$.

	O			**P**	
				$\epsilon|0:\neg C_Gp \vee (p \wedge E_GC_Gp)$	0
	$n := 1$			$m := 2$	
1	$\epsilon|0:\ ?_\vee$	0		$\epsilon|0:\neg C_Gp$	2
3	$\epsilon|0:\ C_Gp$	2		$\otimes$	
				$\epsilon|0:\ p \wedge E_GC_Gp$	4
5	$\epsilon|0:\ ?_{\wedge 2}$	4		$\epsilon|0:\ E_GC_Gp$	6
7	$\epsilon|0:\ ?\ a \in G$	6		$\epsilon|0:\ K_aC_Gp$	8
9	$\epsilon|0:\ ?_1^a$	8		$\epsilon|0_a1:\ C_Gp$	10
11	$\epsilon|0_a1:\ ?\ \langle b,c \rangle \in G^*$	10		$\epsilon|0_a1:\ K_bK_cp$	12
13	$\epsilon|0_a1:\ ?_2^b$	12		$\epsilon|0_a1_b2:\ K_cp$	14
15	$\epsilon|0_a1_b2:\ ?_3^c$	14		$\epsilon|0_a1_b2_c3:\ p$	24
17	$\epsilon|0:\ K_aK_bK_cp$		3	$\epsilon|0:\ ?\ \langle a,b,c \rangle \in G^*$	16
19	$\epsilon|0_a1:\ K_bK_cp$		17	$\epsilon|0:\ ?_1^a$	18
21	$\epsilon|0_a1_b2:\ K_cp$		19	$\epsilon|0_a1:\ ?_2^b$	20
23	$\epsilon|0_a1_b2_c3:\ p$		21	$\epsilon|0_a1_b2:\ ?_3^c$	22

Explanations: moves 1 to 3 are similar to the example 1. Move 5, in accordance to the particle rule of the conjunction and his rank of repetition 1

($n := 1$), **O** has the choice in his challenge but he can play only once. Let us consider that he chooses the second conjunct (we shall consider the other case below). Then **P** utters $E_G C_G p$ in the label $\epsilon|0$ move 6. Thereafter (moves 7-9), **O** chooses the agent a and then the label 1 for a. Obviously, **P** does the corresponding defence uttering $C_G p$ in that label. At move 11, **O** arbitrary chooses the sequence $\langle b, c \rangle$ of agents. According to the particle rule for the common knowledge operator, **P** utters the corresponding embedded sequence of individual knowledge operators. Moves 11 and 13: **O** respectively chooses the label 2 and 3 for agents b and c. Doing so, he compels **P** to utter p in the label $\epsilon|0_a 1_b 2_c 3$, but due to (SR-2), **P** cannot produce that defence for the moment. Hence, **P** counter-attacks move 3 with the sequence $\langle a, b, c \rangle$ of agents at move 16. From moves 18 to 22, he reuses labels chosen by **O** (moves 9, 13 and 15). In his turn, at move 22, **P** forces **O** to utter p in the label $\epsilon|0_a 1_b 2_c 3$. Now, **P** is allowed to produce his defence against the challenge that has not been defended yet. Then he utters $\epsilon|0_a 1_b 2_c 3 : p$ at move 24 and wins.

Now let us consider that instead of the second conjunct, **O** has chosen the first. It provides the dialogue below:

O				P	
				$\epsilon|0: \neg C_G p \vee (p \wedge E_G C_G p)$	0
	$n := 1$			$m := 2$	
1	$\epsilon|0: ?_\vee$	0		$\epsilon|0: \neg C_G p$	2
3	$\epsilon|0: C_G p$	2		$\otimes$	
				$\epsilon|0: p \wedge E_G C_G p$	4
5	$\epsilon|0: ?_{\wedge 1}$	4		$\epsilon|0: p$	8
7	$\epsilon|0: p$		3	$\epsilon|0: ? \langle \rangle \in G^*$	6

Explanations: In the course of that dialogue, **O** forces **P** to utter p in the label $\epsilon|0$. For the same reason as before, **P** cannot defend yet. But at move 6, **P** challenges the move 3 choosing an empty sequence of agent. Doing this, he reverses the charge and then it is **O**'s turn to utter p in the label $\epsilon|0$. Thereafter, **P** can produce his defence in the move 8. It is **O**'s turn to play but there is no other move that he can do. So according to (SR-3) the game is over and **P** wins this dialogue.

Consequently whatever **O**'s choice was on the conjunction, **P** is able to win.

3.3 Example 3

van Ditmarsch (2010) presents an interesting understanding of *Moore Sentence*. The special feature of such sentences is to become false just by their own announcement. Such propositions are true before their announcement but false after that. We now consider such an example in order to test the ability of our rules to deal with case of what is commonly named *unsuccessful update*.[15] Moreover sentences like *Moore Sentence* can help the reader to correctly understand how to play with **DEMAL**'s rules, in particular (SR-A.1).

	O			P	
				$\epsilon\vert 0$: $[p \wedge \neg K_a p]\,(p \wedge \neg K_a p)$	0
	$n := 1$			$m := 2$	
1	$\epsilon\vert 0$: $?_{[\,]}$	0		$\epsilon\vert 0$: $\neg(p \wedge \neg K_a p)$	2
3	$\epsilon\vert 0$: $p \wedge \neg K_a p$	2		$\otimes$	
5	$\epsilon\vert 0$: p		3	$\epsilon\vert 0$: $?_{\wedge_1}$	4
7	$\epsilon\vert 0$: $\neg K_a p$		3	$\epsilon\vert 0$: $?_{\wedge_2}$	6
	$\otimes$		7	$\epsilon\vert 0$: $K_a p$	8
9	$\epsilon\vert 0$: $?^a_1$	8			
				$p \wedge \neg K_a p\vert 0$: $p \wedge \neg K_a p$	10
11	$p \wedge \neg K_a p\vert 0$: $?_{\wedge_2}$	10		$p \wedge \neg K_a p\vert 0$: $\neg K_a p$	12
13	$p \wedge \neg K_a p\vert 0$: $K_a p$	12		$\otimes$	
			13	$p \wedge \neg K_a p\vert 0$: $?^a_1$	14
15	$\epsilon\vert 0_a 1$: $!_{(p \wedge \neg K_a p)}$	14		$\epsilon\vert 0_a 1$: $p \wedge \neg K_a p$	16
17	$\epsilon\vert 0_a 1$: $?_{\wedge_1}$	16		$--$	

Explanations: move 1, **O** challenges the announcement and **P** chooses to reject to commit himself in the announcement. Move 3: **O** challenges the negation. At moves 4 and 6, thanks to his rank of repetition ($m := 2$), **P** plays twice over his challenge on the conjunction of move 3 and he obtains both conjuncts. Move 8: **P** challenges the negation of move 7. As **O** has no possible defence, he challenges move 8 by choosing the label 1, but owing to (SR-2) **P** cannot produce the corresponding defence for the moment. Hence at move 10, he uses his rank of repetition ($m := 2$) in order to change his defence from the challenge on announcement (challenged by **O** at move 1 and already defended by **P** at move 2). Moves 11 and 13 are respectively about conjunction and negation. Move 14: in the label in which both player are committed in

---

[15]See van Ditmarsch and Kooi (2006) for various definitions on *successful* formula and update.

the announcement, **P** chooses to challenge move 13 with the label 1 in order to produce the corresponding defence of the challenge move 9. But **O** has never uttered the announcement in the label 0_a1. Then at move 15, **O** uses the rule (SR-A.1) and compels **P** to utter the announcement in the label 0_a1, what he does at move 16. Move 17, **O** challenges the conjunction of move 16, but once again due to (SR-2), **P** is not able to produce this defence. And as he has no other possible move, he loses and **O** is the winner of the dialogue.

Hence, in **DEMAL**, **P** cannot win a dialogue which states that a Moore Sentence is successful.

4 Conclusion and further developments

4.1 Choice, Announcement and Commitment

As we have tried to underline, the dialogical framework offers an alternative understanding of epistemic operators. On the one hand, all knowledge operators are interpreted in terms of choice: a label for *K*-operator, an agent for *E*-operator and a sequence of agents for *C*-operator. On the other hand, announcement operators represent acts of commitment, either a concession or an assertion taken in charge by the arguers.

Thanks to the dialogical framework the meaning of these operators is dynamically given through the game of challenges and defences between the two arguers of the dialogue. They are defined in their use in an argumentative context, not from an abstract point of view in terms of truth-conditions. The construction of the epistemic operators and the difference between the public announcement and its dual appear in new lights. Through the burden of choice, all epistemic operators lead to a boolean proposition: common knowledge operator changes in a sequence of embedded individual knowledge operator; sharing knowledge operator becomes an individual knowledge operator and the individual knowledge operator simply gives the proposition in a chosen label. Moreover, as it is shown, announcement operators are not operations on models but are acts of commitment of the players of the dialogue. That gives us a new light on what public announcement can be, and we hope to get closer to Plaza (1989)'s intuition about exchange in communicative contexts.

4.2 Further Developments

Therefore, this dialogical reconstruction represents a starting point of further works and researches. As previously said, a soundness and completeness proof of **DEMAL** is given in Magnier and de Lima (2012). One interesting field of further research is found in direction of Yamada's works and principally consists in the exploration in the possible extension of **DEMAL** with an operator that deletes commitments that occur in course of a dialogue.

Another interesting issue using the logic **DEMAL** is on Leibniz's studies about conditional law. Thiercelin (2010) and Thiercelin (2011) underline the fact that Leibniz provides very precise criteria for the juridical modality of the conditional law. The restrictions that Leibniz provides on conditional for his studies in law seem to be (and they are!) very close to announcement operator. However surprising it may seem, most of his criteria exactly correspond to how a public announcement is understood in **DEMAL**. Indeed, it is possible to interpret a sentence like *B is suspended to A* (which corresponds to the juridical modality of the conditional law) as $[A]B$ in the course of a dialogue between what Thiercelin named the 'conditioner' and the 'conditionee'[16] that can respectively be understood as the arguer who utters an announcement and the other one who challenges it. The first step of this exploration is already done in a jointed work in Magnier and Rahman (2012).

Acknowledgements. Special thanks are addressed to all those who have supported and encouraged this field of research, in particular T. de Lima for his useful help and feedback, to V. Fiutek for her many advices and to anonymous referees for their encouraging comments.

Bibliography

Balbiani, P., van Ditmarsch, H., Herzig, A., and de Lima, T., 2010. Tableaux for Public Announcement Logic. *Journal of Logic and Computation*, 20:55–76.

Fagin, R., Halpern, J. Y., Moses, Y., and Vardi, M. Y., 1995. *Reasoning about knowledge*. MIT Press, Cambridge, Massachusetts.

Fontaine, M. and Redmond, J., 2008. *Logique Dialogique : une introduction - Première partie 1 : Méthode de la dialogique : régles et exercices*, volume 5 of col. *Cahiers de logique et Epistémologie*. College Publications, London.

Gerbrandy, J., 1999. *Bisimulation on Planet Kripke*. PhD thesis, University of Amsterdam, ILLC. URL http://www.di.unito.it/~gerbrand/papers/DS-1999-01.text.pdf.

---

[16]see Thiercelin (2011) pp. 251-253.

Hendricks, V. F., 2005. *Mainstream and Formal Epistemology*. Cambridge University Press.

Hendricks, V. F. and Symons, J., 2010. Where's the bridge? epistemology and epistemic logic. *Philosophical Studies*, 128:137–167.

Keiff, L., 2009. Dialogical logic. URL {http://plato.stanford.edu/entries/logic-dialogical/}.

Mackenzie, J., 1985. No logic before friday. *Synthese*, 63(3):329–341.

Magnier, S. and de Lima, T. A Soundness & Completeness Proof on Dialogues and Dynamic Epistemic Logic. 2012 - forthcoming.

Magnier, S. and Rahman, S. Leibniz's Notion of Conditional Right and the Dynamics of Public Announcement. *Logos & Episteme*. 2012 - forthcoming.

Plaza, J., 1989. Logics of public announcements. In Pfeifer, M. S., Hadzikadic, M., and Ras, Z. W. (ed.), *Proceedings 4th International Symposium on Methodologies for Intelligent Systems*, pages 201–216.

Rahman, S. and Keiff, L., 2005. On how to be a dialogician. In Vanderveken, D. (ed.), *Logic, Thought and Action*, pages 359–408. Springer, Dordrecht.

Rahman, S. and Rückert, H., 1999. Dialogische Modallogik (für T, B, S4, und S5). *Logique et Analyse*, 167(168):243–282.

Rebuschi, M., 2009. Implicit vs. explicit knowledge in dialogical logic. In Majer, O., Pietarinen, A. V., and Tulenheimo, T. (ed.), *Games: Unifying Logic, Language, and Philosophy*, pages 229–246. Springer.

Rebuschi, M. and Lihoreau, F., 2008. Contextual epistemic logic. In Dégremont, C., Keiff, L., and Rückert, H. (ed.), *Dialogues, Logics and Other Strange Things. Essays in Honour of Shahid Rahman*, pages 305–335. College Publications, London.

Thiercelin, A. Conditions, conditionnels, droits conditionnels : l'articulation du jeune Leibniz. unpublished manuscript, 2010.

Thiercelin, A., 2011. Epistemic and practical aspects of conditionals in leibniz's legal theory of conditions. In Gabbay, D., Canivez, P., Rahman, S., and Thiercelin, A. (ed.), *Approaches to Legal Rationality*, volume 20 of *Logic, Epistemology, and the Unity of Science (LEUS)*, pages 203–215. Springer, Dordrecht.

van Ditmarsch, H. Dynamic epistemic logic, the Moore sentence, and the Fitch paradox, 2010. URL http://arche-wiki.st-and.ac.uk/~ahwiki/pub/Arche/ArcheLogicGroup10Jun2009/slidesMooreFitch.pdf.

van Ditmarsch, H., van der Hoek, W., and Kooi, B., 2007. *Dynamic Epistemic Logic*, volume 337 of *Synthese Library : Studies in Epistemology, Logic, Methodology, and Philosophy of Science*. Springer, Dordrecht.

van Ditmarsch, H. and Kooi, B., 2006. The secret of my success. *Synthese*, 153(2): 339–339.

Walton, D. N. and Krabbe, E. C. W., 1995. *Commitment in Dialogue: Basic Concepts of Interpersonal Reasoning*. Albany State University of New York Press, New York.

Yamada, T., 2012. Dynamic logic of propositional commitments. In Trobok, M., Miscvic, N., and Zarnic, B. (ed.), *Between Logic and Reality: Modeling Inference, Action, and Understanding.* Springer-Verlag, Berlin, Heidelburg, New York.

PART III

PHILOSOPHICAL AND LINGUISTIC
PERSPECTIVES

Belief Conditional in the Ugaritic Language

Cristina BARÉS GÓMEZ*

ABSTRACT. One of the most important innovations to study the conditional structure was made by Ramsey. The test of Ramsey has been used for many approaches to a non-strict conditional. This is the starting point of the study, and it involves the task of determining the sets of true sentences that constitute an antecedent in order to render true the corresponding counterfactual. In further approaches, the sets of the true sentences are undestood as building agent's belief. In such a context these sets are understood as the belief and knowledge required for a conditional to be true. With this approach to the conditional in the Semitic language, we try to study the belief from the language itself, because the belief is expressed thanks to the different tenses/aspects used. We try to obtain the belief modality by checking and analysing the language itself for building an approach to the conditional statement focusing on their use in the text.

1 The Ugaritic language and our methodology of research

We shall study conditionals the Ugaritic language as belief conditionals, but first of all, we must explain briefly the structure of the language and the methodology that we are going to use. Ugaritic is a Semitic language attested between the XIV and XII century B. C., in the ancient city of Ugarit (Ras Shamra)[1] and the surrounding area, along the Mediterranean coast of modern Syria. This language was written by means of an alphabet of 30 cueneiform signs, incised on clay tablets. We also have evidence of another alphabet of 22 letters. The archive found in the city, back in 1929, contained over one thousand six hundred Ugaritic

---

*Grupo de Lógica, Lenguaje e Información, Universidad de Sevilla, Spain & Centro de Ciencias Humanas y Sociales (CCHS), Consejo Superior de Investigaciones Científicas (CSIC), Spain.

[1]A good general approach to the discovery of Ugarit can be found in Smith (2001).

texts, including myths, legends, rituals, letters, legal and administrative texts, school exercises, etc. It has a three-consonant root, typical of Semitic languages. The strictly consonantal system of the West Semitic alphabet is supplemented by three signs with relevant vocalic elements.[2] The Ugaritic language has been chosen as a prototype to build the structure of a language that could be treated with computational tools. We developed a formalization of the structure of the language taking into account all its levels of research.

Our methodology[3] was named Hermeneumatic[4] and has among its purposes the development of computer applications that could help the researcher in his task of interpretting texts critically. The target is not to achieve an automatic translation of texts because the synonym accuracy between both will never be completed.

In order to reach the structure of the language we have used the Knowledge Structure Manager, KSM.[5] This is a kind of Experts System developed by Jose Cuena and applied to natural language. Our aim is to formalize the expert's reaction when facing a particular problem. The starting point for the computerization of Ugaritic has been the design and development of a Data Bank (UDB). However, many issues remain unsolved. We do not know the exact vocalization of all words, which provides us with the aspect and the declination, the phonetics is known by the three alif, the syllabic text and the rest by comparative linguistics. The syntax and the semantic levels are not completely known.

---

[2]The three signs that the ugaritic aphabet has in contrast with the rest of the West Semitic languages are the 'a, 'u and 'i. An alif (') is a semi-vowel (or a weak consonant). The ugaritic doesn't write the vowels, except if they are preceding for the alif. The vocalic system in semitic languages is important because it give us the tense and aspect of the verbs. With this vocalic system in Ugaritic we have an additional help to understand the morphology and the semantic. The others vocalization usually comes from the comparative linguistic in semitic languages, reconstructing the phonological patterns.

[3]The main idea of our methodology was taken from different projects that were developed by Jesus Luis Cunchillos (CSIC) and José Cuena (UPM). The first project began in June 1990 and it was called "Northwest Semitic Philological Data Bank: Ugaritic, Phoenician, Punic", financed by the Spanish Ministry of Education. The 5th one, still ongoing, is directed by Juan Pablo Vita (CSIC), with the title "Banco de Datos Semíticos Noroccidentales: Desarrollo y aplicación de Nuevas tecnologías para el estudio y conservación de la documentación semítico-noroccidental del II y I milenio A.C." Reference: HUM 2007-65317/FILO.

[4]This terminology was proposed by J. L. Cunchillos. For more information about the Hermeneumatic methodology, see Cunchillos (2000).

[5]An extended explanation of KSM is published in Cuena and Molina (2004).

Several projects are still in the first stage. Among them, one studies the Phoenician language and another the Akkadian language.

1.1 Module I. Ugaritic text (TU)[6]

The first module of the Ugaritic Data Bank (UDB) was to clarify the text line of a clay tablet with all its epigraphical problems. The process spans from the object (clay tablet or inscription) to obtain the text line with epigraphical accidents. The structure of this action has been developed in different sequential steps. These are: Graphematic Chain (CG): once clean, restitution or segmentation; written object, (material context); and text line. We accept the source text and keep physically the text lines with their many readings, collations.

1.2 Module II. Generator of Segmentation, Restoration and Concordance(GSRC)[7]

This module cleans the text, divides the CG and makes the union between different CGs. It treats the broken chain and restores the incomplete CG. After these processes we obtain a word in developed morphology (*Palabras en Morfología desplegada*, PMD). This module has to be completed by the phonological level, still in progress. We encounter many difficulties to treat the phonological level of the Ugaritic language. As we have already mentioned, only the vowels placed next to some weak consonants are written. Besides we have to add some of the problems with Ugaritic phonology such as the contraction of the vowels (*ay>ê aw>ô*); the reduplication of consonants and the loss of the Nun (CvNCv>CvCCv); or the *w>y* when placed first position CwC/CyC, which is unclear in the dicionary. [8]

---

[6]The whole structure of the UDB will not be developed, for it is not the topic of this paper. Therefore, we shall just mention it and include enough bibliography for further reading. There are three publications of this module, two of them in books (Spanish and English) and the other in electronic version Cunchillos and Vita (1993); Cunchillos et al. (2003a). All these projects were made in 4thD, but they are now translated into MSQL and they will be accessible from all platforms. This publication will soon be made available online by CSIC.

[7]The publication of the module II can be found in Cunchillos and al (1996).

[8]After this module, we begin the typical work of Hebrew studies: the concordance of Ugaritic words in this particular case. See Cunchillos and Vita (1995); Cunchillos et al. (2003b).

1.3   Module III. Morphological Analysis (AMU)[9]

We obtained the PMD from the second module. The morphological Analysis (AMU) needs:

Lexicon

We start from the actual knowledge of the language and then we question all the dates and arguments. The lexicon receives feedback in the program itself. It is not completely finished. We cover roots and radicals (radical is a word that cames from a root with the thematic vowel). The root appears in the lexicon in a traditional way for the Semitic roots, in the 3rd person singular of the perfective form in the active voice: "*qatala*".

Each input in the lexicon contains the following philological information:

- Root/ radical Number of homographic terms.

- Grammatical classification.

- Basic meaning.

- Etymology.

- Bibliography.

- Notes.

Morphological modifiers

These are all the invariable elements that are used to differenctiate names (gender and number) and a set of derived elements that we add to the root (such as proffessions, names from some places, etc), suffixes, adjetive-pronoun, and the different conjugations, modes, tenses and pronoun suffixes of verb forms.

Rules. Different levels of analysis

Level 1:   The Developed Morphological Word (PMD) without a modifier. AMU affects on the lexicon and PMD agrees with the root/radical.

Level 2:   The PMD with a morphological Modifier. AMU incides on the lexicon by looking for a root/radical to match with the rest of the graphematic chains.

---

[9]This module was developed by R. Cervigon, all the information about it could be found in Cervigon (2007); Cervigón (2007).

Level 3:   The PMD comes from a weak root.

Level 4:   It describes the theoretical form of the noun which comes from the verbal root or other cases.

1.4   Module IV. Syntax (ASU)[10]

We work with "concatenation of words": what a complete text in a literary unit has inside, as it was proposed by some philologists. The information from each word is added to the other modules. The concatenation of words will give us the input for the next module: the literary module.

Although this module is just in the begining, to build this we have to clarify the syntactic structure of the language. For this purpose, we focus on the structure of the conditional in Ugaritic, the main topic of this paper and one of the less clear logical constants. We will analyse different conditionals that we have found in the text with the help of the modules already developed and of the logic of belief.

1.5   Module V. Semantic Level

The most important methodological principle was established by Cunchillos. We work directly with the texts, with their basic unit, we do not try to mark the unit with frames or labels. When we treat a text it should be progressive and incremental, from epigraphy to semantics. This point of view is essential in our work, so when we try to build the semantics, this semantic will have the same methodological structure. Usually, the specifier of the syntax is found at the lexical level, so we start to build a semantics that is already given. However, our lexicon is not given and it takes all the information from the other levels, for example the morphological level. The regular way for analyzing a text is to know the meaning of the sentences and then, to specify the formalization to give the correct relation. Here, since the semantic does not give us many clues, we do not really know if we are right with the translation or not. Therefore, we need to discover the semantic level with specifiers that are given to us by the other levels. Our research starts to show all the levels involved. Then, we have chosen one type

---

[10]The first approach to the syntax module could be found in Siabra (2007). Nonetheless, the logical approach could be helpful, for this work is still ongoing.

of text, the letters.[11] Up until now, ninety three letters have been found and published.

2 The conditional structure in the Ugaritic language

The theory of the conditional sentence in northwestern Semitic languages is not well developed.[12] We still face many problems to clearly know its structure. In Ugaritic, the most common way to find it is to have the antecedent (protasis) before the consequent (apodosis), but this order may be reversed in some cases. Usually, the antecedent occurs following a conjunction, with *hm*, *im*, *k* or *ky* being the most common. The consequent occurs after the antecedent, with the conjunction *w* or with the preposition *p*.[13] The Semitic languages show a strong preference for conjoining the sentences with paratactic or coordinate constructions over the hypotactic or subordinate ones. In the case of the conditional in Ugaritic we have the same kind of preference. We usually find the two sentences in the same syntactic level and the protasis is not considered a subordinate sentence.[14]

If we analyse the verbs appearing in a conditional, we find the two usual aspects that determine the verbal semantic in semitic languages: perfect (qtl) and imperfect (yqtl).[15] In Ugaritic, the antecedent or protasis, like in Biblical Hebrew, can have the two aspects already mentioned. Moreover, the apodosis or consequent usually appears in the imperfect form and seldom in the perfect form.[16]

We have chosen two letters containing conditional structure and have built our analysis following the methodology already explained. The conditionals that we use have been chosen because they manifest different uses of the various forms: perfect and imperfect.

---

[11]There are several translations of each Ugaritic letter, but for a general view the main translations of the letters are Caquot et al. (1989); Pardee (2002); Hawley (2003); Bordreuil and Pardee (2004).

[12]For an explanation of the conditional form in ugaritic language see §83.23, §83.122g, §97.9 in Tropper (2000).

[13]The consequent is followed by *p* see p. 790 in Tropper (2000).

[14]This is the usual form in the Semitic languages in general and in Ugaritic in particular. Two sentences of the same syntactical level; p. 547 in Lipinski (2001); Verret (1988).

[15]In Ugaritic we have the form YQTLU, but not the YQTLØ in the conditional sentences see p. 909, §76.533 in Tropper (2000). For a general view of the aspect and modality in ancient Semitic using Biblical Hebrew as an example see Hatav (1997).

[16]For a specific table with all the occurrences of the perfect and imperfect forms in conditional sentences see Bares and Solans (2010).

2.1   KTU. 2.10.[17] Conditional QTL→ Imperative[18]

This letter was written by Iwrdr to Plsy. It shows the information that Trgds and Klby give to Iwrdr about some disaster. The sender asks for the confirmation of the information and whatever else he would like to know about the disaster. We have chosen the conditional in the document to analyse its structure.[19]

00-2.10:9   hm[20] . in[21] mm[22]

---

[17]KTU.2. 10=A 2709=CTA 53==M 3330=RS 4.475=UT 54. Museum: It was in the Louvre (AO17.316), but is now in Aleppo (A2709). Find site: Great Priest´s House. Topographic point: 431 Depth: 0 m. Size (Height 65.0, length 49.0, width 19.0),Cunchillos et al. (2003a).

[18]For different transcriptions, translations, notes and analyses of the letter see Dietrich et al. (1975, 1976); Ahl (1980); Lipinski (1981a); Cunchillos (1982); Pardee (1987); Caquot et al. (1989); Pardee (2002); Bordreuil and Pardee (2004).

[19]All those analyses have been made with AMU, however, we have picked the one we think is more suitable out of a wider range of analyses. The levels are the different analysis, they take into account different morphologicals rules. In the analysis we offer the lexicon: Root/ radical, Number of homographic terms, grammatical classification, basic meaning, etymology; and the morphological modifiers, difference names (gender and number) and a derived set of elements (such as proffessions, names of some places, etc), adjetive-pronoun, suffixes and the different conjugations, modes, tenses and pronoun suffixes of verb forms.

[20]This particle connects sentences (individually or groups of them). It could appear as a disjunctive, conjunction or a conditional one. See p. 95, 96, 97, I in Aartun (1978), §83.142, §83.23 in Tropper (2000), p. 725 in Piquer-Otero (2007) p. 167,168 in del Olmo Lete and Sanmartín (1996).

[21]For more information see p. 19-22, II in Aartun (1978), §88.2 in Tropper (2000), p. 37, 38 in del Olmo Lete and Sanmartín (1996).

[22]p. 283,284 in *del Olmo Lete and Sanmartín (1996)*.

Abbreviations: ac: Akkadian; ug: Ugaritic; fen: Phoenician; hb: Hebrew; arm: Aramaic; etiop: Ethiopian languages; arb: Arabic; sem com: common semitic; o. a.: Old Asyrian; sir: Syriac.

N° 2 – Level: 1 – *hm* = *hm*
[Chain = conjunction] AMU RULES: lexicon(hm): conjunction(hm) CONJUNCTION, RADICAL: *hm* conjunction I «if»: ug. *'in/hm* «if»; arb. *'in* «if»; arm. *hen/'i/en* «if»; hb. *'im* «if»;ac. *šumma*.

N° 1 – Level: 1 – *in* = *in*	N° 1 – Level: 1 – *mm* = *mm*
[Chain = negative adverb] AMU RULES: lexicon(*in*) ADVERB: NEGATION, RADICAL: *in* adverb: negation «no/there isn't»; *yānu,yānumma*«no/there isn't» ac.; *'i* «» etiop.; *ynny* «no/there isn't» fen.; *'ayin*, *'ēn* «no/there isn't» hb.	[Chain = undefined pronoun] AMU RULES: lexicon(*mm*)–≥undefined pronoun(mm) UNDEFINED PRONOUN, RADICAL: *mm* undefined pronoun I «anything, all.»; *manman, manma* «anybody»ac.; *mūma* «anybody» hb.

"If we would not be completely beaten (if there is nothing at all) / if they would not be beaten," [23]

00-2.10:10   nḫtu[24] *. w*[25] *. lak*

N° 2 – Level: 2 – *nḫtu* = - + *n*- + *ḫta* + -
[Chain = verbal prefix and afix + verbal prefix+ preformant + verb: regular + verbal afix] AMU RULES: Verbal form(*nḫtu*). Verbal prefix(-);Verbal afix(-);The rest of the chain(*nḫtu*)–≥The rest of the chain(*ḫtu*) –≥ preformant(*n*-); Regular form.verb: regular(*ḫta*). VERBAL FORM: -≥ imperativ 2ª m. s., 2ª f. s., 2ª c. d., 2ª m. pl., 2ª f. pl. CONJUGATION: N -≥ qtl 3ª m. s., 3ª m. d., 3ª m. pl., 3ª f. pl. CONJUGATION: N; ROOT: *ḫta* verb: regular «to snatch, to defeat, to beat.» (≥ *ḫatū* «to knock down» ac.; *ḫatā'* «to bury» arm.

[23] All the translations provided here are approximative using just the archaeological, epigraphical and the morphological analyses and the translations that some semitic rechearchers have made. The syntax will be done later on. Therefore, the semantics are subject to change.

[24] For the analisys of *nḫtu* as QTL in the 3rd person masculine plural and with the conjugation N (nifal) see p. 533 in Tropper (2000), and p. 267 in Pardee (2003-2004).

[25] This conjunction is really used. It has different translations: copulative, explicative, declarative or enphatic functor. It is used for introducing a final conclusion or a consequent of the first sentence. It can also work as a nexus between the protasis and the apodosis in a conditional sentence. See p. 512, 513 in del Olmo Lete and Sanmartín (1996), p. 63-86 in Aartun (1978), p. 782-788 in Tropper (2000), p. 723,724 in Piquer-Otero (2007).

N° 1 – Level: 1 – $w = w$	N° 10 – Level: 2 – *lak* = - + - + *lik* +-
[Chain = conjunction] AMU RULES: lexicon(w)– ≥conjunction(w) CONJUNCTION, RADICAL: w conjunction «and, but, for what, then, so». w «and» sem. com. *wa* «and»o. a.	[Chain = verbal prefix and afix + verbal prefix+ preformant + verb: regular + verbal afix] AMU RULES: Verbal form(*lak*). Verbal prefix(-);Verbal afix(-);The rest of the chain(*lak*). The rest of the chain(*lak*); preformant(-); Regular form.verb: regular(*lik*). VERBAL FORM: -≥ imperative 2ª m. s., 2ª f. s., 2ª c. d., 2ª m. pl., 2ª f. pl. -≥ qtl 3ª m. s., 3ª m. d., 3ª m. pl., 3ª f. pl. CONJUGATION: G, Gp, D, Dp, RAÍZ: *lik* verb: regular «to order, to commission, to send.»(≥ *la'aka* «to send» arb.; la'aka «enviar» etiop.

"send me a mail back".

2.2 KTU.2.30.[26] Conditional QTL→ QTL/ QTL→ YQTL[27]

This letter is a message to the queen and refers to the ascent of the Hittites. This case is particulary difficult because we have two different conditionals in the same letter, different tenses/aspects with different semantics. This letter has been repeatedly used as an example.

00-2.30:16 w[28] . *hm*[29] . ẖt .

N° 1 – Level: 1 – ẖt = ẖt
[Chain = place name]AMU RULES: Lexicon(ẖt)–≥place name(ẖt) RADICAL: ẖt place name, III «Ḫatti, Hittite Country.»/People from this country.

"And if the Hittite(s)"

00-2.30:17 'l . w . *likt*

---

[26]KTU.2.30=DO 4387=PRU 2, 13=RS 16.379=UT 1013. Museum: Damasco. Find site: Royal Palace, central archive, room 64. Topographic point: 537 Depth: 2,0 m. Size (height 62.0, length 48.0, width 22.0), Cunchillos et al. (2003a).

[27]For transcriptions, translations, notes and analyses of the letter see Dietrich et al. (1974, 1976); Cunchillos (1979); p. 428-430 in Ahl (1980);Lipinski (1981b); Pardee (1984), p. 321-324, v.II in Caquot et al. (1989); p. 85, 86 in Bordreuil and Pardee (2004); p. 92, 93 in Pardee (2002).

[28]See all the analysis before and note 25 on the facing page.

[29]The extended analysis appears in note 20.

N° 6 – Level: 2 – *'l* = - + - + *'ly* + -	N° 2 – Level: 2 – *likt* = - + - + *lik* + -*t*
[Chain = afix + verb: 3ª weak radical + sufix] Assimilation or loss of a consonant. Possible theoretical analysis. AMU RULES: Verbal form(*'l*). Verbal prefix(-);Verbal afix(-);The rest of the chain(*'l*); VERBAL FORM: -≥ qtl 3ª m. s., 3ª m. d., 3ª m. pl., 3ª f. pl. CONJUGATION: G, D, ROOT: *'ly* verb: 3ª weak radical, I «to go up, to leave, to attack, to storm, to pounce on, to ascend, Š: to offer, to raise.» (≥ *elū* «to go up, to ascend» ac.; *'alā* «to go up, to ascend» arb.; *'alawa* «to go through, to cross» etiop.; *'ālāh* «to go up, to ascend» hb.; *'allī* «to raise» sir.	[Chain = verbal prefix and infix + verbal prefix + prefix + verb: regular + verbalafix] AMU RULES: Verbal form(*likt*)–≥Verbal prefix(-);Verbal afix(-*t*);The rest of the chain(*lik*); Regular form of the verb: regular(*lik*). VERBAL FORM: -≥ qtl 3ª f. s., 2ª m. s., 2ª f. s., 1ª c. s., 3ª f. d. CONJUGATION: G, Gp, D, Dp ROOT: *lik* verb: regular, «to order, to commission, to send.»(≥ la'aka «to send» arb. ; la'aka «to send» etiop.

"ascend, I would send (a message)"

00-2.30:18 *'mk*[30] . *w* . *hm*

N° 2 – Level: 1 – *'m* = *'m*
[Chain = preposition] AMU RULES: Lexicon(*'m*)–≥preposition(*'m*) PREPOSITION RADICAL: *'m* preposition I «with, to, near» (≥ *'an* «with, to, near to» arb.; *'am* «with, to, near to» arm. ; *'im* «with, to, near to»hb. SUFFIX: pronoun-adj. possessive *'-k'* 2ª m. s., f. s.

"to you, and if"

00-2.30:19 *l* . *'l* . *w* . *lakm*[31]

---

[30]This could appear with different suffixes.

[31]This is an absolute infinitive that works as an internal accusative to give emphasis on the action. See p. 123 in Sivan (1997) and p.680 in Piquer-Otero (2007). The enclitic -m has been also described to emphasize the adverbial sense, but this is not easy to prove. For this see Pope (1951).

N° 2 – Level: *1 – l = l*	N° 10 – Level: *2 – lakm = - + - + lik + -m*
[Chain = adverb: negation] AMU RULES: Lexicon(*l*)–≥adverb: negation(*l*) ADVERB: NEGATION RADICAL: *l* II «no.» (≥ *lā* «no» ac.; *lā* «no» arb.; *lō* «no» hb.; *lā* «no» ug.	[Chain = mimation + verbal prefix+ preformante + verb: regular + mimation] AMU RULES: infinitive with mimation(*lakm*)–≥ mimation(*-m*)–≥ Verbal form(*lak*)–≥Verbal prefix(-);Verbal sufix(-);The rest of the chain(*lak*)–≥ preformante(-); Regular form.verb: regular(*lik*). VERBAL FORM: CONJUGATION: G, Gp, D, Dp, ROOT: *lik* verb: regular «to order, to commission, to send.» (≥ la'aka «to send» arb. ; la'aka «to send» etiop.

"they did not,"

00-2.30:20 *ilak . w . at*

N° 7 – Level: *2 – ilak = i- + - + lik + -*
[Chain = verbal prefix and suffix + verbal prefix + preformante + verb: regular + verbal sufix] AMU RULES: Verbal form(*ilak*)–≥Verbal prefix(*i-*);Verbal sufix(-);The rest of the chain(*lak*)–≥ preformante(-); Regular form.verb: regular(*lik*). VERBAL FORM: -≥ yqtl 1ᵃ c. s. CONJUGATION: G, Gp, D, Dp, ROOT: *lik* verb: regular «to order, to commission, to send.» (≥ la'aka «to send» arb. ; la'aka «to send» etiop.

"I would certainly send one".

3 Formalizing the conditional structure.

1. 2.10: hm QTL → w IMPERATIVE

2. 2.30: hm QTL → w QTL & hm l QTL → w YQTL

The big doubt that we have is how the use of the tense/aspect in the antecedent and in the consequent could change the semantics of the conditional. To our knowledge, there is no clear rules that could differentiate an actual conditional from a counterfactual one, as could be done (more or less) for Hebrew for the particle *lu* and the uses of the QTL in the counterfactual conditional.[32] There are different opinions about this regarding ugaritic,[33] although none of them really clarifies

---

[32]Following p. 126-194 Hatav (1997).

[33]"(...) irreale Konditionalsätze [zeichnen sich] nicht durch spezifische formale" in p. 908 in Tropper (2000); and "Toute distinction lexicale entre conditions réelles et irréelles est encore inconue" p. 86 in Bordreuil and Pardee (2004). In p. 120-121 Segert (1984) says that in Ugaritic "the relationship of the condition to reality are indicated by the use of tense/aspect in the main and subordinate clauses", but after that he only

the conditional structure. There also are have many different translations of the same sentence in various languages. Another thing we need
to consider is the particle that we use for the conditional. Some of the
particles known in Hebrew seem to exist also in Ugaritic. However,
it is still uncertain if they are used similarly. In Biblical Hebrew these
particles could be explained in their uses as follows:[34]

Sentence	Condition	Particle
Hypothetical	Invalid	Antecedent in factual: *lu/y*
	Invalid	Antecedent in non-factual: *lu*
	Possibly true	*im*
Actual	Restricts in time	*ky*
	Does not restrict	another one or none

If we now look at the logical studies, there are different approaches
to the structure of the conditional. First, we have the studies of the
conditional using the possible world semantics to approach the con-
trafactuality in different worlds. The first researcher who did this was
Lewis.[35] He tried to formalize them by looking at the structural relation

explains the variability of the antecedent: the use of the "imperfective" (or a nominal
sentence) in the antecedent indicates a real sentence, in the future (examples like (hm)
YQTLU/nom. → YQTLU), while the use of the "perfect" "may indicate an unreal
condition". As an example, he uses the first conditional of KTU 2.30: w hm QTLA →
w QTLA, and he translates "and if the Hittite had come, I would have sent (a message)
to you", but he does not offer any explanation for the second one (w hm l QTLA
→ w YQTLU). In p. 213 Verret (1988) says "Wir neigen zu der Annahme, die bisher
gedeutete konstruktion bezeichne tatsächlich einen Realis. Da es sich hier eindeutig um
eine Wirklichkeitserfahrung handelt, ist der hauptsächliche Gebrauch des Indikativs
in Vordersatz ... leicht einzusehen. Weiter, da der Nachsatz fast immer einer Form für
die Gegenwart oder Zukunft bedarf, gilt hier dasselbe Verfahren".

[34] For an analysis of these particles in Biblical Hebrew see Meyer (1989) and the justification of this table could be found in Revell (1991). Its condition of invalidity found
in the next table means that we talk about a counterfactuality, we are not analyzing an
strict conditional which could be true or false. The antecedent in factual could mean
that the antecedent is in the indicative mode. The studies of the the counterfactual
conditional in logic do not differentiate a conditional with indicative → subjunctive
from one with subjuntive → subjunctive. Both express a counterfactual statement but
it is not really clear how to distinguish them in the formalization. Usually the most
well-known counterfactual is the defeasible one. This two kinds of counterfactual are
defined in Hebrew for the particle *lu*. In Ugaritic it still remains unknown.

[35] His final presentation of the counterfactual theory could be found in Lewis (1973).
For a complete overview of the conditional logics see Palau (2005).

of a counterfactual: with $\square \rightarrow$, that is the translation of "would"[36] and with $\Diamond \rightarrow$, which is the translation of "might".[37] But he focuses on the case of conterfactuals, and not on the unit of all conditionals. For this purpose, he assigns a function to each possible world m_i with a corresponding sphere of accesibility S_i, so the elements of S_i are the accessible worlds from m_i. The inner spheres are the most similar, the outer spheres being the least similar.

Another study of conditionals is due to Stalnaker. Contrary to Lewis, his approach meant to give a complete theory of conditionals and not only counterfactuals. He interprets Ramsey's test in another way, by using possible worlds and developing a unique semantics for conditional sentences. According to him, all the conditional propositions are hypothetical, so, in some points, the counterfactual with a true antecedent will be reduced to a material conditional. He designs an absurd world λ which is not accessible from any world, where all the contradictions and their consequents are true; and a fuction f, with a proposition and a world as arguments. The function offers the value of a possible world which is more similar to the world in which the sentence is true. Therefore, the conditional $A \rightarrow B$ is true in the world m iff B is true in $f(A, m_i)$ in the selected world m_i where A is true. If not, then $A \rightarrow B$ will be false. If the antecedent is impossible, then the function selects the absurd world. The problem was that the formal structure of the theory depended on the pragmatic supposition that determines the similarity relationship between worlds. Besides, the indicative conditional does not have the same behavior as the counterfactual ones, as we can see in the following sentences:

- If Oswald did not kill Kennedy, someone else did.

- If Oswald would not have killed Kennedy, someone else would have done it.

Instead these approaches to the conditional sentence, we have chosen a logic of belief to study the conditional sentences that we have in the Ugaritic language. Our inspiration comes from Pardee's studies,

---

[36]It expresses an intentional connection between the antecedent and the consequent, but this necessity could be associated with the logical necessity and is not different from the strict conditional.

[37]This operator reduces the relation to a possibility relation.

because he [38] points out that the belief of the agent could be something to take into acount for chosing between the perfective or the imperfective form. This interpretation will still remain unproven, for we should check all the conditional sentences and be able to diferentiate all the conditional sentences in Ugaritic. Still, this could be a first step forward in the study of the structure of the Ugaritic conditional.

First of all, we will express the conditional without translating the tenses:

1. To beat (Perfective) $\rightarrow$ To send (Imperative)

2. To ascend (perfective) $\rightarrow$ To send (perfective)
   Not to ascend (perfective) $\rightarrow$ To send (imperfective)

We are going to formalize the conditional structure by taking into account the belief of the agent. The system that we use is KD45. We consider the knowledge to be true belief, so we will deal with the two operators K and B. The axioms are as follows:[39]

$K_a(\varphi \rightarrow \psi) \rightarrow (K_a\varphi \rightarrow K_a\psi)$	distribution of K_a over$\rightarrow$
$\neg B_a \bot$	consistent beliefs
$B_a\varphi \rightarrow B_a B_a\varphi$	positive introspection
$\neg B_a\varphi \rightarrow B_a \neg B_a\varphi$	negative introspection
From φ and $\varphi \rightarrow \psi$ infer ψ	modus ponens
From φ infer $B_a\varphi$	necessitation of belief

The approach we are going to take for belief change is called AGM's[40] Theory of Belief Revision and its postulates are as follows:

Expansion: We accept φ as new information assuming that our current belief set is K. φ has been accepted. The operator is $\oplus$.

---

[38]"(...) both the protasis and the apodosis may be expressed as either complete or incomplete by the speaker according to his/her view of the situation. This usage is probably one case where aspect reflects realis/irrealis, with the perfective expression used to categorize a condition or an outcome as more real/certain than one expressed by an imperfective. In any case, the expression of conditions and outcomes has nothing to do with time per se, but with the aspect which the speaker accords to each" p. 334 in Pardee (2003-2004).

[39]See van Ditmarsch et al. (2008).

[40]The AGM paradigm comes from the authors Alchourrón, Gärdenfors and Makinson. This information was taken from the book (van Ditmarsch et al., 2008), so all the postulates can be found there.

Contraction: It is when φ is given up as a belief. Contraction yields a set of beliefs from which φ is removed. The operator is $\ominus$.

Revision: The agent, having accepted φ, wants to change his belief. The operator is $\circledast$.

Following Pardee we understand the YQTL as indicating a less possible belief, and the QTL as a more certain belief. But for this we need to give a semantic treatment of belief revision in terms of possible worlds. For that purpose, a definition of truth for belief will be the following:

$M, w \models B_i\varphi$ iff $\forall v(R_i wv \Rightarrow M, v \models \varphi), w \neq v$

The more quantity of worlds an agent considers possible, the less he believes, and viceversa. A possible world coincides with a valuation, and we represent a world like a maximal consistent set of propositional formulas:

$w_0 = \{\varphi \in L_0 \mid w \models \varphi\}$ with φ atomic

A belief set will be:

$K_w = \{\varphi \in L_0 \mid M, w \models B\varphi\} = \underset{Rwv}{\cap} v_0$

This works for expansion $\oplus$. For contraction we add some worlds that the agent considers possible. We add a system of spheres, fall-back theories relative to the agent's current theories. They are linearly ordered by $\supseteq$, and contain the maximun W and the minimun R(w), and for all φ if some S $\in$ *Sphe*(R(w)) intersects with $\| \varphi \|_0$, then there is a $\subseteq$ −smallest S'$\in$ *Sphe*(R(w)) that intersects with $\|\varphi\|_0$. So for contraction, R(w)$\cap\|\neg\varphi\|_0$ should not be empty.

As it was said previously, in Ugaritic we have the particles *ky* and *hm/im*.[41] These particles have a clear deictic character, because they could be used with this function too in the Ugaritic corpus. But we do not have any clear occurrence of the *lu* or *luly* for the antecedent with the hypothetical conditional, as in Biblical Hebrew. The only particle in the antecedent that we have is the *hm l*, but *l* is a negative particle. Thus, we shall focus in the particle *im/hm*, the only one we found in Ugaritic that could be a counterfactuality, or at least hypothetical, if we look at the Hebrew corpus. If we take the *im/hm* as a hypothetical particle, possibly true as in Hebrew, our examples show the counterfactuality. Just to clarify, we will formalize the sentence.

1- $B\varphi \rightarrow \neg B\psi$

2a- $B\varphi \rightarrow B\psi$

2b- $B\neg\varphi \rightarrow \neg B\psi$

---

[41] For an analysis of the exchange of the hm/im see p. 544-553 in Lipinski (2001).

The first case is clear because it expresses a counterfactuality (because of the *im/hm*). The belief of an agent and the possibility to be true lies in the fact that the first one become true and then the second one also become true (although the second is not really believed by the agent). The difference between a counterfactual and a factual is that the factual does not express the belief of an agent and the counterfactual expresses a belief that could be true or false, and since we could add to the antecedent all the postulates of AGM approach, such as $\oplus, \ominus$ and $\circledast$, we respect the Ramsey test. The AGM postulates, that could be added, express the non-monotonicity involved in the definition of a conditional in natural language.[42] The factual will be in the world w, while the operator for belief in the counterfactual is considering more that one world and is capable of changing. This could be regarded as changing the model to make a hypothetical belief. The problem would be differenciating B from ¬B, because both of them express the possibility, although one more than the other. It could be made with the ordering spheres that express different degrees of belief.

Maybe we could have used the function f from the Defeasible Reasoning. This function is a revision operator[43] and represents fA, is A plus all the suppositions associated $A \wedge A_1 \wedge ... \wedge A_n$ in the antecedent of the conditional. This function could work for the factual, but we use for the ugaritic counterfactual the AGM postulates because we need to introduce the hypothetical belief of the agent, we introduce the propositional acttitude.

We have to explain why they use a YQTL in the consequent of the second conditional of example 2 and an imperative in the consequent of example 1. The YQTL is normally used for a real proposition. However if we think of the aspect of the YQTL, it just means an unfinished action, and taking into account the Pardee's quotation, it could be expressing the non belief of the agent who says this. The same happens in the

---

[42]The implication that we have in the natural language conditional is not the classical logical implication. We refer to the conditional ($\rightarrow$) as a connective. The clearest property that fails in the relation of the natural language conditional is the monotonicity. This property does not fail in the strict conditional. If we have $A \rightarrow B$ and we add C to the antecedent we could have $A, C \nrightarrow B$ in the natural language conditional.

[43]More information about this can be found in (Carnota, 1995; Palau, 2005). The definition of this operator comes from Alchourron system DFT or Deontic Defeasible T. This function allows the non-monotonicity typical of the conditional in natural language. (Def.>) $A > B =_{df} fA \rightarrow B$, where $\rightarrow$ is a strict implication. See the caracterizations axioms of expansion, extensionality, limited expansion and jerarquic order in p. 160 Palau (2005).

consequent of example 1. In this case it is less certain for the agent, because it is written in an unfinished form. This is why we use ¬*B*.

But we still have to explain the $B\neg\varphi \rightarrow \neg B\psi$. What we have in the antecedent is *hm l*. If we took the negation as a regular one, we would have this formalization, nonetheless, this negation is a modal-sentential negation[44] in Ugaritic which means the possibility, ¬*B*. Therefore this formalization would be more like $\neg B\varphi \rightarrow \neg B\psi$. $\neg B\varphi$ does not coincide with $B\neg\varphi$, because the former negation expresses the agent's belief and the second the negation of a proposition. Here we would have the normal defeasible counterfactual conditional that will be different from the factual one in Ugaritic. Thus, the two sentences that we showed before will be formalized in a different way:

- If Oswald did not kill Kennedy, someone else did. $\neg\varphi > \psi$

- If Oswald would not have killed Kennedy, someone else would have done it. $\neg B\neg\varphi \rightarrow B\psi$

Another thing that we should bear in mind is that in our system of belief, $B\varphi$ does not mean φ, the property T: $B\varphi \rightarrow \varphi$ may fail. For believe, we change the axiom T for the axiom D: $\neg B\bot$. The belief is not true knowledge, but it has to be consistent for an agent.[45] The agent is ignorant about the truth of his belief, but he has a minimal consistents of his belief. If he believes something does not mean it is true, but he can not believe one thing its opposite. The belief opens the possibility of a revision and a change of the belief, that is, the hypothetical conditional.

4 Conclusion

We have analized the conditional sentences that appear in the Ugaritic letters KTU. 2.10 and KTU. 2.30. Our methodology was developed step by step and following the hermeneutic methodology: archaeology and epigraphy, morphology, sintax and semantics. For the first three steps we have used the UDB and for the other two we have made an approach based on the AGM logic of belief. We have chosen the AGM logic because we think it is the approach that takes us closer to the datas

---

[44]Research about the negation in Ugaritic is still ongoing. This kind of negation could be an expresion of propositional acttitude.

[45]This axion D expresses the Moore principle: $\neg B\bot \rightarrow \neg B(\varphi \wedge \neg\varphi)$, but this could derive in the Moore's paradox in the natural language too. Here is another point where we could see that the belief like propositional attitude is touching the level of pragmatics in natural language.

we have obtained from the other levels. Also, this logic matches better in the linguistic information.

In the Ugaritic conditional we have shown that Pardee's idea about the YQTL and QTL as aspects which could mean some kind of belief, could fit in the belief revision conditional. We could differentiate the factual and the counterfactual conditional if we choose the *hm* as a hypothetical particle, as it is used in Hebrew, and if we analyse the *l* negation as modality negation. The non-monotonicity that is inside the natural language conditional could also be approached too with the AGM.

Thereby, we have tried to take an approach to the conditional by taking all the information that the language gives us into account. This logical connective is important in our work context because, as we said at the beginning, we deal with an expert system that tries to establish the common reasoning in the structure of a language. The non-monotonicity that is inside the conditional structure and the introduction of the belief are points of interest for formalizing natural language. Nevertheless, this is an analysis of just two conditionals of the Ugaritic corpus. We would need to analyse all the conditionals we have and try to understand their structure. Also, analysing all the letters would be really useful too because they are connected. Some are the answer to the others and this way we could compile the change of belief of the different agents.

Acknowledgements

This paper has been made thanks to the I3P grant from the Consejo Superior de Investigaciones Científicas (CSIC). I wish to thank the referees for help to improve this paper.

Bibliography

Aartun, K., 1978. *Die Partikeln des Ugaritischen*. Alter Orient und Altes Testament, Neukirchen-Vluyn.

Ahl, S. W., 1980. *Epistolary texts from Ugarit*. PhD thesis, Brandeis University, Ann Arbor, Michigan, U.S.A.- London, England.

Bares, C. and Solans, B. E., 2010. Analisis formal de ktu 2.72: 17-24 aplicando la metodologia hermeneumatica. In Fernández, D., Gómez-Caminero, E., and Hernández, I. (ed.), *Estudios de Lógica, Lenguaje y Epistemología. IV Jornadas Ibéricas*, pages 3–25, Sevilla. Universidad de Sevilla, Fenix Editora.

Bordreuil, P. and Pardee, D., 2004. *Manuel d'Ougaritique*, volume 2. Paul Geuthner, Paris.

Caquot, A., de Tarragon, J. M., and Cunchillos, J. L., 1989. *Textes Ougaritiques: Textes religieux, rituels, correspondance*, volume II. Les éditions du cerf, Paris.

Carnota, R. J., 1995. Lógica e inteligencia artificial. *Enciclopedia Iberoamericana de filosofía*, Lógica.

Cervigon, R., 2007. Interpretacion critica de textos ugariticos. Master's thesis, Universidad Politecnica de Madrid, Madrid.

Cervigón, R., 2007. Analizador morfológico ugarítico, amu. In Justel, J., Solans, B., Vita, J. P., and Zamora, J. A. (ed.), *Las aguas primigenias. El próximo Oriente Antiguo como fuente de civilización*, volume 1, pages 173–182, Zaragoza. IEIOP.

Cuena, J. and Molina, M. 2004, *Knowledge Engineering and Agent Technology*, chapter Using Knowledge Modelling Tools for Agent-Based System: The experience of KSM. IOS Press, Amsterdam.

Cunchillos, J. L., 1979. Le texte ugaritique ktu.2.30. *Anuario de Filología 5*, pages 73–76.

Cunchillos, J. L., 1982. La lettre ugaritique ktu 2.10. *Materiali Lessicali ed Epigrafici*, (1): 19–23.

Cunchillos, J. L., 2000. *Hermeneumatica*. CSIC, Madrid.

Cunchillos, J. L. and al, 1996. *Banco de Datod Filologicos Semiticos Noroccodentales III: Generador de Segmentaciones, Restituciones y Concordancias*. CSIC, electronic edition.

Cunchillos, J. L. and Vita, J. P., 1993. *Banco de Datod Filologicos Semiticos Noroccodentales I: Textos Ugariticos*, volume 1. CSIC, Madrid.

Cunchillos, J. L. and Vita, J. P., 1995. *Banco de Datod Filologicos Semiticos Noroccodentales II: Concordancia de Palabras Ugariticas en morfologia desplegada*. CSIC, Madrid Zaragoza.

Cunchillos, J. L., Vita, J. P., and Zamora, J. A., 2003a. *The Text of Ugaritic Data Bank*, volume 1-4. Piscataway.

Cunchillos, J. L., Vita, J. P., Zamora, J. A., and Cervigon, R. A concordance of ugaritic words. Electronic Aplication, Piscataway, 2003b.

del Olmo Lete, G. and Sanmartín, J., 1996. *Diccionario de la Lengua Ugarítica*. Aula Orientalis-Suplementa, Barcelona.

Dietrich, M., Loretz, O., and Sanmartín, J., 1974. Die ankündigung eines botem (udr)) im brief. *Ugarit-Forschungen 6*, pages 458–459.

Dietrich, M., Loretz, O., and Sanmartín, J., 1975. Der brief rs4.475=cta53. *Ugarit-Forschungen 7*, pages 529–530.

Dietrich, M., Loretz, O., and Sanmartín, J., 1976. *KTU. Die keilalphabetischen Texte aus Ugarit*. Alter Orient und Altes Testament, Neukirchen-Vluyn.

Hatav, G., 1997. *The Semantics of Aspects and Modality. Evidence from English and Biblical Hebrew*. Jhon Benjamins Publishing Company, Amsterdam-Philadelphia.

Hawley, R., 2003. *Studies in Ugaritic Epistolography*. UMI Microform 3088741, Chicago, online edition.

Lewis, D., 1973. *Conterfactuals*. Blackwell Publishing, Oxford.

Lipinski, E., 1981a. Allusions historiques dans la correspondance ougaritique de ras shamra: Lettre de ewri-sarri à pilsiya. *Ugarit-Forschungen 13*, pages 123–126.

Lipinski, E., 1981b. Ahat-milki, reine d'ugarit et la guerre du mukis. *Orientalia Lovaniensia Periodica, OLP 12*, pages 93–96.

Lipinski, E., 2001. *Semitic Languages Outline of a Comparative Grammar*. Orientalia Lovaniensia Analecta, Leuven-Paris-Sterling(Virginia), second edition.

Meyer, R., 1989. *Gramática del Hebreo Bíblico*. CLIE, Terrassa.

Palau, G. D., 2005. Logicas condicionales y razonamiento de sentido comun.

Pardee, D. 2002, *The Context of Scripture: Archival Documents from the Biblical World*, volume III, chapter Ugaritic Letters. Brill, Leiden-Boston-Köln.

Pardee, D., 1984. Further studies in ugaritic epistolography. *Archivfür Orienrforschung (AfO) 31*, pages 225–226.

Pardee, D. 1987, *Love and Death in the Ancient Near East (Essays in Honor of Marvin H. Pope)*, chapter As Stronge as Death, pages 65–69. Guilford.

Pardee, D., 2003-2004. Recension of ugaritische grammatik,tropper. *Archivfür Orienrforschung (AfO) 50*, pages 1–404.

Piquer-Otero, A., 2007. *Estudios de Sintaxis Verbal en Textos Ugaríticos. El Ciclo de Baal y la "poesía bíblica arcaica"*. Verbo Divino, Navarra, España.

Pope, M., 1951. Ugaritic enclitic -m. *Journal of Cuneiform Studies*, 5(4):123–128.

Revell, E. J. 1991, *Semitic Studies. In honor of Wolf Leslau*, chapter Conditional Sentences in Biblical Hebrew Prose. Otto Harrassowitz- Wiesbaden.

Segert, S., 1984. *A basic Grammar of the Ugaritic Language with selected texts and glossary*. University of California press.

Siabra, J., 2007. El módulo sintáctico del ugaritic data bank (udb). In Justel, J., Solans, B., Vita, J. P., and Zamora, J. Á. (ed.), *Las aguas primigenias. El próximo Oriente Antiguo como fuente de civilización*, volume 1, pages 189–202, Zaragoza.

Sivan, D., 1997. *A Grammar of the Ugaritic Language*. Handbook of Oriental Studies, Brill, Leiden-New York-Köln.

Smith, M. S., 2001. *Untold Stories: The Bible and Ugaritic Studies in the Twentieth Century*. Hendrickson, Peabody, Massachusetts, first edition.

Tropper, J., 2000. *Ugaritische Grammatik*. Alter Orient und Altes Testament, Münster.

van Ditmarsch, H., van der Hoek, W., and Kooi, B., 2008. *Dynamic Epistemic Logic*. Springer, Dordrecht, The Netherlands.

Verret, E., 1988. *Modi Ugaritici. Eine morpho-syntaktische Abhandlung uber das Modalsystem im Ugaritischen*. Orientalia Lovaniensia Analecta.

To Be Is To Be Chosen

A Dialogical Understanding of Ontological Commitment

Mᴀᴛᴛʜɪᴇᴜ FONTAINE* & Jᴜᴀɴ REDMOND†

ABSTRACT. One of the most important contributions of dialogical logic is its understanding of quantification by means of the notion of choice. Adopting a critical position towards the introduction of an existence predicate in free logics, we will outline a new understanding of existence within the dialogical framework: *To be is to be chosen.*

Indeed, against the standard view in free logic, the aim of this paper is to grasp the meaning of quantification by taking into account the relationship between the choice of a constant and the resulting utterance.[1]

1 Introduction

The philosophical reflection on non-existence is an issue that has been tackled at the very start of philosophy and constitutes since the publication of Russell's "On Denoting" (Russell, 1905) one of the most thorny debates in analytical philosophy. Russell's choice was clever: he was keen to show how the new instruments of logic might offer an original approach to some venerable metaphysical and epistemical problems such as the problem of judgment of existence. Actually, the paper gave Russell the opportunity to stress the main contribution of the "modern logic": the notion of "quantifier" that could now bring an unexpected twist to Kant's remark that "existence is not a real predicate".

*Univ Lille Nord de France, F-59000 Lille France;
UdL3, STL, F-59653 Villeneuve d'Ascq France;
CNRS UMR8163.
†Centro da Filosofia das Ciências da Universidade de Lisboa (CFCUL).
[1]The following paper is part of an unpublished paper written some years ago in French (Fontaine et al., 2009) and is the original source of some central ideas of recent publications and researches on the dialogical approach to the logic of nonexistents and fictionality. See also (Rahman, 2001) and (Rahman et al., 1997).

Roughly, Russell's definite description theory consists in conceiving grammatical names not as genuine names but rather as disguised definite descriptions. Replacing names by definite descriptions, Russell solves the problem of negative existential statements[2] by means of quantification and empty predicates. Let "Pegasus" be synonymous for "the two-winged horse", all that we can say is that it is not the case that there exists something satisfying the description. Consequently, though "Holmes does not exist" is true, all of the following statements are false:

1. Holmes is a detective.

2. Holmes is not a detective.

3. Holmes is a character imagined by Conan Doyle.

4. Holmes is Holmes.

The uniform falsity of these statements is linked to the lack of reference of the name "Holmes". However, as stressed by Leonard (Leonard, 1956), although quantifiers enable us to deal with empty predicates, Russell's solution (and more generally classical logic) is grounded on a tacit existential presupposition with respect to singular terms.[3] This presupposition is expressed in a formal language by the two following principles:

$\forall x \varphi \rightarrow \varphi[x/k_i]$ (Specification)

$\varphi[x/k_i] \rightarrow \exists x \varphi$ (Particularization)

Intuitively, the former means that if every object in the domain satisfies φ, then k_i satisfies φ. Conversely, the latter means that if k_i satisfies φ, then there exists an object in the domain that satisfies φ. For example, if Holmes satisfies the property of being a detective, then there exists someone who is detective. In other words, these principles establish that every singular term k must refer to something lying in the range of ontologically loaded quantifiers.

---

[2]How to deny the existence to something that does not exist? Do we have first to assume a reference of which we say it does not exist? If there is not reference at all, what would be denying the existence about?

[3]"The modern logic has made explicit the logic of general existence, but it has retained a tacit presupposition of singular existence." (Leonard, 1956).

Different kinds of free logics have challenged these principles. Semantically, the idea is that some singular terms might be without reference or have a reference lying beyond the range of ontologically loaded quantifiers. In this way, the principles of particularization and specification are not valid anymore. Karel Lambert called those logics *free logics*, for logics free of ontological commitment with respect to singular terms (Lambert, 1960). Lambert distinguishes between negative, positive and neuter free logics, the semantics of which will be sketched thereafter.

2   Explicit Existence in Free Logics

Negative free logic is directly inspired by Russell's theory. Indeed, although singular terms are not conceived as disguised definite descriptions, if a name does not refer to something existent it does not refer at all, it is an empty name. And every statement in which such an empty name occurs is false, excepted from negations of atomic formulas. Syntactically, the language is the same as the one for classical logic to which is added an existence predicate ($E!$) and an identity symbol. We now define briefly this semantics:

[D1]   A model M for negative free logic is a tuple $\langle D, I \rangle$ where D is the domain of quantification and I a partial interpretation function (that is, a function which is not defined for every singular term: it is not defined for empty names).

[D2]   Interpretation for negative free logic:

1. For every singular term k, either $I(k)$ belongs to D or $I(k)$ is not defined.

2. For every n-ary predicate P, $I(P)$ is an n-tuple of members of D.

3. Every member of D has a name.

[D3]   Truth in model for negative free logic:[4]

(i) $V_M(Pk_1, \ldots, k_n) = 1$ if and only if $I(k_1), \ldots, I(k_n)$ are defined and $\langle I(k_1), \ldots, I(k_n) \rangle \in I(P)$.

---

[4]We give only the relevant truth conditions. The truth conditions for the other connectives $\neg$, $\vee$, $\wedge$, $\rightarrow$, $\leftrightarrow$ are defined as usual. It will be the same for the other free logics defined below.

(ii) $V_M(k_i = k_j) = 1$ iff $I(k_i)$ and $I(k_j)$ are defined and $I(k_i)$ is the same as $I(k_j)$.

(iii) $V_M(E!k_i) = 1$ iff $I(k_i)$ is defined.

(iv) $V_M(\forall x\varphi) = 1$ iff $V_M(\varphi[x/k_i]) = 1$ for every k_i such that $I(k_i)$ is defined.

(v) $V_M(\exists x\varphi) = 1$ iff $V_M(\varphi[x/k_i]) = 1$ for at least one k_i such that $I(k_i)$ is defined.

As a direct consequence, if the interpretation of an individual constant k_i is not defined, then every atomic formula containing this k_i will be false (but its negation is true). Thus, we can easily check how specification and particularization are not valid anymore. If instead formulas containing empty names are said to be undetermined, then we get a neuter free logic.[5]

Unlike negative free logic, positive free logic is such that identity statements such as $k_i = k_i$ are always true. Indeed, positive free logicians think that identity formulas such as the mentioned above express an analytic truth, and this is so whether k_i refers or not. They are thus committed to understand this kind of name not as empty but rather as referring to nonexistent entity. To distinguish between existent and nonexistent individuals, the domain of the discourse is divided in an innerdomain D_I (containing the existents) and an outerdomain D_O (containing the nonexistents). We now briefly define the relevant features of their semantics:

[D4]   Interpretation for positive free logic:

1. For every singular term k, $I(k)$ belongs to $D_I \cup D_O$.

2. For every n-ary predicate P, $I(P)$ is an n-tuple of members of $D_I \cup D_O$.

3. Every member of $D_I \cup D_O$ has a name.

[D5]   Truth in a model for positive free logic:

---

[5]Notice that indeterminacy is to be conceived either as strong or weak. In the weak version, indeterminacy of atomic sentences does not affect the clauses for the other connectives. In a strong version, it is contagious to the whole formula. How to deal with indeterminacy is in fact another matter, and can be done by means of supervaluation method (see Section 6).

(i) $V_M(Pk_1, ..., k_n) = 1$ iff $\langle I(k_1), ..., I(k_n) \rangle \in I(P)$.

(ii) $V_M(k_i = k_j) = 1$ iff $I(k_i)$ is the same as $I(k_j)$.

(iii) $V_M(E!k_i) = 1$ iff $I(k_i) \in D_I$.

(iv) $V_M(\forall x \varphi) = 1$ iff $V_M(\varphi[x/k_i]) = 1$ for every k_i such that $I(k_i) \in D_I$.

(v) $V_M(\exists x \varphi) = 1$ iff $V_M(\varphi[x/k_i]) = 1$ for at least one k_i such that $I(k_i) \in D_I$.

These different ways of dealing with existence in logic have the merit of rendering explicit the ontological commitment of (some) singular terms in the object language. However, the criticism against these logics is precisely grounded in this use of the existence predicate. Indeed, we think that such an understanding of existence is linked to a specific omission namely the relation between the act of choosing a singular term and the resulting assertion. In what follows, we will display a way of dealing with ontological commitment that gives a central role to the notion of choice. This can be tracked back to the natural deduction system of Jaśkowski.

3 Explicit Choice in Natural Deduction

The first attempt to implement choices in natural deduction is to be found in Jaśkowski (Jaśkowski, 1934). This natural deduction system was built in order to be applied to inclusive logics — that is logics with possibly empty domain. The problem is the following: if the domain is possibly empty, how to be sure that an individual constant is available to instantiate a quantifier? The solution of Jaśkowski relied on the idea that, while instantiating a quantifier in a proof-process, we have to make explicit the supposition of a singular term. More precisely, Jaśkowski built a system that allows to introduce in the object language two new metalinguistic symbols that express two different kinds of suppositions:

1. Any supposition of a formula is prefixed by the symbol $\mathcal{F}$.

2. Any supposition of a singular term is prefixed by the symbol $\mathcal{C}$.

In this paper, we are concerned with the second kind of supposition: the supposition of a singular term. According to Jaśkowski, universal instantiation can be applied only if the supposition of a singular term has been previously introduced in the object language. This idea suggests the following formulation of tableau rules for free logic:

δ-type rules		γ-type rules	
k_i is new		k_i is arbitrary	
T $\exists x\varphi$	F $\forall x\varphi$	T $\forall x\varphi$	F $\exists x\varphi$
T Ck_i	T Ck_i	T Ck_i	T Ck_i
		...	...
T $\varphi[x/k_i]$	F $\varphi[x/k_i]$	T $\varphi[x/k_i]$	F $\varphi[x/k_i]$
		(the utterance of T $\varphi[x/k_i]$ assumes the occurrence of T Ck_i)	

As a consequence, the validity of specification assumes the occurrence of the supposition of the adequate singular term. Thus, the following formulation of specification does not hold: $\forall x\varphi \rightarrow \varphi[x/k_i]$:

1. F $\forall x\varphi \rightarrow \varphi[x/k_i]$

2. T $\forall x\varphi$

3. F $\varphi[x/k_i]$

The tableau-proof ends without closing at step 3 since T Ck_i does not occur in the branch. In fact, Jaśkowski did not really condition the use of quantifiers in the style of nowadays free-logic, he rather added as a rule that a singular term supposition can always be assumed and thus obtained classical logic. Jaśkowski acknowledges that the act of choice should be rendered explicit as a separated distinguishable step in a proof. Unfortunately, he implemented this idea by the introduction of a new type of formula. The resulting system at the very end is not that different of introducing an existence predicate: replace Ck_i with $E!k_i$ (where $E!$ is the existence predicate) and a standard free logic with an existence predicate obtains. As we will discuss below, we endorse the idea that the meaning of quantifiers involves two steps, however one of these steps is an action, the choice, and the other is a proposition, the result of the act of choice.

4   Do it in Dialogic! The Introduction Rule

From the dialogical point of view free logic is the logic where the choices of the proponent are conditioned by previous choices of the opponent. Existence is thus herewith understood as the result of an interaction. Moreover, we will not assume that the domain of discourse is a static collection of data given by a model, but that this domain result from a dialogue conceived as a process of construction. It is precisely these dynamic features of dialogical logic that allows avoiding the use of the existence predicate.

For an arbitrary φ, the particle rules that establish the *local semantics*[6] for quantifiers are the following:

Utterance	Attack	Defense
$X - ! - \exists x \varphi$	$Y - ? \ \exists$	$X - ! - \varphi[x/k_i]$
$X - ! - \forall x \varphi$	$Y - ? \ \forall/k_i$	$X - ! - \varphi[x/k_i]$

The local meaning of quantifiers displayed above can be seen as consisting in a double move, involving an action, the choice of a singular term, and the utterance of the formula that results after that choice. Indeed, in the case of the existential quantifier, the defender chooses an individual constant and then utters the resulting (instantiated) formula. In the case of the universal quantifier, the challenger chooses an individual constant and asks the other player to instantiate the formula. Stated in such a way, there is no restriction with respect to the availability of individual constants used by both of the players. Notice that strategically, the opponent will usually introduce new individual constants and the proponent will try to use individual constants previously given by the opponent. But this has nothing to do with the local rules that are stated independently from the player at stake.

If the standard rules for classical and intuitionistic logic are assumed we obtain, as shown below, the validity of the principles of specification and particularization:

	O			P	
				$Ak_1 \rightarrow \exists x Ax$	0
1	Ak_1	0		$\exists x Ax$	2
3	$?\exists$	2		Ak_1	4

---

[6]We will not present here the whole rules for dialogical logic, furthermore, we will ignore in our examples the issue on "ranks" since they are not really relevant for our issue. For a presentation of the dialogical rules, see N. Clerbout's contribution in the present volume. See also Fontaine and Redmond (2008), Keiff (2009) and Rahman and Keiff (2005).

	O			P	
				$\forall x Ax \rightarrow Ak_1$	0
1	$\forall x Ax$	0		Ak_1	4
3	Ak_1		1	$?\forall / k_1$	2

In order to obtain a dialogical free logic, we must add restrictions on the application of these rules. In other words, the particle rules for quantifiers remain the same - that is the local meaning is not different from the one of classical and intuitionistic logic, however the so-called *global* meaning displayed by the structural rules will be different. More precisely, dialogical free logic requires a structural rule, stated below and called *Introduction Rule*, that establishes that the (proponent's) availability of singular term is a function of the choices made by the opponent during the dialogue.[7] By contrast with the logics we mentioned before, ontological commitment of quantifiers is captured by means of the application of a particular rule that fixes the meaning of those quantifiers in the context of a game (for short, by means of the application of a particular structural rule). We can therefore delete from our language the existence predicate "*E!*". In the dialogical versions of free logic presented in the present paper we will assume on the one hand that quantifiers are ontologically loaded (i.e. they only range over existents) and on the other hand that individual constants are not necessarily so.[8]

In order to formulate the *Introduction Rule*, we define first the notion of introduction (of singular terms):

[D6]   Introduction - A singular term k_i played by X is said to be introduced if and only if:

1. X utters the formula $\varphi[x/k_i]$ while defending a formula of the form $\exists x\varphi$ and k_i has not been used to attack or to defend a quantifier before,

2. X chooses k_i by means of the move $\langle ? \ \forall/k_i \rangle$ while challenging a formula of the form $\forall x\varphi$ and k_i has not been used to attack or to defend a quantifier before.

---

[7]See Rahman (2001).

[8]In Rahman's original paper (Rahman, 2001), two different kinds of quantifiers were used, namely ontologically loaded and non-ontologically loaded quantifiers. In the present paper, we will only assume ontologically loaded quantifiers.

[RS-6]   Introduction Rule: Only O is allowed to introduce singular terms.

Intuitively, this rule means that availability of a singular term is determined through the choices of the opponent. If we allow us to use a model-theoretic vocabulary, we could describe this process as one in which the opponent was building a counter-model by his concessions and by the same way building the domain of existent entities. Thus, ontological commitment is now understood with respect to the introduction rule: only the individual constants introduced by the opponent are ontologically loaded. As a consequence of [RS-6], the principles of specification and particularization are not valid anymore, as it is shown in the following dialogues:

	O			P	
				$Ak_1 \rightarrow \exists xAx$	0
1	Ak_1	0		$\exists xAx$	2
3	$?\exists$	2			

Explanation: Although Ak_1 has been conceded by O (move 1), P cannot defend himself when O challenges the existential quantifier (move 3) by means of k_1 because O did not introduce it. Therefore, O wins the dialogue and the particularization is not valid.

	O			P	
				$\forall xAx \rightarrow Ak_1$	0
1	$\forall xAx$	0			

Explanation: P cannot attack the universal quantifier stated by O (move 1) since no individual constant has been introduced so far, that is no individual constant is available for P.

These two dialogues show how specification and particularization do not hold in dialogical free logic. In fact, these principles are not valid in positive and negative free logics, but in neuter free logic things are a bit different. Indeed, in a neuter free logic, they are undetermined. The aim of the next section is to develop a more fine-grained system able to introduce further distinctions between different approaches to free logic.

5 Positive, Negative and Neuter Dialogical Free Logics

In the context of positive and negative free logics *without identity*, we just have to apply the standard dialogical rules enlarged by the *Introduction Rule* [RS-6]. However, the main difference between negative and positive free logics rests on the understanding of identity. As we mentioned above, while in negative free logic identity is conceived as synthetic and dependent on the existence of the entity at stake, in positive free logic, identity is thought to be analytic and independent on the existence. Thus, in order to differentiate these logics, we will implement different rules for identity in our dialogical framework.

The following rule involving identity yields *dialogical positive free logic*:[9]

[RS-FL$_+$]   At the start of every dialogue for positive free logic, O concedes $k_i = k_i$, and P can ask to substitute k_i by any k_j played in the dialogue.

With this rule, the opponent is forced to concede that identity holds for every individual constant occurring in a dialogue. Consequently, the proponent is free to state without any justification that $k_j = k_j$ for every individual constant that occurs in a dialogue, including those that have not been introduced.

In *dialogical negative free logic*, identity holds only for the existents, that is for the individual constants that have been previously introduced. In order to implement this notion, we add the following rule:

[RS-FL$_-$]   At the start of every dialogue for negative free logic, O concedes $\forall x(x = x)$.

Notice that because of the Introduction Rule, the proponent will be allowed to challenge the conceded universal only if the opponent has previously introduced an individual constant.

What else do we need to develop a neuter free logic? In dialogical neuter free logic, every formula where an individual constant occurs the ontological commitment of which has not been specified will be

---

[9]We also assume a rule for substitution of individual constants. Briefly, this rule says that if a player X concedes $k_i = k_j$ and further concedes $\varphi[x/k_i]$, the player Y is allowed to ask him to substitute k_j with k_i in the formula φ and X will have to defend himself by uttering $\varphi[x/k_j]$. It follows from the formal rule for atomic formulae that while applying this rule, the role of X will be played by the opponent and the role of Y will be played by the proponent.

undetermined. Stated in more dialogical words, if certain individual constants that occur in a dialogue have been used but not introduced, then there is no winner. More precisely, a dialogue for dialogical neuter free logic will be played with the [RS-FL_] rule of dialogical negative free logic[10] but with a different winning rule, namely the following one:[11]

[RS-FL$_N$] Winning Rule - X wins iff both of the following conditions are fulfilled:

1. It is Y's turn to play and he cannot or the dialogue contains two occurrences of the same atomic formula respectively labeled X and Y.

2. Every individual constant k_i that occurs in the dialogue has (eventually) been introduced or is identical with a constant k_j that has (eventually) been introduced.

In all other cases, nobody wins (and the thesis is claimed to be undetermined).

Applying this rule, particularization is undetermined (and not valid). The dialogue is the same as the one displayed above (see section 4) though the result is different: there is no win, neither for the proponent nor for the opponent. Indeed, despite the impossibility for P to answer the O's challenge on the existential quantifier (move 3), O does not win because the constant k_1 occurs and this constant has not been introduced in the whole dialogue.

All these dialogues show how to understand ontological commitment by means of ontologically loaded quantifiers. This framework displays how to deal with nonexistents in a dialogue and what are the consequences of taking them in account. This is a logic without the tacit presupposition decried by Leonard (Leonard, 1956). Moreover unlike the traditional free logics, it is not subject to the usual criticism against the use of an existence predicate. As a conceptual result, we achieve a new dynamic understanding of ontological commitment grasped in

---

[10]That is we deal with identity as in dialogical negative free logic.

[11]We rely here on a strong notion of indeterminacy according to which as soon as an indeterminacy occurs in a formula it contaminates the whole formula. A weaker notion of indeterminacy allows to win a dialogue despite the indeterminacy of a particular individual constant insofar as there is no move of the opponent where an atomic formula has been uttered and this particular constant occurs.

terms of these choices and their interaction essential for the meaning of quantification. In a dialogue, *to be is to be chosen*.

Let us come back once more to Jaśkowski's calculus and let us compare it with the dialogical approach. In the dialogical framework, as stressed above, the local meaning of a quantifier consists in a double move: choosing a singular term and uttering the resulting formula. This double act inherent to the meaning of quantification matches Jaśkowski's double step: the assumption of a singular term and the instantiation of the quantifier. However, contrary to Jaśkowski's approach, the dialogical approach does not convert this action into a formula: quantification is, according to our view, the interaction of actions and propositions.

6 Supervaluation and Superdialogues

Van Frassen (van Fraassen, 1966) and Bencivenga (Bencivenga, 1986) contested on one hand the metaphysical commitment of positive and negative free logics and on the other hand the truth-values gaps that produce the indeterminacy of neuter free logic. According to Bencivenga, logic should be neutral in relation to metaphysical assumptions on the basic underlying semantics. It is crucial to point that in the dialogical context the above approach to neuter free logic can be seen as jeopardizing the whole project of a dialogical logic. Indeed, originally, dialogical logic was developed with the aim to provide a dialogue-definite notion of propositions (namely to be part of dialogue where necessarily exactly one of both players wins) even for those propositions that might be indeterminate from the truth-value point of view: consider the dialogical approach to intuitionistic logic, where the opponent wins and the dialogue is definite, though from the truth-value point of view third-excluded is neither true nor false. A solution would be to change the notion of non-validity for neuter free logics in such a way that a formula is not valid iff (1) the opponent wins and (2) every individual constant k_i that occurs in the dialogue has (eventually) been introduced or is identical with a constant k_j that has (eventually) been introduced. If (2) is not the case, we say that the formula is indeterminate (however it is *dialogue-defined*). However, it is not that clear if the solution is really satisfying, this leads us to the approach we call below *superdialogues*.

In the following we will describe Bencivenga's own proposal that extends van Frassen's method of supervaluation to first-order logic (van Fraassen, 1966). Let us start with van Frassen's theory of supervaluations where models consist in *partial valuations, classical extensions* and *supervaluations*:

- *Partial valuations* allow truth-value gaps such as in some three-valued logics. In other words an assignment of truth to some propositions, falsity to the others and no value to the rest.

- Consider all ways of extending a partial valuation to a total valuation by arbitrarily assigning values (consistent with the truth conditions - if a given proposition is arbitrarily made true, then any disjunction containing this proposition will be made true too) to those propositions that the partial function yields a lack of value. Call these the *classical extensions* of the original partial valuation.

- A supervaluation is defined as follows: A proposition is true according to the supervaluation if it is true in all classical extensions; false according to the supervaluation if it is false in all classical extensions and has no (super-)value if it takes different values in different classical extensions.

Logical consequence: A proposition is a logical consequence of another proposition if there is not partial valuation every classical extension of which makes all the premises true and the conclusion false.

Validity: A proposition is valid according to supervaluation if there is no partial valuation the classical extension of which renders that proposition false.

Take for instance the principle of non-contradiction. We assume that the proposition φ might be undetermined — such as a first-order formula in which an empty name occurs — and a partial valuation as described in the matrix below by the lines 2 to 4. The third line is the case with undetermined truth value:

1	φ	$\neg\varphi$	$\neg(\varphi \wedge \neg\varphi)$
2	1	0	1
3	#	#	#
4	0	1	1
5	1	0	1
6	0	1	1

The first of the two possible classical extensions (line 5) assign true to φ and accordingly false to its negation while the second extension (line 6) assigns the dual values. According to both of these extensions $\neg(\varphi \wedge \neg\varphi)$ is true, and thus so is its supervalue. Non-contradiction is thus valid according to the supervaluation.

One way to read supervaluation is to read classical extension as *if-valuation*. In other words, some propositions are neither true nor false, e.g. those involving fictional terms, but we do — by means of classical extensions — as if they were true or false. However, the framework is still incomplete. Supervaluations are only efficient at the propositional level. What about quantifiers? What about $k_i = k_i$? Is it true, false or does it lack a value? If we consider equalities to be atomic propositions then identity will lack a supervalue. Bencivenga accomplished the task to extend the supervaluational framework to first-order logic by combining outerdomains with supervaluations.

Bencivenga (Bencivenga, 1986) does not consider at all classical extensions. Instead he considers all ways of assigning a denotation to the empty names, and the total valuations which will result from that.

Let us assume that k_i in $\varphi[x/k_i]$ is empty, and thus the interpretation function undetermined. The idea is to evaluate this formula with respect to an hypothetical context in which k_i would have a reference, whatever it is.

To be able to that, we consider a partial model U that consists in a domain D and an interpretation I which is partial with respect to singular terms. Then, we add an extension of this model, U', which ascribes to the partial interpretation I an extension I'. This superinterpretation I' assigns an arbitrary value to initially empty singular terms. Let us take for example $\neg(Pk \wedge \neg Pk)$: If $I(k) = \#$, then $V(Pk) = \#$ and $V(\neg(Pk \wedge \neg Pk)) = \#$. To validate the principle of non-contradiction, we complete I with an I' in order to assign an arbitrary value to k. Now, whatever would k denote, it would render $\neg(Pk \wedge \neg Pk)$ true. The same holds for $k = k$ because whatever k might be, it would be identical with itself.

However, a problem remains: the principles of particularization and specification would now be validated. Bencivenga recommends the following solution: If it is relevant to take into account the extension for the expression lacking interpretation in the initial model, it is not the same for the one which have value in the initial model. Indeed, if for example $\forall x\varphi$ has a value in the initial model, this value has the priority over the extension. Then, we could have that $\forall x\varphi$ is true in the initial model and $\varphi[x/k]$ as undetermined. Moreover, by applying I' to k, we could have that $\varphi[x/k]$ is false. Hence there is a counter-model to specification.

Another more simple explanation given by Woodruff (1971), and also endorsed by Read (1995), consists in taking into account a *free extension* rather than superinterpretation. In this framework, the extension I' of the partial interpretation I ranges over an outerdomain and applies to individual constants whereas the initial interpretation I ranges over the innerdomain and applies to quantifiers. Therefore, the interpretation of k might lay beyond the range of the quantifiers and that is why specification is no longer valid.

The implementation of the Bencivenga-Woodruff strategy in the dialogical approach is pretty straightforward and amounts to the concatenation of a neuter free logic with a positive free logic. We might call this concatenation a *superdialogue*. Superdialogues result from applying the following rules:

[RS$_{SD}$-1]   Every dialogue is first played by applying the rules that define dialogical neuter free logic.

[RS$_{SD}$-2]   If a dialogue finished with [RS$_{SD}$-1] has been won neither by O nor by P, the dialogue starts again with the rules for positive free logic.

Hence, specification and particularization are still non-valid whereas a formula like $\exists x Ax \rightarrow (\exists x Ax \vee Ak_1)$ is valid — notice that the latter is not valid in (dialogical) neuter free logic.

7   To be Chosen and To be Symbolic

Dialogical free logics as presented previously are too restrictive. Because of the introduction rule, every existentially quantified formula turns out to be non-valid. In a model theoretical framework this can be seen to be a consequence of the possibility of having empty domains.[12]. Therefore, each time the proponent has to choose first, he will lose. As a result, the equivalence between formulas like $\exists x(Ax \rightarrow \forall x Ax)$ and $\exists x \neg Ax \vee \forall x Ax$ does not hold anymore. This suggests that in a dialogue, even if the domain is possibly empty, a kind of move, that we will call *symbolic*, should be allowed.[13] Such moves should indicate that the

---

[12]Such kind of free logics are *inclusive*.

[13]Although we use "symbolic" in a somewhat different manner, this notion has its roots in the philosophy of Hugh MacColl. For more details on this point, see Rahman and Redmond (2008), Section 1.2.1, pp. 27 sq.

decision about the ontological status of the constants involved have not been taken yet — recall that the ontological status is determined by the opponent's choices. Indeed, sometimes it is due to the interaction that takes place during a dialogue that new information arises about the ontological status of a given individual constant. In order to describe a dialogical system where the status of some individual constants at some stage of the dialogue might have an undetermined ontological status the rule [RS-6] has to be replaced with the rule [RS-FL$_S$] formulated as follows:

[RS-FL$_S$]   While defending an existential quantifier or challenging an universal quantifier P must use totally new individual constants or individual constants previously introduced by O.

We also need the following definitions:

[D7]   An individual constant is said to be totally new if and only if it does not occur in the initial thesis, or if it has not been previously introduced.

[D8]   We call symbolic an individual constant totally new or an individual constant occurring in the initial thesis.

[D9]   An individual constant is said to be ontologically loaded if and only if it has been introduced by O.

The principles of particularization and specification are still non-valid though the explanation is somewhat different to the one of the dialogues for free logic described in the precedent sections:

	O			P	
				$Ak_1 \rightarrow \exists x Ax$	0
1	Ak_1	0		$\exists x Ax$	2
3	?∃	2			

Explanation: According to [RS-FL$_s$], P must defend the challenge on 3 either with a totally new constant or with a constant previously introduced by O. Yet k_1, the individual constant required to answer the O-challenge occurs in the initial thesis and has not been introduced. Therefore, P cannot defend the existential quantifier and O wins: Particularization is not valid.

As already mentioned, in relation to non-validity of particularization and universal specification the dialogues that make use of symbolic individual constants do not differ from those of free logic described in the previous sections. By contrast, the case of existentially quantified formulas such as $\exists x(Ax \rightarrow \forall x Ax)$ makes a difference. As it is shown in the dialogue below, a symbolic constant without determined ontological status occurs at the beginning of the dialogue. However, in the course of the dialogue the opponent introduces another individual constant which is used by the proponent to update the defense of the quantifier with this very same individual constant that is ontologically loaded since it has been chosen by the opponent:

	O			P	
				$\exists x(Ax \rightarrow \forall x Ax)$	0
1	$?\exists$	0		$Ak_1 \rightarrow \forall x Ax$	2
3	Ak_1	2		$\forall x Ax$	4
5	$? \forall / k_2$	4		Ak_2	8
				$Ak_2 \rightarrow \forall x Ax$	6
7	Ak_2	6			

Explanation: P defends the existential quantifier (move 2) with a totally new individual constant. There begin the symbolic use of the individual constant k_1 and the dialogue continues without having determined its ontological status. Later, O introduces an individual constant, namely k_2, to challenge the universal quantifier (move 5). So, P updates his defense of the existential quantifier with this ontologically loaded individual constant (move 6). The dialogue continues with the usual rules and P wins (move 8).

The interesting point of the dialogical framework is that we can continue the dialogue despite a while of indeterminacy. One essential feature of this dynamic free logic is indeed the possibility for the proponent to update his defense making profit of new pieces of information conceded by the opponent's action. This symbolic process followed by an update gives the opportunity to the proponent to develop a winning strategy for existentially quantified formulas in a free logic context. Notice that by contrast with supervaluation, the idea is not to give an arbitrary interpretation to singular terms, but to allow for the use of singular term, the ontological status of which is not determined.

This dialogic is now properly called dynamic. Indeed, in addition to a meaning based on actions, the ontological status of individual constants can change during the game with respect to the opponent's choices. In a model-theoretic formulation, we might say that the dialogue begins with a symbolic domain, where the division between existents and nonexistents is not settled — we can think of it also as the union of the innerdomain and outerdomain. After the introduction of k_2 (move 5), the game is played with an (ontologically loaded) domain which contains at least one individual.

In dialogic, the application of the introduction rule can also be seen as producing a change of the context of argumentation. Indeed, after the introduction of k_2, we play with ontologically loaded quantifiers.

8   Conclusion

To conclude, notice that we never understand quantifiers from a model-theoretic viewpoint, as if it should be objectual or substitutional, nor from a proof-theoretic viewpoint. Indeed, we propose here an alternative semantics proper to game-theoretic approaches in which meaning is given in a relation between an act of choice and a resulting assertion. Moreover, the individual constants are not interpreted with respect to a model. Therefore, it does not matter whether or not the ontological commitment has to be understood with respect to a name or with respect to an object. The ontological commitment here makes sense only in a game; through a sequence of challenges and defenses.

So far so good, but some conceptual problems remain: How to define the conditions for the winning strategies and the notion of validity in this dialogical free logic? Indeed, we face an alternative.

(1) On the one hand, we could understand the meaning of the quantifiers dynamically. That is the ontological commitment of the quantifiers would be understood in such a way that it could change with respect to specific moves in the dialogue. From this perspective, at the start of the dialogue, the quantifiers are not ontologically loaded, that is their ontological commitment can be said to be symbolic. More precisely, the quantifiers are said to be symbolic if and only if the decisive constant to win the dialogue is symbolic. In the dialogue displayed above (see section 7) the last individual constant played, namely k_2, is ontologically loaded, that is, it has been introduced by the opponent. Thus the existential quantifier is eventually considered to be ontologically loaded, though at the start this quantifier was symbolic.

By contrast, if the decisive individual constants are still symbolic at the end of the dialogue, we say that the ontological commitment of the quantifiers is still symbolic and that the quantifiers are understood as not being ontologically loaded. Let us see this in an example:

	O			P	
				$\exists x(Ax \rightarrow Ax)$	0
1	$?\exists$	0		$Ak_1 \rightarrow Ak_1$	2
3	Ak_1	2		Ak_1	4

Explanation: The individual constant k_1 played by P in order to defend the existential quantifier (move 2) has not been introduced. However, he wins the dialogue anyway by stating Ak_1 (move 4), an atomic formula previously conceded by O (move 3). According to our definitions the existential quantifier is not ontologically loaded.

(2) On the other hand, we might think that the symbolic status qualifies individual constants and not quantifiers. Furthermore we might think that the quantifiers must always *eventually* be ontologically loaded. That is, the proponent can start using symbolic constants but at the end of the game, the constants occurring in the very last atomic formulas must be ontologically loaded. In this case the winning rule must be formulated as follows: The proponent wins only if he wins by using an ontologically loaded constants. In this case, the proponent would lose $\exists x(Ax \rightarrow Ax)$, but he would have won the game for $\exists x(Ax \rightarrow \forall xAx)$.

Finally, let us point out that the dialogical free logic presented here is not properly speaking a logic of fictionality. Indeed, though this logic is able to express the difference between symbolic and ontologically loaded constants, it does not furnish any tool to determinate if an individual is a fiction or not. It simply shows how to develop a dialogical argument if the thesis involves fictions. In order to extend this free logic to the study of fictionality, some further technical developments are required (as the introduction of a fictionality operator for example) as well as a more precise ontological definition of what a fictional entity is.[14]

---

[14]In order to develop the first main ideas for a dialogic of fictionality Fontaine and Rahman (2010) implement A.-L. Thomasson's (1999) approach to fictional entities — conceived as ontologically dependent entities — and combine it with a fictionality operator. Rahman and Tulenheimo (2010) developed a model-theoretical semantics that combines the notion of ontological dependence with fictionality operators.

Bibliography

Bencivenga, E., 1986. Free Logics. volume 166 of *Studies in Epistemology, Logic, Methodology, and Philosophy of Science*, pages 373–427. Dordrecht/Hingham, Kluwer.

Fontaine, M. and Rahman, S., 2010. Fiction, Creation and Fictionality: An Overview. *Methodos*, 10. http://methodos.revue.org.

Fontaine, M. and Redmond, J., 2008. *Logique Dialogique : Une Introduction. Volume I. Méthode de Dialogique : Règles et Exercices*, volume 5 of *Cahiers de Logique et d'Épistémologie*. London: College Publications.

Fontaine, M., Redmond, J., and Rahman, S., 2009. Être et Être choisi - Vers une logique dynamique de la fiction. URL http://stl.recherche.univ-lille3.fr/textesenligne/etre_et_etre_choisi.pdf/.

Jaśkowski, S., 1934. On the Rules of Supposition in Formal Logic. *Studia Logica*, 1:5–35.

Keiff, L. Dialogical Logic. Stanford Encyclopedia of Philosophy, 2009. URL http://plato.stanford.edu/entries/logic-dialogical/.

Lambert, K., 1960. The Definition of E(xistence)! in Free Logic. In *Abstracts: International Congress for Logic, Methodology and Philosophy of Science*. Stanford, CA, Stanford University Press.

Leonard, H., 1956. The Logic of Existence. *Philosophical Studies*, 3(4).

Rahman, S., 2001. On Frege's Nightamre : Ways to Combine Paraconsistant and Intuitionistic Free Logic. In Wansing, H. (ed.), *Essays on Non-Classical Logic*, pages 64–85. World Sientific, London.

Rahman, S. and Keiff, L., 2005. On How to Be a Dialogician. pages 359–408. Springer Verlag, Dordrecht.

Rahman, S. and Redmond, J., 2008. *Hugh MacColl et la naissance du pluralisme logique - Suivi d'extraits majeurs de son oeuvre*, volume 3 of *Cahiers de Logique et d'Épistémologie*. London, College Publications.

Rahman, S. and Tulenheimo, T. Fictionality Operators and the Artifactual Theory of Fiction. submitted, 2010.

Rahman, S., Rückert, H., and Fischmann, M., 1997. On Dialogues and Ontology. The Dialogical Approach to Free Logic. *Logique et Analyse*, 160:357–374.

Read, S., 1995. *Thinking about Logic*. Oxford, Oxford University Press.

Russell, B., 1905. On Denoting. *Mind*, 14:479–493.

Thomasson, A.-L., 1999. *Fiction and Metaphysics*. Cambridge Studies in Philosophy. Cambridge, Cambridge University Press.

van Fraassen, C., 1966. Singular Terms, Truth-Value Gaps and Free Logics. *Journal of Philosophy*, 67:481–495.

Woodruff, P. Free logics, modality and truth. Unpublished manuscript quoted by Bencivenga (1986), 1971.

Logical Dialogues from Middle Ages

AUDE POPEK*

ABSTRACT. The mediaeval form of dialectical disputations known as *Obligationes* was very popular in fourteenth century. We shall focus on the best known obligational disputation called *Positio*. In addition to the usual presentation of the General rules that determine the course of the game, we shall display some less known rules that we shall call Internal rules, aiming at describing the way a proposition can be defended according to its main connective as well as to what the players know. From this point of view, there is a striking similarity between the mediaeval and dialogical approach to logic. The aim of the paper is to present, besides the general rules of Walter Burley, some Internal rules and their features.

Introduction

The '*Obligationes*' name a special kind of dialectical disputations widely practised during the Middle Ages and especially during the fourteenth century. Briefly, an *Obligatio* is a dialogue led by two participants: an Opponent and a Respondent. The disputation starts with Opponent introducing a proposition (also called *obligatum*) that Respondent is committed to defend as true, false or doubtful for the sake of the disputation. The disputation goes on with Opponent introducing other propositions (one at a time) that Respondent must either grant, deny or doubt on the basis of certain consequence relations between the *obligatum* and the propositions previously introduced by Opponent. Nonetheless, if there is no such relations, Respondent answers propositions on the basis of a set of background knowledge shared with Opponent. The disputation is over when its given time has run out or if Respondent badly answered the propositions.

*Univ Lille Nord de France, F-59000 Lille France;
UdL3, STL, F-59653 Villeneuve d'Ascq France;
CNRS UMR8163.

The use of the word *'obligationes'* comes from the fact that Respondent is *committed* to uphold a proposition (previously put forward by Opponent) with respect to precise constraints. We notice that there were two main streams relative to the way of driving such disputations, which Robert Fland called the *antiqua responsio* and *nova responsio*, each of them respectively symbolized by Walter Burley's and Roger Swyheshed's views.[1] The main difference between the *antiqua* and *nova responsio* relies on the way to answer propositions. In the *antiqua* version of the game, propositions are answered on the basis of their relation with the *positum* or with other previously introduced propositions. If there is no logical relation between the new proposition and the *positum* or *other already introduced ones*, the proposition must be answered on the basis of a certain set of knowledge or beliefs. Such set of knowledge or beliefs plays a significant part in the way to answer propositions introduced by Opponent and then, in the outcome of the disputation. Conversely, in the *nova responsio*, each proposition must be answered only on the basis of their relation with the *positum*. Moreover, the answer given to irrelevant proposition, i.e., propositions that do not follow from the *positum*, can change during the disputation. For a deep scrutiny of the *nova responsio* and more particularly on Roger Swyneshed's treatise, see Ashworth (1996), Spade (1977), Dutilh Novaes (2006). In this paper, we shall exclusively focus on Walter Burley's *Tractatus de Obligationibus* which is among the best known theory on this topic.[2] Burley's treatise gathers six types of obligational disputations: *Institutio, Petitio, Positio, Depositio, Dubitatio* and *Sit verum*. In the disputation called *Instituto*, the players deal with the change of meaning of some utterance. In *Petitio*, Opponent coerces Respondent into doing something, mostly into answering in a particular way. For instance 'I state that you affirmatively respond to God exists'. In *sit verum*, the proposition that Respondent must uphold as true should include mention of our knowledge. For example, 'You know that you are running'. Finally, the three other kinds of disputations, *Depositio, Dubitatio* and *Positio* are the same, except that in a *Depositio* Respondent is committed to maintain the *depositum* as false and in the *Dubitatio*, the *dubitatum* as uncertain.

---

[1]See P. V. Spade in Spade (1978).

[2]Walter Burley (or Burleigh b. 1274/5; d. after 1344). For a detailed survey of Burley's life and works, see Martin (1964) and Ottman and Wood (1999) and the extended bibliography in Weijers. Burley's treatise dates from 1302. It has been edited in Green (1963).

We shall exclusively focus on Burley's theory of *Positio* which is usually considered as spelling out the paradigmatic version of *Positio* for fourteenth century. Several sets of rules govern the *Positio* and more generally the *Obligationes*: Rules of the *Obligational Art* and rules *de bene esse*.[3] Rules *de bene esse* are rather regulative than constitutive rules of this art. They specify how to properly answer each propositions in the disputation.[4] Rules of *Obligational art* constitute the core of the disputation. They specify how the disputation should proceed with respect to a proposition stated as *obligatum* (or *positum* if we are in a *Positio*) and a set of knowledge stipulated by the participants before playing the disputation. We shall present in details the rules of *Obligational Art* for a *Positio* in section 1. Besides those rules traditionally discussed, we find another set of rules in the passage devoted to the *Positio* that we shall call for convenience Internal rules. The part devoted to the *Positio* in Burley's treatise is itself divided into sub-sections. Each subsection provides a set of Internal rules. Some of them describe the way to defend a *positum* (that is the proposition that must be maintained as true) with respect to its main connective. Thus, we find for instance in the *Positio* a sub-section called *Conjunctive Positio* providing rules for defending a conjunction inside the *Positio*. We shall present each subsection of the *Positio* in section 2. In section 3 and section 4, we shall provide and discuss two sets of Internal rules, respectively those of a *Positio of disjunction* and *Disjunction of Positio*.

1 Burley's rules of *Positio*

A *Positio* is led by two participants: an Opponent (**Op**) and a Respondent (**R**). The disputation starts with **Op** putting forward a proposition that **R** can either deny or accept. If **R** denies the proposition, the disputation is over. If **R** accepts the proposition put forward by **Op**, the proposition is then called a *positum* and **R** is committed to respond as if it were true. If the proposition stated as *positum* is a false contingent one, it has to be considered as true for the sake of the disputation and thus, the disputation is played as if it has been true. However, if the *positum* is a false proposition, this must have been noticed, mostly by **R**, we shall see in example 1 below why, but let us for the moment return to our first step in the disputation. We have said that **R** can either deny or accept the

---

[3]See Burley in Green (1963): "Sciendum quod quaedam regulae sunt de esse istius artis, et quaedam de bene esse." p. 46, l. 19-20.

[4]See Burley in Green (1963): "Sequitur de regulis quae non sunt de esse istius artis, sed solum utiles." p. 52, l. 1-2.

226 A. Popek

first proposition put forward by **Op**, but he cannot arbitrarily do it. The rule given in Burley's treatise says that **R** must deny any contradictory proposition put forward by **Op** and then close the disputation before it begins. If **R** accepts a non-contradictory proposition, the disputation then goes on with **Op** successively putting forward other propositions (*proposita*) that **R** can either deny, grant or doubt with respect to four General rules (rules of obligational art). **R** must answer each one at a time. The disputation ends by **Op** saying *Cedat tempus* (time is over) either when the time allocated to the disputation has run out or when **R** badly answered a proposition, i.e., he did not follow the rules.[5] Burley gives four general rules that constitute the practice of this art and that provide an abstract way to answer each proposition introduced in the disputation. The rules are the following ones:[6]

GR1 Everything that is posited and put forward in the form of the *positum* during the time of the *Positio* must be granted.[7]

GR2 Everything that follows from the *positum* must be granted. Everything that follows from the *positum* either together with an already granted proposition (or propositions), or together with the opposite of a proposition (or the opposites of propositions) already correctly denied and known to be such, must be granted.[8]

GR3 Everything incompatible with the *positum* must be denied. Likewise, everything incompatible with the *positum* together with an already granted proposition (or propositions) or together with the opposite of a proposition (or the opposites of propositions) already correctly denied and known to be such, must be denied.[9]

GR4 If it is irrelevant, it must be responded to on the basis of its own quality; and this [means] on the basis of the quality it has relative

---

[5]That is, granting (respectively denying) two contradictory propositions or by granting AND denying the same proposition during the disputation.

[6]We use here the translation of Yrjönsuuri in Yrjönsuuri (2001) of the Obligational rules. The rules have, however, slightly differences w.r.t. the *Depositio* and *Dubitatio*.

[7]See Burley in Green (1963): "Omne positum, sub forma positi propositum, in tempore positionis, est concedendum." p.46, l. 24-25.

[8]See Burley in Green (1963) "Omne sequens ex posito est concedendum. Omne sequens ex posito cum concesso vel concessis, vel cum opposito bene negati vel oppositis bene negatorum, scitum esse tale, est concedendum." p. 48, l. 24-27.

[9]See Burley in Green (1963) "Omne repugnans posito est negandum. Similiter omne repugnans posito cum concesso vel concessis, vel opposito bene negati vel oppositis bene negatorum, scitum esse tale, est negandum." p. 48, l. 28-31.

to us. For example, if it is true [and] known to be true, it should be granted. If it is false [and] known to be false, it should be denied. If it is uncertain, one should respond by saying that one is in doubt.[10]

GR1 states that the *positum* should be granted whenever it is introduced in the disputation. Burley add, however, an exception to the rule. Let 'Marcus is running' be the *positum* and we assume that the players know that 'Marcus' and 'Tullius' denote the same person. Therefore, **R** should also grant 'Tullius is running' whenever it is introduced in the disputation.[11] However, if **R** does not know that 'Marcus' and 'Tullius' refer to the same person, then **R** should answer 'doubtful' to the proposition 'Tullius is running'.[12] **GR2-3-4** specify the conditions under which **R** should respond 'grant', 'deny' and 'doubtful' to each proposition introduced by **Op** other than the *positum*. Those rules rely on the notion of relevance.[13] A proposition is said *relevant* in the obligational disputation if and only if it is either *consequently relevant* or *incompatibly relevant*.[14]

Definition 1.1 (Relevance). Two kinds of relevance:

1.1 (Consequently relevant): A proposition is called *consequently relevant* when it follows from previously introduced proposition(s) in the disputation.

---

[10]See Burley in Green (1963): "Omne propositum aut est pertinens aut impertinens. Si sit impertinens, respondendum est secundum sui qualitatem, et hoc, secundum qualitatem quam habet ad nos. Ut, si sit verum, scitum esse verum, debet concedit. Si sit falsum, scitum esse falsum, debet negari. Si sit dubium, respondendum est dubie." p. 48, l. 17-21.

[11]Notice that this example of Burley's is an instance of the principle of the substitutivity of identicals, that is, if **R** knows that 'Marcus is running' and that 'Marcus is Tullius' then he also knows that 'Tullius is running'. For a thorough scrutiny of the substitutivity of indenticals, see Priest (2005).

[12]See Burley in Green (1963): "Et ponitur haec particula: sub forma positi propositum, quia si proponatur sub alia forma quam sub forma positi, non oportet quod concedatur. Ut si Marcus et Tullius sint nomina eiusdem, et ponatur Marcum currere, non oportet concedere Tullium currere. Aut enim est notum quod Marcus et Tullius sunt nomina eiusdem aut non. Si sit notum, et ponatur Marcum currere, est concedendum Tullium currere, quia sequens. Si non sit notum, respondendum est ad hanc dubie: 'Tullius currit'. Et ponitur haec particula: 'in tempore positionis', quia, si proponatur extra tempus, non oportet quod concedatur." p. 46, l. 25 - p. 47, l. 5.

[13]We translate the Latin word 'pertinens' as 'relevant'.

[14]We respectively translate 'pertinens sequens' and 'pertinens repugnans' to 'consequently relevant' and 'incompatibly relevant'.

1.2 (Incompatibly relevant): A proposition is called *incompatibly relevant* when it is the negation of a consequently relevant one(s).

A proposition is then called *irrelevant* when it is not relevant.[15] **GR2-3-4** therefore specify how **R** should respond to relevant and irrelevant propositions. We assume that to grant an incompatibly relevant proposition is the same as denying a consequently relevant one, and conversely to deny an incompatibly relevant proposition is equivalent to grant a consequently relevant one.

Remark. The term 'follows from' (*sequens*) in **GR2-3-4** is not defined in Burley's *De Obligationibus* but in his *De Consequentiis* and in his *De Puritate Artis Logicae*.[16] The former presents a collection of rules of consequence and the latter a precise definition and a division of different kinds of consequence. Roughly, three main kinds of consequence are distinguished: natural consequence, accidental consequence and as-of-now (*ut nunc*) consequence. The two first ones are also absolute (*simplex*) consequence. Natural consequence, such as defined by Burley in his *De Puritate Artis logicae. Tractatus Longior* means that the "consequent is *included* in the antecedent" and the "antecedent cannot be true without the consequent".[17] We find the same definition in Burley's *De Consequentiis* where the natural consequence is also called consequence *simpliciter bona*.[18] Burley means by consequence *bona* (or good consequence) that the antecedent cannot be true without the consequent.[19] It is worth noting that the consequence *bona* have two main properties: transitivity and contraposition.[20] Conversely, accidental consequence means that the "consequent is not included in the antecedent" and the

---

[15]'Impertinens'

[16]See Grenn-Pederson (1980) and Burleigh and Boehner (1955).

[17]See Burley in Burleigh and Boehner (1955): "Consequentia simplex est duplex: quaedam naturalis; et est quando antecedens includit consequens et talis consequentia tenet per locum intrinsecorum..." p. 61, 6-8 and "Consequentia naturalis est quando consequens est de intellectu antecedentis, nec antecedens potest esse verum nisi consequens sit verum." p. 128, 70.

[18]See Grenn-Pederson (1980), p. 141-142, §116.

[19]See Grenn-Pederson (1980): "Et sciendum quod ad bonitatem condicionalis non plus requiritur, nisi si antecedens sit verum consequens erit verum." p. 128, §68.

[20]"quidquid sequitur ad consequens, sequitur ad antecedens; quidquid antecedit ad antecedens, antecedit ad consequens" and "Ex opposito contradictorie consequentiis debet inferri oppositum contradictorie antecedentis; quidquid repugnat consequenti, repugnat antecedenti".

consequence relation holds in virtue of 'extrinsic rules'.[21] Finally, in an as-of-now consequence, the antecedent cannot be true without the consequent, but at a specific time. The as-of-now consequence holds at certain moments of time while the absolute consequence holds necessarily. Besides those distinctions, Burley provides ten rules of inferences as well as rules following from these main rules.[22] A formulation of some of them in Gentzen-style sequent calculus is given in DutilhNovaes (2008). Burley's theory of consequence as spelling out a natural deduction system in the sense of Gentzen is discussed in King (2001). Nothing is said in the treatise *De Obligationibus* about the consequence relation that holds in the different *Positio* except in the part devoted to the *Impossible Positio*. Burley says that in an *Impossible Positio* (*Positio* played with a *positum* known as impossible[23]) the *natural consequence* does not hold. We can then reasonably assume that it holds in the other sub-sections of *Positio*.[24]

Finally, the last general rule **GR4** must be used whenever **GR1-2-3** cannot. **GR4** defines the way to answer irrelevant propositions, i.e., propositions that do not follow from a previously introduced one. By this rule **R** should answer irrelevant propositions according to what he knows or believes and regardless of the proposition stated as *positum*. Moreover, an important precision is brought about the way to understand "its own quality" as "the quality it [irrelevant proposition] has relative to us". It seems that Burley refers here to a certain agreement between the participants. If so, **R** should also answer irrelevant propositions according to what is accepted or believed by **Op** (and any other attendees) and not only by himself. In such case, the participants must agree on certain facts about the world, i.e., the truth or not of certain contingent propositions at least before running the disputation. The precision may at first seem surprising but it can easily be explained. Among other reasons, **R** can lose the disputation if he fails to correctly answer the irrelevant propositions, in other words, if he denies (respectively grants) a proposition known as true (respectively as false). But how could **Op** know whether **R** answers well if irrelevant propositions

---

[21]See Burley in Burleigh and Boehner (1955) "Consequentia accidentalis est quae tenet per locum extrinsecum, et est quando antecedens non includit consequens, sed tenet per quandam regulam extrinsecam", p. 61, 8-10.

[22]See Burleigh and Boehner (1955).

[23]For more explanations, see section 2.

[24]For a deep scrutiny of Burley's theory of consequence and the impossible positio, see D'Ors (1990).

must be answered only on the basis of what he really knows or believes? It is then clear that we need a criteria according to which **Op** or any other attendees could say if **R** answers well or not. **Op** (and any other attendees) should be able to judge if **R** is wrong or not with respect to each irrelevant proposition. A useful assumption is then to assume that the participants agree on a certain amount of facts or propositions before playing the disputation. However, this assumption can lead us to several difficulties, mostly about the possible properties of such a set of knowledge or beliefs. Should we define, for instance, a set closed under known entailment or not? The closure under known entailment is the epistemic principle that, for any propositions p and q, if a subject **R** knows that p (is true) and knows that p implies q, then he knows that q (is true). This principle can also be rewritten with multiple premises. If **R** knows that p (is true) and knows that q (is true), and **R** comes to know r by correctly deducing if from both p and q, then **R** knows r (is true). Those principles simply say that **R** can add to what he knows things deduced from what he already knows. If we now rephrase our previous question in obligational terms, it would be: should **R** grant each irrelevant proposition deduced from $\mathbb{K}$? The answer is yes. If we assume that the set is closed under known entailment, we also have to assume that each proposition deduced from the set $\mathbb{K}$ is also known by the participants. This assumption settles the problem of judging **R**'s answers. In this paper, we shall assume that a set of background knowledge ($\mathbb{K}$) closed under known entailment is determined before running the disputation and that there is an agreement between the participants on the members of $\mathbb{K}$. Each *Positio* is therefore associated with a non-empty set $\mathbb{K}$ of propositions. $\mathbb{K}$ is consistent and stands for the partial view that the players have over the world (or model). The view is partial insofar as some propositions will not get the value 'true' or 'false' but 'doubtful'.

Let us give now a very basic example from Burley's treatise of *Positio*:

Example 1. $\mathbb{K} = \{$you are not in Rome, you are not a bishop$\}$

	Op	R	Rules
1	you are in Rome	accepted	*positum*
2	You are not in Rome or you are a bishop.	granted	irrelevant and true.
3	You are a bishop	granted	consequently relevant.
4	*Cedat Tempus*		

$\mathbb{K}$ is the set of background knowledge shared by the participants. The left column indicates the order in which propositions are introduced whereas, the right column indicates which rule is applied by **R**. At first, **Op** puts forward a contingent (false) proposition that **R** accepts, so 'you are in Rome' becomes the *positum* and must be held true during the time of the disputation. The dialogue goes on with **Op** introducing, at the second round, 'you are not in Rome or you are a bishop' that **R** also grants since it is irrelevant and true according to $\mathbb{K}$. 'You are not in Rome' is true according to $\mathbb{K}$, then 'your are not in Rome or you are a bishop' is also true and must be granted. Finally, 'you are a bishop' is introduced at round **3** and must be granted because it 'follows from' **1-2**. In this example, **R** wins the dialogue even if 'you are a bishop' contradicts $\mathbb{K}$ because he succeeded in maintaining the consistency into his set of answers.[25]

The purpose of this kind of example is to show that any false proposition compatible with the *positum* can be 'proved' in the disputation without **R** losing it. By false proposition we mean proposition contradicting the content of $\mathbb{K}$. As C. Dutilh-Novaes has already thoroughly pointed out in Dutilh Novaes (2007), the consistency maintenance is the central notion behind the *Obligationes*. The reason why it is possible to maintain consistency during the game is expressed by one of the rules *de bene esse*: All responses must be directed to the same in-

---

[25]On the consistency maintenance in Burley's theory, see C. Dutilh-Novaes in Dutilh Novaes (2007).

stant.[26] In other words, it is considered that **R**'s answers are given as
if they were given at the same time. This restriction is necessary since
the participants play mainly with contingent propositions. **GR4** is a
clear statement that **R** should answer irrelevant propositions according
to a certain set of knowledge but nothing prevents us to revise what
we know during the disputation except this rule. It is quite striking
that we can find the same underlying idea in Hintikka's *Knowledge and
Belief*: "It is clear that a standard of logical consistency is applicable to
a number of statements only when they are fully comparable; and this
presupposes, among other things, that the temporal distance between
them (including what happens in the interval) is irrelevant".

2 Burley's division of *Positio*

A *Positio* is not solely played by means of the general rules. We find in
Burley's treatise another set of rules that we call Internal rules. Some of
them define the way to defend the *positum* with respect to its outmost
form. Thus, if the *positum* is, for instance, a complex proposition such
as a disjunction, **R** should then follow the general rules coupled to
the internal rules defining the way to defend the disjunction. We find
therefore several subsections in the part devoted to the *Positio* in Burley's
treatise. Each of them provides rules defining the way to defend a
positum of a certain kind. The different subsection are listed at the
beginning of Burley's treatise:[27]

> *Positio*, as the term is used here, is a prefix to something
> statable [indicating that the statable thing] should be held
> to be true. And it is divided, because one sort of *Positio* is
> possible and the other sort is impossible. And each of these
> is subdivided, because [the *Positio*] covers either a simple or

---

[26]See Burley in Green (1963): "Alia regula est: omnes responsiones retorquendae
sunt ad idem instans." p. 61, l. 22-23. We used the translation of Kreztmann and
Stump (1988).

[27]We use Kreztmann/Stump's translation in Kreztmann and Stump (1988). Burley
in Green (1963): "Positio, secundum quod hic sumitur, est parefixio enuntiabilis ad
habendum pro vero. Et dividitur, quia quaedam est positio possibilis, quaedam est
impossibilis. Et utraque subdividitur, quia aut cadit super enuntiabile simplex aut
compositum. Et si super enuntiabile compositum, aut illud est compositum mediante
coniunctione copulativa et dicitur positio coniuncta, aut mediante coniunctione disiunctiva et dicitur indeterminate. Similiter, in positione aliquando est conditio, et tunc
est dependens positio. Ad quam reducuntur positio cadens et positio renascens.", p45,
l.12-21.

a composite statable thing. If it covers a composite statable, either it is a composite formed by means of a copulative conjunction - in which case it is called conjoined *Positio* - or it is formed by means of a disjunctive proposition and is called indeterminate *Positio*. Likewise, sometimes there is a stipulation in a *Positio*, and then the *Positio* is dependent. *Positio cadens* and *positio renascens* are included under dependent *Positio*.[28]

Positio is first divided into two main parts: *Possible Positio* and *Impossible Positio*. If the *positum* is a proposition regarded as possible then we should follow the rules belonging to the part of *Possible Positio*, but if it is regarded as impossible we should apply the rules belonging to the part of *Impossible Positio*. As a result, only either possible or impossible propositions should be stated as *positum*, and then played in this kind of disputation. Two main questions immediately arise: How should we understand the words 'possible' and 'impossible'? And why is *Positio* narrowed to only those both types? Burley gives more details on what should be a possible and impossible Positio in each of the relevant parts, we shall return to it below. Possible and Impossible Positio are themselves divided into four subsections: *Conjunctive Positio, Indeterminate Positio, Dependent Positio* and *Positio Vicaria* (that does not appear in the quote above). Indeterminate Positio is itself divided into *Positio of disjunction* and *Disjunction of Positio*. And Dependent Positio is also itself divided into *Cadens Positio* and *Renascens Positio*.

The part called *Conjunctive Positio* provides rules to defend a conjunction. If a *positum* is of the form of a conjunction then **R** should grant each conjunct whenever they are introduced in the disputation. Indeterminate *Positio* consists of *Positio* of disjunction and Disjunction of *Positio*. In the former, a disjunction must be stated as *positum* whereas in the latter one of the disjuncts is stated as *positum* but **R** does not know which one.[29] In other words, a disjunction is supposed to be true but **R** does not know which disjuncts is true, or more precisely, which one must be upheld as true. In *Positio* of disjunction, **R** has to

---

[28] A graphical representation of the divisions is provided in Appendix.

[29] See Burley in Green (1963): "Positio indeterminata fit duobus modis: aut quando ponitur dictum disiunctivae, aut quando ponitur altera pars disiunctivae. Quando disiunctiva ponitur, tunc est positio disiunctionis. Sed quando altera pars disiunctivae ponitur, tunc est disiunctio positionis.", p. 72, l. 16-20. And: "Et sit disiunctio positionis ita quod altera pars determinate ponitur, tibi tamen indeterminate.", p. 75, l. 12-13.

uphold a disjunctive proposition as true. For he needs to grant one of the disjuncts whereas **Op**'s strategy would be to force him into denying both disjuncts. From this point of view, disjunction of *Positio* is quite different. The disjunction itself is not the *positum* and the core of the game is not to defend a complex proposition by trying to grant its consequences and to remain consistent at the same time since **R** does not actually know which proposition is the *positum*. In some sense, this kind of disputation reaches a certain pragmatic view of the disjunction in which to assert a disjunction would mean to not be able to assert one of its disjuncts. Stated otherwise, the two disjuncts do not belong to the set of players' knowledge. For in a disjunction of *Positio*, **Op**'s strategy is quite different since it consists in forcing **R** into denying at least one of the disjunct and especially, the one that was posited. Conversely, **R**'s strategy merely consists in avoiding denying both disjuncts.

The subsection called *Dependent Positio* handles cases in which the *positum* is stated under conditions, for instance "α is *positum* if β holds" or "if you do β then α is *positum*".[30] Burley's example is the following one: "If you affirmatively respond to the first proposition, [then] "you are running" is *positum*, and not otherwise". The rules provided in *Cadens Positio* (*falling positio*) determine the conditions under which the *positum* that was stated under condition ceases to be *positum* during the game.[31] It is of the form "I state that α is *positum* till β". Each *Cadens Positio* is a *Dependent Positio* but the opposite is not necessarily true. Burley's example is: "Socrates is black. I state that Socrates is black till something that must be denied is proposed". The part called *Renascens Positio* determines the conditions under which the *positum* that has ceased to be *positum* becomes again *positum*.[32] All *Renascens Positio* are *Cadens Positio* but the opposite is not necessarily true.

Finally, *Positio Vicaria* deals with issues related to definite description. It seems that this part deals with cases in which the denotation of a term

---

[30]See Burley in Green (1963): "Dependens positio est quando ponitur aliquid cum aliqua conditione, et fit hoc modo: si affirmative respondeas ad primum propositum, sit 'te currere' positum, et non aliter." p. 76, l. 16-17.

[31]See Burley in Green (1963): "Et est positio cadens quando aliquod enuntiabile cessat esse positum, alia causa subveniente quam cum dicitur 'cedat tempus'; et ideo, in hac positione superfluit dicere 'cedat tempus'." p. 79, l. 18-19.

[32]'renascens' means coming back to life. See Burley in Green (1963): "Ad hanc positionem habet reduci positio renascens, nam omnis positio renascens est cadens, et utraque est dependens; non enim renascitur nisi prius ceciderit, et fit hoc modo: sit 'te negative respondere' positum, quamdiu est verum, et quam cito sit falsum, cadat, et cum iterum sit verum, iterum sit positum." p. 80, l. 17-21.

may change during the disputation. Burley lists three different kinds of *positio vicaria*.[33] One in which **R** should not answer on his own behalf, for instance, 'you must reply as Burley did'. Another one in which a proposition stands for another one, for example, 'Socrates is running' stands for 'Plato is running'. And the last one in which the denotation of the terms of a proposition changes during the disputation. Burley's example is the following one: 'Socrates is running', the name Socrates really denotes what is usually denoted by Socrates, that is the philosopher of the ancient Greece but, at another time of the disputation, the name Socrates may denote what is for example denoted by the name Plato. Then, the proposition 'Socrates is running' would stand for the proposition 'Plato is running'. We shall not go into each subsection of *Positio* but only focus on Indeterminate Positio, that is *Positio of disjunction* and *disjunction of Positio*. Before presenting their rules in section 3 and section 4, we shall come back to our previous question about the terms 'possible' and 'impossible' in the obligational context.

At the beginning of the section dealing with possible *Positio*, Burleys states that only 'false contingent proposition', 'true uncertain proposition' and even, in some case, 'truth known to be true' should be stated as *positum* in a possible *Positio*.[34] This restriction immediately excludes propositions being always true and propositions being always false, i.e., tautological and contradictory propositions. According to Burley's examples, it seems that we should understand 'false contingent propositions' as propositions that contradict $\mathbb{K}$, that is to say, what it is known by the players at a certain moment of time. One of his examples that can illustrate this interpretation is

We know that Socrates is black; I posit 'Socrates is white'.

So the *positum* clearly contradicts what the players present as really being true. In the passage devoted to the *Impossible Positio*, Burley distinguished different types of impossible propositions, those that are

---

[33]See Burley in Green (1963): "Sequitur de positione vicaria, et fit positio vicaria multis modis. Uno modo quando una persona obligatur pro alia. Alio modo quando una propositio ponitur pro alia. Tertio modo quando ponitur una propositio uno tempore pro seipsa et alio tempore pro alia." p. 81, l. 12-16.

[34]See Burley in Green (1963): "Primo tamen, dicendum est de positione possibili. Et primo videndum est quid in hac positione debet poni. Et sciendum quod in positione possibili debet poni falsum contingens et verum dubium et aliquando, verum scitum esse verum, verbi gratia, ut contra protervientes, qui aliquando verum negant scitum esse verum; non enim semper verum scitum esse verum habetur pro vero." p. 45, l. 23-29.

contradictory in themselves and those that are not. Propositions that are contradictory in themselves should not be accepted as *positum*.[35] The reason is simple, anything follows from a contradiction, then each proposition that could be introduced in the disputation would be consequently relevant, and then should be granted. Therefore only propositions that "does not formally include opposites" should be accepted in an impossible *Positio*. Burley says then that two principles can not take place in this kind of disputation: "From the impossible anything follows" and "the necessary follows from anything".[36] The rejection of the former amounts to the rejection of the *ex falso quodlibet sequitur* principle (that is anything follows from what is (logically) false), if by 'false' and 'impossible' we mean self-contradictory.

3 *Positio* of disjunction

In a *Positio* of disjunction, a disjunction is stated as *positum* and **R** is committed to maintain it as true. Burley's rules for *Positio* of disjunction rely on a slightly different notion of relevance. For convenience, we shall call it *mutually relevance* and differentiate it from Definition 1.1. This notion of mutually relevance only takes place in *Positio* of disjunction and it is used to characterize the relation that may hold between the two disjuncts. Burley calls two disjuncts 'mutually relevant' if one *follows from* the other.[37] Let us rephrase Burley's definition as follows:

Definition 3.1 (Mutually Relevance). For any φ and ψ such that $\varphi \vee \psi$ is the *positum*, φ and ψ are mutually relevant if and only if either $\varphi \Rightarrow \psi$ or $\psi \Rightarrow \varphi$, where '$\Rightarrow$' is a relevant implication.

Notice that it is not the case that for *any* φ and ψ, either $\varphi \Rightarrow \psi$ or $\psi \Rightarrow \varphi$, that is to say, there are propositions occuring in a disjunction

---

[35]See Burley in Green (1963): "Sequitur de positione impossibili, et est positio impossibilis quando propositio impossibilis ponitur. Et ideo, in hac positione nihil debet poni nisi impossibile. Non tamen est quodlibet impossibile ponendum, quia impossibile formaliter includens opposita non debet hic poni. Quia, si poneretur repugnans posito, esset concedendum, quia repugnans posito esset sequens ad positum. Et ideo, solum impossibile non includens opposita formaliter debet hic poni. Et quidam dicunt quod solum impossibile opinabile debet hic poni." p. 83, l. 10-18.
[36]See Burley in Green (1963): "Et sciendum quod in hac positione non sunt istae regulae sustinendae: ex impossibili sequitur quodlibet; necessarium sequitur ad quodlibet." p. 83, l. 19-21.
[37]See Burley in Green (1963): "Si autem partes sint possibiles, aut igitur sunt pertinentes aut impertinentes. Si autem pertinentes, ita quod una pars sequatur ad aliam, consequens debet concedi ubicumque proponatur, quia si consequens negetur, oportet negare antecedens; et ita, oporteret negare disiunctivam quae ponitur." p. 73, l. 6-10.

that are not mutually relevant. Stated otherwise, we do not assume that the implication relation at stake between both disjuncts is the material classical one, therefore it is not the case that for any two propositions $(\varphi \rightarrow \psi) \vee (\psi \rightarrow \varphi)$ is valid.

Positio of disjunction is governed by the following rules:

PoD1 If each part is necessary then each part must be granted (whenever it is proposed).

PoD2 If each part is impossible then it must be admitted only in impossible *Positio*.

PoD3 If one part is possible and the other impossible, the possible part must be granted (whenever it is proposed).[38]

PoD4 till **PoD10** concern the case where disjuncts are possible. In such case, they are either mutually relevant or not:

PoD4 (mutually relevant) The one that follows must be granted (whenever it is proposed).

PoD5 (not mutually relevant) If each is true, each when first proposed must be granted.

PoD6 (not mutually relevant) If each is false, each when first proposed must be denied.

PoD7 (not mutually relevant) If one is true and the other false, the true part must be granted and the false part must be denied.

PoD8 (not mutually relevant) If each part is doubtful, one must respond doubtfully to each.

PoD9 (not mutually relevant) If one part is true and the other doubtful, the true part must be granted and the doubtful one must be responded doubtfully.

---

[38]See Burley in Green (1963): "Si autem disiunctiva ponatur, videndum est aut utraque pars sit necessaria, et tunc utraque pars est concedenda ubicumque proponatur; aut utraque pars sit impossibilis, et tunc non debet admitti, nisi in positione impossibili. Si autem una pars sit possibilis et alia impossibilis, pars possibilis debet concedi ubicumque proponatur, ...", p. 72, l. 22-27.

PoD10 (not mutually relevant) If one part is doubtful and the other false, one must respond doubtfully to the doubtful part when first proposed, and later, if the false part is proposed, it must be denied. And then if the doubtful part is proposed, one must respond affirmatively to it.[39]

PoD1 to **PoD10** should be slightly recast in epistemic terms. So **Pod1** should actually be read as "If each part is [known to be] necessary then each part must be granted". The other rules should be read in the same way.

Rule **PoD1** is difficult to understand. Let, for instance, two propositions φ and ψ be considered as necessary by both players. The *positum* is $\varphi \lor \psi$, that is to say, a false proposition with respect to what is known by the players. The question is then why it is necessary to grant φ AND ψ (if they are introduced by **Op**) in order to maintain the *positum* as true. It would be enough to grant at least one of the disjuncts. Unfortunately, there is no explanation at all in Burley's treatise. **PoD2** simply says that we should consider the rules developed in the part of Impossible *Positio*. However, there are no specific rules developed for disjunction in this part. **PoD3** is as difficult to understand as **PoD1**. Burley says that the disjunct considered as possible should always be granted if the other one is impossible. But if a proposition is considered as possible that does not mean that it is true. Let, for instance, $\varphi \lor \psi$ the disjunction in which φ is a false possible proposition and ψ an impossible proposition. The *positum* is $\varphi \lor \psi$ and the first proposition introduced by **Op** is φ. What should **R** do? To grant or to deny the proposition? Stated otherwise, is φ a consequently relevant proposition or an irrelevant proposition? If φ is an irrelevant one then it should be denied according to **GR4**. If φ is a consequently relevant proposition, then rules **PoD4** to **PoD10** would not make sense. Burley's solution is to say that **R** must grant

---

[39]See Burley in Green (1963): "Si autem pertinens, ita quod una pars sequatur ad aliam, consequens debet concedi ubicumque proponatur, quia si consequens negetur, oportet negare antecedens...", p. 73, l. 7-9, and "Si autem partes sint impertinens, aut utraque est vera, aut utraque est falsa, aut una vera et alia falsa. Si utraque sit vera, utraque primo proposita est concedenda. Si utraque sit falsa, utraque primo proposita est neganda. Si una sit vera et reliqua falsa, pars vera debet concedi et pars falsa debet negari. Si utraque pars sit tibi dubia, ad utramque respondendum est dubie. Si una sit vera et alia dubia, pars vera debet concedi, et ad partem dubiam respondendum est dubie. Si una sit dubia et alia falsa, ad partem dubiam primo loco propositam est respondendum dubie; et postea, si proponatur pars falsa, illa debet negari. Et si tunc proponatur pars dubia, ad illam respondendum est affirmative, quia est sequens.", p. 73, l. 24-p. 74, l. 1.

the possible proposition φ even if it is false, in other words, **R** does not take into account **GR4**.[40] **PoD4** merely says that the consequent of an implication should always be granted. Therefore, for any φ and ψ such that $\varphi \vee \psi$ is the *positum* and $\varphi \Rightarrow \psi$, then ψ should be granted by **R** whenever it is introduced by **Op** in the disputation. The reason is simple, if **R** denies the consequent, he should also deny the antecedent, and then he would fail to defend the *positum*. Notice that nothing is said about the antecedent, that is wether we have to grant or deny it. Rules **PoD5** to **PoD7** are the result of the successive application of the general rule **GR4** and the rule of elimination of the disjunction.[41] For instance, let $\varphi \vee \psi$ be the *positum* in which φ and ψ are false according to the players' knowledge ($\neg\varphi$ and $\neg\psi$ are in $\mathbb{K}$) and φ is first introduced by **Op** in the disputation. Then, according to **PoD6** and **GR4**, φ should be denied since it is irrelevant and false. Thus, if ψ is next introduced in the disputation, it should be granted.

4 Disjunction of *Positio*

Disjunction of *Positio* is a very special game among the set of obligational disputations since it is the only one where **R** does not know the proposition stated as *positum* that he is committed to defend. So how does the game run? According to the part devoted to disjunction of *Positio* in Burley's treatise, it seems that a disjunctive proposition is assumed to be true before playing the disputation, and then the main difficulty is to find a way to maintain the disjunction as true but without knowing which disjunct is or must be maintained as true[42] (that is which one is stated as *positum*). In such a case, **Op**'s role mostly consists in compelling **R** to deny the disjunct that was posited. Burley's rules thus consist in giving **R** a way to avoid denying propositions introduced in the disputation. Before displaying the rules, we shall come back to the previous definition of mutually relevance. Burley slightly modified the definition for disjunction of *Positio*. In a disjunction of *Positio*, the definition is the following one:

---

[40]See Burley in Green (1963) l. 29 p. 72 - l. 5 p. 73.

[41]Which is sometimes written $\varphi \vee \psi$, $\neg\varphi \vdash \psi$.

[42]See Burley in Green (1963): "Positio indeterminata fit duobus modis: aut quando ponitur dictum disiunctivae, aut quando ponitur altera pars disiunctiva... Sed quando altera pars disiunctivae ponitur, tunc est disiunctio positionis." p. 72, l. 16-20 and "Et sit disiunctio positionis ita quod altera pars determinate ponatur, tibi tamen indeterminate." p. 75, l. 12-13.

Definition 4.1 (Mutual Relevance). We say that two disjuncts φ, ψ are mutually relevant if and only if:

- Either $\varphi \Rightarrow \psi$ or $\psi \Rightarrow \varphi$,

- Or φ and ψ are *incompossible*.[43]

The case of *incompossible* propositions has been added to the previous definition of mutual relevance.[44] Unfortunately, Burley did not give any precise definition of the property of 'incompossibility' (nor of its converse, the property of 'compossibility'). We may however attempt to characterize it by means of Burley's examples and set the following definition:[45]

Definition 4.2 (Compossible/Incompossible). For any φ and ψ such that $\varphi \vee \psi$, φ and ψ are *incompossible* if and only if $\varphi \Rightarrow \chi$ and $\psi \Rightarrow \neg\chi$ for some χ. The propositions are *compossible* is they are not *incompossible*.

In other words, two propositions are incompossible if one implies the opposite of what is implied by the other. The rules for disjunction of *Positio* are the following ones:

DoP1 Each disjuncts are true then each must be granted.

DoP2 Each disjuncts are false then each must be responded to doubtfully.

DoP3 One disjunct is true and the other false then the true disjunct must be granted and the false irrelevant one must be responded to doubtfully.

DoP4 Each disjuncts are dubious or only one of them, one must respond to doubtfully to any doubtful irrelevant one, whichever it is.

---

[43]See Definition 4.2 below.

[44]See Burley in Green (1963): "Si autem sit disiunctio positionis et partes sint pertinentes, aut igitur partes sunt incompossibiles aut se habent sicut antecedens et consequens." p. 75, l. 3-5.

[45]See Green (1963): "Exemplum tertii: ponatur te sedere. Deinde proponatur: te sedere et tu numquam respondisti ad Deum esse sunt similia. Haec debet concedi, quia vera et impertinens. Deinde: Deus est. Haec debet concedi, quia necessaria. Deinde: numquam respondisti ad Deum esse. Hoc debet concedi, quia sequens, et tamen est impossibilis per accidens, et in concessione huis 'Deus est', primum propositum devenit *incompossibile* posito." p. 56 l. 4-10.

The rules for mutually relevant propositions are the following ones:[46]

DoP5 If the disjuncts are incompossible with each others then one must respond doubtfully to each.

DoP6 If there is an implication relation between the disjuncts then **R** must always grant the consequent.

From **R**'s point of view, there is no definite *positum*, therefore each disjunct is regarded as an irrelevant proposition and then, **R** should answer according to the set of knowledge. Thus, if each disjunct is true or doubtful, **R** should grant or doubt both (**PoD1** and **PoD4**). Actually, if each disjunct is true or doubtful, there is no difficulties at all. It is not the case when at least one of the disjuncts is false. **R** cannot deny a disjunct without taking the risk to deny the *positum*. **DoP2** and **DoP3** then advise to doubt each false disjunct. **PoD5** simply says that the disjuncts should not be granted nor denied. If **R** denies one of the disjuncts, then he takes the risk to deny the *positum* and if one of the disjuncts is granted then the other one should be denied since they are incompossible. Besides, one of the possible kind of disjunction with incompossible propositions is the excluded middle. We can put in the sentence letter P for φ and χ and ¬P for ψ. Thus, we obtain P ⇒ P and ¬P ⇒ ¬P, and then the *positum* is P ∨ ¬P. We can therefore have a better understanding of the need to doubt each disjunct. **PoD6** is the same as **DoP4** except that **R** should never deny the antecedent.

The approach in *Disjunction of Positio* seems to be the opposite of the approach in *Positio of disjunction*. It seems that the purpose is to find the proposition from which one can derive the disjunction supposed to be true. From this point of view, it is not far from a certain pragmatic approach of the disputation. Asserting a disjunction is the evidence that we are not able to assert one of the disjuncts. However, there is a big difference between looking for the true disjunct, from which one can derive the disjunction, and looking for which disjunct is the *positum*, since in a possible *Positio* the *positum* is not necessarily a true proposition. The *positum* can be a "false contingent proposition" supposed to be true

---

[46]See Burley in Green (1963): "Si autem sit disiunctio positionis et partes sint pertinentes, aut igitur partes sunt incompossibiles aut se habent sicut antecedens et consequens. Si sint incompossibiles, ad utramque respondendum est dubie; neutra tamen poterit negari, quia tunc forte negatur positum, nec concedi, quia, concessa una parte, oportet negare aliam et ita forte negatur positum. Si una pars sequatur ad aliam, pars, quae sequens est, semper est concedenda, quia vel est posita vel sequens ad positum." p. 75, l. 3-10.

for the sake of the disputation. It is fairly obvious that we cannot put the disjunction of *Positio* on the same level than the *Positio* of disjunction, or even than the conjunctive *Positio*. What is at stake here is not to defend a complex proposition by trying to draw its consequences and remaining consistent at the same time. Besides, in a certain sense, disjunction of *positio* is remarkable since it combines the behaviour of conjunction and disjunction. Consider the case where the disjuncts are irrelevant.[47] Both should be granted if they belong to $\mathbb{K}$. The other cases listed by Burley are more or less similar to what happens in *Positio* of a disjunction.

5 Conclusion

The *Positio* and more generally the *Obligationes* are a highly stylized form of disputations. We have shown that the disputation called *Positio* actually is the result of the application of two different sets of rules: the general rules that we have presented in section 1 coupled with a set of internal rules. We have only presented a part of them, those defining a *Positio of disjunction* (in section 3) and *disjunction of Positio* (in section 4). Even if the general rules are the core of the oligational practice, the internal rules define different and specific types of games.

The attempt to provide a global logical framework for the *Obligationes* as well as for the *Positio* seems therefore to be quite difficult to conceive. We had the opportunity to show in the section 2 that the *Positio* itself gathers several kinds of disputations. This presentation is a preliminary step towards a thorough scrutiny of the *Oligationes* by means of dialogical approach to logic. It is interesting to notice that the *Positio* shares some characteristic of the dialogical approach such as developped by Rahman and Keiff in Rahman and Keiff (2005) and that this approach could provide us tools for throwing light on some of their aspects.

A Appendix

Distinctions displayed into Possible *Positio* also hold into Impossible *Positio*.

---

[47]See rule **DoP1** above.

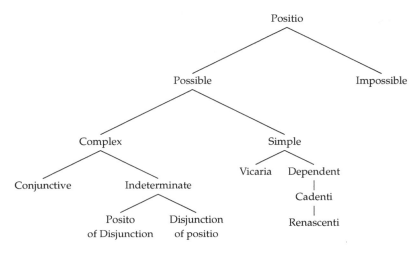

Bibliography

Ashworth, E. J., 1996. Autour des Obligationes de Roger Swyneshed: la nova responsio. *Les Etudes Philosophiques*, (3):341–360.

Burleigh, W. and Boehner, P., 1955. *De Puritate Artis Logicae Tractatus Longior: With a Revised Edition of the Tractatus Brevior*. The Franciscan Institute.

D'Ors, A., 1990. Ex impossibili quodlibet sequitur. *Archives d'histoire doctrinale et littéraire du moyen-âge*, 57:121–154.

Dutilh Novaes, C., 2006. Roger Swyneshed's obligationes: a logical game of inference recognition? *Synthese*, 151(1):125–153.

Dutilh Novaes, C., 2007. *Formalizing Medieval Logical Theories: Suppositio, Consequentiae and Obligationes*, volume 7 of *Logic, Epistemology, and the Unity of Science*. Springer, Berlin.

DutilhNovaes, C., 2008. 14th century logic after Ockham. In Gabbay, D. and Woods, J. (ed.), *Handbook of the History of Logic Volume 2*, pages 433–504. Elsevier.

Green, R., 1963. *An Introduction to the Logical Treatise De Obligationibus: With Critical Texts of William of Sherwood (?) and Walter Burley*. PhD thesis, Université catholique, Institut Supérieur de Philosophie.

Grenn-Pederson, N. J., 1980. Walter Burley's De Consequentiis: An Edition. *Franciscan Studies*, 40:102–166.

King, G., 2001. Conseqeunce as inference: Medieval proof theory 1300-1350. In *Yrjön-suuri (2001)*, pages 117–145. Kluwer.

Kreztmann, N. and Stump, E., 1988. *The Cambridge Translations of Medieval Philosophical Texts. Vol. I: Logic and the Philosophy of Language*. Cambridge University Press, Cambridge.

Martin, C., 1964. Walter Burley. In Hinnebush, W. H. (ed.), *Oxford Studies Presented to Daniel Callus*, pages 194–230. Oxford University Press, Oxford.

Ottman, J. and Wood, R., 1999. Walter of burley: His life and works. *Vivarium*, 37(1): 1–23.

Priest, G., 2005. *Towards non-being: The logic and metaphysics of intentionality*. Oxford University Press, USA.

Rahman, S. and Keiff, L., 2005. On how to be a dialogician. In Vanderveken, D. (ed.), *Logic, Thought and Action*, pages 359–408. Springer.

Spade, P., 1977. Roger swyneshed's obligationes: edition and comments. *Archives d'histoire doctrinale et littéraire du moyen-âge*, 44:243–285.

Spade, P., 1978. Robert Fland's Insolubilia: An Edition, with Comments on the Dating of Fland's Works. *Mediaeval Studies*, 40(-1):56–80.

Weijers, O. Le travail intellectuel à la Faculté des arts de Paris: textes et maîtres (ca. 1200-1500). *Répertoire des noms commençant par G (Studia artistarum 6)(Turnhout, 1998)*, pages 37–62.

Yrjönsuuri, M. (ed.), 2001. *Medieval formal logic: Obligations, Insolubles, and Consequences*, volume 49 of *The New Synthese Historical Library*. Kluwer, Dordrecht.

CONTACTS

Editors of the Series
- Shahid RAHMAN: shahid.rahman@univ-lille3.fr
- Nicolas CLERBOUT: nicolasclerbout@wanadoo.fr
- Matthieu FONTAINE: fontaine.matthieu@gmail.com

Editors of the Volume
- Cristina BARÉS GÓMEZ: crisbares@gmail.com
- Sébastien MAGNIER: sebastien.magnier@bbox.fr
- Francisco J. SALGUERO: salguero@us.es

Contributors
- Hans van DITMARSCH: hvd@us.es
- Virginie FIUTEK: fiutek.virginie@gmail.com
- Laura LEONIDES: laura@ciencias.unam.mx
- Aude POPEK: audepopek@gmail.com
- Juan REDMOND: juanredmond@yahoo.fr
- Pablo SEBAN: seban.pablo@wanadoo.fr
- Fernando SOLER-TOSCANO: fsoler@us.es
- Tero TULENHEIMO: tero.tulenheimo@univ-lille3.fr
- Fernando V.-QUESADA: fernandorvelazquezq@gmail.com